CLASSICAL TEXTS AND THEIR TRADITIONS

Scholars Press
Homage Series

No Famine in the Land: Studies in Honor of John L. McKenzie
   James W. Flanagan and Anita W. Robinson, editors

Israelite Wisdom: Theological and Literary Essays in Honor of Samuel Terrien
   John G. Gammie, editor

Selected Papers of Lionel Pearson
   Donald Lateiner and Susan A. Stephens, editors

Classical Studies in Memory of Karl K. Hulley
   Harold D. Evjen, editor

Classical Texts and Their Traditions: Studies in Honor of C. R. Trahman
   David F. Bright, and Edwin S. Ramage, editors

Hearing and Speaking the Word: Selections from the Works of James Muilenburg
   Thomas F. Best, editor

Greek Poetry and Philosophy: Studies in Honour of Leonard Woodbury
   Douglas E. Gerber, editor

CLASSICAL TEXTS AND THEIR TRADITIONS

Studies in Honor of C. R. Trahman

edited by

David F. Bright
and
Edwin S. Ramage

Scholars Press
Chico, California

CLASSICAL TEXTS AND THEIR TRADITIONS

Studies in Honor of C. R. Trahman

edited by

David F. Bright
and
Edwin S. Ramage

©1984
Scholars Press

Library of Congress Cataloging in Publication Data
Main entry under title:

Classical texts and their traditions.

   (Scholars Press homage series ; no. 6)
   1. Classical philology—Addresses, essays, lectures.
2. Paleography—Addresses, essays, lectures. 3. Transmission
of texts—Addresses, essays, lectures. 4. Trahman, C. R.
(Carl R.) I. Trahman, C. R. (Carl R.) II. Bright, David F.
III. Ramage, Edwin S., 1929-   . IV. Title. V. Series.
PA26.T73C57   1984   938   84-1326
ISBN 0-89130-729-X

Printed in the United States of America

CONTENTS

Acknowledgements	ix
Preface	xi
Dissertations directed	xv
Tabula gratulatoria	xvii
An unpublished manuscript of *Moralium dogma philosophorum* DAVID F. BRIGHT, University of Illinois at Urbana-Champaign	1
Metamorphosis in the twelfth-century *Metamorphosis Golye episcopi* JOHN R. CLARK, Fordham University	7
Beinecke Library, Yale University: an unpublished *Vitae sanctorum* DIANNE L. CREASY, University of Cincinnati and BARBARA A. SHAILOR, Bucknell University	13
Deceptum errore: Images of Crete in the *Aeneid* LESLIE PRESTON DAY, Wabash College	25
A reconsideration of Cicero's *princeps civitatis* in the light of new evidence from a sixth-century political treatise ATHANASIOS S. FOTIOU, Carleton University	41
The Vergilian manuscripts M, P and R ROBERT E. GAEBEL, University of Akron	59
A reference to the *chora basilike* of Alexander the Great (Plut., *Phokion* 18.5) A.J. HEISSERER, University of Oklahoma	67
A fourth redaction of the *Histoire ancienne jusqu'à César* JEFFREY H. KAIMOWITZ, Trinity College, Hartford	75
The adultery mime reconsidered PATRICK H. KEHOE, Wichita State University	89
The rhetorical value of the similes in Lucretius ANNE LEEN, Furman University	107

Counterfeit man DANIEL B. LEVINE, University of Arkansas	125
Time's mirror: a reflection of Phaedra's isolation and self-consciousness CECELIA A.E. LUSCHNIG, University of Idaho	139
The Statilius-subscription and the editions of late antiquity DONALD E. MARTIN, Rockford College	147
Cicero's *Pro Sestio* in London, British Library, Ms Harley 4927 TADEUSZ MASLOWSKI, University of California, Los Angeles	155
Historical development in Livy RICHARD E. MITCHELL, University of Illinois at Urbana-Champaign	179
Clodia in Cicero's *Pro Caelio* EDWIN S. RAMAGE, Indiana University	201
The cup and the lip JAMES S. RUEBEL, Iowa State University	213
The wrath of Aeneas: two myths in *Aeneid* X ROBIN R. SCHLUNK, University of Vermont	223
Encolpius and Asianism (*Satyricon* 2.7) BRENT W. SINCLAIR, Smith College	231
Pseudolus as Socrates, poet and trickster EVA STEHLE, Wheaton College	239

ACKNOWLEDGEMENTS

It is a pleasure for the Editors to record their indebtedness to a large company who have supported this project at every stage. Primary credit must go to the friends and former students of Carl Trahman who encouraged the idea of a testimonial gathering in Cincinnati on the occasion of his retirement (April 1982). By the time of that event, the plan for a Festschrift had already attracted wide support. The project has found many eager backers, and we should like to express our thanks to all who have made the publication of this book possible. Particular thanks are due to the Department of Classics in the University of Cincinnati for its generous subvention from the Semple Fund.

The volume has been prepared and typeset on the UNIX system at the University of Illinois at Urbana-Champaign. Professor Brian Dutton (Department of Spanish, Italian and Portuguese) was most helpful in offering his expert advice in the planning stage. Mr. Fred W. Jenkins performed a host of services as Research Assistant, and we are grateful to the Research Board of the Graduate College, University of Illinois, for funding which went in part to support this work. Androula Panayiotou prepared copy with her customary accuracy and good cheer. But our most profound thanks are due to Pamela Patton, Computer Consultant in the School of Humanities at the University of Illinois: on her has devolved the greatest burden of entering, formatting and correcting the copy for UNIX and overseeing every stage of the production. The book simply would not have come about without her patient labors.

PREFACE

This collection of essays is offered to Carl R. Trahman by his friends, especially his former graduate students, on the occasion of his retirement as John Miller Burnam Professor of Latin and Romance Palaeography in the University of Cincinnati, after a career which has affiliated him with that institution for more than forty years. It is a measure of the loyalty and affection he has inspired that the papers contained in this volume have been contributed by persons who studied under Professor Trahman at various times from the 1950's to the 1980's.

Carl Trahman's preparation in Classical Studies began at Union College in Schenectady NY, where he won numerous distinctions including election to Phi Beta Kappa and took his degree in 1938. From there he went directly to Cincinnati for graduate study. The Department of Classics in the University of Cincinnati during the 1930's was a scene of scholarly training at its liveliest, and Trahman was able to work under such eminent figures as Carl Blegen, R.K. Hack, George Karo, Malcolm McGregor and Rodney Potter Robinson.

It was with Robinson that Trahman wrote his dissertation, a work which showed a characteristic breadth of interest: the knowledge of Latin in the Greek world. From Robinson also he gained his abiding concern with palaeography; and as Robinson had succeeded his mentor John Burnam and continued the study of Visigothic palaeography for which Burnam was renowned, so the Professorship was in turn entrusted to his student Carl Trahman.

Indeed, not only the faculty then teaching in the Department were to be viewed as distinguished. Among Trahman's fellow graduate-students were John L. Caskey, Cedric Boulter, Donald W. Bradeen and Peter W. Topping. Each of these was to attain broad repute in a different field, a fact which attests to the range and thoroughness of preparation which the Department demanded of its students.

Upon receiving his doctorate in 1942, Trahman immediately entered the service of his country, and spent the next four years as a cryptanalyst with U.S. Naval Communications and the Signal Intelligence Service, including time in Australia, the Philippines and Japan.

In 1946 he returned to academic life as an Instructor in Classics at Yale University, and in 1948 was invited to return to Cincinnati as a faculty member in the program which had trained him. He remained a central figure in that program for the next thirty-four years, moving through the ranks until in 1964 he was honored with the John Miller

Burnam Professorship of Latin and Romance Palaeography. He held that Chair until his retirement as Professor Emeritus in 1982.

Two qualities above all marked Carl Trahman's contribution to his Department: breadth of learning backed up with careful and first-hand familiarity with both the ancient sources and the modern scholarship; and a passionate devotion to teaching. Over the years, Trahman was responsible for most of the Latin programs at both the undergraduate and graduate levels, and was universally acknowledged to be an outstanding teacher across the entire span of courses which thus fell to his stewardship. Whether he was conveying the rudiments of grammar to beginners or presenting (to the despair of his composition classes) polished specimens in the style of a half-dozen Latin authors, untangling cursive scripts or Tacitean politics, he was meticulous and enthusiastic. Being in Carl's classroom was never dull and never unprofitable, and many of his students have set as their goal a comparable commitment to teaching as a primary academic function.

Carl always takes an obvious pleasure in seeing a student's interest sparked, and has always been quick to encourage that interest as far as it will go. Frequently this has taken the form of helping a graduate student shape into a dissertation topic an idea which might, in other hands, have been held back for personal publication. The result has been a corpus of dissertations representing a career's worth of publication, from early Latin literature to Giraldus Cambrensis, and from palaeography to physiognomy. Carl published relatively few papers, but instead invested his learning and his energy in steering his students' work, often on the ideas which have always come so readily to him. When directing a dissertation, Carl was as meticulous as in every area of his teaching. He blended firmness with support, and especially with a willingness to foster the evolution of an idea. The success of his efforts may be gauged from the papers and books which have resulted from theses he directed.

Another reflection of his effectiveness as a teacher lies in the fact that, although the Department for many years rested its international reputation chiefly on its dazzling achievements in pre-classical archaeology, yet over these same years Trahman directed more dissertations than anyone else in the Department.

The same wit and care and zest went into Trahman's scholarly writing. His article on the lies of Odysseus (*Phoenix* [1952] 31 ff.) is still constantly cited, and his reviews of Pease's monumental edition of Cicero's *De natura deorum* are models of discernment and erudition (*AJP* 1958 and 1961). He also edited three sets of Semple Lectures, ranging from Alister Cameron on Plato to Steele Commager on Propertius and Henry Rowell on Ammianus. But his most characteristic contribution to scholarly discussion consists of some two dozen public lectures on a most improbable array of topics, showing again his breadth and his learning. Among the topics: the attitude of the Roman administration towards Greek and Latin; Marx and Epicurus; the Marxist interpretation of ancient materialism; Latin prose rhythm; A.E. Housman and the Latin poets; Insular illuminated Gospel Books; the painted book; and Roman attitudes towards Nature and the Environment.

Yet it is as an extraordinary teacher that Carl Trahman has chiefly earned the respect and gratitude both of his colleagues and of so many who have passed through the Department at Cincinnati during the past four decades. This was indeed his own preferred area of impact. He commented at the time of his retirement: "My greatest satisfaction and joy over the years have been the success and achievement of my students. Several of these are now distinguished professors in leading colleges and universities, productive scholars contributing regularly to our knowledge with books and articles. They have outshone their professor: this is certainly the way it should be."

One purpose of this collection of essays, all written by former students (many of whom wrote their dissertations under his supervision) is to convey the range and versatility which characterize Carl Trahman's own interests. The papers vary considerably in length; some treat relatively narrow topics while others are on rather general problems; and the subject matter ranges from Hesiod to the Renaissance. But all the papers have in common a desire to convey some small measure of thanks for the energy and concern which Carl has lavished on his students. It is with appreciation, respect and deep affection that we present these papers to our mentor, colleague and friend on the occasion of his retirement.

David F. Bright
Edwin S. Ramage

DISSERTATIONS DIRECTED

1950   Gerard Sullivan: Pagan Latin Poets in Giraldus Cambrensis

1957   Paul J. Armleder: Quotation in Cicero's Letters

            Edwin S. Ramage: *Urbanitas, Peregrinitas, Rusticitas:* the Roman View of Proper Latin

1964   Elizabeth Rottenberger: Gerbert and the Classics

            Robin R. Schlunk: The Homeric Scholia and the *Aeneid*

1966   Anthony Damico: *Otium:* Roman Views on the Proper Use of Leisure

            Mildred F. Smith: Comparative Studies in Latin Poetry: Cave and Grove

1967   David F. Bright: The Origins of the Latin Uncial Script

            Athanasios S. Fotiou: A Sixth-century Greek Dialogue: *On Political Science*

1968   Robert E. Gaebel: A Study of the Greek Word-lists to Vergil's *Aeneid* Appearing in Latin Literary Papyri

1969   Patrick H. Kehoe: Studies in the Roman Mime

            Tadeusz Maslowski: Lucretius and Cicero

            Daniel E. Pilarczyk: *Hominum vultus* in Tacitus

1970   Jeffrey H. Kaimowitz: Studies of Imagery in Selected Plays of Plautus

1971   Eva M. Stehle: The Unity of Physics and Ethics in Lucretius

1975	Charles J. Lowry: The Influence of Quintilian on the Historical Works of Tacitus
	Donald E. Martin: Studies in the Editing of Latin Classical Authors in the Late Roman Empire
	Norman W. Merrill: Cicero and Early Roman Invective
	Barbara A. Shailor: The Scriptorium of San Pedro de Berlangas
1980	Anne Leen: Didactic Uses of Rhetoric in Lucretius
	Brent W. Sinclair: Valerius Maximus and the Evolution of Silver Latin
1983	Dianne L. Creasy: The Development of the Formal Latin Gothic Script of Spain: Toledo (ca. 1140-1275)

In Progress:

>Wanda Finney: Hymns and Prayers in Horace's *Odes*

>Andrew McGurgan: The Political Significance of Cicero's Late Philosophical and Rhetorical Treatises (46-43 BC)

TABULA GRATULATORIA

Professor & Mrs. Van Meter Ames
Professor James A. Barthelmess
Professor Emmett L. Bennett, Jr.
Professor & Mrs. Cedric G. Boulter
Mrs. Mary Lou Bradeen
Professor & Mrs. David F. Bright
Professor & Mrs. Gerald Cadogan
Professor Elizabeth G. Caskey
Professor A.J. Christopherson
Professor John R. Clark
Professor Getzel M. Cohen
Mr. J. Rawson Collins
Dr. Dianne L. Creasy
Professor & Mrs. Anthony Damico
Professor Jack Davis
Professors Joseph and Leslie Preston Day
Miss Wanda Finney
Professor & Mrs. Athanasios S. Fotiou
Professor & Mrs. Robert E. Gaebel
Professor Kathryn J. Gutzwiller
Professor & Mrs. A.J. Heisserer
Mr. & Mrs. David R. Hensley
Mr. Fred W. Jenkins
Dr. & Mrs. Jeffrey H. Kaimowitz
Professor & Mrs. Patrick H. Kehoe
Professor & Mrs. Donald R. Laing, Jr.
Professor Anne Leen
Professor Daniel B. Levine
Dr. Charles J. Lowry and Ms. Lorna Petersen
Mr. & Mrs. Lance Luschnig
Drs. Donald and Sherrilyn Martin
Professor Tadeusz Maslowski
Susan Butler McBeath
Malcolm & Marguerite McGregor
Mr. & Mrs. Andrew McGurgan
Professor & Mrs. Gottfried Merkel
Dr. & Mrs. Norman W. Merrill
Professor Ann Michelini
Professor & Mrs. Richard E. Mitchell
Most Rev. Daniel E. Pilarczyk

Mr. Samuel F. Pogue
Miss Stephanie Pope
Professor & Mrs. Edwin S. Ramage
Professor & Mrs. Charles H. Reeves
Professor & Mrs. James S. Ruebel
Professor & Mrs. Michael M. Sage
Professor & Mrs. Robin R. Schlunk
Professors Barbara A. Shailor & Harry W. Blair
Professor & Mrs. Brent W. Sinclair
Professor Eva Stehle
Professor & Mrs. Peter W. Topping
Dr. William F. Vocke
Professor Gisela Walberg
Professor & Mrs. Donald Wellington
Mrs. Priscilla R. Young
Department of Classics, University of Cincinnati

AN UNPUBLISHED MANUSCRIPT OF
MORALIUM DOGMA PHILOSOPHORUM

DAVID F. BRIGHT

Habent sua fata libelli. From the late twelfth century until the fifteenth, one of the most popular school texts of moral philosophy was a handbook which now goes under the name *Moralium dogma philosophorum* (*MDPh*) - the first three words of the text - because its title is not known.[1] We have nearly ninety Latin manuscripts of the work,[2] and it was also translated into vernacular tongues soon after its composition.[3] The name of its author is likewise not beyond dispute. My purpose in this paper is to draw attention to a version of the *MDPh* which differs in certain respects from the published texts.

The dispute over the authorship of *MDPh* has subsided - though probably not ended - and the prevalent view is that the work should be attributed to Guillaume de Conches (ca. 1090-1160).[4] A Norman by birth, Guillaume spent many years in Chartres, both as a student of Bernard de Chartres and as a teacher of philosophy, and in Paris. Unfortunately, his knowledge of classical philosophy was apparently greater than his grasp of theology, and he found himself under sustained attack by those who opposed classical learning (the so-called Cornificians). Among his chief antagonists was Guillaume de St.-Thierry, who published *de erroribus Guillelmi a Conchis* (*PL* CLXXX. 333-340). In fact, Guillaume's work on ancient philosophy and grammar was quite considerable: he wrote on Plato's *Timaeus,* on Boethius and Priscian, and on Macrobius' *de somnio Scipionis.* But his major

---

[1] The standard edition is *Das Moralium dogma philosophorum des Guillaume de Conches,* hsg. J. Holmberg (Uppsala 1929). A very unsatisfactory edition by V. de Vit may be found in Migne *PL* CLXXI. 1003-1056, where the work is attributed to Hildebert.

[2] Holmberg pp. *12-15* lists fifty MSS, and the tally was expanded by his reviewers and in other work made possible by his edition. See esp. J. Williams, "The Authorship of the *moralium dogma philosophorum*", *Speculum* 6 (1931) 392-410; and for a complete list see Delhaye (below, n. 4) 228 n.4.

[3] Holmberg pp. 85 ff. presents Old French and Middle Low Franconian versions.

[4] Ph. Delhaye's exhaustive study of the question, and his judgment in favor of Guillaume, should end the debate: "Une adaptation du *De officiis* au XIIe siècle", *Rech. théol. anc. méd.* 16 (1949) 227-258; *id.* 17 (1950) 5-28. Among the contenders supported by scholarly opinion: Hildebert of Lavardin, Gauthier de Châtillon, Alain de Lille and Bartholomaeus of Pisa. A few MSS attribute this work - filled with quotations of Seneca, Boethius and Isidore - to Cicero.

work was *de philosophia mundi,* which gave evidence to support the remark by his pupil John of Salisbury that Guillaume was the greatest philosophy teacher of his day after Bernard de Chartres. He also wrote a *Dragmaticon philosophiae,* which recast the material of *de phil. mundi* into dialogue form.

But it was as a teacher that Guillaume was mainly renowned. After the brouhaha attending his writings, he retired in dismay from the schools about 1140 and assumed the position of tutor to the Norman court. Among his pupils was the future Henry II of England, to whom *MDPh* is perhaps addressed.[5]

This work, then, is a presentation of moral tenets compiled for school use. From among the many titles found in the MSS, Delhaye's support for *Moralis philosophia* seems well-placed.[6] In general the work follows the outline of Cicero's *de officiis,* from which it quotes liberally. Its parts are *de honesto* (and *de comparatione honestorum*), *de utili* (with *de comparatione utilium*) and *de conflictu honesti et utilis.* Worked in with the material taken broadly or exactly from Cicero is a florilegium from such sources as Sallust and Seneca, Juvenal and Horace, Publilius Syrus, Lucan, Isidore etc., presenting useful or memorable comments on topics of concern to the moralist; but there is nothing novel in the treatise.[7]

As befits the popularity of the *MDPh,* the number of manuscripts is large, but many of them are valueless. Holmberg describes the nine he used consistently for his edition, and touches upon seven others, but he lists fifty in all. It is clear that, as commonly with mediaeval works of this type, it is impossible to construct a stemma of any kind.[8] Holmberg reports the following grouping for the MSS he consulted (p. *21*):

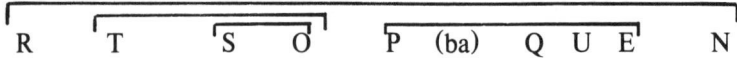

[5] The preface addresses *vir optime et liberalis Henrice R* (but the MSS are not unaminous in reporting *Henrice R*: cf. Delhaye 253 n. 111, and Holmberg 7). Delhaye is cautious: the addressee is probably a king named Henry. Holmberg is certain that this is Henry Plantagenet, while contrariwise Manitius regards the form of address *vir optime et liberalis* as precluding a royal addressee (*Gesch. lat. Lit. Mitt.* III [München 1931] 219). But if Guillaume speaks as a tutor to the Plantagenet prince before he assumed the throne, the address is not inappropriate.

[6] Delhaye 234. The MSS also give e.g. *liber philosophiae de honesto et utili, compendium morale, isagoge in moralem philosphiam.*

[7] Indeed Holmberg (p. *8*) comments: "Es könnte fast scheinen, als stünde diese auf alle originalität verzichtende kompilation mit dem, was wir sonst von Guillaume kennen, kaum in einklang."

[8] Cf. Holmberg *23* on the "variantenkomplex, der jeder einfachen stemmaformel hohn spricht."

The University of Cincinnati Library possesses a copy of *MDPh,* apparently acquired through private purchase by Rodney Potter Robinson in the late 1920's: no acquisition records are now to be found. This codex, Cinc. Univ. 16, was not known to Holmberg when he prepared his edition, and indeed is first listed among the MSS of *MDPh* by M. P. Vernet in 1947.[9] Thus the evidence of Cinc. 16 has never been brought to bear upon the text.

Cinc. 16 is a vellum codex of 36 leaves normally 18.5cm x 13.8 cm. The text is written in a single column within an area 13.5 x 8.8 cm. Rulings on the flesh side: horizontal rulings .6 cm apart in the first gathering, and .7 cm elsewhere. Initials are set off between double vertical rulings (.5 cm on the inner margin, and .3 on the outer). Prickings are distinct triangular perforations (flesh side) still mostly observable.

The gatherings vary in size. The first was a quaternion, from which the middle bifolium is now lost. The second and third are complete quaternions, the fourth a quinion and the fifth a binion. In the first gathering there are 21 lines of text per page, in all others 22.

The last gathering has suffered extensive damage. F. 34 is torn away at the lower outer corner, resulting in the loss of some text; and there is a gap at the bottom of foll. 31-36 averaging 5 cm in width, which however has not resulted in the loss of any text. In addition, several leaves throughout the codex have sustained water damage, most notably in 33-36. Fol. 36v is severely faded and very difficult to read now.

Initial letters of sections of the text are set off in red or blue, and within the text there are some initial letters larger than the text hand and executed unpredictably in red or blue. Even their occurrence is impossible to predict, as they are unrelated to sentence or section. There are also several places where the copyist wrote in the letter but the initialer failed to complete his task (e.g., 18v20, 19r6). Moreover, through the initial letter of each sentence is a simple vertical stroke in red. Quotations are indicated by the name of the author written in red and normally placed in the text immediately preceding the quotation. When this was inadvertently omitted, it was supplied in the margin.

Scattered through the MS are notations and corrections in several later hands. Frequently (e.g., 1r, 11r, 14r, 23r) the original writing has been retraced — not always correctly — where it had faded. On 36v appear two notations in different hands, both upside down to the text. One is now quite illegible; the other reads *Amesius* (erased) .. *Amesius*

---

[9] M.F. Vernet, "Un remaniement de la 'Philosophia' de Guillaume de Conches", *Scriptorium* 1 (1947) 243-257 (Cinc. 16 listed p. 143 n. 2).

permissione divina abbas, whom we may presume to have possessed the volume at some time.

The manuscript may be assigned to the early fourteenth century. The various Gothic hands indicate that the volume was copied in northern France, i.e. in the area of Guillaume's activities. This is where the vast majority of the MSS of *MDPh* were prepared.

Word separation is absolutely clear, except that prepositions such as *in* and *ad* are regularly treated as proclitics. Within words, letters are usually joined whenever it is possible without requiring finials or leading strokes solely for this purpose. *I* is never elongated, and *A* is not very closed, even in its most broken form (23-32).

Apparently a different copyist was responsible for each gathering. The differences are in some instances a matter of general effect rather than clearly definable features, but the conclusion is unavoidable.

Fol. 1-6 The hand of the first gathering is fairly compact, with close connections of letters within words. Individual *i* is marked with a slash as well as double *i*; it does not occur consistently, and there are some gratuitous strokes (e.g., óptímum 4v3). *Est* is abbreviated only by ē. The copyist of these pages was careful to leave room for the names of authors being quoted, to be inserted by the rubricator.[10] In other gatherings, the names are more frequently found in the margin. And, as noted, this gathering is unique in having 21 lines per page rather than 22.

Fol. 7-14 In these pages, the hand is slightly rounder and noticeably less concerned to connect letters within words. Again, *i* is slashed even when single. Here we find *est* abbreviated by both ē and ;. *R* assumes the 2-shape more frequently, but still not consistently.

Fol. 15-22 This gathering is distinguished by the larger module of the hand, and therewith the more generous spacing between words. Letters are more loosely constructed than elsewhere, most notably *g* and *a.* The cross-stroke of *e* is often omitted. In all, the hand suggests a less skillful (or less experienced) copyist than the others. I may add that his spelling is also slightly more degraded than the others.

Fol. 23-32 The hand of this largest gathering is much more broken than any other in the MS, and stands out most clearly from its fellows, although it is not distinguished by any particular traits. The ink in these pages is consistently more faded than in the rest of the volume, even where it has not apparently suffered water damage. It is likely that the ink is different in composition.

---

[10] There is one apparent exception (4v21), but there it may have been set into the margin so as not to detract from the elaborate initial with which the quotation begins.

Fol. 33-36 It is difficult to form a fair impression of the hand in these leaves because of the water damage they have sustained. The writing is fuzzy where it is legible, and the pages are wrinkled and incomplete. Yet the relatively careless formation of the letters and the lack of uniformity of line length indicate a change of hand.

Thus each gathering was assigned to a different copyist, an unusual situation for a manuscript of such modest proportions. One might conjecture that the volume was to be prepared in relatively short order, and several copyists were set to work on it. This would fit with the unequal distribution of material as reflected in the unequal size of the gatherings, and the omissions by initialer and rubricator.

The manuscript presents the full text of *MDPh* except for the lost bifolium and the incidental damage to f.34. Two features may be noted. First, Cinc. 16 contains at the very end of the text a passage from Boethius *de consol.* V which is not reported for many other MSS, and which would connect it at least indirectly with PQUE.[11] We should note that of these, P, Q and E are among the earliest of the MSS (all saec. XIII), and the presence of the passage in our MS supports the belief that it belongs in the text.

Second, the MS presents one portion of the text in a form different from other editions to date. The dialogue *de securitate* (I. C.3 in Holmberg, pp. 32-36) is in all versions a pastiche of the possibly Senecan *de remediis fortuitorum* 2-13, and quotations from other authors. Normally the first part is a dialogue between Timor and Securitas, the second between Homo and Securitas. Cinc. 16 shows some distinctive features. The entire section includes virtually all of the relevant parts of *de rem. fort.* Holmberg notes that some other MSS have more extensive excerpts than he prints, especially Padua 101 (used by de Vit for *PL*), Erlangen Univ. 396 (E) and Paris. BN 5137 (N). None has so complete a version as Cinc. 16. Moreover, our MS has somewhat rearranged the passages, and altered the text, of *de rem. fort.* And finally, the entire dialogue has been unified into an exchange between Timor and Securitas (in the Senecan model, the interlocutors are not identified).

Questions occur at this point to which I cannot yet have answers. In how many other MSS does this fuller version occur? Holmberg's observations cover about one-third of the MSS, but there has been no complete collation for any part of the text. Perhaps this paper may serve to raise the question of which other manuscripts report a similar text. Until that is known, we cannot say anything conclusive on the question of interpolation vs. authenticity. It would seem likely on first

---

[11] Cf. Holmberg *22.*

glance that the extra material is intrusive. But note that all the MSS known to contain a more extended text stand early in the tradition. Cinc. 16 is not elsewhere deformed by interpolation. And the simpler dialogue format with only two interlocutors would seem to be earlier as well. I suspect that a fresh look is indicated: it is possible that the early MSS with fuller text, and the simpler dialogue format, may both reflect a more authentic version of what Guillaume compiled. It may be worth remembering that Guillaume was attracted to the dialogue form for teaching purposes, as his recasting of *de phil. mundi* in the *Dragmaticon* shows. But more information is still needed.[12]

University of Illinois
Urbana, Illinois

---

[12] I am grateful for the assistance of Mrs. Jean S. Wellington, Classics Librarian in the University of Cincinnati; and of C.R. Trahman on an earlier occasion.

METAMORPHOSIS IN THE TWELFTH-CENTURY
METAMORPHOSIS GOLYE EPISCOPI

JOHN R. CLARK

The *Metamorphosis Golye episcopi* is an anonymous twelfth-century poem of goliardic verse in 59 quatrains. The poem survives in only two manuscripts of miscellany, an English manuscript of the mid-thirteenth century (Harley MS 978) and a French manuscript of the early fourteenth century (St. Omer MS 710), neither of which provides a completely accurate text. Thomas Wright first edited the poem in 1841 on the basis of the Harley manuscript in his *Latin Poems Commonly Attributed to Walter Mapes.*[1] A more modern version of the text was made by Robert B.C. Huygens in 1962 by incorporating the readings of the St. Omer manuscript.[2] Huygens' edition confirmed many of the emendations made by Karl Strecker back in the mid-1920s, when he aptly compared various readings of the poem with the fifth century *De nuptiis Philologiae et Mercurii* by Martianus Capella.[3] The *Metamorphosis Golye episcopi* is in many ways simply an expanded commentary on the first two books of Martianus Capella, which describe the betrothal and wedding of Philology or Wisdom to Mercury, the god of Eloquence.

Our poem is in the form of a dream vision, in which the poet seems to enter a beautiful grove. Within the grove is an equally beautiful palace, from which emanates the joyful sound of celestial harmony. The vision of the dreamer moves within to survey the divine guests assembled for the marriage of Mercury and Philology--the significance of each being explained in a typically medieval glossing fashion. Juno and Jupiter are seen presiding over creation; Jupiter symbolizing the heat infused into creative life and Juno the proper balance of the elements. The virgin Pallas, the *Mens Altissimi,* ordains the laws and destinies of nature. Next we see the groom and the bride, Mercury and Philology; eloquence and wisdom must be joined together. There follows a lengthy description of Phronesis, the mother of Philology, the

---

[1] Thomas Wright, ed., *The Latin Poems Commonly Attributed to Walter Mapes* (London 1841) 21-30.

[2] Robert B.C. Huygens, "Mitteilungen aus Handschriften," *Studi medievali* 3 (1962) 764-72.

[3] Karl Strecker, "Die Metamorphosis Goliac und das Streitgedicht Phyllis und Flora," *Zeitschrift für deutsches Altertum* 62 (1925) 180; and "Kritisches zu mittellateinischen Texten, III: zur Metamorphosis Goliae," *Zeitschrift für deutsches Altertum* 63 (1926) 111-15.

appearance of Sol, the four urns which represent the four seasons, the nine Muses, and the three Graces, each with an edifying gloss.

Into this harmonious setting now intrude the jarring notes of Silenus and the drunken satyrs, heralding the approach of Venus and her wanton son Cupid. The goddess Pallas Athena, as the champion of *pudicitia* or modesty, steps forward to oppose Venus. Their various supporters do battle, but the outcome is left in doubt. Without attempting to resolve the conflict between Venus and Pallas which he himself had raised, the poet-dreamer proceeds with an introduction of the classical philosophers and poets who were also present. There then follows the poet's major innovation to Martianus Capella's wedding assembly, his inclusion of the major twelfth-century masters at the schools of Chartres and Paris among the participants. It is noticed, however, that Abelard is missing. The leader of the hooded monks is found to be responsible, he "who had caused silence to be imposed on the great poet" (st. 55.4). This reference brings to mind the condemnation of Abelard at the Council of Sens in 1140 under the leadership of Bernard of Clairvaux. The poet then comments on this evil crowd of monks, calling them the heirs of Pharaoh, religious on the outside, but superstitious within. The gods gathered at the wedding assembly join in this judgment and decree that the monks should not hear the secrets of philosophy, but be confined instead to the dungheap of the mechanical arts. The poem ends with the poet's prayer that the monks be banished from the schools of philosophy.

The word *metamorphosis* in the title of the poem seems singularly inapt to describe the events in the poem to which our poet is a witness. Other titles in the goliardic corpus, such as *Praedicatio Golie* or *Confessio Golie,* are much more exact in describing the contents of their poems. As a result, Winthrop Wetherbee concludes that since the title *Metamorphosis* bears no clear relation to the poem, it was "no doubt added later because of the poem's similarity to other 'Goliard' verse."[4] John Benton suggested that a more accurate title would have been *De nuptiis Golie,* by analogy with the *Apocalypsis Golie,* which is a parody of the Apocalypse of St. John.[5]

The title *Metamorphosis Golye episcopi* is given in the Harley manuscript (with a second hand adding the letter h to spell *Methamorphosis*). There is no title in the later St. Omer manuscript,

---

[4] Winthrop Wetherbee, *Platonism and Poetry in the Twelfth Century* (Princeton 1972) 128 n. 4.

[5] John Benton, "Philology's Search for Abelard in the 'Metamorphosis Goliae,'" *Speculum* 50 (1975) 205.

but then other titles are also often not listed in this manuscript.[6] Two scholars have made attempts to salvage the title as given in the Harley manuscript. Edward A. Synan, although he sees nothing that can be understood as a metamorphosis in the contents of the poem, suggests that the word echoes indirectly the title of Apuleius' well-known *Metamorphoses,* which provided a source and model for Martianus Capella's first two books.[7] This would have to be a most indirect echo, however, since our poet shows no direct influence of Apuleius whatsoever.[8] Peter Dronke takes his cue from the end of the poem with its condemnation of the monks. "Bishop Golias is the subversive mock-bishop of the Feast of Fools, who while the feast lasts can sanction even outrageous criticism of the church's establishment. His 'metamorphosis' is both the way he would like to see the world changed and his own raptness as dreamer--the visionary state in which (so he would have us believe) true insight is possible. A Carolingian letter to a (genuine) bishop speaks of his consecration as turning him 'by a certain wondrous metamorphosis (*quadam mirabili metamorphosi*) into another man ... introducing him into the powers of God, the treasures of wisdom and knowledge, cognizant of divinity.' "[9]

Dronke's emphasis on the extended meaning of the word *metamorphosis* does, I believe, hold the key to a proper understanding of the poem's title, but we need not quote a Carolingian letter to appreciate its significance. By returning to the description of the dream-vision in the first part of the poem, we will be able to see the particular relevance of the word to Martianus Capella's *De nuptiis* and to our poet.

The description of the beautiful, harmonious grove in which the poet-dreamer finds himself (stanzas 2-9) contains a number of verbal parallels to the Delian grove in Martianus, where Mercury and Virtue go to seek the advice of Apollo on Mercury's future wife.[10] In Martianus, Mercury, Virtue and Apollo then ascend to the palace of

---

[6] *Catalogue général des manuscrits des bibliothèques publiques des départements.* Tome III (Paris 1861) 314: "La plus grande partie de ce volume se compose de fragments assemblés sans titres."

[7] Edward A. Synan, "A Goliard Witness: The *De Nuptiis Philologiae et Mercurii* of Martianus Capella in the 'Methamorphosis Golye episcopi,' " *Florilegium* 2 (1980) 122.

[8] The mention of Apuleius and Pudentilla in stanza 46.3 comes from Sidonius Apollinaris, *Epistle* II.x.5. The reference to the classical love poets and their beloveds (st. 45.2-3) also comes from Sidonius, although previous scholarship has identified Apuleius' *Apologia* 10.4-9 as the source. Cf. Karl Strecker, "Kritisches," 115; and Max Manitius, *Geschichte der lateinischen Literatur des Mittelalters,* Band III (Munich 1931) 269 n. 7.

[9] Peter Dronke, *Abelard and Heloise in Medieval Testimonies* (Glasgow 1976) 18.

[10] Strecker, "Die Metamorphosis," (above, n.2) 180, and "Kritisches'" (above, n.2) 113; also Synan, (above, n.7) 133.

Jupiter, where they secure his assent to the marriage of Mercury and Philology. In the *Metamorphosis Golye episcopi* the dreamer comes upon the lavish palace set within the grove itself, from which he can survey the cosmic wedding assembly. In our poem, before the poet describes the palace and glosses the wedding guests, he seems to be reborn:

> Nemoris in medio campus patet latus,
> violis et alio flore purpuratus,
> quorum ad fraganciam et ad odoratus
> visus michi videor esse bis renatus.   (st. 9)

"In the middle of the grove lies a broad plain, made purple with violets and other flowers; by their fragance and scent I seem to myself to be twice reborn." In Martianus Capella, before Apollo and Mercury reach the palace of Jupiter, they are metamorphosed into their respective planets: "atque ita metamorphosi supera pulchriores per Geminos proprietate quadam signi familiaris invecti augusto refulsere caelo ac mox Tonantis palatium." "Thus enhanced by this transformation into celestial bodies, they were carried through Gemini, a sign kindred to them, and they shone forth in the majestic sky and soon sought the palace of the thunderer."[11] This is the only example of the word *metamorphosis* in Martianus, but its use here and the use of the word *renatus* by the goliardic poet in a parallel context are not coincidental. Our poet-dreamer is reborn or metamorphosed so that he can properly see and understand the *involucra* and *figurae* which underlie this cosmic assembly.[12] This ennobling or empowering metamorphosis has its counterpart in twelfth century theological writing, in man's quest to be reunited with God. Alain de Lille refers to the metamorphosis which comes about through ascending to a contemplation of the heavens; best is an apotheosis which occurs when man is snatched up to a contemplation of the divine.[13] To comprehend the cosmos fully, the goliardic poet

---

[11] Martianus Capella, *De nuptiis Philologiae et Mercurii* I.30, ed. Adolf Dick, addenda et corrigenda iterum adiecit Jean Préaux (Stuttgart 1925, rpt. 1978) p. 20, 11. 13-16. Translation by William Harris Stahl and Richard Johnson with E.L. Burge, *Martianus Capella and the Seven Liberal Arts*, Volume II: *The Marriage of Philology and Mercury* (New York 1977) 17.

[12] *Totum sub involucro, totum sub figura* (st. 11.4) is part of the poet's description of the engravings on the palace walls and can be extended to include those assembled inside.

[13] "Sed aliquando excedit homo istum statum ... ascendendo in coelestium contemplationem: et talis excessus dicitur exstasis sive metamorphosis ... Excessus autem superior dicitur apotheosis, quasi deificatio; quae fit, quando homo ad divinorum contemplationem rapitur." Alain de Lille, *Regulae Theologicae* 99, in J.P. Migne, *PL* 210.673C.D. See Wetherbee (above, n.4) 192 n. 11, and Robert Javelet, *Image et Ressemblance au douzième siècle de Saint Anselm à Alain de Lille* (Strasbourg 1967) Vol.

must be transformed and himself become supra-terrestrial. Like the metamorphosis of Mercury and Apollo in their ascent, our poet must be reborn in order to gain true insight into the significance of the marriage of Mercury and Philology.[14]

Appendix

> Nupta sibi comes est de stirpe divina,
> vestis de cyndalio, partim hyalina,
> vultus rutulancior rosa matutina
> quem nec sox decoxerat nec lesit pruina.   (st. 22)

"His bride and companion is of divine stock, her clothes silken and glass-green; her face is ruddier than the early morning rose which neither *sox* had cooked nor hoar-frost damaged." This entire stanza was omitted in the St. Omer manuscript. The Harley manuscript gives the nonsensical word *sox* in line 4. Thomas Wright, in 1841, emended *sox* to *nox* on the basis, I assume, of the pluperfect tense of *decoxerat* and by comparison to the other noun *pruina*. Huygens simply prints the word *sox* with no comment on the passage. Edward A. Synan has recently accepted Wright's emendation. Yet surely the answer lies in the meaning of the word *decoxerat,* "to cook, boil, or injure," and the mistake in the word *sox* lies not with the first letter, the *s,* but rather with its last letter, the *x.* *Sol,* the sun, not *nox* or night, has yet to "cook" the early morning rose. Perhaps the scribe was thinking ahead to the *x* in *decoxerat* and mistakenly wrote *sox.*

There is a somewhat similar passage in the *Anticlaudianus* of Alain de Lille, written between the years 1181-84 (about 40 years after the *Metamorphosis,*):

> nec enim rosa mane puella
> Vespere lanquet anus, sed vultu semper eodem
> Gaudens, eterni iuvenescit munere veris.
> Hunc florem non urit hyems, non decoquit estas.   (I.65-68)[15]

I.265 and *passim.* I would like to thank Professor Winthrop Wetherbee of the University of Chicago for calling my attention to the Javelet book.

[14] See also Wetherbee (above, n.4), 110 n. 99 for Bernard Silvestris' "gloss on the ascent of Apollo and Mercury in the *De nuptiis,* with its similar emphasis on the 'introductory' role of poetic language (Cambridge U.L. Ms. 1.18, f. 24va): 'In hoc ascensu cum Mercurio et virtute Apollo incedit, quia in itinere ad creatorem quid bonum est sapientia concipit, eloquentia aperit.' "

[15] *Alain de Lille,* ed., R. Bossuat (Paris 1955) 59.

"For the rose does not play the young girl in the morning and droop like an old maid in the evening; but rejoicing in a never-changing appearance, it is young with the gift of eternal spring. Winter does not nip this flower, nor summer wilt it." There is a natural contrast between winter and summer (with the verb *decoquit*), as there would be between hoar-frost and the sun. Our goliardic poet had inverted the natural order and put his word *pruina* last in order to fit his end-rhyme.

Fordham University
Bronx, New York

BEINECKE LIBRARY, YALE UNIVERSITY: AN UNPUBLISHED *VITAE SANCTORUM*

DIANNE L. CREASY

BARBARA A. SHAILOR

The Beinecke Rare Book and Manuscript Library of Yale University has recently acquired a manuscript produced in Spain during the late twelfth century. It is remarkable not only for its size, decoration and contents, but for its date: few archives in the United States, with the exception of the Pierpont Morgan Library and the Hispanic Society in New York City, possess manuscripts written in Spain before the thirteenth century. We shall outline briefly those aspects of Beinecke MS 625 which may be of interest to paleographers, art historians and hagiographers.

The manuscript consists of 106 large folios of thick and rather stiff parchment, each measuring approximately 520 x 365 mm. The writing area (370 x 235 mm.) is surrounded by spacious margins, and contains two columns of 38 lines each. Ruling is done in brown crayon, with double horizontal bounding lines at top, center and bottom of the written space, and single vertical bounding lines on either side of each column.[1] Prickings are visible only in the gutter. This precise arrangement of physical format, although on a smaller scale, is found in MS 10108 of the Biblioteca Nacional in Madrid, dated 1218 and probably from Toledo.[2]

The present collation is as follows: I^4, II^8, III^6, $IV\text{-}VI^8$, $VII\text{-}VIII^6$, IX^8, $X\text{-}XII^6$, XIII^8, XIV^4, XV^6, XVI^8. Judging from the gaps in the text, all or nearly all of the quires once had eight folios, with the hair side of the parchment facing out. Catchwords appear in the lower margin of the last folio of the quire, verso, centered below the second column; only two remain (ff. 34v and 88v).

---

[1] The only exceptions to this pattern are in quires I, III, XI and XII, where a second vertical bounding line is added on the side near the gutter.

[2] For Madrid, B.N. 10108 (a copy of the *Planeta* of Diecus de Campus Hispanus) see S. H. Thomson, *Latin Bookhands of the Later Middle Ages* (Cambridge 1969), no. 115; Z. García Villada, *Paleografía española* (Madrid 1923) p. 286 and lámina 76; J. Domínguez Bordona, *Manuscritos con pinturas* (Madrid 1933), v. 1, no. 729 and fig. 255; and A. Canellas Lopez, *Exempla scripturarum latinarum in usum scholarum, Pars altera*[2] (Zaragoza 1974) pp. 81-82 and lámina 45.

The manuscript was written by a single scribe in an early form of gothic script.[3] The letters, made with a broad, sharply-cut pen held at a 45-degree angle, are quite large (minims of about 4 mm.), well spaced, and even. They tend to slant very slightly toward the left. The normal letter space is taller than it is wide, but ascenders and descenders are nearly as long as the minims, and spaces between the lines are generous. Compression is marked, and the connection between letters made by the one-stroke serifs makes each word appear a compact unit. Serifs occurring on the tops of the ascenders are slightly forked, giving the script a spiky appearance. There is some angularity at the top of *m* and *n*, and in the curves of *o, c, e* and so on.

Among the minuscule letter forms, one notes that *a* is always of the uncial type, with the bow joining the shaft very near the top. The minuscule *d* is more common than the uncial. Only with *o* and *p* is *r* found in union. At the end of a word the looped *s* is always used. Both diagonals of *x* end on the line; often the letter appears to have been made in three strokes.[4] The *y* is dotted, as is common in Spanish manuscripts of the twelfth and early thirteenth centuries, and a short stroke to the right is added at the base of the tail. Rustic capitals are used within the text as one-line capitals.

The *e* caudata is rarely found in Beinecke MS 625, and the ampersand — a tall form with a nearly vertical shaft — is used only when *et* begins a sentence. Both these features were fading in Spain in the late twelfth century, and are uncommon by the first quarter of the thirteenth. The tironian *et* is composed of a long straight horizontal stroke and a shorter vertical stroke ending in a hairline extending toward the right. A suprascript *a* represents *ur*. The abbreviation for final *us* is the usual one, with the circle closed and the tail reaching barely below the top of the minims. An *e* with a bar over it stands for *est*, a semi-colon for *-et* or, after *s*, for *-ed* (S; = *sed*). The various cases of *Christus* may be represented by $\overline{xpo}$, $\overline{xpi}$, and so on, or by *x* with a suprascript *i* or *o*. Both forms are common in other Spanish manuscripts of this period. An unusual feature is the abbreviation for *-que*, which consists of a *q* followed by a check-mark above a comma, both attached to the shaft of the *q*. A similar form appears in documents of the last quarter of the twelfth century at León, and a few

---

[3] The same scribe made some corrections and additions. The latter are marked in the text by a majuscule *I* slightly askew. The addition, preceded by the same symbol, is written in the side or lower margin and enclosed on three sides by a line which sometimes ends in the same curled-leaf motif used in the colored initials (see below).

[4] The Visigothic *x* often had a similar form in the preceding period. Cf. C. U. Clark, *Collectanea Hispanica* (Paris 1920) pl. 1, 1.4 and pl. 52, 1.4; and A. Millares Carlo, *Tratado de paleografía* (Madrid 1932), p. 88, fig. 3.

times elsewhere.[5] Considering this, along with other abbreviations and the letter forms, the Beinecke manuscript should probably be dated to the last quarter of the twelfth century, in the same period as such codices as the Bible of San Isidoro dated 1162 (León, S. Isidoro, Vitr. A, no. 3).

The script of Beinecke MS 625 can, however, be more closely compared to that of four manuscripts now in the library of the Cathedral of Toledo: MS 37-27, a *Sacramentarium* and *Pontificale* of Toledo; MS 10-26, a *Vitae Patrum*, and MSS 44-9 and 44-10, companion volumes containing the *Homilarium* of Smaragdus and the *Homilarium* of Paulus Diaconus, respectively.[6] These last two bear a very close resemblance to the Beinecke manuscript in size and page format, as well as script. The same hand may well have written the Beinecke manuscript and the two volumes of homilies, since the letter forms and abbreviations are nearly identical, including the form of the ampersand, the distinctive form for -*que*, and the distortions in the shape of the one-line rustic capitals. This resemblance suggests strongly that Beinecke MS 625 was also written in Toledo.

Our hypothesis is supported by a study of the decoration of the Beinecke manuscript, which is of high quality and distinctive design. Six historiated initials enclose profile heads of saints: on f. 5r, Oranus; f. 12v, Copres (see pl. I.1); f. 15r, Abbas; f. 19r, Apollonius; f. 19v, Dioscurus; f. 60r, Valerius and Donadeus [?]: These initials vary from 12 to 4 lines high. The letter itself is done in flat medium blue or orange-tinted red, sometimes split by a strip of the parchment ground or a row of red scallops. The head within the letter is drawn in brown outline with stylized waves for the hair, thick curved brows, round eyes looking upward, and a frowning mouth. Corners of the initial are filled by curled leaves covered with scales or hatching. The same curled-leaf motif appears around the outer edges of the initial, often sprouting from the shaft. Green and yellow are sometimes added to the predominantly blue and red color scheme, and once (f. 12v) a flesh-tone is added to the face. This type of historiated initial is rare among Spanish

---

[5] E.g., Madrid, Archivo Histórico Nacional, Clero, carpetas 964, no. 21 (A.D. 1180) and 965, no. 14 (A.D. 1191). Both are from the monastery of S. Pedro de Eslonza (León).

[6] Descriptions of the Toledo manuscripts are in J. Janini and R. Gonzálvez, *Manuscritos litúrgicos de la Catedral de Toledo* (Toledo 1977). MS 37-27 is entry no. 116, pp. 132-35, and lamina 9; dated s. XII^{ex}. MS 10-26 is mentioned in no. 5, p. 59, and dated to s. XII-XIII. MSS 44-9 and 44-10 are no. 173, pp. 183-84 and laminas 13 and 14; dated s. XII^{ex}. None of these manuscripts has an explicit with place or date. However, MS 37-27 is for the use of Toledo, and all four manuscripts have the type of binding usually put on codices in the Cabildo library in s. XVI. There is no indication that these codices were written or ever belonged elsewhere.

manuscripts of the period. There is one similar profile head, much smaller, in the border of an initial in Toledo Cathedral MS 44-10 (f. 194v; see pl. I.2).

The remaining colored initials range in size from 31 to 2 lines. Again the letter is done in flat blue or red, with filler and marginal extensions in either or both colors, and an occasional touch of green or yellow. The two largest, on ff. 96v and 105v, are partially composed of elongated dragons similar to those in Madrid, B.N. 10108,[7] but are more skilfully executed (see pl. III.5). Next in size are two initials done entirely in red (ff. 33v and 54v), with elaborate extensions in which the curled-leaf motif is again prominent. There is a similar, although much smaller, initial *a* on f. 60r of Escorial MS M.III.2, also probably from Toledo.[8] More initials of this type appear in Toledo Cathedral MSS 44-9 and 44-10, for example on ff. 39r and 240v. The smallest colored initials are from 14 to 2 lines high. The filler in these may be a single large curled leaf or a solid palm leaf; the more complex type is again paralleled in Toledo, Cathedral, MSS 44-9 and 44-10 (compare plates IV.7 and II.3 with II.4). The simpler ones bear a striking resemblance to those in Escorial M.III.2, although the same type was in use in much of Spain during this time. But the similarity between the initials with more elaborate filler in the Beinecke codex and the two volumes of homilies is such that it seems impossible that they were executed by different artists, much less in different regions.[9] Thus the decoration in Beinecke MS 625, by reason of its resemblance to Madrid, B.N. 10108, Escorial M.III.2, and especially the two Toledo Cathedral manuscripts, supports the theory that the codex was produced in Toledo.

The contents of Beinecke MS 625 provides additional information concerning its origin. There were many compilations of saints' lives circulating in the Iberian peninsula during the Middle Ages. Among those manuscripts containing *vitae* which were copied before the twelfth

---

[7] See note 1. Thomson, García, Domínguez and Canellas all illustrate f. 14r, which is unusual: it is the only folio which contains a human figure as well as a dragon.

[8] For Escorial M.III.2, dated A.D. 1188 and probably from Toledo, judging from the laws it contains, see I. Kirchner, *Scriptura gothica libraria* (Munich and Vienna 1966), no. 6; J. Burnam, *Paleographica iberica* (Paris 1912-25) v. 2, no. 33; Thomson, *Latin Bookhands*, no. 113; Canellas, *Exempla ... altera*, pp. 77-78 and lámina 42; and G. Antolín, *Catálogo de los Códices latinos de la Real Biblioteca del Escorial* (Madrid 1910-23) v. 3, pp. 86-88.

[9] Toledo, Cath. 44-9 and 44-10 are unquestionably more elaborate. Gold and silver-gilt leaf are used on the initials, as well as flat colors, and MS 44-9 contains two extremely well done miniatures. This perhaps explains why those two manuscripts have no small, simple initials comparable to those in Beinecke MS 625: in the Toledo manuscripts the large initial with curled-leaf filler is the plainest type used.

inuuiii vaoiauucs. ꝛ iaiui iiiia
aulo obftupefcerent. fcrocis uehem
tiam nō fcrentes. congregauerunt
sup eum harene moles inmenfas.
ļ ftante tam ibidem patre amone,
qꝛa nec sic quidem cum moꝛtua
fuiſſ; beſtia suse ipso appꝛinquaꝛe
audebant. Incipit de ſcō copꝛete.

r ar quidam pibr m
ipsa heremo habens
monasterium copꝛis
nomine uir ſcs amo-
cauit sepnagmus. ꝛ ipse mitas
uirtutes faciens. languoꝛes curás.
et efficiens sanitates. ſ, et demones
fugiens. ꝛ mlta mirabilia faciens.
ex quib; nō nulla etiam mi pñ-
cia esseruit. hus ꞇ cum audiſſ; nos
et osculo salutaſſet. atq; ex moꝛe
post oratōem etiam pedes lauiſſet.
rogabat ex nobis qui aderant ın
ſꝭ. sibi aut ꝛogabam; eum ut
ipse magıs nobis de sinıs geſtis aliq̃
narraret. exquut? aelbꝰ quib; u-

coꝛpoꝛatos dei filius ad patris dextꝛam
collocauit. qui uiuit ꞇ regnat cum dō
patre omipotente ꞇ ſpu ſcō : in ſcła ſcłoꝝ.

a m · ē · H · Is̄ · reg Leonis ꝓ
De aſcenſione Dn̄i. i.

ACH AOETo̅ ꝙ o dilectiſſi
m saluas nr quam paſ-
sangumis sui uniuersitans
condidit estimauit. a die
coꝛpoꝛalis oꝛtus . usq; ad exitum passio
nis :. p diſpenſationem humilitatis in-
pleam ē. Et licet qaam multa informa
servi diuinitatis signa radiauerint: pri-
pꝛie tamen illius tempoꝛis actio ad de-
monstrandam susceptam hominis pꝛınıut

1 (left): Bein. 625, fol. 12v
2 (right): Tol. 44-10, fol. 194v

3 (left): Bein. 625, fol. 82r

...semp cum deo in secula secu[lorum]...
Incipit ipsum beati ieronimi...
uita sci ysidori...
...erpatr?ueram...
...monis habuit...
inuoco spm s[anctu]m...
ill. langue...
...mdn ad narrandis eas...
tribuit. facta dicens e[st]...
...e[ss]e enim gloria. qui fr[atr]...
res ut ait xps. uana...
tum eam uerb? oriente...
picturam ingenua. Alexan...
macedo. quem u[squ]e arre...
dum. u[squ]e hurum captam...
uocat. cum ad achillis tu...
ueansi. Ethesor? & u...
magnum fuens pione...

4 (right): Tol. 44-9, fol. 39r

Incipit ep[isto]la b[eat]i pauli ap[osto]li ad Corinthios:
...t...s: Oramur uos ne inuacuū
grām dei recipiatis. In uacuum
grām dei recipit. qui uocatus
in xpo: uexra adhuc legis instaura[?] fe-
tatur. Sit enim. Tempore accepto ex-
audiui te. et in die salutis adiuui te.
Tempus acceptum & dies saluus in
hac uita e[st]: sic aut saluari. Ambulare
dum lucem habeas: ne tenebre uos
comprehendant? uia in illo s[e]c[u]lo nulla emendatio potest e[ss]e: sic legimus
q[uo]d non e[st] in morte qui memor sit tui.
modo solum possimus inuenire salutem: quia iuxta ap[osto]lm testimonium in
inferno nemo confitebitur. Ecce nunc
tempus acceptabile: ecce nunc dies salutis. Sicut alibi. Ego dum tempus

que de obitu ei' dicere cepamus. Igitur cum scs paulin' debitum do spm reddidisset: ita niueo candore uult' ei' et omne corp' effectum e: ut omis inter singultum et lacrimas benedicerent dnm dm nrm qui educet scos suos in magnificentia. ut ostendat seruis suis quia hec e glia oib' scis eius. et ideo laudet in dno aia eius. omnib' timentib' dnm quia concupiunt in mandatis dei sui. et intellexit sup egenum et pauperem ut potens est: in sclm semen ei' et iusticia ei' maneret in sclm scli. Veruntam et hoc qd ad meritum sci paulini pertinet: uenera cio tua debet agnoscere. Quod

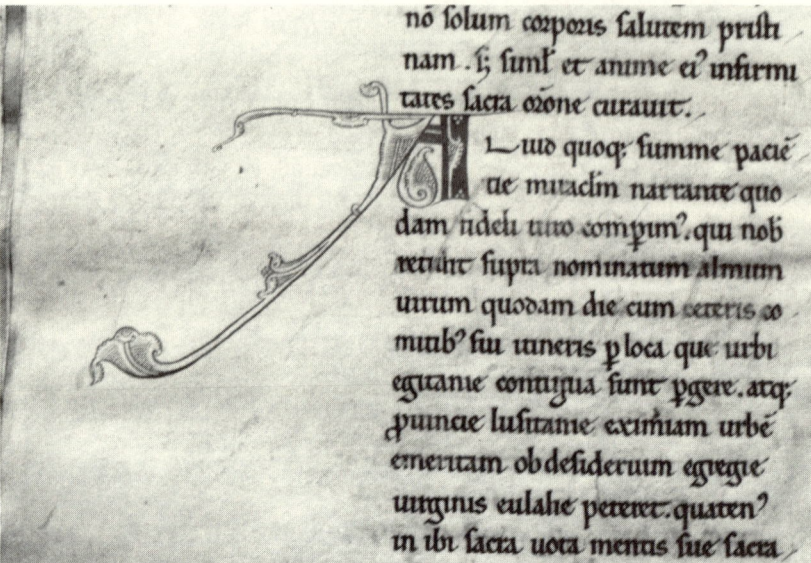

6 (upper): Bein. 625, fol. 33v
7 (lower): Bein. 625, fol. 25v

century we can include Escorial a.II.9; Madrid, Biblioteca Nacional 494; Madrid, Real Academia de la Historia Códices X and XIII; Paris, Bibliothèque Nationale nouv. acq. lat. 2178; and a sixteenth-century copy of a lost manuscript of Carracedo from the tenth century, now Escorial &.III.8. There is no doubt, however, that Beinecke MS 625 is most closely related to the earliest surviving collection of *vitae*, found in Madrid, Biblioteca Nacional 10007, a Visigothic manuscript dated 902 and formerly in Toledo.[10]

The similarities between the Yale codex and that from Toledo can be seen from the following transcriptions of incipits and explicits in Beinecke MS 625. Each work is followed by the appropriate bibliographical citation and the corresponding folios in B.N. 10007.[11]

1. ff. 1r-5r end of the Prologue: //tis. palmam requirant. *Explicit pphm* [sic] *orani presbyteri. Incipit vita sancti iohannis.* Primum igitur tanquam uere fundamentum nostri operis ... uitentur et perfectam pacientie palmam requirant. (Folios missing between 1-2, 2-3, and 4-5)

   Madrid, B.N. 10007: ff. 2v-12v.

2. f. 5r-v *Incipit uita sancti orani.* Uidimus et alium apud thebaidam mirabilem uirum nomine oranum hic mutorum ... uirtutum celestium. in hymnis et laudibus dei per uigiles uiderentur.

   Madrid, B.N. 10007:ff. 139r-140v.

3. ff. 5v-6r *De sancto amone.* Vidimus autem in tebaydam etiam alium uirum nomine amonem pater trium milium ... his abstinere que in oculis habentur et in manibus.

   Madrid, B.N. 10007: f. 140v.

---

[10] Madrid, B.N. 10007 ends on f. 263v: "Explicit in era dccccxl [A.D. 902] regnante domno adefonsum princeps Armentarius Indignus et graue onus peccatorum depressus scripsit. Hora pro me sic Inueniad requiem anime tue. Amen." Although it is not possible to say with certainty that B.N. 10007 was produced at Toledo, we know that it was preserved there by the 11th century. A note dating from that period is located in the lower margin of f. 147v: "Hunc librum dedit domnus pe [erasure of ca. 7 letters] ti deo et ecclesia sancte marie sedis toletane pro redemtione anime sue et omnium parentorum suorum. in tali uero ratione, ut ullus nec episcopus nec clericus uel etiam laicus eundem librum ab eadem ecclesia auferat, sed semper ibi maneat." See Ramon Fernández Pousa, "Los manuscritos visigóticos de la Biblioteca Nacional," *Verdad y Vida* 10 (1940) 16; also *idem, San Valerio, Obras* (Madrid 1942) 1-18.

[11] Items 1-18 are from Rufinus Tyrannius, *Historia monachorum* (PL 21. 391-462). The remaining texts have the bibliographical reference, when available, following the transcription.

4. f. 6r *De sancto beno.* Vidimus et alium senem mansuetudine omnes homines precellentem benum nomine ... cocodrillum ab eo alio tempore fugatum perhibetur.

   Madrid, B.N. 10007:ff. 140v-141r.

5. f. 6r-v *De sancto oxirinco.* Uidimus autem in ciuitate tebaydis quendam nomine oxirinco in qua tanta religionis ... alios in abstinentia. alios in signis et uirtutibus ministrantes.

   Madrid, B.N. 10007: f. 141r-v.

6. ff. 6v-7r *Incipit de sancto theone.* Vidimus et alium non longe ab urbe eadem parte qua mittit ad heremum ... circa eius cellulam plurima deprehendebantur.

   Madrid, B.N. 10007:ff. 141v-142r.

7. ff. 7r-11v *Incipit de sancto appollonio.* Uidimus et alium uirum sanctum nomine appollonium apud thebaidam in finibus ... et uideatis que bona sunt in ierusalem omnibus diebus uite uestre amen.

   Madrid, B.N. 10007:ff. 142r-149v.

8. ff. 11v-12v *Incipit de sancto ammone xvi.* Qve audiuimus de sancto ammone quodam uiro cuius etiam locum in quo ... cum mortua fuisset bestia sine ipso propinquare audebant.

   Madrid, B.N. 10007:ff. 149v-151v.

9. ff. 12v-15r *Incipit de sancto coprete.* Erat quidam presbyter in ipsa heremo habens monasterium copres nomine uir sanctus annorum ... dupplicem leticiam gessimus et pro salute hominis et pro beneficijs diuinis.

   Madrid, B.N. 10007:ff. 151v-155r.

10. f. 15r-v *Incipit de sancto abbate.* Addebat ad huc etiam hec abbas in quid syrus aliquando et ysaias et paulus occurrent sibi ... tradidit spiritum et continuo uident ipsi ab angulis// (Two folios missing between 15-16; *De Heleno, De Elia,* and the beginning of the Life of Apelles, which are in B.N. 10007, are lacking in Beinecke MS 625.)

    Madrid, B.N. 10007: ff. 155r-156r.

11. f. 16r-v Life of Apelles begins imperfectly: //At illa clamans et euilans aufugit ita ut omnes fratres ... nonnullis fortasse audientium uix crediblie.

    Madrid, B.N. 10007: ff. 158v-159v.

12. ff. 16v-18v *Incipit de sancto paphnuncio.* Uidimus et monasterium sancti paphnuncij hominis dei qui nominatissimum in illis locis ... suscipi hymnum canentibus et conlaudantibus deum.

Madrid, B.N. 10007: ff. 159v-162r.

13. f. 18v *Incipit de ysidori monasterij.* Uidimus apud thebaidam etiam ysidori nominatissimum monasterium amplissimis apacijs ... ad hoc ipsum recubans spiritum letus emittet.

Madrid, B.N. 10007: f. 162r-v.

14. ff. 18v-19r *xxiiii. de sancto serapione.* Sed et in regione arsenoyte serapionem que ... ipsa esse in quibus frumenta tunc congregata sunt.

Madrid, B.N. 10007: f. 162v.

15. f. 19r-v *Incipit de sancto appollonio.* Tradebant autem seniores horum fuisse quendam persecutionis tempore monachorum ... est dominus adducere et uota nostra orationesque complere.

Madrid, B.N. 10007: ff. 162v-163v.

16. ff. 19v-20r *Incipit de sancto dioscoro.* Vidimus et alium uenerabilem patrem apud thebaidam dioscorum nomine ... cui anima et spiritus sanitas expetenda est.

Madrid, B.N. 10007: ff. 163v-164r.

17. ff. 20r-24v *Incipit de nitrie monasterijs.* Uidimus autem et nitriam famosissimum in omnibus egipti monasterijs locum qui quadraginta ferme milibus abest ... in summa admiratione uite eius iusticie atque animi eius uirtutes habuisse mirabatur.

Madrid, B.N. 10007: ff. 164r-169v.

18. ff. 24v-26v *Incipit de sancto paulo.* Fuit quidam inter discipulos antonij paulus nomine cognomento simplex ... periculis liberauit et tota nobis hostendit mirabilia ipsi gloria in secula seculorum.

Madrid, B.N. 10007: ff. 169v-172v.

19. ff. 26v-29r *Incipit uita sancti malchi captiui monachi.* Qvi nauali prelio dimicaturi sunt. ante in portu et in tranquillo ... christo deditum posse mori. non posse superari. per iesum christum dominum ... seculorum.

BHL no. 5190; PL 23.55-60; Madrid, B.N. 10007: ff. 172v-176r.

20. ff. 29r-31r *Incipit uita sancti frontoni.* Edificationis uestre memor et mei solacij curam ferens. decreui aliqua ... et uniuersis fratribus

legite gratias agentes domino nostro iesu christo filio dei patris ... seculorum amen.

BHL no. 3190; Madrid, B.N. 10007: ff. 176r-178v.

21. ff. 31r-36r *Incipit uita uel memoratio mirabiliorum que deus pro boni obsequij famulatum sanctissimi fructuosi episcopi ad corroborandam fidem credentium statuit ad salutem.* Postquam antiquitas mundi tenebras superne ueritatis noua irradiauit claritas ... merens eius inuictum postulauerit auxilium statim plenum a domino peticionis sue consequitur fructum.

F. C. Nock, *The Vita Sancti Fructuosi: Text with a Translation, Introduction, and Commentary* (Washington 1946: The Catholic University, Studies in Mediaeval History N.S., v. VII) pp. 87-129; BHL no. 3194; Madrid, B.N. 10007: ff. 178v-185v.

22. ff. 36r-51r *Incipit epistola beati iohannis constantinopolitani episcopi ad theodorum monachum de reparatione labe* [sic]. Qvis dabit capiti meo aquam et oculis meis fontem ... Quamquam certus sim quod si hec libenter legas alia ultra medicamenta non queres. (Folio missing between 42-43, 48-49, 49-50)

Bibliotheca Casinensis (Monte Cassino 1876: v. III, Florilegium Casinense) pp. 389-411; Madrid, B.N. 10007: ff. 185v-211v.

23. ff. 51r-54r *Incipit uita sancte pelagie ceterum que secuntur.* Magnas domino gratias referre debemus qui non uult perire ... patribus et in locum mundissimum collocatum ad laudem et gloriam patris et filij et spiritu sancti amen. [epilogue:] Ego uero iacobus ... Cum qua uos deus faciat inuenire misericordiam in illa die. quoniam ipsi est honor et potestas in secula seculorum amen. (Folio missing between 53-54)

BHL no. 6605; Madrid, B.N. 10007: ff. 211v-216v.

24. ff. 54r-56v *Incipit uita sancti symeonis scripta ab eius discipulo nomine antonio die quarto kalendas augusti.* Sancte igitur recordationis beatus symeon cuius depostionem hodie celebramus ... christus operare dignatus est qui cum deo patre et spiritu sancto uiuit et regnat ... seculorum.

BHL no. 7959; PL 73. 325-34; Madrid, B.N. 10007; ff. 216v-220v.

25. ff. 56v-57r *Incipit de monachorum penitentia recuperationis.* Frater quidam impugnabatur a fornicatione. Contigit autem uenire ... De cetero attende temet ipsum et esto sollicitus. Respondit ei frater. Ecce amo tecum ero donec moriar.

PL 73. 884-85; Madrid, B.N. 10007: ff. 220v-221r.

26. ff. 57r-58r *Item alia. xxvi.* Monachus quidam solitarius antiquus in conuersationem proficiens. sedebat in montem in partes ... Etiam post aliquos dies mortis sue reuelatum est senibus de transitu eius.

PL 73. 886-88; Madrid, B.N. 10007: ff. 221r-222v.

27. f. 58r-v *De exultacione diaboli in monachorum. uel perseuerantia et labore perfectorum.* Dicebat quidam de thebeis senibus quod filius esset sacerdotis ydolorum quia ... Valde bonum est oratio monachorum. et placuit deo donare michi salutem. et egressus factus sum monachus.

PL 73.885-86; Madrid, B.N. 10007: ff. 222v-223r.

28. ff. 58v-60r *Item epistola beatissime egerie laude conscripta bergidensium monachorum a ualerio collata.* Qvesto et intento corde presentis sancti et deo placiti ... Quia qualis hinc quis egreditur talis in iudicio presentatur. ut recipiat unus quisque secundam opera sua.

PL 87.421-26; Madrid, B.N. 10007: ff. 223r-225r.

29. f. 60r-v *Dicta beati ualerij ad beatum donadeum scripta.* et ut de his duabus retributionibus sepe dictis manifestius pateat quod ... agens demum penitentiam iterum migrauit e corpore.

PL 87.431-33; Madrid, B.N. 10007: ff. 225r-226v.

30. ff. 60v-61v *Item de bonello monacho.* Hec igitur tue beatitudini narrans. aliud huiuscemodi simile reminiscor. Quidam religiosus ... et usque hodie ibidem perseuerat.

PL 87.433-35; Madrid, B.N. 10007: ff. 226v-227v.

31. ff. 61v-62r *De celeste reuelacione.* Dum holim sancte memorie beatissimus fructuosus ... et presentibus auferens luctum ad epti sunt consolationis gaudium.

PL 87.435-36; Madrid, B.N. 10007: ff. 227v-228v.

32. f. 62r-v *De monachorum penitentia uel recuperationis post ruinam.* Dvo fratres inpugnati a fornicationis spiritu. abierunt et acceperunt uxores ... et reminiscens assidue misericordiam dei mei letabar. Et dixerunt senes. Equales est amborum penitencia.

PL 73. 882-83; Madrid, B.N. 10007: f. 228v.

33. ff. 62v-65v *Incipit doctrina mandatorum duodecom sancti athanasij episcopi ad anthiocum.* Dux aliquis nomine anthiocus ueniens ad sanctum athanasium episcopum in graui ... Et nos oramus ut nos

omnes mereamini ingredi ibi per gratiam domini nostri iesu christi ... seculorum amen. (Folio missing between 62-63)

Cf. PG 28.555-75 (the Latin translation differs somewhat from the printed text); Madrid, B.N. 10007: ff. 228v-234r.

34. ff. 65v-68v *hinc sequitur uita ipsius antiochi abbatis.* Hec igitur audiens anthiocus et scribens ea in libro cordis. et ... dum tempus est curramus ad dominum saluatorem nostrum quia apud eum est fons uite et radix bonitatis. ipsi est gloria in secula seculorum.

    Cf. PG 28.575-90 (the Latin translation differs somewhat from the printed text); Madrid, B.N. 10007: ff. 234r-238r.

35. f. 68v *xlviii. Incipit de monachis perfectis.* Iam dudum animis nostris insedit dilectissimi fratres monachorum singularis ... conuersatio sursum in celis est. Et hec quidem in omni ecclesia catholica// (One folio and one quire [?] plus one folio missing between 68-69)

    R. Fernández Pousa, *San Valerio. Obras* (Madrid 1942) pp. 122-29; Madrid, B.N. 10007: ff. 238r-239r.

36. ff. 69r-82r The Life of St. Antony begins imperfectly: //ore eius procedunt lampades accense. Crines quoque incendijs sparguntur. Ex naribus eius fumus egreditur quasi fornacis estuantis ... ut demones quos illi deos esse arbitrantur. conculcent atque deiciant. Deceptores scilicet omnium. et tocius corruptionis artifices. Igitur beatus antonius .xvi. Kalendas februarij recessit e seculo ... amen. (Folio missing between 74-75, 75-76, and 79-80)

    PL 73.138-68; Madrid, B.N. 10007: ff. 17v-48r.

37. ff. 82r-89v *Incipit pphm* [sic] *beati ieronimi presbyteri de uita sancti ylarionis* [added in a later hand:] *monachi.* Scripturus uitam beati ilarionis habitatorem eius inuoco spiritum sanctum ... *Incipit uita sancti ylarionis.* Ilarion ortus huicothauta. qui circiter quindecim milia a gaza ... Qui respondens ait. Procuratorem fuisse uille ad quaem [sic] ortulus quoque// (Two folios missing between 88-89, one between 89-90.)

    PL 23.29-54; Madrid, B.N. 10007: ff. 48r-63v.

38. ff. 90r-96r The Prologue to the Life of Germanus begins abruptly: //illatis obtutibus ebetat oculorum aciem lumen confundit ... malo quod meminem. *Incipit uita sancti germani.* Igitur germanus altisidionensis oppidi indigena fuit. parentibus splendidissimis ... *Explicit uita sancti germani episcopi.* Sanctus germanus episcopus

pridie kalendas augusti de hoc corpore ... ut suffragia illius misericordiam deum consequantur. (Three folios missing between 92-93.)

Madrid, B.N. 10007: ff. 64v-80v.

39. ff. 96r-103v *Incipit uita sancti ambrosij episcopi.* Ortvs uenerabilis pater augustine ut sicuti uiri atanasius episcopus et ... cum unum de turba deprecaretur ut scirent quis essent uiri audierit ambrosium eius consortem. (One folio missing between 98-99.)

PL 14.27-46; Madrid, B.N. 10007: ff. 80v-95v.

40. ff. 103v-106v *Incipit epistola orani presbyteri ad paccatum de uita sancti paulini episcopi.* Domno sancto et uenerabili paccato oranius presbyter in christo salutem ... Vt et hij qui non uiderunt eos in corpore eorum discentes uitamque eis perfectam lectionis inditio colligentes. ad emulationem sancti operis in//

PL 53.859-66; Madrid, B.N. 10007; ff. 133v-139r.

Both volumes are fragmentary and are no longer in their original bindings,[12] so it is not surprising that the order of the *vitae* differs somewhat. What is remarkable is the number of the works which the two manuscripts share. As is evident from the above list, for every work in the Beinecke manuscript there is a corresponding life in the codex of 902.[13] In addition, if one compares the *incipits* and *explicits* of the following three passages from B.N. 10007 with those listed above (nos. 4, 15 and 17), the similarities are apparent:

(4) *De sancto beno.* Vidimus et alium senem mansuetudine omnes omines precellentem benum nomine ... corcodrillum ab eo alio tempore fucatum peribetur.

---

[12] The quires of Beinecke MS 625 were unbound for some time, and many folios show signs of water damage sustained then. Apparently the manuscript was laid against others while damp: offset color from initials of this and other mansucripts can be seen on several folios. The manuscript was recently bound according to the specifications of Laurence Witten in blind-tooled brown calf. All the flyleaves are modern. Madrid, B.N. 10007 is bound in deer skin, with clasps; see Fernández, (above, n. 10) 16.

[13] There is no such correspondence of texts between the Yale codex and the other early Spanish collections mentioned above. Indeed, there are usually differences in both the number and arrangement of the lives. See, for example, the comparison of the contents of Madrid, B.N. 10007 (listed as Toletanus 10.25) and Madrid, Academia de la Historia Códice XIII, in D. de Bruyne, "L'héritage littéraire de l'Abbé Saint Valère," *Revue Bénédictine* 32 (1920) 5-7. One can, however, compare the contents of the Beinecke MS with a later manuscript, Toledo, Cathedral 10-26, apparently produced at Toledo in the first quarter of the 13th century (see footnote 6). The contents of MS 10-26 have not been published; rubrics, *incipits* and *explicits* were checked on a visit to Toledo in 1982.

(15) *Incipit de sancto apollonio.* Tradebant ergo seniores orum fuisse quendam persecutionis tempore monachorum ... est dominus adducere et uota nostra orationesque conplere.

(17) *XXUII Incipit de nitre monasteriis.* Venimus autem et nitriam famosissimum in omnibus egipti monasteriis locum qui quadraginta ferme milibus abest ... in summa admiratione uitę eius iustitie atque animi eius uirtutes abuisse mirabatur.

In other passages there are errors which are easily explained by a glance at the Visigothic manuscript, for some of the rubrics of B.N. 10007 are in yellow, and are extremely difficult to read against the glossy, yellowish parchment. Thus the heading in no. 22 ends in *lapsi* in B.N. 10007 (f. 185v), but reads *labe* in the Beinecke codex.

Is it therefore possible to theorize that Beinecke MS 625 is a direct copy of B.N. 10007? A close analysis of the text does not support this hypothesis, since the number and type of variant readings suppose at least one intermediary text. Simple orthographical changes such as the addition or omission of *h,* and the confusion of *b* and *v* or of *c* and *g* can be readily understood. What is difficult to attribute to scribal error is the change from *ergo* (B.N. 10007) to *autem* (Beinecke 625), from *uenimus* to *uidimus,* or from *gloria* to *honor* (a variant reading in no. 22). We suspect that at least one copy of the 902 manuscript intervened, although judging from those portions of the texts compared, it was an accurate transcription of the exemplar.

On the basis of the text, script and decoration it is evident that the Beinecke *Vitae sanctorum* was produced in Toledo toward the end of the twelfth century. Given the importance of Toledo in this period, the manuscript merits further study of both its codicological features and its contents.

University of Cincinnati
Cincinnati, Ohio

Bucknell University
Lewisberg, Pennsylvania

DECEPTUM ERRORE: IMAGES OF CRETE IN THE *AENEID*

LESLIE PRESTON DAY

The island of Crete or people, places, and objects associated with Crete appear with some frequency in Vergil's *Aeneid*.[1] Aeneas himself visits Crete on his wanderings; scenes of Cretan legend are depicted sculpturally on the doors of the Temple of Apollo at Cumae; and Crete's association with craftsmanship and archery is evoked in images and descriptions throughout the poem. References are made to the island itself (either in nominal or adjectival form), to specific cities or sites on Crete (Cnossus, Gortyn, Cydonia, Mount Ida, Mount Dicte), or to historical and mythological personages associated with the island (Minos, Pasiphae, Ariadne, Phaedra, Androgeos, the Minotaur, Daedalus, Idomeneus, and the Curetes). A close examination of these references shows us something of Vergil's technique, in particular his use of image as symbol. Cretan names and images have been inserted not only for ornament or erudition, as suggested by many commentators,[2] but also they create a complex set of associations which Vergil uses to move his poem forward on a symbolic level. It is not by chance that Crete is associated with many of the major events and characters of the *Aeneid*; it is part of Vergil's scheme to weave various levels of meaning into the dense texture of his poem. It is necessary to look at the passages which contain Cretan references to understand their significance for the poem.

Crete is first mentioned in Book III (104-17), where Anchises wrongly interprets the command of the oracle of Apollo on Delos to

---

[1] The idea for this article was suggested by the title of a paper by Andreas Panagopoulos delivered at the Fifth Cretological Congress in Ayios Nikolaos, Crete, in September of 1981, and subsequently published as "Kriti sto ergo tou Birgiliou," *Politeia* 2 (1981) 65-76. Mr. Panagopoulos' examination of the depictions of Crete in ancient literature shows that they were basically negative. Because Crete was a backwater of the ancient world and a major base for pirates, ancient authors — in particular Polybius and Nepos — expressed a prejudice against the island. See also M.I. Finley, "The Rediscovery of Crete," *Aspects of Antiquity* (London 1968) 7-23. Panagopoulos, however, does not see this kind of attitude in Vergil's writings. While I agree that Vergil is not negative toward Crete in the same way as other ancient authors, I do not believe that he is as positive as Panagopoulos would have us believe.

[2] For example, R.D. Williams, *The Aeneid of Virgil, I-VI* (London 1972) 340, 418; *VII-XII* (London 1973) 296, 429; R.G. Austin, *Virgil, Aeneid IV* (Oxford 1963) 45.

seek the original Trojan homeland as a reference to Crete:

> Creta Iovis magni medio iacet insula ponto,
> mons Idaeus ubi et gentis cunabula nostrae.   105
> centum urbes habitant magnas, uberrima regna,
> maximus unde pater, si rite audita recordor,
> Teucrus Rhoeteas primum est advectus in oras,
> optavitque locum regno. nondum Ilium et arces
> Pergameae steterant; habitabant vallibus imis.   110
> hinc mater cultrix Cybeli Corybantiaque aera
> Idaeumque nemus, hinc fida silentia sacris,
> et iuncti currum dominae subiere leones.
> ergo agite et divum ducunt qua iussa sequamur: 115
> placemus ventos et Cnosia regna petamus.
> nec longo distant cursu: modo Iuppiter adsit,
> tertia lux classem Cretaeis sistet in oris.

This first and longest reference to Crete should be and is of great importance for our understanding of Vergil's use of Cretan imagery. The description of Crete here seems straightforward; it is the island of 100 cities of the *Iliad* (II.649), it is associated with Jupiter as in the *Georgics* (IV.149-152) and it is connected with Troy by the similarity of place names, especially Mount Ida. There is, however, more here than is at first evident. The island itself occupies the significant first position in the passage, and it is *Creta Iovis,* Jupiter's Crete. It is his because of the tradition that he was born and raised on the island, but this strong association with the god may have further significance. It is Jupiter who has devised the plan for the creation of the Roman race, and the wanderings of the Trojans are part of his plan for educating Aeneas. The fact that the Trojans land on Jupiter's island may therefore indicate that Create is part of his overall design. Not only is Crete Jupiter's, but it is also *cunabula gentis,* the cradle of the Trojan race and the place from which Teucer came to found Troy. It is associated with the early nurturing of the Trojans, and the connections between Troy and Crete are explicated. Cretan civilization is seen as having primacy over the Trojan culture, and, indeed, throughout the poem there are many references to superior Cretan craftsmanship.[3] To complete this nurturing

---

[3] It is interesting to note that modern archaeology and scholarship have confirmed that the first true civilization in the Aegean was on Crete and that during the flowering of Minoan culture the products of Cretan craftsmanship were valued throughout the Mediterranean. Vergil is therefore reflecting an historical occurrence, in a manner that may be fortuitous or may have been derived from a continuous folk memory. Vergil may also be reflecting the chance finds of Bronze Age objects which were constantly being made in antiquity.

image of Crete, Anchises also associates the island with the Magna Mater and describes it as a pastoral landscape, devoid of human activity, where the gods still dwell.

In spite of these positive associations, the important fact about this description of Crete, which the audience knows but the characters have not yet learned, is that it is false. Anchises is deceived in his belief that Crete is the new homeland ordained by the gods for the Trojans. Crete is another stage in the attempt to rebuild Troy, and during Book III Aeneas gradually learns the impossibility of recreating the empty image of old Troy and comes to the understanding that he must attempt to build something new. He cannot return to the cradle of the race; he must go forward. Crete, then, is a false homeland for Aeneas, but it is part of Jupiter's plan that Aeneas learn from his mistaken belief.

As the Trojans proceed to Crete, they hear that it is deserted (III.121-3):

> Fama volat pulsum regnis cessisse paternis
> Idomenea ducem, desertaque litora Cretae,
> hoste vacare domum sedesque astare relictas.

Commentators have pointed out that the departure of Idomeneus and his followers has left space for Aeneas and the Trojans and has eliminated the possibility of war between the two groups, so recently enemies in the Trojan War.[4] This could be seen as a positive indication to Aeneas of the success of the Cretan venture, but the very mention of Idomeneus is possibly the first hint that the Cretan attempt will fail. Idomeneus, like Daedalus, can be seen as a precursor of Aeneas. Servius tells us that Idomeneus was caught in a storm on his return from Troy and vowed that if saved he would sacrifice the first thing he saw on landing.[5] It turned out to be his son, and after he killed the boy a plague came, and Idomeneus was forced to flee to Italy. Like Aeneas, Idomeneus performed an act of *pietas* to the will of the gods, an act which involved the death of a son, just as *pater* Aeneas will be responsible for the deaths of so many innocent young people as he accomplishes the destiny the gods have appointed for him. As will happen to Aeneas, Idomeneus was driven out of Crete by disease and fled to Italy. The mention of Idomeneus at this point, then, is not just a way to eliminate a potential problem for the Trojans; it is a foreshadowing of what will happen to Aeneas on Crete and in Italy. The

---
[4] T.E. Page, *The Aeneid of Virgil, Books I-VI* (repr. London 1967) 286.
[5] Servius *ad Aen*.III.121.

association between the two men is strengthened by possible verbal echoes of the description of Crete abandoned by Idomeneus (123) in the passage relating the departure of Aeneas from the island (190):

> hanc quoque deserimus sedem paucisque relictis.

Finally (III.129-190), the Trojans arrive on the island, *antiquis Curetum oris* (131). Mention of the Curetes again calls to mind Jupiter, since the Curetes protected the god in his infancy, but they will not protect the Trojans. The Trojans found their new Troy, calling it Pergamum, and the people "rejoice in the old familiar name" (*laetam cognomine*). Disease, however, comes upon them immediately, a disease similar to that which afflicted the Greeks in the *Iliad*, (I.59f) and it is seen as a sign that the gods do not favor the settlement. Finally, the Penates appear to Aeneas in a dream, tell him that he must seek Italy, and explain that Crete is not his new homeland (III. 161 f.):

> mutandae sedes. non haec tibi litora suasit
> Delius aut Cretae iussit considere Apollo.

Crete is denied to the Trojans by the will of Jupiter (171):

> Dictaea negat tibi Iuppiter arva.

When Aeneas tells the dream to Anchises, the old man admits his earlier mistake (181):

> seque novo veterum deceptum errore locorum.

This is an image of Crete which will persist throughout the *Aeneid*, an image of deception, here self-deception. Crete may be the *cunabula gentis*, but Aeneas has learned that he cannot return to the past. It is an important lesson for Aeneas, and Crete is used again in the poem to point up the deception of false goals or ideas.

The image of Crete as deceptive did not originate with Vergil, though his use of it is unique. Crete plays an important role in the *Odyssey*, Vergil's foremost epic model in the first six books of the *Aeneid*. Odysseus three times tells similar lies about his identity, first to Athena, then to Eumaeus, and finally to his wife Penelope.[6] In all three lies he identifies himself as a Cretan, a follower of Idomeneus, or at least claims to have seen Odysseus on Crete. Odysseus is a man

---

[6] *Odyssey* XII. 256 ff.; XIV. 199 ff.; XIX. 172ff. On these lies, cf. C.R. Trahman, "Odysseus' lies." *Phoenix* 6 (1952) 31-43.

seeking to return home, and for him Crete is a false homeland. For Aeneas, who has abandoned his home and is seeking a new one, Crete is also a false homeland; it is false both because it cannot be the old Troy and because it is not the divinely appointed home which awaits him. It is wrong both for the past and the future and as false as the Crete of Odysseus' lies. However, Odysseus uses Crete to deceive deliberately in order to achieve his true homecoming, while Aeneas is deceived through ignorance of his true home. Crete is for him a deception through ignorance — *deceptum errore,* as Vergil says of Anchises. Throughout the *Aeneid* Crete will continue as an image of deception.[7]

There is a final mention of Crete in Book III, a reference to Idomeneus by Helenus, who warns Aeneas to avoid the eastern coast of Italy, where the Greeks, including Idomeneus, have settled (400 f.):

> ... et Sallentinos obsedit milite campos
> Lyctius Idomeneus; ...

Helenus' advice works on several levels because of the inclusion of Idomeneus here. On the surface, he refers merely to the political situation, that there are Greeks on the east coast of Italy who would be hostile to Aeneas and the Trojans. The advice to avoid areas of Cretan settlement is also a warning against the establishment of a false homeland on the east coast, an especially apt and ironic bit of advice, since Helenus' new home also should be perceived as a false new Troy. There is room for optimism, however, since Idomeneus, as a forerunner of Aeneas, also suggests the end of Aeneas' wanderings and the eventual success of a settlement in Italy.

References to Crete by no means stop after Book III. Early in Book IV Crete appears again in an extremely interesting pair of similes which describe Dido and Aeneas. In the famous simile likening Dido to a wounded deer, she is placed in a specifically Cretan setting, a setting which is emphasized by repetition (IV. 68-74):

> uritur infelix Dido totaque vagatur
> urbe furens, qualis coniecta cerva sagitta,
> quam procul incautam nemora inter Cresia fixit
> pastor agens telis liquitque volatile ferrum
> nescius: illa fuga silvas saltusque peragrat
> Dictaeos; haeret lateri letalis harundo.

---

[7] W.R. Johnson, *Darkness Visible* (Berkeley 1976) 81, 96 suggests this idea, but does not elaborate on it.

Somewhat later, Aeneas is compared with Apollo among his followers, who include Cretans (IV. 144-6):

> ... Apollo
> instauratque choros, mixtique altaria circum
> Cretesque Dryopesque fremunt pictique Agathyrsi.

The Cretan setting of the deer simile has been explicated as adding color or making the picture more vivid.[8] Duclos quite rightly sees Crete in this image as part of a pattern of similes in which Dido is first likened to Diana, the huntress (I. 500 f.), then to a wounded deer, while Aeneas is compared to Apollo, who will "complete the fatal conquest."[9] Duclos further suggests that the Cretan imagery is meant to evoke Ariadne, who was deserted, as Dido will be, by the man she loved.[10] The similarities both in verbal echoes and theme, between Book IV of the *Aeneid* and Catullus 64, which describes the desertion of Ariadne, are too numerous to ignore,[11] and they support the identification of Dido with Ariadne. The Cretan setting of this simile strengthens the association of the two women, and the simile of Aeneas as Apollo places Aeneas in the same setting.

We have already seen, however, that Crete was an image of falseness and deception in Book III, and such an image also applies here. The point of the simile is to show love's effect on Dido and Aeneas' role in it, as well as to foreshadow the unhappy ending of the affair and to give psychological insights and coloring. The Cretan setting not only warns us that the outcome will parallel what happened to Ariadne, but it shows that the love of Dido and Aeneas is false. Dido is deceived into thinking that Aeneas will stay with her, and Aeneas deceives himself into believing that he can give up his quest. Carthage with Dido's love is another false homeland for him. In the end, Dido will be another innocent and tragic victim sacrificed to Aeneas' destiny, as Idomeneus and Daedalus sacrificed their sons. The references to Crete in Book IV are not, then, purely ornamental, but they weave new levels of meaning into the fabric of the story of Dido and Aeneas. The Cretan imagery, along with echoes of Catullus 64, evokes the story of Ariadne and Theseus, but it also points out the falseness of Dido and Aeneas' love and the deception which will result in Dido's tragic end.

---

[8] Williams, (above, n.2) I-VI. p. 340; Austin (above, n.2), p. 45.
[9] G. Duclos, "Nemora inter Cresia," *CJ* 66 (1971) 193-5.
[10] *Ibid*, p. 194.
[11] D.H. Abel, "Ariadne and Dido," *CB* 38 (1961-2) 57-61.

During the funeral games for Anchises in Book V, Cretan references appear three times. After the ship race, the unlucky Sergestus, whose return in his disabled ship is compared to a wounded snake, is given a Cretan woman as a booby prize (V. 284 f.):

> olli serva datur operum haud ignara Minervae,
> Cressa genus, Pholoë, geminique sub ubere nati.

The woman, skilled in weaving, is described in terms which resemble Homeric fomulas,[12] but the Cretan origin for such women does not appear in Homer. Sergestus is a minor character in the *Aeneid,* and it is difficult to see why he would be connected with Crete or the idea of deception associated with it elsewhere. Sergestus, however, was the founder of the Sergian house, whose later descendant was the infamous Catiline. The image of the broken snake has been seen as a reference to the scotching of Catiline's consipiracy,[13] and if this is so, the association with Crete may suggest the deceit and trickery of Sergestus' descendant.

Other Cretan objects are given as prizes in the funeral games. The first prize for the foot race is a pair of Cretan arrows and an axe (V. 306-07):

> Cnosia bino dabo levato lucida ferro
> spicula caelatamque argento ferre bipennem.

It is Euryalus who wins the race, through a certain amount of trickery on the part of his lover Nisus, an event which foreshadows the tragic deaths of the two in Book IX. The arrows are here designated as Cretan, not only because of the association of the island with archery, but also to point up the trickery of Euryalus' victory and to suggest the falseness of the young men's goals. It is interesting to note that Euryalus will be presented with a Cretan sword before going out on the ill-fated expedition in Book IX (305).

At the conclusion of the games, Ascanius and the Trojan youths perform the *lusus Troiae,* a difficult maneuver whose complexity is likened to the Cretan labyrinth (V. 588-93):

> ut quondam Creta fertur Labyrinthus in alta
> parietibus textum caecis iter ancipitemque
> mille viis habuisse dolum, qua signa sequendi
> frangeret indeprensus et inremeabilis error;

---

[12] R.D. Williams, *Virgil, Aeneid V* (Oxford 1960) 100; cf. *Il.* XXIII.263; IX.128 f.

[13] R.A. Hornsby, *Patterns of Action in the Aeneid* (Iowa City 1970) 63.

> haud alio Teucrum nati vestigia cursu
> impediunt texuntque fugas et proelia ludo ...

The games here described were revived by Julius Caesar and established by Augustus as a regular institution, and hence they establish a connection between the founders of the Julian house and its most notable descendants. Much has been written about the *lusus Troiae* and the whole magical significance of the labyrinth image which appears here and on the doors of the temple of Apollo at Cumae in Book VI (see below).[14] Here the labyrinth image has been employed to describe the complexity of the boy's figures and their order and design, yet the simile actually suggests the opposite.[15] The whole image is not one of order, but rather of confusion and wandering (*inremeabilis error, parietibus caecis*) and deliberate deceit (*dolum*), like the other Cretan images since Book III. Part of the deceit is that these complicated maneuvers are not real; they are games performed by boys in imitation of the real battles which follow.[16] The labyrinth image is not completely worked out here, as the games are interrupted by the ship burning; but it is repeated and its full significance suggested at the beginning of Book VI.

The doors of the Temple of Apollo at Cumae have been sculpted by Daedalus with scenes of the Cretan labyrinth, and are described in VI.14-33, the longest Cretan reference outside Book III.

> Daedalus, ut fama est, fugiens Minoia regna
> praepetibus pennis ausus se credere caelo   15
> insuetum pariter gelidas enavit ad Arctos,
> Chalcidicaque levis tandem super astitit arce.
> redditus his primum terris tibi, Phoebe, sacravit
> remigium alarum posuitque immania templa.
> in foribus letum Androgeo; tum pendere poenas   20
> Cecropidae iussi (miserum!) septena quotannis
> corpora natorum; stat ductis sortibus urna.
> contra elata mari respondet Cnosia tellus:

---

[14] J.L. Heller, "Labyrinth or Troy Town?" *CJ* 42 (1946) 123-139; W.F.J. Knight, *Cumaean Gates* (Oxford 1936); R.W. Cruttwell, *Virgil's Mind at Work* (Oxford 1946) 37, 83-97, 165-82.

[15] M. DiCesare, *The Altar and the City: A Reading of Virgil's Aeneid* (New York 1974) 83-4; M.C.J. Putnam, *The Poetry of the Aeneid* (Cambridge, Mass. 1965) 88.

[16] Cruttwell (above, n.14) 87-9 sees verbal echoes of these games in the shield of Aeneas in Book VIII and in the fight between Turnus and Aeneas in Book XII. There are other links between the description of the *lusus Troiae* and the shield of Aeneas, particularly in the dolphin imagery in both (V.594-5, VIII. 673-4). The shield of Achilles in the *Iliad* also had scenes of Cnossus depicted on it, and the audience may be meant to make the connection.

> hic crudelis amor tauri suppostaque furto
> Pasiphae mixtumque genus prolesque biformis
> Minotaurus inest, Veneris monimenta nefandae;   25
> hic labor ille domus et inextricabilis error;
> magnum reginae sed enim miseratus amorem
> Daedalus ipse dolos tecti ambagesque resolvit,
> caeca regens filo vestigia. tu quoque magnam   30
> partem opere in tanto, sineret dolor, Icare, haberes.
> bis patriae cecidere manus.

The passage is one of three *ekphraseis* in the *Aeneid* (including the paintings in the Temple of Juno at Carthage and the Shield of Aeneas), and although its significance has been overlooked by many scholars,[17] it forms the climax of the Cretan imagery. Aeneas here learns the meaning of Crete.

First of all, the temple and its sculpture are said to have been the work of Daedalus, the preeminent ancient craftsman, representative of the primacy of Cretan arts and crafts. There may have been a connection between Daedalus and Cumae which prompted Vergil to include him here,[18] but Daedalus also forms an important paradigm for Aeneas because of the numerous parallels between the two men.[19] Both were forced to travel from Crete over the sea to Italy.[20] Both were fathers, and while Daedalus lost his son, Aeneas lost his father. Daedalus' grief for Icarus is poignantly described by his inability to depict his son on the reliefs, while Aeneas' loss has motivated the journey to the Underworld which brings him to Cumae. These references to Daedalus not only parallel certain events which have occurred to Aeneas, but they also show the depth of feeling between father and son, not just between Aeneas and Anchises, but between *pater* Aeneas and all the innocent young men and women who have lost or will lose their lives because of his destiny. These events and feelings have further significance for Vergil's own society, since there is a possible parallel of Daedalus and Icarus with Augustus and Marcellus,[21] a parallel which is strengthened by the association of Augustus with the reconstruction of

---

[17] For example E. Norden, *P. Vergilius Maro. Aeneis Buch VI* (Berlin 1916) 120, suggested that it holds up the action.

[18] R.G. Austin, *Virgil, Aeneid VI* (Oxford 1977) 39 and references.

[19] DiCesare (above, n.15) p. 95; M.O. Lee, *Fathers and Sons in Virgil's Aeneid: Tum genitor natum* (Albany 1979) 58-62.

[20] The description of Daedalus' journey uses nautical imagery (*enavit, remigium alarum*). See DiCesare, p. 95.

[21] Putnam (above, n.15), p. 211, n. 8.

the Temple of Apollo at Cumae.[22] This symbolic reference to the Augustan age is particularly fitting here, since it is the vision of the Roman future, with Augustus and Marcellus at its center, which will form the climax of Aeneas' journey to the Underworld.

The significance of the sculptured labyrinth on the temple doors has been widely discussed. It may in part have been suggested to Vergil by the fact that Minos was traditionally one of the judges of the dead, and the poet may also have known of the connections of labyrinths with tombs and the underworld.[23] The scene has been seen as a symbol of the rites of initiation and the tortuous passage through the Underworld, linked to primitive rites and superstition in Italy as well as other parts of the world.[24] The labyrinth, according to these theories, is an archetypal image which works below Vergil's consciousness, but, as Brooks has pointed out, even if this is true, it has little to do with Vergil's conscious poetic craft which we are examining here.[25] The same might be said of modern Jungian interpretation of the labyrinth, which equates it with the confusing world of matriarchal consciousness.[26] Certain details indicate that Vergil meant the labyrinth to serve as a symbol for Aeneas' journey in the Underworld; the description of his trip in Book VI contains verbal echoes of the labyrinth of both Books V and VI: for example, *inremeabilis error* (V. 591) is echoed in *inremeabilis undae* (VI. 425), and *hic labor ille domus* (VI. 27) is repeated by the Sibyl at the start of the journey, *hic labor est* (VI. 129). As Aeneas gazes at the doors he is seeing a symbolic representation of the journey he is about to make, the maze-like and tortuous path he will take through the Underworld.[27] This will be the last of his *errores*[28] and the last stage of his initiation, and he sees that the ending will be successful. The first scene Aeneas sees on the door is the death of Androgeos and the punishment for it which set in motion Theseus' destruction of the labyrinth. The *urna* of 1. 22 is echoed in the Underworld by the *urna* which Minos uses to judge the dead (VI. 432). The description of illicit love foreshadows the meeting

---

[22] Austin (above, n.18), p. 42.

[23] P. Enk, "De labyrinthi imagine in foribus templi Cumani insculpta (Verg. *Aen.*VI.27)," *Mnemosyne* 11 (1958) 322-30.

[24] W.F.J. Knight (above, n.14), p. 172.

[25] R.A. Brooks, "Discolor Aura: Reflections on the Golden Bough," *AJP* 74 (1953) p. 261, n.2.

[26] Lee (above, n.19) pp. 148-50.

[27] Putnam (above, n.15) pp. 211, n.8; M. Verrall, "Two Instances of Symbolism in the Sixth *Aeneid*," *CR* 24 (1910) 44.

[28] Putnam (above, n.15), p. 87.

with Dido. Theseus' successful completion of the maze with Ariadne's thread implies Aeneas' successful passage through the Underworld.

Aeneas also learns something of his own past, an important step before the vision of Rome's future which he will see in the Underworld. The Athenian scenes on one of the doors show the death of Androgeos and the selection by lot of seven victims to be sent to Crete as reparation, the first events of the cycle that leads to the destruction of the labyrinth. On the other door, the Cretan scenes show the passion of Pasiphae, the mating and monstrous birth, the labyrinth to contain the monster, and the solving of the maze by the thread given by Daedalus to Ariadne. The labyrinth is symbolic of Aeneas' wanderings, and at its center is the product of illicit passion, *Veneris monimenta nefandae,* which is both a reminder and a warning to Aeneas.[29] This illicit love is parallel to the passion of Dido and Aeneas,[30] and it is interesting to note verbal echoes here of Catullus 64, echoes which in Book IV were used to strengthen the identification of Dido with Adriadne. Lines 29-30 seem to recall Catullus 64. 112-13:

> inde pedem sospes multa cum laude reflexit
> errabunda regens tenui vestigia filo.

Although the Sibyl's sudden appearance prevents us from seeing Aeneas' reaction to these scenes, Vergil makes quite clear the pity Daedalus felt for Ariadne, feelings which must parallel Aeneas' pity for Dido's tragic fate, which are made clear later on. The audience is meant to judge Dido kindly, as Daedalus judged Ariadne, and to see her as an innocent victim, as Ariadne is presented in Catullus 64. Finally, Vergil gives a poignant picture of Daedalus' grief for his son, and this is the sort of pity which Vergil displays towards the fates of all the innocent followers of *pater* Aeneas who will die so that Rome's destiny will be fulfilled.

Through his description of the Cretan labyrinth, Vergil has presented Aeneas with a vision of his past and a warning for his future. After Book VI, Aeneas will give up trying to recreate the past, which, like all things Cretan, is a false goal. He has confronted the deceptive power of passion and has seen that it brings destruction. This is the first stage in the education which he receives in the Underworld.

---

[29] Austin (above, n.18), p. 44.

[30] Hornsby (above, n.13), p. 53; Putnam (above, n.15) p. 87, infers that the connection of the labyrinth image with Dido was initially suggested by the fact that Ascanius rode the horse given to him by Dido in the *lusus Troiae.* This idea, however, ignores the general importance of Cretan imagery in the *Aeneid.*

Among other Cretan images in Book VI, we see Minos and Rhadamanthus as judges (VI.432 f., 566-9):

> quaesitor Minos urnam movet; ille silentum
> conciliumque vocat vitasque et crimina discit.
>
> Cnosius haec Rhadamanthus habet durissima regna
> castigatque auditque dolos subigitque fateri
> quae quis apud superos furto laetatus inani
> distulit in seram commissa piacula mortem.

Minos seems to be reviewing judgments of the dead in formal Roman legal language,[31] while Rhadamanthus makes judgments on the basis of crimes which have been kept hidden in life. The association of Crete with deception is again strong, and who better than a Cretan to judge the trickery of others? Aeneas also sees a crowd of women in the Underworld, among whom are two Cretans, Phaedra and Pasiphae (VI. 445-7). All these women have been introduced as a backdrop for the meeting with Dido, and modern commentators have been mystified as to the reasons for Vergil's selection of these particular examples.[32] To a certain extent these women appear because they were part of the canonical list of women encountered in the Underworld by Odysseus (*Od.* XI.321 ff.); yet the inclusion of Pasiphae should come as no surprise, since she was used by Vergil as a parallel to Dido, and Phaedra strengthens this association of Dido with Crete and the deceptive power of passion.

After Book VI, images of Crete are neither so frequent nor so extensive, but where they do occur they continue to carry the association of deception. Because of Aeneas' lessons in the Underworld, however, the precise nature of the deception changes, and after the arrival in Italy Crete becomes a symbol of false values, rather than a false homeland.

It is interesting to note that when the Trojans finally reach their appointed home, the image of Crete reappears (VII.135-40). Aeneas and his followers place their food on flat wafers of bread, which they subsequently consume, thus fulfilling the prophecy of Celaeno (III.250 ff.) that Aeneas would not found his city before hunger forced the Trojans to eat their tables. So wary of false homelands has Aeneas become, however, that he seeks confirmation of the omen; he invokes all the possible local deities, the Nymphs, the earliest gods (Tellus,

---

[31] Austin, *Virgil, Aeneid VI* p. 156.
[32] Austin, p. 162; Williams, *The Aeneid of Virgil, I-VI*, pp. 485, 487.

Nox), the signs of the heavens, both his parents, and Jupiter and Cybele to send him a sign that he is not deceived. He specifically calls on Idaean Jupiter and the Magna Mater, both of whom have been firmly associated with Crete in Book III. It is Jupiter who gives the sign that there is no deception involved and confirms Italy as their homeland. Crete is thus again associated with deception, that is, the deception of a false home which Aeneas fears. Furthermore, the positive nurturing associations of Crete found in Book III are also evoked; as Crete was the *incunabula gentis* for the Trojans, so does Jupiter show that Italy will fulfill the same role for the Roman race.

Crete appears again in Book VIII, where Evander's people sing in their prayer to Hercules about that hero's slaughter of the Cretan bull, one of his canonical labors (VIII.294 f.):

> ... tu Cresia mactas
> prodigia et vastam Nemeae sub rupe leonem.

If Hercules is a paradigm for the manner in which Aeneas is to rid Italy of *furor* and tyrants,[33] then it is significant that he has also overcome the bull from Crete; that is, he has overcome the deception of false values. It is also possible that Vergil is making a connection between this bull and the one who inspired Pasiphae's passion. As Hercules overcame the Cretan bull, so has Aeneas overcome the deception of false values and illicit love. Vergil has here changed the myth of Hercules and the Cretan bull to emphasize his meaning; normally the bull is said to have been taken alive, not killed.[34] In addition, if Cacus, whose subjection at the hands of Hercules is an important theme in Book VIII, is a parallel for Turnus, then the Cretan bull, also subdued by Hercules, might recall the passion of Turnus for Lavinia, which is proven to be false — as false as Turnus himself believes Aeneas' love for Lavinia is.

As a Cretan weapon played a role in the foot race involving the trickery of Nisus and Euryalus in Book V, so also does one figure in their tragic end in Book IX (303-5):

> sic ait inlacrimans; umero simul exuit ensem
> auratum, mira quem fecerat arte Lycaon
> Cnosius atque habilem vagina aptarat eburna.

---

[33] Putnam (above, n.15), p. 132.

[34] P.T. Eden, *Commentary on Virgil Aeneid VIII* (*Mnemosyne Supplement* 35) (Leiden, 1975) p. 101.

Here it is a Cretan sword presented by Iulus to Euryalus before the nocturnal foray which results in the death of Nisus and Euryalus. Both are betrayed by love and by the desire for spoils, and the Cretan sword foreshadows their fate and symbolizes the deception of false values. It also serves as a link with Book V, in which we saw a foreshadowing of their death.

In Book XI (264 f.) we again hear of Idomeneus when Diomedes refuses to help the Latins. He tells the envoys of the ability and *pietas* of Aeneas and the Trojans and cites the disasters which befell the victors in the Trojan War. One of those victorious Greeks who suffered disasters was Idomeneus, forced to flee Crete when his people turned against him (*versos penatis*). This passage is basically a catalogue of the *nostoi* of the Greek heroes, and Idomeneus was a canonical part of such a list from the *Odyssey* on.[35] Diomedes here, however, is using these examples to warn the Latins of the futility of war with the Trojans. Such a war results in disaster for both the victor and the conquered, and the desire for the glory of war is a false value. War between the Trojans and Latins is, as Diomedes warns, a false goal, and embedded in his message is a Cretan symbol of its falseness.

Crete appears again in Book XI as a clear image of deception in the story of Camilla. Camilla is lured into false action by the splendid golden arms of Chloreus, a priest of Cybele. These arms include Cretan arrows and a Lycian bow (XI. 773), objects which have been seen as included for ornament.[36] Inspired by a desire for these as booty, Camilla rushes into action, only to meet death at the hands of Arruns. As in the Nisus and Euryalus episode, the Cretan weapons represent the false values which lead the noble Camilla to her death, and as with all who are led astray by these deceptive goals, Vergil is full of pity for her.

Finally, in the last book of the *Aeneid,* Crete appears twice, both times in connection with the gods rather than mortals, and with the same contradictory associations encountered in Book III. When Aeneas has been wounded and the physician cannot heal him, Venus cures her son unawares with a Cretan herb (XII. 411-15):

> hic Venus indigno nati concussa dolore
> dictamnum genetrix Cretaea carpit ab Ida
> puberibus caulem foliis et flora comantem
> purpureo; non illa feris incognita capris
> gramina cum tergo volucres haesere sagittae.

---

[35] *Odyssey* III. 191ff.
[36] Williams, *The Aeneid of Virgil, VII-XII,* p. 429.

The idea, no doubt, came from the story reported by Aristotle and Cicero that dictamnum made arrows fall out of goats' bodies,[37] but the image does not seem to carry the association of deception. Venus does, however, deceive Aeneas by acting secretly, and the very act of trying to stop Aeneas by wounding him mortally is based on false premises. Aeneas is destined to win and to create the Roman race, as Juno herself finally learns in Book XII. The belief that he can be defeated is false, and the ease with which Venus heals him with a Cretan herb points this up. The emphasis of this passage, however, is on the healing properties of Crete and its maternal association. *Venus genetrix* here is the Augustan ideal, and she recalls the *mater cultrix Cybeli* of Book III. Associated with the gods then, Crete becomes a positive image of nurturing; only for mortals does it represent a false value.

The final image of Crete is once again negative. The Dira sent by Jupiter to eliminate Juturna from the battle and make way for the death of Turnus is compared to a poisonous Cretan or Parthian arrow (XII. 856-9).

> non secus ac nervo per nubem impulsa sagitta
> armatam saevi Parthus quam felle veneni
> Parthus sive Cydon, telum immedicabile, torsit,
> stridens et celeris incognita transilit umbras.

As the first reference to Crete in the *Aeneid* connected the island with Jupiter, so does the last; Crete again plays a role in Jupiter's overall plan. Though the image here is apparently one of open violence, there is still something deceptive about it; the arrow is unseen and works by hidden poison.[38] The action of the Dira here directly determines the fate of Turnus, and the simile points up in a most violent and destructive way the falseness of his values and his self-deception in fighting the Trojans. The very violence of the image strips away Turnus' false values; it is a sign of his error and the anger of Jupiter.[39]

An examination of the images of Crete shows us something of Vergil's masterful technique. References are made to Cretan places, people, and objects throughout the *Aeneid*, where they add color and erudition. However, Vergil does more than simply decorate his poem with learned references, and his choice of Cretan images is significant. From its first appearance, Crete becomes a symbol of deception and false goals, like the false Pergamum which the Trojans tried to build on

---

[37] Arist., *Hist. An* 9.6.1; Cic. *ND* 2.50. Cf. also Theophr. *Hist. plant.* 9.16.
[38] Johnson (above, n.7), p. 96.
[39] Putnam (above, n.15), p. 169.

the island. Though Crete is the cradle and mother of the Trojan race, associated with Jupiter, Apollo, and Cybele, it is a symbol of the futility of trying to return to the past. Aeneas must go forward, and the images of Idomeneus and Daedalus show him what he must do and what the cost will be in human suffering. After his love affair with Dido, Aeneas is shown the labyrinth, symbol of his wanderings, and he recognizes the falseness of illicit love at its center. As Aeneas is shown the labyrinth, symbol of his wanderings, and he recognizes the falseness of illicit love at its center. As Aeneas learns the future in Book VI, so does he also learn the past, and the falseness of its values for him and for Rome is emphasized by the appearance of all the doomed Cretans he sees in the Underworld. Cretan images are scarcer after Book VI, since Aeneas no longer needs the warning of the falseness of past values nor does he need the comfort of the paradigms represented by Daedalus and Idomeneus; he is firmly committed to the future and has learned true values. Others, however, still adhere to the false values of the past, as the Cretan imagery associated with Euryalus, Camilla, and Turnus indicates. The false goals lead to the destruction of these otherwise noble characters, and their destructiveness is most clearly shown near the end of Book XII, where Jupiter sends one of the Furies to earth like a Cretan arrow. Through this image Vergil shows Jupiter's will, that the new race must abandon the old ideals. Crete has played an important role as the cradle of civilization and the source of many arts and crafts, and as a stage in the educative process of Aeneas and mankind, but its value lies in the past. The true values for Jupiter lie in the future with Rome.

Wabash College
Crawfordsville, Indiana

A RE-CONSIDERATION OF CICERO'S *PRINCEPS CIVITATIS* IN THE LIGHT OF NEW EVIDENCE FROM A SIXTH-CENTURY POLITICAL TREATISE

ATHANASIOS S. FOTIOU

The state of the last three (and apparently most important) books of Cicero's *De republica*,[1] is so ruinous that they continue to defy the scholar's attempts to reconstruct their argument. From Book IV, the theme of which is the social classification of citizens and their education, only two short passages survive in the Vatican manuscript. Only four folios are extant from Book V which deals with the qualifications and position of the ideal statesman, the *princeps* or *rector civitatis*. The duties of the statesman and the rewards of his labours are the subject of Book VI, of which nothing survives in the Vatican palimpsest.

Most of the information about the final Books comes from quotations, paraphrases or summaries made by writers in late antiquity[2] such as Lactantius, St. Augustine, Nonius and Macrobius who has preserved the *somnium Scipionis*. Until the fifth century, Cicero's *De republica* was known and used in the West by Christian apologists in their polemic against paganism. To the Greeks of late antiquity, however, Cicero's treatise was little known. Apart from a brief reference to it by the third century writer Aristides Quintilianus (cf. Cic., *Rep.* IV 12,14), there is no other evidence pointing to any knowledge of it by Greeks in the eastern part of the Roman Empire.[3] It is not until the early sixth century that the *De republica* is referred to again in the fragments of an anonymous dialogue *On Political Science* (περὶ πολιτικῆς ἐπιστήμης). The work originally comprised six books but only fragments of Books IV and V survive in a Vatican palimpsest. It is with these fragments that this paper is concerned. Angelo Mai,[4] who first discovered and edited them, dated the treatise to the reign of Justinian and attributed it to Peter the Patrician, the Master of Offices to

---

[1] There is an excellent introduction in the recent edition by E. Bréguet, *Cicéron, La république*, 2 vols. (Paris: Budé 1980) 41ff.

[2] Bréguet 162-65.

[3] D. Claudius Didymus, a grammarian of the early Empire, was the first Greek known to have written a commentary entitled περὶ τῆς Κικέρωνος πολιτείας; cf. Breguet 163 n. 2.

[4] A. Mai, ed. *Scriptorum veterum nova collectio*, vol. II (Rome 1827).

Justinian.⁵ For the purpose of this paper, it will suffice to state that the work should be dated more correctly to the first quarter of the sixth century and should remain anonymous for reasons I have discussed elsewhere.⁶

Of Book IV which deals with the military class (φύλακες) and their training, only the final section, still incomplete, is extant. Book V deals with the ideal statesman, the king, being the monarchical component of a mixed constitution, the other elements being the aristocratic and the democratic. The fragments of these two Books, though not very extensive, are important for the student of Latin literature because they afford some idea of the extent to which Latin writers were known in sixth-century Byzantium. It is interesting to note that the Anonymous author quoted not only Cicero with whom he was most familiar, but also Cato the Elder,⁷ Livy,⁸ Juvenal⁹ and a certain Etruscan Firminus.¹⁰ The ultimate purpose of this essay, then, is twofold: first, to discuss the extent to which the Anonymous made use of Cicero, in particular his *De republica,* and second, to find out whether the author's use of Cicero's *De republica* can shed any light on the Ciceronian *princeps,* who has been the subject of considerable controversy among scholars.

There are six or possibly seven references, quotations or paraphrases taken from Cicero in the extant fragments. In fact, Cicero is the most quoted author, followed by Plato with five citations. The single citation in Book IV, Fol. 293ᵛ, runs as follows:

> Οὐκ ἀνάξιον δέ, οἶμαι, ὦ Θωμάσιε, κἀκείνου
> μνησθῆναι, ὃ Κικέρων ἱστορεῖ, τοῦ παρὰ
> Ῥωμαίοις πεζικοῦ περὶ στρατοῦ· φησὶ γὰρ
> τὰ μὲν ὅπλα οὕτω φέροντας ἀχωρίστως
> ἔχειν ἀεὶ οἷόν τινα μέλη τοῦ σώματος

---

⁵ Mai 573-74.

⁶ In the introduction to a forthcoming edition of the fragments. For reasons of convenience, I shall refer to the author of the treatise as the Anonymous.

⁷ Fol. 350ᵛ. A quotation extending to six manuscript lines comes from a speech Cato delivered in Rome. The quotation cannot be located in the existing fragments of Cato's speeches. It is possible that the Anonymous found the quotation in the *De republica* of Cicero, who was very fond of Cato. See A. S. Fotiou, "A new fragment of Cato the Elder" *C&M* 33 (1981-82) 125-33.

⁸ Fol. 331ᵛ. This citation is a paraphrase of Livy 6.23.7; the second, Fol. 349ᵛ, probably taken from Livy, is a paraphrase concerning tax arrangements in early Republic.

⁹ Fol. 350ᵛ: a brief paraphrase on the theme of justice.

¹⁰ Bk. IV, Fol. 293ᵛ: the author is unknown. Mai suggested Frontinus but there is no evidence to support this. The quotation, which has a poetic ring to it, most probably came from a rhetorical writing.

οἰομένους καὶ πρός γε τροφὴν σφίσι πέντε ἀποχρῶσαν ἡμέρας. ἀνάγκης τε ἄνευ τινός, καὶ εἰ παρεῖναι συμβαίνοι νωτοφόρα ζῷα, ὃ συνηθείᾳ μακρᾷ βεβαιωθὲν νόμος παρ' αὐτοῖς ἐγίγνετο, ὡς καὶ τιμωρίαν ἐπικεῖσθαι εἴ τις παραβαίη.

Mai found a similar idea expressed in Cicero's *Tusculanae Disputationes* (2.16.37):

> ferre plus dimidiati mensis cibaria, ferre si quid ad usum velint, ferre vallum. Nam scutum, gladium, galeam, in onere nostri milites non plus numerant, quam humeros, lacertos, manus. Arma enim membra militis esse dicunt.

There are, however, some serious differences in style and content between the two passages which make the identification questionable. First, the ideas are reversed in the Greek paraphrase; secondly, the Byzantine author does not list the name of the arms borne by Roman infantrymen; thirdly, the important detail of a half-month's rations is changed to five days — although the suggested emendation to read <δέκα> πέντε is very attractive; fourthly, the concluding clause, ἀνάγκης τε ἄνευ ..., about pack animals and disciplinary measures, reads as part of the original passage. Mai[11] suggested that the Anonymous author borrowed the citation from a lost book, perhaps Book V, of Cicero's *De republica*. A likelier source, in my opinion, would have been Book IV, where the Roman military class and its training were discussed. Book IV of the Byzantine treatise, probably modelled to an extent on the same book of Cicero's *De republica*, is entirely devoted to φυλάκων πέρι καὶ τῆς πολεμικῆς ἐπιστήμης. It seems plausible that the Anonymous, who was interested in restoring Roman military tactics and discipline in the Byzantine armed forces, had been attracted by Cicero's account (ἱστορήσας) of Roman infantry discipline.

In Book V, Fol. 292ʳ, there is a citation concerning Socrates:

> εὖ γὰρ ὀνομάζει Κικέρων Σωκράτη ἀρχηγόν, καὶ ἵνα ἑκὼν ῥωμαΐσω καὶ αὐτός, πρίγκιπα τῆς ὅλης καὶ ἀληθοῦς φιλοσοφίας ἀποκαλῶν.

---

[11] Mai (above, n.4) 593, note 2.

Cicero's *De oratore* 3.16.60 has been proposed as a possible source. C.A. Behr, however, called the connection "tenuous" and suggested that "the citation may be another lapse of the author's,"[12] that is, a confusion of Plato's name with Socrates', both of whom are mentioned close together in Book II of the *De republica: nam princeps ille* (11.21) for Plato and *ut facit apud Platonem Socrates* (11.22). The context, however, in which these expressions are found is so different from the context of the Anonymous citation that the possibility of confusion becomes very questionable. It is likely that Cicero in one of the books of the *De republica* called Socrates *principem omnis et verae philosophiae*.

A third reference to Cicero's *De republica* which can be found in the tenth heading of the table of contents to Book V, Fol. 297ʳ, is of great interest. It reads: παράθεσις τῆς κατὰ Πλάτωνα καὶ Κικέρωνα πολιτείας. The comparison has not survived in the extant fragments. There is, however, evidence that the Anonymous criticized Plato's *Republic* as Cicero had in his *De rep.*, and preferred certain aspects of Cicero's political treatise. First, the ninth heading of the table of contents to Book V explicitly mentions that the two interlocutors of the dialogue, Menodorus and Thomasius, "objected to certain ideas of Plato."[13] Secondly, Patriarch Photius, who wrote a brief summary of the Byzantine dialogue,[14] informs us that the author ἐπιμέμφεται δὲ τῆς Πλάτωνος δικαίως πολιτείας. The Anonymous' criticism of Plato's *Republic* must have made a strong impression on Photius for him to include it in a resumé of only ten lines. Photius, on the other hand, says nothing about Cicero's *De republica* itself. Indirectly, however, he allows us to see in the concluding phrase of the resumé what in fact attracted the Anonymous to Cicero's work:

> "Ἢν δ' αὐτοὶ πολιτείαν εἰσάγουσιν, ἐκ τῶν τριῶν εἰδῶν τῆς πολιτείας δέον αὐτὴν συγκεῖσθαί φασι, βασιλικοῦ καὶ ἀριστοκρατικοῦ καὶ δημοκρατικοῦ, τὸ εἰλικρινὲς αὐτῇ ἑκάστης πολιτείας συνεισαγούσης, κἀκείνην τὴν ὡς ἀληθῶς ἀρίστην πολιτείαν ἀποτελειούσης.

---

[12] C.A. Behr, "A New Fragment of Cicero's *De Republica*," *AJP* 95 (1974) 141-149, at 147. In Fol. 296ʳ the Anonymous quotes Cleanthes' prayer but calls it that of Socrates. The error was probably caused by a confusion, since both Socrates and Cleanthes are known to have resigned to the will of the gods.

[13] Fol. 297ʳ: ἐν ᾧ καὶ ἔνστασις πρός τινα τῶν τῷ Πλάτωνι εἰρημένων.

[14] *Bibliotheca*, codex 37.

This passage clearly states that the Anonymous' πολιτεία was a mixed constitution, which lay at the heart of Cicero's *De republica* also. According to Photius' testimony, the Anonymous called his constitution 'dicaearchan' (δικαιαρχικόν) and claimed that it was a novel type. The author's claim is supported by the ninth heading of the table of contents which informs us that "the two interlocutors expressed different views about their *politeia* from those expounded by the ancient writers."[15] The term δικαιαρχικόν is not to be related with Δικαίαρχος, the fourth century Peripatetic philosopher, but rather was formed from δικαιαρχία which broken into its components δικαία ἀρχή simply meant "the rule of justice or the just."[16] The novel character of the Anonymous' constitution lay in the fact that the monarch representing the ideal statesman in a mixed constitution became an official elected by members of the other components of the constitution, the aristocratic and the democratic. In a revealing fragment describing the procedure whereby an ἄριστος (*optimus*) is elected to the throne, the author remarks that the entire election should be "based on the decision of the subjects and the counsel of the best men."[17]

Cicero announced that the theme of his *De republica* was *de optimo civitatis statu et de optimo cive*.[18] For Cicero, the ideal state was the mixed constitution which is superior to the other three simple constitutions: kingship, aristocracy and democracy.[19] As an example of a mixed constitution which approximated the ideal, Cicero in Book II expounded the political organization of the early Roman Republic. This approach was criticized by Tubero, one of the speakers, who thought that Cicero was being too specific in dealing with the ideal state:

> Laudavisse mihi videris nostram rem publicam, cum
> ex te non de nostra, sed de omni re publica
> quaesisset Laelius.
>
> (*De rep.* II.38, 64)

---

[15] Fol. 297ʳ: ὅτι ἀνόμοια περὶ τῆς πολιτείας εἴρηται τοῖς ὑφ' ἑτέρων εἰρημένοις.

[16] On this subject see my article "Dicaearchus and the Mixed Constitution in Sixth Century Byzantium. New Evidence from a Treatise *On Political Science*," *Byzantion* 51 (1981) 533-47.

[17] Fol. 344ʳ: νόμιμον δὲ τόδε εἶναί φημι καὶ οὕτω γιγνόμενον δίκαιον τῇ μὲν γνώμῃ τῶν βασιλευομένων, τῶν δὲ ἀρίστων γίγνεσθαι βουλῇ.

[18] *Ad Quintum fratrem* III 5, 1-2; *ad Atticum* VIII 11, 1.

[19] *De rep.* I 35, 52; 45, 69; II 23, 41.

The same sort of criticism in reverse is found in a fragment of the Anonymous' *On Political Science* in which Menodorus, the major speaker, is pressed by Thomasius, the disciple, to be more specific in his approach. The fourth citation or reference to Cicero reads (fol. 185ʳ):

> Ἡμεῖς δὲ ἦν ἁπλῶς οἶμαι πολιτείαν σώφρονά τε δηλαδὴ καὶ ἀρίστην καὶ οὐ τήνδε ἢ τήνδε ἰδίως, ὡς ὁ Κικέρων τὴν τῶν Ῥωμαίων, ἐπισκοπεῖν ἐνεστησάμεθα.

The citation is another proof of the Byzantine author's close familiarity with Cicero's *De republica*.

This statement by Menodorus came as a response to Thomasius' pressure on him to specify the number of magistrates (ἄρχοντες) to be appointed for the governing of the state. Menodorus yields and specifies that the number is ten, a point on which Thomasius then comments. Below is the fifth and most illuminating citation from Cicero:

> Ταῦτα λέγων, ὦ Μηνόδωρε, Κικέρωνι συμφήσεις ὅλην σχεδὸν λέγοντι τὴν βασιλικὴν φροντίδα περὶ δέκα ἐπιλογὴν ἀνδρῶν ἀρίστων καταγίγνεσθαι προσήκειν οἳ καὶ ἐξαρκέσουσιν ἱκανοί γε ὄντες καὶ ἄλλων ἀνδρῶν ἐπιλογὴν ποιήσασθαι οἷς ἂν χρῷτο πρὸς τὰς τῆς πολιτείας διοικήσεις.
> (Fol. 185ʳ-185ᵛ)

The main elements of the quotation, or rather paraphrase, are:

1. The ruler or head of state is called 'King' as the phrase βασιλικὴν φροντίδα clearly denotes.
2. The king's responsibility is the selection of ten best men (ἄριστοι) who become the highest officials (ἄρχοντες).
3. The ten highest officials, in turn, select other officials to fill in the higher positions of the administration. The paraphrase in all probability comes from Cicero's *De republica* and more specifically from Book V, where the qualifications and the political position of the ideal statesman, the *rector* or *princeps rei publicae* were delineated.[20]

In an important fragment where the "lawful proclamation" — that is, the election of the king — is described, the Anonymous refers to the King's duties among which he stresses the σωτηρία τῶν πολιτῶν: "he should receive kingship for the salvation of the citizens and live

---

[20] For an analysis of Book V, see P. Bréguet, (above, n.1) vol. I, pp. 79-83.

not for himself but rather for his citizens."[21] In this context, the Anonymous cites "definitions" of kingship borrowed from Plato and Cicero (our sixth reference):

> Εὖ γὰρ τὴν βασιλείαν ὡρίσατο Πλάτων μὲν
> οὐ τῷ ἔχοντι ἀλλὰ τοῖς ἀρχομένοις εἶναι
> συμφέρον, Κικέρων δὲ τοῦ ἔχοντος ἴδιον
> μὲν πόνον ἀλλοτρίας δὲ φροντίδα
> σωτηρίας.

No such 'definition' of kingship occurs in the extant parts of the *De republica*. The only other possibility is that the 'definition' had been found in a text which discussed the duties of the ideal statesman, the *princeps*, and such a text could only have been in Book V or VI. Again Cicero's *princeps* is called βασιλεύς and his government βασιλεία. In the paraphrase from Plato's *Republic*, the Byzantine author adopted the same approach. Plato speaks about the 'genuine ruler' who sacrifices his own advantage to that of his subjects (*Rep.* I 347d 5):

> Τῷ ὄντι ἀληθινὸς ἄρχων οὐ πέφυκε τὸ αὑτῷ
> συμφέρον σκοπεῖσθαι ἀλλὰ τὸ τῷ
> ἀρχομένῳ.

In the Anonymous' paraphrase, Plato's ideal ruler has been identified with the ideal King.[22]

At this point, having considered the Anonymous' citations from Cicero's *De republica*, we should compare Cicero's *princeps* and the Anonymous' βασιλεύς on the basis of what can be gleaned from the extant fragments. I shall begin with an examination of their respective political positions and their duties, and then turn to their virtues.

In the fragments of the Byzantine treatise, the most common title of the ideal statesman is βασιλεύς, or βασιλικὸς ἀνήρ;[23] he is also referred to as πολιτικός. The identification of the two concepts,

---

[21] Fol. 344ʳ: σωτηρίας δὲ μᾶλλον ἕνεκα τῶν πολιτῶν ὅμως καταδεχόμενον, οὐχ αὑτῷ μᾶλλον ζήσοντα ἢ ἐκείνοις.

[22] Political writers of the Hellenistic and Roman periods following the example of Plato's identification of the πολιτικός with the βασιλικός in his *Statesman* (259d; 267c, etc.), deliberately presented the virtues and duties of the two figures as interchangeable. G.J.D. Aalders, *Political Thought in Hellenistic Times* (Amsterdam 1975) 88ff.; L. Delatte, *Les Traités de la Royauté d'Ecphante, Diotogène et Sthénidas* (Liège-Paris 1942).

[23] Fol. 343: τὸ συγκινεῖσθαι τὸν ὄντως βασιλικὸν ἄνδρα οὐρανῷ τε καὶ κόσμῳ. Fol. 343ʳ: ἀνάγκη οὖν τὸν πολιτικὸν ἢ πάντας τοὺς πολίτας ...; Fol. 343ᵛ: εἰ μὲν τοῦτο, ... ἐπηγγέλλετο ὁ πολιτικός ...; cf. also 350ʳ. The king is also called κυβερνήτης τῶν ἀνθρώπων (Fol. 331ᵛ) and

βασιλικός and πολιτικός, accords with the author's philosophical argument that βασιλική επιστήμη and πολιτική φιλοσοφία are identical since both have as their aim the imitation of God.[24]

Kingship is only one component, the monarchical, of the tripartite mixed constitution.[25] As such, the king is not a hereditary and absolute monarch but a constitutional one. Above all, kingship is an elective office;[26] the two other constitutional bodies, 'aristocracy' and 'democracy' hold the right to elect the king according to a νόμος πολιτικός set up especially for this purpose. Another state law prescribes the king's retirement from office either because of old age or illness.[27]

The king is elected in accordance with a 'civil law' which reads: "The man who aspires to become king and to be called by a name after the heavenly king would justly receive kingship as a gift of God and an offering by the citizens."[28] Such a king is 'legal' (νόμιμος) and his kingship 'lawful' (έννομος). There are three steps to be followed for the 'lawful proclamation' (έννομος ανάρρησις) of a king:[29]

ποιμήν λαών (Fol. 331ʳ) or simply ποιμήν (Fol. 350ᵛ).

[24] Fol. 354ʳ: ὅτι ταυτὸν βασιλεία τε καὶ πολιτικὴ φιλοσοφία, οἷα θεοῦ μίμησις οὖσα.

[25] The idea of kingship as part of a mixed constitution can be traced back to Plato's *Laws* (693d) and *Menexenus* (238cd) and Aristotle's *Politics* (1297a). According to Osann's plausible assumption, it was Dicaearchus who first expanded on the idea contained in Plato's writings in his *Tripoliticus* which was made up of two sections, a theoretical, and a practical, the latter being a sketch of the Spartan constitution as the best μικτὸν γένος πολιτείας. F. Osann, *Beitrage zur griechischen und romischen Literaturgeschichte*, vol. II (Cassel-Leipzig 1839) pp. 23ff.; S. E. Smethurst, 'Cicero and Dicaearchus', *TAPA* 83 (1952) 224-32; G.J.D. Aalders, *Die Theorie der gemischte Verfassung im Altertum* (Amsterdam 1968); K. von Fritz, *The Theory of the Mixed Constitution in Antiquity* (New York 1954).

[26] Hans Georg Beck, *Das byzantinische Jahrtausend* (Munich 1978) puts it in strong terms when he writes "Keinesfalls is der byzantinische Herrscher ein absoluter Monarch" (p. 40); certain institutions and forces limited the imperial power and rendered the Byzantine state or *Wahlmonarchie* (p. 67). See also the article by the same author, "Res Publica Romana. Vom Staatsdenken der Byzantiner" *SBAW* Phil.-Hist. Kl. (1971) 7-41.

[27] Fol. 331ᵛ. The king has two alternatives, either to retire and let another ἄριστος be elected to succeed him, or choose an assistant (βοηθός) who would gradually take over the administration of the state.

[28] Fol. 354ᵛ: τῶν μὲν νόμων, ὦ Θωμάσιε, πρῶτος θετέος αὐτῇ ὑπ' αὐτῆς τῇ βασιλεία, τῆς ἐννόμου χάριν ἀναρρήσεως, ὡς ἂν ὁ ὅμοιος αὐτῇ καὶ ἐπώνυμος ἀνὴρ συγγίγνεσθαι μέλλων δικαίως, ὡς προερρήθη, παρὰ θεοῦ τε διδομένην καὶ τῶν πολιτῶν δέξοιτο προσφερομένην.

[29] Fol. 344ᵛ is one of the passages newly discovered and deciphered by the present writer. It contains a definition of what the Anonymous means by 'legal' as applied to kingship; it is the election of the king according to an enacted law.

1. The heads or leaders (πρωτεύοντες) of all the city orders (τῆς πόλεως τάγματα) will take an oath to the effect that in nominating the most suitable men for the kingly office they will use their objective and sound judgement.

2. Each head will name perhaps three candidates from among the 'best men' (ἄριστοι) whom they regard as worthy of kingship. An ἄριστος should be selected for possessing the following qualities: virtue (ἀρετή), that is, moral and intellectual superiority; expertise in state laws and political matters; high rank (τάξις), appropriate age (χρόνος) and the proper standing (ἀξία).

3. All the citizens (πολῖται) of the city, by votes cast in four 'houses' within three days, will select the king from among the nominated candidates.

In the following passage where the distinct roles of the 'best men' and the people are referred to, the two concepts of 'legal' (νόμιμον) and 'just' (δίκαιον) are used synonymously:

> Let the king regard such a choice as a heavy burden upon himself as well as a good service for which he is accountable before divine judgement and perhaps before men too; he should receive kingship for the salvation of the citizens and live not for himself but rather for his citizens ... This is, then, my definition of 'legal;' if it is done as I said, it would be 'just' since the lawfulness of the king will be based on the decision of his subjects and the counsel of the 'best men.'[30]

Finally, the man who is elevated to the highest state office by such a 'democratically' instituted procedure "will be in harmony with the majority opinion."[31] This opinion by which a man was granted — the verb most commonly used is προσφέρειν — the powers of his office also acts as a restricting force which "reduces the king's license;"[32] the king should willingly accept such a limitation.

---

[30] Fol. 344ᵛ. The concluding clause of the passage is a clear statement about the role of the electing bodies; the best men offer their counsel by nominating the candidates and the 'people' make the final decision as to which candidate should be king: τῇ μὲν γνώμῃ τῶν βασιλευομένων, τῶν δὲ ἀρίστων γίγνεσθαι βουλῇ. The contribution of the citizens in the election is emphasized in this phrase also: ἀλλὰ καὶ δόξῃ πλείονι τῶν πολιτῶν προνοεῖν ἐλέσθαι [ἀξίως] γιγνομένῃ. Fol 331ʳ.

[31] Fol. 33ᵛ: πλὴν οὐκ ἄτοπον συμφέρεσθαι ἐν πολιτείᾳ, ὡς φῂς αὐτός, τῇ τῶν πολλῶν δόξῃ ὅσον κάλλιστα.

[32] Fol. 331ʳ: τῇ τῆς [ἀδείας] ἐλαττώσει [τ]ῇ πλείονι δόξῃ.

To summarize: the king is an ἄριστος who is first nominated together with others by a group called πρωτεύοντες, leaders of the city's τάγματα, and then he is elected by the citizens of the capital. But who were these πρωτεύοντες and what did the city's τάγματα represent?

The πρωτεύοντες are members of a group (τάξις)[33] comprised of two hundred ἄριστοι who come from a larger class variously called simply ἄριστοι or ἀρίστων κατάλογος 'register of best men', and ἀρίστων σύστημα or τάγμα 'system or class of best men.' The class of 'best men' make up the second component of the mixed constitution, the aristocratic for which the Anonymous reserved an important position in his ideal state. The qualifications which entitled a man to become a member of the aristocratic class were nature, upbringing and education (φύσις, τροφή, παιδεία), that is, the ingredients of virtue (ἀρετή).[34] The Anonymous' system of meritocracy leaves no room for such traditional claims as birth, ancestry, power and wealth. A state, writes the Anonymous, should employ the art of 'discovery' and 'midwifery' in determining who is to be classified as ἄριστος. For this reason, he allows an upward and downward mobility in the class of 'aristocracy.'

The class of 'best men' was assigned certain positions and functions in the mixed constitution. First, they were elected members of the senate;[35] second, they filled the ten highest positions of the administration;[36] and third, a select group of two hundred ἄριστοι, divided into twenty units, exercised the supervision (ἐπιστασία, ἐποπτεία) of the 'state orders' (τάγματα πολιτείας or πολιτικά) of the imperial administration;[37] these 'orders' were of two distinct kinds, military (τάγματα στρατιωτικά) supervised by one hundred ἄριστοι and civic (τάγματα ἀστικὰ) supervised by the second group of one hundred ἄριστοι. Although the references to these 'orders' are general and vague, we may reasonably assume them to have been the various clerical ranks of the administration which made up a class

---

[33] Fol. 349ᵛ: Menodorus concludes his description of the functions of the best men as follows: ἐμοὶ μὲν οὖν τὰ δόξαντα, ὦ Θωμάσιε, τῆς τῶν ἀρίστων περὶ τάξεώς τε καὶ ταξιαρχίας τῇδε εἰρήσθω.

[34] Fol. 352ʳᵛ deals with the criteria employed in the selection of the best men.

[35] Fol. 354ᵛ: δεύτερος (νόμος) περὶ τῆς τῶν ἀρίστων συγκλήτου βουλῆς, τροφῆς τε αὐτῶν ἕνεκα καὶ παιδείς, τιμῆς τε καὶ τάξεως ἔτι δὲ καὶ ταξιαρχίας, ᾗ ἐρρήθη, γιγνομένης.

[36] Fol. 354ᵛ: τέταρτος (νόμος) περὶ τῶν μεγίστων ἀρχῶν καὶ τῆς τῶν ὁμοίων ἀρχόντων ἐκ τῶν ἀρίστων ἐπιλογῆς.

[37] Fol. 334ʳ: οὕτω δὴ καὶ ἡμᾶς τοὺς ἀρίστους ἐπιστήσαντας τῆς πόλεως καὶ πολιτείας τάγμασιν.

distinct from the 'system of best men.' The phrase πρωτεύοντες τῶν ταγμάτων should be connected with the twenty units of ἄριστοι in charge of the civic and military 'orders.' Thus, the leaders of the 'city orders' are twenty ἄριστοι who hold first rank in each of these units. If this assumption is correct, then twenty leaders would nominate a total of sixty ἄριστοι from whom one ἄριστος, supposedly the best, would be elected king by the people.

Next comes the question of the relative position held by the τάξις of the two hundred ἄριστοι within this political system. I believe that this group of select ἄριστοι should be connected with the senate; they were not, however, the senate itself, which must have been a larger body, but a rather large committee of the senate. Whereas the members of this distinct group had a definite duty[38] to perform, perhaps over a limited period of time, the members of the senate were appointed for life and were assigned, it seems, other deliberative, advisory, legal and, possibly, legislative responsibilities.[39]

The fragments of Book V contain information which, though vague in language, is important for understanding the character of this select group of ἄριστοι. Their privileged position allows them to pursue an independent course of action and lifestyle within the political and administrative organization.[40] The continuous supervision, however, which they exercise over the lower ranks of the administration will not be oppressive but, on the contrary, beneficial and humane, since its aim is to prevent powerful men from transgressing the law and committing injustice toward the weaker clerks. Through this *patrocinium* they will acquire the friendship and loyalty of the subordinate *ordines*.[41] They will

---

[38] Fol. 349^{rv} deals with the supervision of the group of two hundred ἄριστοι over the administrative τάγματα, military and civil.

[39] H.G. Beck, 'Senat und Volk von Konstantinopel' in *Bayerische Akademie der Wissenschaften (Philos. — Hist. Klasse), Sitzungsberichte* — Heft 6, Munich 1966, pp. 3-30; A.H.M. Jones, *The Later Roman Empire* (Oxford 1964) vol. I, pp. 329ff.; L-P. Raybaud, *Essai sur le sénat de Constantinople* (Paris 1963) especially 51-62.

[40] Fol. 334^r: μόνους τοὺς βίους καταζητοῦντας ἰδιοπραγεῖν ἐν τούτοις ἐν οἷς ἂν τύχοιεν τεταγμένοι.

[41] Fol. 334^r: καὶ ἐπὶ τοῖς δικαίοις καὶ νομίμοις οὐκ ἐῶντας πρὸς τῶν ἰσχυροτέρων ἀδικεῖσθαι. Protection of the lower ranks from the arbitrary actions of their superior officers was a paramount concern to the Roman emperors in late antiquity. A.H.M. Jones writes that Roman emperors "relied on the clerical grades, perhaps not altogether in vain, as a check against the far more arbitrary extortions and illegalities of the administrative officers, the provincial governors in particular." See "The Roman Civil Service (Clerical and Sub-clerical Grades)," *JRS* 39 (1949) 38-55. This explains why the Anonymous assigned supervisory duties to a group of ἄριστοι who were not part of the administration proper but acted independently to ensure that law and justice were done. In such capacity these ἄριστοι were able to become acquainted with public opinion within the administration as well as in society at large.

be careful, however, not to interfere with the work of the higher officials (ἄρχοντες) whose duty will be to make sure that the administrative machine under the direction of the heads of departments and bureaux (ἀρχαί) operates smoothly. The administration (διοίκησις) of the state is thus a three-tiered structure made up of the ἄριστοι as supervisors, the higher officials as overseers of the operation of the administrative apparatus and the clerical orders who were the actual operators of the machine. "In this way," as our author notes, "the king's political providence would move through the best men and the appropriate offices and orders below them to their final destination."[42] The Anonymous was much concerned to draw a line between the functions of the ἄριστοι as supervisors and the ἄρχοντες as chiefs of the *officia*. Menodorus defines the role of the select group of ἄριστοι in the overall administration of the state as follows:

> I maintain, in fact, that these men (ἄριστοι) should be elevated as far as possible from this (i.e., the duties of the higher officials); they should be placed on a higher plane where they can seek to act independently over their sphere of influence ... Whatever, then, is accomplished by the 'best men,' some of whom may have served at times as high officials, will remain on a more solid ground and in some other way will be based on a cogent argument.[43]

The efficient function of the administrative machine at all levels will have wider effects on the state and society at large:

> Then on this basis, each citizen would perform his duties in harmony, like a lyre, and the state moving to the strains of an all harmonious symphony would

---

Their knowledge of public opinion in turn helped them to nominate the most suitable ἄριστοι for the throne.

[42] Fol. 295ᵛ: ... τὰς πολιτικὰς προνοίας, διὰ δὲ τῶν ἀρίστων καὶ τῶν μετ' αὐτοὺς προσφόρων ἀρχῶν τε καὶ ταγμάτων πρὸς ἕκαστα ἐπιπορευομένας ἰθύνοντα (τὸν βασιλέα).

[43] Fol. 334ʳ: ἐγὼ δ[ὲ τ]ούτου μὲν ἐκείνους ὡς ἀπωτάτω γίγνεσθαι ἢ μᾶλλον ἀνωτάτω φέρεσθαι χρῆναί φημι μόνους τοὺς βίους καταζητοῦντας ἰδιοπραγεῖν ἐν αὐτοῖς ἐν οἷς ἂν τύχοιεν τεταγμένοι ... ὃ διὰ τῶν ἀρίστων καὶ ὄντων κατὰ καιρὸν ἀρχόντων γιγνόμενον, αὐτό τε εὐσταθέστερον ἂν εἴη καὶ ἄλλως ἀναγκαίῳ γίγνοιτο λόγῳ.

be all the more founded on justice and grounded on stability.⁴⁴

Let us now return to the fifth citation from Cicero and consider it in the light of what has been said about the βασιλεύς and the ἄριστοι in the Anonymous' *politeia*. There are two vexing questions which the contents of the quotation raise: first, how did Cicero's ideal statesman attain such a high position that he had the power to appoint magistrates? Second, who are the so-called ἄριστοι from whom the ten magistrates were selected? Unfortunately, the *De republica* provides no clear answers to these questions. Practically everything connected with the *optimus civis* whom Cicero announced as the theme of his treatise has become the subject of heated debate among modern scholars. There is even little agreement on the meaning of the various titles used to describe the position and the function of the chief of state. His titles are *princeps, princeps civitatis, rector, rector rei publicae, rector patriae, rector et gubernator civitatis*. Less common are *moderator rei publicae, tutor et procurator rei publicae, summus vir* or simply *vir*. It is not my purpose to repeat in detail the long and complicated arguments advanced by various scholars. The reader is referred to Bréguet's introduction to his recent Budé edition of the *De republica* for a summary of scholarly opinion,⁴⁵ and a few words about the controversy will be sufficient here. The authorities are divided into two camps.

The first group is represented by R. Reitzenstein and E. Meyer⁴⁶ who saw in the *princeps/rector* a "monarch without a crown." The terms *rector* and *princeps* are used, according to these scholars, synonymously to describe a privileged, quasi-monarchical position. The leading representative of the second group is R. Heinze⁴⁷ who

---

⁴⁴ Fol. 295ᵛ: καὶ τῶν πολιτῶν ἕκαστος ἐναρμονίως, λύρας τύπῳ τὰ ἴδια πράττων ἥ τε πολιτεία ταῖς ὅλαις τῆς παναρμονίου συμφωνίας κινουμένη χορδαῖς δικαιοτέρα τε καὶ εὐσταθεστέρα γένοιτο.

⁴⁵ E. Bréguet (above, n.1), in particular pp. 128-42 of the Introduction to Vol. I, where he discusses the issues concerning Cicero's *princeps*.

⁴⁶ R. Reitzenstein, "Die Idee des Principats bei Cicero und Augustus", *Nachrichten von der Gesellsch. Wiss. zu Göttingen, Phil.-Hist. Kl.* (1917) 399-436 and 481-98 is devoted to a discussion of the *princeps;* idem, "Zu Cicero *De re publica*" *Hermes* 59 (1924) 356-62. E. Meyer *Caesars Monarchie und das Principat des Pompeius*, 3 ed. (Stuttgart-Berlin 1919); cf. also P. Grenade, "Autour du *De re publica*" *REL* 29 (1951) 162-83. For a more recent survey of the problems relating to the *De republica*, see P. Boyancé, *Études sur l'humanisme ciceronien* (Coll. Latomus 121. Brussels 1970) 180-96.

⁴⁷ "Cicero's Staat als politische Tendenzschrift" *Hermes* 59 (1924) 73-94, reprinted in *Vom Geist des Römertums*, ed. E. Burck, 3d ed. (Stuttgart 1960) 141-59. Cf. also E. Lepore, *Il princeps ciceroniano* (Naples 1954); L. Wickert, art. "Princeps" *RE* XXII.2 coll. 1998-2296, especially 2227-2229.

envisaged the *princeps* as a type of the ideal statesman, as a member of a class of men. Furthermore, Heinze maintains that *princeps* indicates a political position of first rank among the traditional Roman aristocracy, whereas *rector* signifies moral and intellectual superiority.[48] The evidence in the *De republica* is vague enough to make both these tenable, although Heinze's theory has found more followers.

But the evidence of the Byzantine treatise leaves no doubt which thesis it supports. Reitzenstein's view of the *princeps* as a "monarch without a crown" seems to be closer to the import conveyed by the contents of the citation. The right of the election of the magistrates has been taken away from the Roman Assemblies, the *curiae*, and given to the *princeps*, whom the Anonymous calls βασιλεύς. This is a constitutional change of great consequence, and it is most puzzling if indeed Cicero proposed it. There is no discussion of the *magistratus* in the extant portions of the *De republica*, though Cicero in his *Laws* states that he treated this subject in general *in illis libris*,[49] meaning the books of the *De republica*. Perhaps the clearest and most important statement about the magistrates is made in connection with the mixed constitution in which, Cicero insists, there should be a balance (*conpensatio*) of rights, duties and functions among the three components: *ut et potestatis satis in magistratibus et auctoritatis in principum consilio et libertatis in populo sit*.[50] There is practically nothing else said about them in the *De republica* as it survives. The number ten, however, to which the Anonymous refers in his citation may be correct. The source again is Cicero's *Laws;* in Book III,[51] which is wholly devoted to the discussion of the magistrates, Cicero informs us that the few innovations he has suggested will contribute to the balanced type of constitution praised in the *De republica*. Since the treatment of magistrates, which probably occurred in Book V, is lost, we cannot of course identify the changes.

---

[48] Heinze 79.

[49] *De leg.* III 5, 13. All references are to the edition by C. W. Keyes, *Cicero: De Re Publica. De Legibus* (London 1928).

[50] *De rep.* II 33, 57. Cicero calls the best element in the mixed constitution *quiddam in republica praestans et regale* (*De rep.* I 45, 69). Reitzenstein argued that Cicero does not refer to the powers of magistrates but to the position and influence of one man. "Zu Cicero" (above, n.46) 360.

[51] *De leg.* III 5, 12: *omnium magistratuum descriptio, sed ea paene nostrae civitatis, etsi a te paulum adlatum est novi*. Cicero is unequivocal about the magistracies he is describing; they will be practically the same as those of the early Roman Republic. Elsewhere (*de leg.* III 1, 4) Cicero informs us that the system of laws concerning the magistrates he is introducing is intended for his ideal state. The question is not so much what kind of magistrates there were but who elected them. Although Cicero is not very explicit on this issue, yet implicitly he acknowledges the right of election to the *curiae* which traditionally held it. See *de leg.* III 3, 8; 4, 10.

Cicero, however, offers us a list of magistrates and their familiar duties: two praetors or consuls, two censors, an unspecified number of aediles and quaestors in a number to be determined by need.[52] Since for Cicero these magistrates represent the administration of the early Roman Republic, the aediles and the quaestors should have shared between them the remaining number of positions, i.e., six.

In view, then, of the above discussion, can the Anonymous' citation be accepted as authentic? Three arguments may be advanced against its authenticity. First, a source, usually a *florilegium* or lecture[53] notes upon which a Byzantine writer commonly drew, may have supplied him with the wrong information. This assumption, however, is highly unlikely in view of the familiarity the Anonymous claimed to have had with Cicero's political treatise. Second, the following passage from Book II of the *De republica* (II. 37, 62) may have supplied the Anonymous with all the data he was looking for: *erat penes principes tota res publica praepositis decemviris nobilissimis*. The Anonymous, or his source, mistook the *decemviri* as δέκα ἄρχοντες, *nobilissimis* as ἄριστοι and the *principes* as βασιλεύς (despite the plural number in the Latin). The determining factor in the matter of authenticity, however, lies in the concluding clause of the citation, which certainly reads as if it were part of the original Latin quotation. Thus, the content of the phrase immediately following *nobilissimis* is totally unrelated to the concluding clause of the Anonymous' citation: *non oppositis tribunis plebis, nullis aliis adiunctis magistratibus, non provocatione ad populum contra necem et verbera relicta*. The Anonymous describes the right of the ten magistrates to choose their own subordinate officials who would assist them in administering the state, whereas the Ciceronian phrase describes the arbitrary and cruel behavior of the *decemvirs*. Third, our author's citation may be reflecting the exceptional powers granted to the *princeps/rector* in critical times.[54] Just as extraordinary powers were given traditionally to a *dictator* who was chosen to save the state from a crisis threatening it, so Cicero in Book IV of his *De republica* may have proposed that a *rector rei publicae* in critical times be elevated to an

---

[52] *De leg.* III 3, 7-8.

[53] M. Richard, "'Ἀπὸ φωνῆς," *Byzantion* 20 (1950) 191-222.

[54] R. Reitzenstein believes that Cicero's *princeps*, like Augustus a little later, took over a 'magistrate Befugnisse' whenever a crisis threatened the state; 'Zu Cicero ...,' (above, n.46) 362. Augustus' powers (mainly military) cannot be compared to those of the *princeps* who "depends wholly on example, knowledge of the laws and influence over public opinion," E. Rawson, *Cicero. A Portrait* (London 1975) p. 152. Cicero envisages Scipio as a restorer of the Roman Republic: *hunc qui unus potest ... his tam periculosis rebus subvenire* (I 19.31); he calls Scipio *principem rei publicae* (I 21, 34) and compares him to a dictator (VI 11, 11-12). On this see R. Meister, "Der Staatslenker in Ciceros *De re publica*," *Wiener Studien* 57 (1939) 57-112, especially 57f. and 87f.

exceptional position and given the power to elect new magistrates as his assistants. The Anonymous, of course, in his citation did not bring out this important distinction. The assumption is quite plausible, in fact the most plausible of the three. And yet, how could an author like the Anonymous who was obviously fond of Cicero's *De republica* fail to notice and record such a distinction which Cicero must have made abundantly clear? This final assumption, then, must also be rejected, even though the authenticity of the Anonymous' citation itself should be maintained.

The second question raised by the Anonymous' citation concerns the class of the Ciceronian ἄριστοι from whom ten high officials were selected. Who were they, and what was their position in relation to the *rector*? In our earlier discussion we argued that the Anonymous conceived of his ἄριστοι as a unique and important class; membership in which depended on certain qualifications which he clearly defined. Likewise Cicero, dissatisfied with the conventional and popular notion that recognized *opes* and *potentia* as the sole requirements of Roman nobility, offered his own definition of these requirements. To the question *qui enim iudicatur iste optimus?* (*De rep.* I. 33, 50), Cicero replies *doctrina, artes, studia* and above all *virtus* (I. 34, 51).[55] These should be the qualities of all those who come under the title *principes* and *optimates*, terms which Cicero frequently employs to designate his aristocratic class.[56] The names were characteristically Republican terms and carried the idea of superiority in them: *principes* referred to members of the senatorial class and the senate itself; the closest equivalent in Greek was ἄριστοι; *optimates* were the first among the senators. The singular *princeps*, was employed by Cicero to render the Platonic/Aristotelian πολιτικός for which there was apparently no precise equivalent.[57]

Concerning the relationship that Cicero envisaged between the *principes/optimates* and the *rector/gubernator rei publicae,* apart from the unequivocal statement that he was *auctor publici consilii,* leader of the senate, nothing else is known. Certainly, the question of relationships between classes and governing bodies must have been dealt with in the final three books and especially in Book V of the *De republica*. Can we

---

[55] *Ibid.* 34, 51. The qualitities of an *optimus vir* by which he should govern the state are *virtus et animus.*

[56] The term *princeps/principes* which was employed by Cicero in many of his writings has become the subject of research by H. Wagenwoort, "Princeps" *Philologus* 91 (1936) 206-11; Lepore (above, n.47); J. Hellegouarc'h, *Le vocabulaire latin des relations politiques* (Paris 1963) 327-61; and P. Drexler, "Princeps-principes" *Maia* 10 (1958) 243-80, to mention only the most important authors.

[57] Heinze (above, n.47) 79f.; Boyancé (above, n.46) 194f.; Brèguet vol. I, 136ff.

assume, then, that some information concerning political relationships in the *De republica* influenced the Anonymous to some degree, just as an aspect of the political functions of Cicero's ideal statesman had certainly affected his concept of the βασιλεύς? It is tempting to reconstruct Cicero's *optimus status rei publicae* on the evidence provided by a sixth-century political treatise, fragmentary though it is. I believe that some kind of reconstruction is possible if we bear in mind that the Anonymous looked to the Roman Republic as seen through the eyes of Cicero in the *De republica* for certain ideas which he made the cornerstone of his *politeia*. The main ones were:

1. the superiority of the mixed constitution over the simple constitutions, for the mixed constitution guarantees equilibrium, hierarchy of ranks and stability.[58]

2. the supremacy of law and justice as the foundation stone of the state. A law determines the election of the king as it had also in early Rome.[59]

3. the political pre-eminence of aristocracy in making up two important organs of the state, the senate and the magistrates.[60]

We should think, of course, that the Byzantine author adapted these and other ideas he borrowed to the realities of his own time, but on the whole, the framework must have stayed unchanged. The βασιλεύς must have corresponded to the *rector rei publicae*, the τάξις of two hundred ἄριστοι to the *optimates*, the τάγμα or σύστημα ἀρίστων to the *principes* from whom members for the senate and magistrates were selected. If we wish to extend the parallels, we may suggest that the *rector*, just as the βασιλεύς, was one of the *principes*, i.e., one of the ἄριστοι, and as such was not only a *princeps* but also a model for all *principes* because of the superior rank to which he was elected. If he had the right to select the magistrates, as the Anonymous wishes us to believe, then certainly he must have been

---

[58] Cicero praises the mixed constitution as superior to the simple ones in Book I where he discusses the good and the bad types of constitution (I 35, 52; 45, 69) and in Book II where he describes the Roman constitution as close to the ideal or at least the best ever realized (II 23, 41-2; 33, 57). Likewise, the Anonymous must have included a debate on constitutional forms in his early books; there is no reference to the mixed constitution in the extant fragments.

[59] Cicero presents three kings, Numa Pompilius (II 13, 25), Ancus Marcius (II 18, 33) and Lucius Tarquinius (II 20, 35) as elected by the people; the advice of the nobility, of course, *patribus auctoribus*, must have been paramount before each election. It is possible that Cicero's description of Roman kingship as elective had influenced the Anonymous' idea of a *Wahlmonarchie*.

[60] Unfortunately no discussion has survived on these important components of the state in the *De republica*; only the Anonymous' fragments contain a few scraps of information.

chosen by the people of Rome — the *curiae* — from a list of candidates submitted by the aristocrats.[61]

In the absence of sufficient evidence from Cicero's *De republica*, the above parallels, of course, must remain largely assumptions. But contents of the quotation from Cicero and the description of the Anonymous' *politeia* have provided a stimulus for rethinking some of the assumptions about the Ciceronian *princeps*.

Carleton University
Ottawa, Canada

---

[61] Certainly Cicero's concept of the *rector*, even if he was *sapientissimus et unus* (Tacitus, *Dial.* 41), as he may well may have been, must have differed substantially from the idea of the Byzantine king as presented by the Anonymous. It is important to emphasize the fact that both Cicero and the Anonymous attempted to build their 'ideal statesman' on the Platonic/Aristotelian model of the πολιτικὸς/βασιλικὸς (*ad Q. fr.* 3, 5, 1-2; *de fin.* 5, 11, Anonymous fol. 299ᵛ 93f.). Moreover, both authors, and particularly the Byzantine were influenced by Hellenistic ideas about kingship. A modern scholar has summed it up: "he (Cicero) is ... rather seeking to fit into the antimonarchical Roman system the virtues associated with monarchy." J. Ferguson, *Utopias of the Classical World.* (London 1975) 160; L. K. Born, "Animate Law in the *Republic* and the *Laws* of Cicero" *TAPA* 64 (1933) 128-137.

THE VERGILIAN MANUSCRIPTS M, P AND R

ROBERT E. GAEBEL

For the text editors of modern times, three manuscripts have furnished the basic text for the works of Vergil. They are the Mediceus, the Palatinus, and the Romanus,[1] written in rustic capital scripts dated variously from the fourth to the sixth centuries. Fragments of five other capital manuscripts of the same period survive and these make occasional contributions to our knowledge of the text in late antiquity.[2] The list is completed by nineteen fragments from the Near East, most of which are papyri from Egypt.[3] In general, the latter are not of great value and Geymonat alone seems to have used them for a text edition.[4] Later manuscripts exist by the hundred, but because I wish to examine the character and quality of M, P and R alone, I shall ignore them in the present study. In order to make the task manageable I have restricted myself to the *Georgics,* except where it was useful to cite examples from the other works.

There are three questions about M, P and R which I should like to answer. They are: 1) By ancient standards, what is the textual quality of these manuscripts? 2) By modern standards, what is their quality? and 3) When they left the hands of their respective scribes, how readable and usable were they? Question 3 differs from 1 and 2 because a superficially correct text may contain many variant readings which scan correctly and are intelligible in context. This is, in fact, frequently the case in the Vergilian text, and too often it is impossible to determine the original reading. Implicit in these three questions is a fourth: Which manuscript — M, P or R — is the best (or perhaps better expressed, the most useful)? It may seem strange that this has not been definitively decided after more than a hundred years of repeated examinations of these manuscripts, but that is the case. For example,

---

[1] Mediceus Laurentianus lat. XXXIX, 1. (M); Vaticanus Palatinus lat. 1631 (P); Vaticanus lat. 5867 (R).

[2] For a description of these see M. Geymonat, *P. Vergili Maronis Opera* (Turin 1973) XIX-XX.

[3] For the text of these see R. Cavenaile, *Corpus Papyrorum Latinarum* (Wiesbaden 1958), nos. 1-19. For the pedagogical use of these texts see R. Gaebel, "The Greek Word-lists to Vergil and Cicero," *Bulletin of the John Rylands Library* 52.2 (Spring 1970) 284-325.

[4] *Op. cit.* Geymonat lists eighteen of them and includes many of their readings in his critical apparatus.

M was preferred by Conway,[5] P by Ribbeck and Sabbadini.[6] Funaioli, on the other hand, believed that the readings of neither were inherently superior.[7] R has been largely ignored.

My answers to these questions rest on complete collations of facsimiles of these three manuscripts against a modern standard, in this case the text of Geymonat. Since Geymonat's critical apparatus for the majuscules provides a complete record of the deviations of these manuscripts, and since he had access to the originals, I have usually trusted his judgement where the scripts are difficult to decipher. Errors and omissions in his apparatus are extremely rare, sufficiently so that I feel that it alone could be used as the basis of research on the capital manuscripts.[8]

It is not altogether easy to find out what standards of correctness the buyer of books demanded. Cicero, in a letter to his brother, complained about the difficulty of obtaining good copies: "de Latinis vero, quo vertam me, nescio, ita mendose et scribuntur et veneunt" (*ad Q. Fr.* III. 5/6.6). Pliny the Younger experienced the same problem: "quos (i.e., libellos) ... recognoscendos emendandosque curem." (*Ep.* IV. 26) Unfortunately, this was probably a common lament, but good copies may have been obtainable too, for Gellius mentions a copy of the *Annals* of Quintus Fabius Pictor in which a *grammaticus* could find only one error (*NA* 5.4.1-2). Any hand-copied text would, of course, have more than one error, yet this episode, in which the *grammaticus* was called in to inspect the copy before purchase, does suggest that there were some demanding customers. For a more precise answer, we must examine the surviving manuscripts themselves, even if they are few in number and perhaps not representative of the mass of copies which once existed.

After recording the results of the complete collations, I distinguished and grouped four types of deviation from Geymonat's standard text. These are: 1) intelligible Latin words (many of which are true variants); 2) unintelligible corruptions; 3) variations in orthography and spelling; 4) alternative -*es*/-*is* spelling of the accusative plural

---

[5] R.S. Conway, "The value of Med. cod. of Virg.," *Bulletin of the John Rylands Library* 15 (1931) 336f.

[6] Otto Ribbeck, *Prolegomena* (Leipzig 1866) 320. R. Sabbadini, *P. Vergili Maronis Opera* (Rome 1930) 23. K. Buchner, *P. Vergilius Maro, Der Dichter der Römer,* (Stuttgart 1959) coll. 455-6, claimed Ribbeck and Janell (1930²) both preferred M, but Ribbeck's own statement (*Prolegomena* 320) shows that he preferred P to M, and M to R.

[7] G. Funaioli, "Il valore del Mediceo nella tradizione manoscritta di Virgilio," *Atti della Società italiana per il progresso delle scienze* 4 (1932) 132.

[8] At *Georgics* III, 291, he fails, for example, to record the reading *set* for *sed* in M.

of -*i*-stem words.⁹ The accompanying tabular presentation of these data (Fig. 1) shows that there is a consistent variation in quality among these manuscripts which permits one to make some definitive statements about their relative merits. All the data are from the *Georgics*. The number in parentheses records the number of lines extant in each manuscript by book. Following this is the number of corruptions. The group 1/*x* indicates frequency of occurrence, i.e., 1 deviation for every *x* lines. The larger *x* is, the fewer are the deviations.

I employed a different format for the data from the accusative plurals of *i*-stem words. Not only did I wish to show the number of instances of both -*es* and -*is*, but I am also reluctant to accept Geymonat's choice of either -*es* -*is* (for reasons given in my article cited in note 9), and for present purposes feel it is necessary to show only relative numbers of occurrences of either -*es* or -*is*. I have included the results of alterations made to the Mediceus by M², Turcius Rufius Apronianus Asterius, consul ordinarius A.D. 494, which seem to show the preference of later ages for the -*es* spelling.

Ms[11]	Bk. 1		Bk. 2		Bk. 3		Bk. 4	
	-*es*	-*is*	-*es*	-*is*	-*es*	-*is*	-*es*	-*is*
M	16	35	30	28	25	51	19	39
M²	27	24	40	18	41	35	23	34
P	17	16	16	31	20	53	7	40
R	41	11	21	16	36	39	15	24

Only the intelligible and unintelligible corruptions seem to be of importance in evaluating the textual quality of these manuscripts. It is true that classical orthography in a manuscript may indicate greater fidelity to the original but this cannot be guaranteed and may merely reflect an archaizing tendency. The same considerations apply to *i*-stem words. Yet one wonders whether the relatively poor orthography of R has encouraged editors to prefer M or P.

In looking at the data cited above, it must be remembered that they reflect the condition of the manuscripts as they left the hands of the scribes, except for a few corrections made by the copyists themselves. For the entire four books of the *Georgics*, these corrections by the original scribes amount to 15 for M, 22 for P, and only 6 for R. Many of the remaining corruptions were corrected later by other hands,

---

[9] I placed the *i*-stem words in a separate category because detailed study has convinced me that they are not merely a type of orthographic variation. See my article "The Varied Use of -*es* and -*is* for the Accusative Plural of i-stem Words in Vergil's *Georgics*," *Latomus* 41 (1982) 104-131.

FREQUENCY OF TYPES OF DEVIATION

	M			P			R	
Intelligible								
Bk. 1	(514)	79	1/6.5	(322)	58	1/5.5	(514)	80	1/6.4
Bk. 2	(542)	149	1/3.6	(404)	84	1/4.8	(328)	57	1/5.7
Bk. 3	(566)	149	1/3.8	(566)	118	1/4.8	(566)	110	1/5.1
Bk. 4	(566)	155	1/3.6	(461)	127	1/3.6	(452)	93	1/4.8
Total	(2188)	532	1/4.1	(1753)	387	1/4.5	(1860)	340	1/5.5
Unintelligible								
Bk. 1	(514)	27	1/19.0	(322)	49	1/6.5	(514)	16	1/32.0
Bk. 2	(542)	37	1/14.6	(404)	67	1/6.0	(328)	16	1/20.5
Bk. 3	(566)	40	1/14.2	(566)	60	1/9.4	(566)	24	1/23.6
Bk. 4	(566)	35	1/16.2	(461)	46	1/10.0	(452)	13	1/34.7
Total	(2188)	139	1/15.7	(1753)	222	1/7.9	(1860)	69	1/26.9
Orthographic								
Bk. 1	(514)	60	1/8.5	(322)	38	1/8.5	(514)	92	1/5.6
Bk. 2	(542)	82	1/6.6	(404)	49	1/8.2	(328)	47	1/6.9
Bk. 3	(566)	92	1/6.1	(566)	48	1/11.8	(566)	103	1/5.5
Bk. 4	(566)	103	1/5.5	(461)	33	1/13.9	(452)	69	1/6.5
Total	(2188)	337	1/6.5	(1753)	168	1/10.4	(1860)	311	1/5.9

Figure 1

especially in M, but until that was done one wonders how usable these manuscripts were. Given the number of intelligible, but incorrect, corruptions, of which perhaps one-third make some sense in the context, plus the unintelligible errors, it is questionable whether they were readable in any meaningful sense. The data show that R, in its uncorrected state, had the fewest intelligible and unintelligible corruptions. In fact, it was by far the most carefully copied text, since both M and P show a slightly higher incidence of intelligible errors and of the unintelligible type, M has almost twice as many as R, whereas P has more than three times as many. Thus the answer to my third question is that these manuscripts, in their uncorrected state, were only barely readable, and would not have met the standards of a discriminating reader. This is confirmed, I think, by the thorough and generally accurate alterations made to M by M^2. The result was that M and M^2 together represent a reasonably good text, whereas M alone does not. P too was subject to extensive correction, but in the *Georgics,* this was limited to Book 1. R has very few corrections, although it did not require as many. Two examples will show the flaws in one of these manuscripts in its original state. They are from P: *Bucolics* 10.32-42; *Georgics* 2.534-540. Corruptions are underlined and Geymonat's choice of the correct reading is listed below each passage.

B. 10.32 MONTIBUS HAEC NOSTRIS SOLI CANTARE PERITI
ARCADES. O MIHI TAM QUAM MOLLITER OSSA QUISSANT
34 VESTRA MEOS OLIM SI FISTULA DICAT AMORES.
ATQUE UTINAM EX VOBIS UNUS VESTRIQUE FUISSEM
36 AUT CUSTOS GREGIUT MATURAE VENITUR UVAE.
CERTE SIVE MIHI PHYLIS SIVE ESSET AMYNTAS
38 SEU QUICUMQUE FUROR QUIT TUM SI FUSCUS AMYNTAS?
ET NIGRE VIOLE SUNT ET VACINNIA NIGRA
40 MECUM INTER SALICES LENTA SUB VITE IACERES
CERTA MIHI PHYLLIS LEGERET CANTARET AMYNTAS.
42 HIC GELIDP FONTES HIC MOLLIA PRATA LYCORI

32. VESTRIS, 33. TUM, QUIESCANT, 36. GREGIS AUT, VINITOR,
37. PHYLLIS, 38. QUID, 39. NIGRAE VIOLAE, VACCINIA,
40. IACERET, 41. SERTA, 42. GELIDI

G. 2.534-540
534 SCILICET ET RERUM FACIA ET PULCHERRIMA ROMA
     SEPTEMQUE UNA SIBI MURO CIRCUMDEDIT ARCES.
536 ANTE ETIAM CEPTRUM DICTAET RGIS ET ANTE
     IMPIA QUAM CAESIS GENS IST EPULATA IUVENCIS
538 AUREUS HANC VITAM IN TERNIS SATURNUS AGEBAT:
     NECDUM ETIAM AUDIERANT INLARI CLASSICA NECDUM
540 INPOSITOS DURIS CREPETARE INCUDIBUS ENSES.

534. FACTA EST, 536. SCEPTRUM DICTAEI REGIS, 537. EST,
538. TERRIS, 539. INFLARI, 540. IMPOSITOS, CREPITARE

These passages exhibit a higher incidence of error than the statistical average, but they are not unique and do reflect the alternation of relatively clear passages with highly corrupt ones. I should note in passing (from my own examination of about twenty later MSS) that virtually none of the uncorrected unintelligible errors found in these three MSS turns up in the medieval texts. This may suggest that M, P and R do not form the basis of the medieval tradition. Indeed there is no *a priori* reason why they should, since hundreds (if not thousands) of these early MSS of Vergil are now lost. On the other hand, the absence of these errors in later MSS may indicate only that some extensive editorial work was carried on which eliminated them. M^2 would be an example of this. In the one case of which I know in the Vergilian tradition where a ninth century MS is a direct copy of one of these surviving majuscules (portions of Bern. 172 are copied from R),[10] the scribe was extremely faithful to his exemplar.

Even without referring to texts other than M, P and R, an answer may be offered to the first question I raised: what is the quality of these manuscripts by ancient standards? M and P are inferior to R in respect to intelligible and unintelligible corruptions. R, in its turn, is inferior to P in orthography. If we combine the best of M, P and R, and take that as a standard of scribal accuracy, it is clear that all three are below the ancient potential, itself a standard quite inferior to the modern. Evidence from other surviving early MSS of Vergil supports this. This information comes from two fragmentary MSS, Palimpsestus Ambrosianus Cimel. ms.3 (the Ambrosian) and Vaticanus lat. 3256 (the Augusteus). The Ambrosian survives in four fragments comprising 78 lines (*Aen.* I 588-607, 649-668, 689-708, 729-748, with lines 734 and 744 missing). When intelligible, unintelligible and orthographic deviations for these passages are tabulated and compared with the data

---

[10] See my article, "The Palatinus and Gudianus MSS of Vergil," *Vergilius* 27 (1981) 52-56.

from the same passages of M, P and R, the Ambrosian shows itself notably superior to M & P.[11]

Errors

	Total	Intelligible	Unintelligible	Orthographic
M	33 1/3.3	12 1/6.5	11 1/7	10 1/7.8
P	29 1/2.7	12 1/6.5	5 1/15.6	12 1/6.5
R	17 1/4.6	10 1/7.8	1 1/78	6 1/13
Amb.	17 1/4.6	7 1/11	0 0/78	10 1/7.8

A similar pattern turns up in the case of the Augusteus. In the *Georgics* this MS is extant for 240 lines in Book I (41-280) and for 40 lines in Book III (181-220).

Errors *G.* I 41-280

	Total	Intelligible	Unintelligible	Orthographic
M	72 1/3.3	28 1/8.5	13 1/18.5	31 1/7.7
P	99 1/2.4	38 1/6.3	39 1/6.1	22 1/11
R	88 1/2.7	40 1/6	7 1/34	41 1/5.8
A	69 1/3.5	33 1/7.3	8 1/30	28 1/9.6

G. III 181-220

	Total	Intelligible	Unintelligible	Orthographic
M	22 1/1.8	13 1/3	2 1/20	7 1/5.7
P	14 1/2.8	7 1/5.7	2 1/20	5 1/4
R	20 1/2	7 1/5.7	0 0/40	13 1/3
A	14 1/2.8	9 1/4	1 1/40	4 1/10

In regard to unintelligible errors, the Augusteus is superior to M and P and about the equal of R. It is noteworthy that, in general, the relative number of corruptions in M, P and R in these passages accords well with their overall character in the *Georgics* as a whole. This supports the use of data from the surviving fragments of the Ambrosian and the Augusteus. These data confirm the earlier observation based on M, P and R alone: M and P especially, and R to a lesser degree, do not exhibit the best possible efforts of the scribes of late antiquity. Thus, the answer to my first question is that even by ancient standards they are not the best representatives of their class.

---

[11] I have hereafter omitted the variations in the accusative plural of *i*-stems as insignificant.

By modern standards they are woefully inadequate and the superiority of a text such as that of Geymonat is full justification for the efforts of modern palaeographers and text editors.

Although the data presented here seem to support R's claim to be the best or the most useful manuscript, I am not prepared to make that assertion without a great deal more detailed work, in particular on the nature of the intelligible corruptions. The many unintelligible errors of M and P are easy to eliminate by examining R and the medieval tradition (where they do not turn up). Orthographic variations may be easily standardized, although it is not certain that Vergil was completely consistent in this respect. Without the suggested further study of the intelligible corruptions it remains an open question which of the three MSS would be of most use in deciding between two variant readings in those many places in the text of Vergil where two contextually acceptable variants survive. At the very least, R should not be considered inferior to M and P until there is enough evidence to support that judgement.

The University of Akron
Akron, Ohio

A REFERENCE TO THE *CHORA BASILIKE* OF ALEXANDER THE GREAT (PLUT., *PHOKION* 18.5)

A.J. HEISSERER

Scholars have long been fascinated by the topic of royal holdings among the possessions of the Hellenistic kings in Asiatic territory, and in particular where those domains were located and how they were acquired or lost.[1] Alexander the Great initiated this process of acquiring royal lands with his invasion of Asia Minor in 334, and the purpose of the present note is to draw attention in a fresh way to a disputed passage that indicates the existence of *chora basilike*.

Plutarch alone, in his life of Phokion (18.5), tells the tale of how in 324 Alexander offered this Athenian general the revenues from any one of four Asiatic cities he might choose: Kios, Gergithos, Mylasa, or Elaia (Plutarch's order).[2] Aelian (*VH* 1.25) substitutes Patara for Gergithos, a point that will be discussed below. Phokion, to be sure, declined the gift, but the issue concerns whether there is any historical substance to the passage, i.e., whether there is evidence to suggest that these towns had passed into Alexander's hands in such a manner that he felt free to offer any one of them to Phokion. Long ago Tarn, in an effort to reject Bickermann's thesis that the Conqueror regarded the

---

[1] M. Rostovtzeff touched on this topic in many places in his monumental *The Social and Economic History of the Hellenistic World*, 3 vols. (Oxford 1941). See also the comments of E. Hansen in her *The Attalids of Pergamon*, 2d ed. (Ithaca 1971) 166-70, 183-86. The latest work that discusses aspects of this topic is by G. Cohen, *The Seleucid Colonies* (*Historia, Einzelschriften*, Heft 30, 1978) 45-70 (with full bibliography).

[2] There has not been much treatment of the *logos*. A. Baumbach, *Kleinasien unter Alexander dem Grossen* (Jena 1911) 88-89, commented briefly that the story reveals Alexander's attitude toward his conquered lands in Greek Asia Minor. W.W. Tarn, *Alexander the Great*, vol. 2, *Sources and Studies* (Cambridge 1950) 222-27, discussed the passage by way of illustration for his special view that Alexander had never "freed" the Greek towns of Asia Minor because they had never lost their freedom *de iure* (199-227). No comment is forthcoming in Hans-Joachim Gehrke, *Phokion* (*Zetemata*, Heft 64, München 1976), although on pp. 144-45 he has some general remarks on the Conqueror's efforts at largesse. R. Flacelière, *Plutarque, Vies*, vol. 10 of ed. Budé (Paris 1976), 34 n.1, provides the Greek text of Aelian and reminds the reader about how Artaxerxes similarly offered to Themistokles three towns in Asia Minor (Plut., *Them.* 29). To judge from Seneca, *De Beneficiis* 2.16, Phokion's consistent refusal of Alexander's gifts became proverbial.

Greek cities in Asia as his own property, declared the Plutarchian passsage to be "pure invention."[3]

My primary concern here is Elaia (see map). Located at the innermost recess of the Bay to which it gave its name, it was not many kilometers distant from two other small Aiolic towns, Pitane on the northern shore and Gryneion on the southern shore of the Bay. A piece of information about these two neighboring towns comes from Diodoros of Sicily, who states that in 335 the Macedonian general Parmenion took Gryneion by storm and sold its inhabitants into slavery,[4] but while besieging Pitane was compelled to retire by Memnon, the Greek general who led the forces of Dareios (17.7.9). Parmenion had been sent the preceding year into Asia Minor by Philip II for the purpose of "liberating" Greek towns from Persian rule;[5] he had been quite successful, since it appears certain that he had reached as far south as Ephesos (Arrian, *Anab.* 1.17.10-12). But in the summer of 335 Memnon's vigorous activity pushed the Macedonian forces all the way back to the Hellespont, "liberating" the same towns in turn. Alexander was too preoccupied in Greece to provide any assistance, so that only in 334 was the conqueror able to make a clean sweep of Asia Minor.

Parmenion was unusually harsh toward Gryneion; and the text of Diodoros implies that he would have sold as slaves the inhabitants of Pitane also, had not Memnon intervened. What had these towns done to deserve such treatment? The answer may be found by comparison with events that took place at Eresos on Lesbos island, directly opposite the Bay of Elaia. Epigraphic evidence from the town shows that in 336 Eresos had been freed from a family of pro-Persian tyrants (very likely by Parmenion although this is not explicitly stated), and in gratitude to

---

[3] Tarn (above, n.2) 227, who emphasized that the four towns were not truly Greek, even though the sources he cited demonstrate the opposite. E. Badian has astutely criticized Tarn's whole thesis: see "Alexander the Great and the Greeks of Asia," in *Ancient Society and Institutions: Studies presented to Victor Ehrenberg on his 75th birthday* (Oxford 1966) 37-69.

[4] N.G.L. Hammond, *Alexander the Great* (Park Ridge, N.J. 1980) 78, contrasts Parmenion's (i.e., Philip's) treatment of Gryneion with Alexander's own humane actions at Ephesos in the next year. But we are not certain whether Parmenion in 335 had learned of the death of Philip and was acting on orders from the new King.

[5] Diod. Sic. 16.91.2. Gryneion, like Pitane and all the surrounding area, had long been under Persian rule, except for a brief respite during the fifth century as a member of the Delian Confederacy. On Gryneion see Tarn (above, n.2) 219-20, and, more recently, George E. Bean, *Aegean Turkey* (New York 1966) 110-12; for the situation of Elaia and Pitane, *ibid.*, pp. 112-14 and 115-17 respectively.

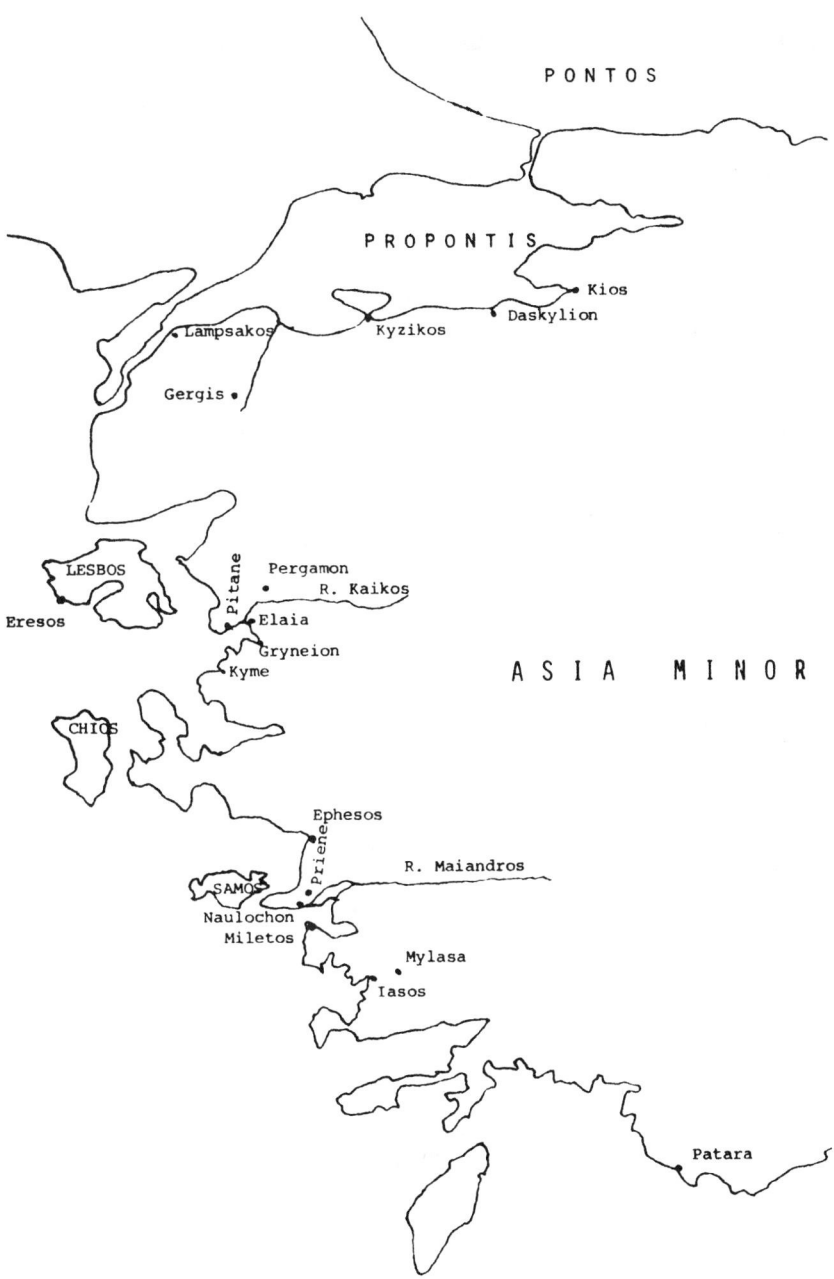

its benefactor it had erected altars to "Zeus Philippios."⁶ In the following spring, however, the approach of Memnon to Aiolis provided the circumstances in which two pro-Persian tyrants seized control of Eresos, dug up the altars to Zeus Philippios, and declared themselves in favor of Dareios; indeed, the stele declares that Agonippos, one of the tyrants, "made war on Alexander and the Greeks," when the Macedonian army and the forces of the League of Korinth appeared in the spring of 335. No doubt similar events will have occurred on the Aiolic mainland, many towns having been first freed from Persian rule by Parmenion, then having reverted to their previous overlord through pressure from Memnon, and finally freed again by Alexander himself. Diodoros also relates that, when Parmenion was besieging Gryneion, Memnon made an attempt on Kyzikos and shortly thereafter crossed over the hinterland of the Troad in order to come to the aid of Pitane (17.7.8). Apparently Parmenion, after his initial victories, was surprised to find Memnon in his rear; Diodoros' passage is best interpreted as meaning that the Macedonian general, retreating in 335 toward the Hellespont, was punishing those states discovered to have gone over to the Persian cause. The sack of Gryneion, similar in attitude if not in scale to Alexander's destruction of Thebes in the same year, was intended to be a lesson for those states that had deserted, or were considering deserting, the Macedonians.

The point to be noticed is that if both Gryneion and Pitane had reverted to the Persian cause in 335, it is virtually certain that Elaia did the same. Nor is there any doubt that betrayers of the "Macedonian peace" suffered punishment of some kind. At Eresos the two tyrants were executed in accordance with Alexander's instruction. At Chios the Conqueror ordered (either in 334 or 332) that escaped betrayers were to be "exiled from all the cities that share in the peace," while those who had been captured were to be brought back and "judged in the *synhedrion* of the Greeks."⁷ Furthermore, it was in 334 that Alexander, as he passed on down the coast of Asia Minor, pronounced an edict regulating the affairs of Priene and its surrounding territory. The opening lines of this inscription read as follows:

>From King Alexander.
>Of those residing in Naulochon,
>as many as are Prienians are to
>be independent and free, possessing

---

⁶ *IG* 12.2.526. Full discussion of the inscriptions from Eresos can be found in A.J. Heisserer, *Alexander the Great and the Greeks: The Epigraphic Evidence* (Norman, Okla. 1980) 27-78.

⁷ Heisserer (above, n.6), 80-81.

the land and all the houses in the
city and the countryside ...⁸

Part of the following clause is lost, wherein reference was made to a specific area, but we can still read the following portion: "I decree the ... *chora* to be mine, and those dwelling in these villages are to pay the tribute." Priene occupied the route that Alexander followed as he approached Miletos. His own fleet surprised the enemy by seizing the harbor of Miletos and Lade island, an action that forced the Persians to obtain water and supplies "from the mouth of the Maiandros" (Arr. 1.19.7). Naulochon, the harbor of Priene and located near this same mouth, will have come under Persian control, and it must have been its complicity with the enemy that led Alexander to assign Naulochon to Priene and to confiscate the adjacent territory. These conditions strongly suggest the manner in which Elaia could be offered to Phokion in 324: ten years earlier Alexander had declared the community to be a part of his royal domain.⁹

With respect to the remaining towns in Plutarch's list we are on much less certain ground, but a situation similar to that at Priene may well have occurred at Mylasa, a town that had long existed within the

---

⁸ Heisserer 146.

⁹ Our knowledge of the legal status of the Greek cities of Asia Minor before the arrival of the Macedonians derives from our general understanding of events that had transpired earlier in the century. The King's Peace of 387 had drawn a boundary line demarcating the Great King's territory from that of the autonomous Greek states, and the Second Athenian Confederacy had gone to great lengths not to impinge upon that arrangement (see T.T.B. Ryder, *Koine Eirene. General Peace and Local Independence in Ancient Greece* [Oxford 1965], esp. chaps I and III with app. III). Since the mainland of Asia Minor (including Klazomenai and Kypros) belonged to the Great King, towns such as the four listed in our Plutarchian passage were his to dispose of, even if in practice they appear to have been generally left alone. Many islands in the Aegean, such as Lesbos and Chios, joined the Second Confederacy and did not thereby violate the oaths of 387. But when Philip in 338 dissolved the Second Confederacy and simultaneously established his own Korinthian League, the cities of these islands were bound to no power. If, however, they could be induced to join Philip's League, then they were participating both in a peace that supplanted the King's Peace and in an alliance that declared war on Persia (Ryder, *ibid.*, app. X). Indeed, the armed alliance soon invaded the Great King's land and, inasmuch as the literary and epigraphic evidence suggests that the Macedonians felt the most effective way to maintain political and military control of the Aegean islands was to enroll their towns in the Korinthian League, it is likely that the same procedure was followed for those Greek towns along the littoral of western Asia Minor during Alexander's campaign of 334. Such a procedure gave first Philip and then Alexander a wide latitude for interfering in the affairs of a League town, as we see in the case of Naulochon and Priene, and if a town for whatever reason went over to the Persian cause, a legal pretext easily existed for Alexander to punish the deserter by declaring part of its land his own *chora*. Probably many Greek cities of Asia Minor, chafing under the age-old domination of Persia, welcomed Alexander's appearance in 334, without realizing that

Persian orbit. Its neighbor, tiny Iasos, lay on the sea some kilometers west of Mylasa and had opposed Alexander's army in 334 (Arr. 1.19.11), but soon changed sides, for this remote *polis* was the home of one of Alexander's most trusted Greek supporters, Gorgos of Iasos.[10] At some unknown date Gorgos and his brother were instrumental in recovering and restoring to their homeland the so-called "little sea." Although the precise identity of this body of water has never been determined, nevertheless it is clear that certain territories exchanged hands, with Alexander's blessing, and it is quite possible that a settlement had been made to the detriment of Mylasa; if Alexander could arrange for Iasos to possess a sea lane that likely affected the trade of Mylasa, he could easily have declared Mylasa or part of its lands royal territory.

Gergis was an old native town of the Troad and has been successfully identified with the modern Karincali.[11] The name of its inhabitants, the Gergithians, and the places they came to inhabit, have caused some confusion. Strabo in one passage (13.616) refers to a place called Gergitha near the sources of the Kaikos river, "to which Attalos transferred those in the Troad after he had destroyed their place." But archaeological evidence has shown that Gergis in the Troad maintained a continuous life throughout the Hellenistic period.[12] In another passage, however, Strabo mentions a "place called Gergithion" in the territory of Lampsakos, a second place of the same name "in the territory of Kyme near Larissa," as well as a "city called Gergitha from the Gergithians in the territory of Kyme" (13.589). Part of the difficulty here is that the antiquity of the places named Gergithion and the city called Gergitha near Kyme are unknown, but nevertheless we can reject Tarn's statement that "no *polis* named Gergithos ever existed" (p. 224) because Steph. Byz. (*s.v.* "Gergis") explicitly says, "It (sc. Gergis) is also called Gergithos, a feminine in the nominative taken from the genitive case." Plutarch's Gergithos, therefore, likely means Gergis, a town that was not far from the very site of Alexander's battle at the Granikos. For this reason it is preferable to excise Aelian's Patara,

---

Macedonian "freedom" could entail the diminution of their own "autonomy."

[10] Heisserer (above, n.6) 169-204. For the latest treatment of the situation of Mylasa, see George E. Bean, *Turkey Beyond the Maeander,* 2d ed. (London 1980) 13-24.

[11] Full discussion of ancient Gergis and its modern topography is found in J.M. Cook, *The Troad* (Oxford 1973) 347-51.

[12] *Ibid.,* p. 351.

which was both larger and better known, and a city that had easily submitted to the Conqueror (Arr. 1.24.4).[13]

Kios must remain a mystery. Tarn rejected its notice on the ground that, "all through Alexander's reign it was in the hands of a Persian dynast, Mithridates, uncle of the founder of the kingdom of Pontus, who ruled there from 337 to 302" (p. 225). Unfortunately, the very source that Tarn cites for this information (Diod. Sic. 20.111.4: 302 B.C.) also makes it clear that some members of that dynasty owed allegiance to at least Alexander's successors (19.40.2; cf. Plut., *Demet.* 4). Furthermore, after Granikos in 334 Alexander sent his general Kalas out as satrap of Hellespontine Phrygia, ordering him to collect the same tribute that had been paid previously to Dareios (Arr. 1.17.1). At about the same time Parmenion was sent to occupy Daskylion (Arr. 1.17.2), the old capital of that satrapy and only a short distance from Kios.[14] The Macedonian king, therefore, seems to have controlled the major portion of Hellespontine Phrygia, and accordingly his offer of the revenue from one of its towns to Phokion is not an extravagant gesture.

I admit that there is a certain hazard in making speculations of this nature. But it is the very obscurity of the places mentioned without elaboration by Plutarch that inclines one to believe that his passage contains a kernel of historical truth rather than the "pure invention" of Tarn. Plutarch's citation of Elaia, when combined with the references in Diodoros and the inscribed decrees from Eresos, makes good historical sense and urges the conclusion that the entire passage represents an authentic reference to the *chora basilike* of Alexander the Great in Asia Minor.

The University of Oklahoma
Norman, Oklahoma

---

[13] *Contra* George E. Bean, *Lycian Turkey* (London 1978) 84, who accepts Patara without any discussion.

[14] On Kalas see H. Berve, *Das Alexanderreich,* vol. 2 (München 1926), no. 397, and for Parmenion's occupation of Daskylion, A.B. Bosworth, *A Historical Commentary on Arrian's History of Alexander,* vol. 1 (Oxford 1980) 128.

A FOURTH REDACTION OF THE
HISTOIRE ANCIENNE JUSQU' À CÉSAR

JEFFREY H. KAIMOWITZ

An illuminated chronicle in The New York Public Library's Spencer Collection, MS. 41, of distinguished provenance, reflects the evolution towards a 'scientific' historiography during the Renaissance. A massive compilation of ancient history, both Biblical and classical, written in French, it retains characteristics of medieval historical writing, while betraying the clear impress of the new age of learning.

Spencer 41 in the form in which it is preserved may well be unique. Research so far has not turned up another example of this particular text, though it is possible that other copies of the compilation have now been lost or are yet to be identified. To a large degree, however, the MS. is based directly on an earlier compilation of ancient history, given the name *Histoire ancienne jusqu'à César* by Paul Meyer, who discussed it in an article written over ninety years ago.[1] According to Meyer and G. Raynaud de Lage,[2] who alone of recent scholars has done important work on the *Histoire ancienne,* this earlier compilation in its first redaction dates roughly to the first quarter of the 13th century.

Meyer,[3] followed by Raynaud de Lage,[4] finds the *Histoire ancienne* divided into seven parts of unequal length. It is useful to list these parts to indicate something of the scope of the earlier work, which was so important in the formation of our MS. These parts, including the length of each in the 13th century Bibl. Nat. MS. fr. 20125 and their sources as identified by Meyer[5] and Raynaud de Lage[6] are as follows: 1: Genesis, ff. 3r-82v (based on Petrus Comestor's *Historia*

---

[1] "Les premières compilations françaises d'histoire ancienne", *Romania* 14 (1885) 1-81.

[2] In the *Dictionnaire des lettres françaises: Le moyen âge* (Paris: Arthème Fayard 1964) 377. Bibliography on the *Histoire ancienne jusqu'à César* can be found in the *Dictionnaire des lettres françaises,* 378, R. Bossuat's *Manual bibliographique de la littérature française du moyen âge* (Melun & Paris: Librairie d'Argences 1951-1961) nos. 3797-3799; 7833-7834, and Brian Woledge's very useful *Bibliographie des romans et nouvelles en prose françaises antérieurs à 1500* (Geneva, Droz, 1954), nos. 77-79, with its *Supplément 1954-1973* (Geneva Droz 1975) under the same numbers.

[3] *Op. cit.* (above, n.1) 36-63.

[4] "Les 'romans antiques' dans l'*Histoire ancienne jusqu'à César*", *Le moyen âge* 63, 4ᵉ série, 12 (1957) 268-269.

[5] *Op. cit.,* (above, n.1) 36-75.

[6] *Le moyen âge,* 268-269 (cf. above, n.2).

2: Assyria & Greece, ff. 83r-88v (after Orosius), 3: Thebes, ff. 89r-117r (*Roman de Thèbes*), 4: Minotaur, Amazons, Hercules, ff. 117v-123v (after Orosius), 5: Troy, ff. 123v-148r (after Dares Phrygius), 6: Aeneas, ff. 148v-178v (after Vergil), 7: Rome, ff. 179r-375v (various sources).

The original *Histoire ancienne*'s successor work, of which Spencer MS. 41 seems to represent only a portion, is on a far vaster scale. Its possible extent will be discussed shortly. At this point it is enough to say that the whole of the 'First Redaction' could be fitted into the two large[7] volumes (240 ff. & 198 ff. respectively) of Spencer 41, which comprises only Books 6-10 of the "premier volume" of the later compilation.

Contents and Sources

An understanding of the nature of the compilation can be gained by a brief, systematic examination of the MS., book by book. Though the work as a whole is incomplete, there is enough to provide an excellent idea of the typical content to be found and the sources used to produce it.

Like the original *Histoire ancienne,* MS. 41 contains both Biblical and classical material. *Book VI* (Vol. I, ff. 1r-67r; 36 numbered chapters), the first book in our MS., is typical. The Biblical portions encompass the whole of the book of *Joshua* and the book of *Judges* through Thola. The source however is not the Bible, but secondary sources. Most notable are the *Antiquitates Judaicae* of Flavius Josephus and the *Historia Scholastica* of Petrus Comestor (12th century), which was also a source of the "First Redaction" of the *Histoire ancienne.* Extensive narrative is the quality that characterizes the work of both these authors. The compiler tends to prefer one or the other according to which has the fuller account, often changing sources several times within one chapter. A further source, though of much less importance due to its dearth of narrative, is the *Speculum historiale* of Vincent of Beauvais (13th century).

The chapters of classical material reveal the same principles of composition evident in the Biblical chapters. The primary sources here are Boccaccio's *Genealogia deorum gentilium* and the first five books of the *Bibliotheca historica* of Diodorus Siculus. The compiler relies more on Boccaccio as a source through most of the book, Diodorus being used to introduce variant opinion, but in the final long chapter on

---

[7] The page size of Spencer 41 is 392 x 280 mm. The written surface is 295 x 185 mm. in double columns. The script throughout is *lettre bâtarde.*

Hercules, Diodorus is more in evidence. There are many references to other authors, but these almost all are lifted directly from the text of Boccaccio.

In *Book VII* (Vol. I, ff. 67v-105v; 58 numbered chapters), the contents are classical in subject. Chapters 1-53, which cover the story of Thebes from the birth of Oedipus to the city's fall to the Epigoni, utilizes a rather full version of the Thebes section (Meyer's part 3) of a redaction of the *Histoire ancienne* as the main source. In the earlier portion (chapters vi and vii), in the narration of the story of Oedipus, material from Boccaccio's *De casibus virorum illustrium* and the *Oedipus* of Seneca is introduced. The final chapters (54-58) are based mostly on section 4 of a redaction of the *Histoire ancienne* with additions in chapters 54-55 from the *Historiae adversus paganos* of Orosius.

Book VIII (Vol. I, ff. 106r-237r; 142 numbered chapters +4 additional unnumbered chapters) is devoted almost exclusively to the story of the sack of Troy with its preliminaries and aftermath. The narrative is for the most part a direct and full translation of the *Historia destructionis Troiae* by Guido delle Colonne (13th century). I may note incidentally that, although there are known French translations of Guido's work,[8] this particular version is unrecorded. Interspersed in the manner of the two previous books are passages drawn from other sources, notably Boccaccio's *Genealogia deorum gentilium,* Seneca's tragedies, and Diodorus Siculus, introducing additional or variant material.

The final unnumbered chapters (ff. 235v-237r) provide information on the Biblical judges Abeson, Ahialon, and Abdon based on Petrus Comestor and Josephus. To fill out his text, for the information available on these judges is scanty indeed, the compiler has laced the chapters with regnal synchronisms for Assyrian, Egyptian, Athenian, Mycenaean (Argive) and Sicyonian kings drawn from the *Chronicon* of Eusebius, and added the story of king Mnestius from Boccaccio's *Genealogia deorum gentilium.*

Books IX and *X* are undivided and comprise all of Vol. II of MS. 41 (156 unnumbered chapters).[9] The contents are mixed but in a more complex fashion than in the books in Vol. I. Biblical material constitutes a large part, covering the period from the birth of Samson through the destruction of the Northern Kingdom of Israel by the

---

[8] See Woledge (above, n.2), nos. 176-178 and Alphonse Bayot, *La légende de Troie à la cour de Bourgogne* (*Soc. d'Emulation de Bruges, Mélanges,* I, Bruges 1908) 19-23.

[9] Vol. II of Spencer 41 is written by a scribe other than the one who wrote Vol. I. In general, it presents a less finished appearance than Vol. I, for there are no lists of rubrics, chapters are unnumbered, and the painted initials in red and blue are not adorned with scrollwork.

Assyrians (ca. 721 B.C.). The same sources are employed as in Book VI.

Of the remaining portions of IX-X, only the most prominent need be discussed. Ff. 1r-23r are devoted to the adventures of Aeneas, beginning with his arrival in Carthage and ending with his death. The main source is a redaction of the *Histoire ancienne,* with additional material in part drawn from the first book of Livy's history, Boccaccio's *Genealogia deorum gentilium,* and the *Facta et dicta memorabilia* of Valerius Maximus. Ff. 71r-80v contain a detailed account of Brutus of Great Britain, the source of which is identified in the text (f. 71r) as the *Brut,* probably the *Roman de Brut* of Wace (12th century), but it is also heavily and directly indebted to the *Historia regum Britanniae* of Geoffrey of Monmouth (1100?-1154) from which in large measure Wace's narrative is taken.[10] In addition, spread throughout the book are short sections of narrative and lists of kings based on Eusebius's *Chronicon,* the *Epitomae in Trogi Pompeii Historias Philippicas* of Justin (3rd century), and the other sources already identified as used in IX-X.

Date of the Compilation

The latest work employed in the compilation is Boccaccio's *Genealogia deorum gentilium,* which was in a continuous process of revision until near the author's death in 1375.[11] Diodorus Siculus' *Bibliotheca historica,* however, was only translated into Latin by Poggio Bracciolini in 1449.[12] Since it is unlikely that the compiler would have employed the Greek text for his work, it is probable that the compilation can be safely put after 1449. The Middle French in which the MS. is composed is not discordant with such a conclusion.

The "Fourth Redaction"

To summarize briefly the dependence of MS. 41 on the *Histoire ancienne jusqu'à César,* the over-all design of our MS. and the order of its contents follow that of the earlier work. Furthermore, most of Book VII (Thebes) and the first part of the combined Books IX-X (Aeneas) are taken directly from the *Histoire ancienne.*

---

[10] *Le Roman de Brut,* edited by Ivor Arnold (Paris: Soc. des anciens textes français 1938-40) I, lxxxix.

[11] *Dizionario biografico degli italiani* (Rome: Istituto della Enciclopedia italiana, 1960-) X, 851.

[12] *Ibid.,* XIII, 645. Poggio translated only the first five books.

Meyer discussed two later versions of the *Histoire ancienne* usually called by modern scholars the "Second Redaction" and the "Third Redaction".[13] The latter, described by Meyer as a new compilation "se rattachant à la seconde rédaction de notre histoire ancienne", is preserved only in two 15th century MSS.[14] It seems even closer to MS. 41 than the "First Redaction" of the *Histoire Ancienne*. Unfortunately, Meyer summarizes it only briefly in a footnote, but he gives enough information for us to recognize its importance as a closer precursor of MS. 41. Meyer points out that it is a combination of the first two redactions and the *Trésor de Sapience* (of Brunetto Latini?). From his indication of where its various sections begin, it seems to be on a larger scale than the two earlier versions, but on a smaller scale than MS. 41. Like the "Second Redaction", it includes a large section of Troy based on the *Roman de Troie* of Benoît de Sainte-Maure, not on the work of Guido delle Colonne.[15] Like Spencer 41, however, it goes much farther than the earlier two redactions in encompassing Biblical history, going all the way up to the period of the prophet Jonah (8th century B.C.). Also like 41, it tends to integrate Biblical and non-Biblical narrative in a way not observable in the earlier versions. Finally, again like 41, it is incomplete, breaking off at the beginning of the history of Rome, its last words announcing a second volume that is not preserved or perhaps was never completed. It seems clear that the "Third Redaction" was a more immediate source of Spencer 41 than the two earlier versions, but, even from Meyer's short summary, it is obvious that our text represents a new compilation, which for convenience we might call the "Fourth Redaction".

Reconstruction

MS. 41 opens with Book VI of the "First Volume" of the work. The colophon at the end of the MS., Vol. II, f. 198r provides more information:

> "nous ferons fin ycy a ce x^e. liure et p(ar) conseque(n)t a ce premier uolume contenant dix liures et po(ur) uenire al xi^e. liure de n(ost)re oeure qui fera le co(m)mencement du second uolume ou quel co(m)mencement sera traitte de la fondation et

---

[13] Meyer (above, n.1), 63-75.

[14] *Ibid.*, 64, n. 2. The MSS. are Arsenal 3685 and Bibl. Nat. fr. 15455.

[15] Guido's *Historia destructionis Troiae* is itself also based on Benoît de Sainte-Maure's *Roman de Troie*.

construction de celle cite faitte p(ar) Remus & Romulus."

It is clear that the work as a whole was conceived on a tremendous scale. MS. 41 contains half of the "First Volume". The "Second Volume" would presumably be comparable, making the work very possibly at the least four times the size of what is preserved.

Since, with regard to the Biblical material, the compilation is designed to provide a very full account, it is not unlikely that the first five books of the "First Volume", if they ever existed, followed the *Pentateuch,* using the Biblical sources already discussed. What makes this hypothesis more plausible is that material from the *Pentateuch* beyond *Genesis* forms the first part of the "Third Redaction" of the *Histoire ancienne.* It may well be, in accordance with the mode of compilation observable in Books VI-X of 41, that classical elements would be scattered among the Biblical portions.

As to the continuation of the compilation, if it was completed, we know from the colophon to the "First Volume" that the history of Rome beginning with Romulus and Remus was intended to open Book XI, the first book in the "Second Volume". It seems reasonable to surmise that in a way similar to what has been observed in the books we have, the books of the "Second Volume", perhaps also numbering ten, would have been based on or inspired by a redaction of the *Histoire ancienne,* but executed on a much larger scale than its predecessor. It is perhaps significant that in the two complete versions of the *Histoire ancienne* for which there are tables of contents available the section on the history of Rome represents just about exactly half of the total work.[16]

As in the first two redactions of the *Histoire ancienne,* the subject matter would be the history of Rome from its founding to the middle of the first century B.C. It is very likely the remaining Biblical history not covered in the "First Volume" would also be included.

We can speculate on the possible sources for the "Second Volume". For Roman history, it is probable that Livy's *Ab urbe condita* would have been used. Though incomplete, it offers a very full narrative for the periods for which it is preserved. There is a long verbatim quote from Livy in Spencer 41, Vol. II, f. 23r at the end of the story of Aeneas. This is one of the earliest occasions on which Livy's narrative could have been utilized and it is likely in the "Second Volume" that his work would have had a prominent part. Justin's history, also employed in the "First Volume", would likely have been a source. For

---

[16] Cf. above, nn.3 & 4.

Historical Method

In character the text of Spencer 41 is basically a compilation, in the original languages or in translation or paraphrases, from the sources sketched above. The controlling principle seems to be the desire to make the content as full as possible. The compiler is not troubled by inconsistencies. Thus extracts from Petrus Comestor include both narrative and explication, while the material drawn from Guido delle Colonne is straight narrative. Not surprisingly, a critical historic overview or conception informing the work is not observable. In this respect, it is similar to many other examples of historical writing from the Western European Middle Ages.[17]

However, the aim to completeness is in itself a new factor. Up to this time, most medieval historical works concerned with the ancient world in its totality were on a smaller scale. The desire for a fuller account reflects a more thorough and inquiring approach.

In addition, the compiler follows certain principles that reveal something of a new critical spirit. He frequently, though far from consistently, identifies various sources he employs, so that for example, in Book VI, such a rubric as "selon comestor vincent et iosephe" is often to be found.[18] At the same time, when his sources conflict, the compiler will indicate both opinions, crediting each to its proper source. For instance, in Book VIII we find: "Et ce selon guy de la coulompne mais diodorus autem aut(re)ment le met en son quint liure la ou il dit ..." (f. 111r).

Characteristic of a critical spirit is the manner in which the compiler eschews the fantastical in his accounts of mythology and tries to take on a more objective tone. This leads to rather peculiar results in Book VI in the story of Procne, Philomela, and Tereus, which is paraphrased from Boccaccio's *Genealogia deorum gentilium*. Boccaccio presents a rationalized explanation of the metamorphosis of the three main characters into birds. The compiler of MS. 41 avoids all reference to the metamorphosis, but retains the information relating to the

---

[17] For a fine account of the medieval conception of history, see G.W. Coopland, *The tree of battles of Honoré Bonet* (Cambridge: Harvard University Press 1949) 38-47.

[18] Two of the medieval authors used by our compiler (Vincent of Beauvais in his *Speculum historiale* and Boccaccio in his *Genealogia deorum gentilium*) carefully cite their sources and it is possible that our compiler's tendency to citation of sources is owing to their inspiration.

rationalization. Translation of both passages provides an opportunity to observe our compiler's technique in borrowing and offers some of the flavor of his rather prolix style.

Boccaccio:[19]

" ... <Procne> dressed with thyrsus and skins went to the forest and led Phylomena dressed in like fashion to the palace. Fired up with rage, when she had thought a great deal <about vengeance> against her husband, she poured out her wrath against her little son Ythis who was greeting her, killed him by cutting his throat, and presented him cooked to her husband who was dining in the morning as was his wont. When he, unaware of what was going on, called for him [Itys] and Prognes continually replied: "He is present" and he <still> did not know before getting up from the table, Phylomena coming from a room presented him the head of his son which had been reserved for this purpose. <Tereus> then suddenly aroused by this pursued the sisters with a sword, but the gods took pity on them so that Prognes was turned into a swallow and proper in appearance for her <dead> son dwelt in her house. Her sister was changed into the bird of her name [nightingale] and sought the woods which she had left at night. Thereus however became a hoopoe; so all the royal house was transformed. The meaning however of such a story, in the opinion of Barlaam, is this. Thereus was a fierce and wicked man, seeking and taking nothing except through war, and for this reason he deserved Mars for a father, though he was the son of Astogirus, leader of the Bystonides. Although he dared do nothing against his wife because of his own crime, she because of shame for the cruel act she had committed never went down into the royal hall, but, dressed in black clothing, in the upper part of the house bewailed her wickedness and her sister's misfortune. <Barlaam> gave this explanation of her [Procne's] metamorphosis, while in Phylomena's case the name as well as her return to the forest was the reason. Thereus however they said was turned

---

[19] The translation is based on the text edited by Vincenzo Romano, *Genealogie deorum gentilium libri* (Bari: G. Laterza 1951) II, 456-457.

into a hoopoe, because the hoopoe is a crested bird, and its song is shrieking, and dung is its food so that by the crest the nobility of his royal head is indicated, and through the shrieking the laments for his lost son, and by the stinking food the rejected and disagreeable memory of the child he ate."

Spencer MS. 41, f. 24v:

This day [Festival of Bacchus] Prognes dressed with thyrsus and skins in the manner of that one [Bacchus] led her sister philomena into the royal residence of thereus thus dressed as she was; and in the rage of grief she bore for the crime committed by her husband against her sister, after she had thought a great deal how she would be able to take vengeance on him, she cut the throat of her little son ythis who ran up to greet her. Keeping his head aside, she had his body cooked all of which she gave to her husband thereus to eat who took no notice of what it was. Thereus several times asked for his son ythis and, each time his wife said that he was there, he did not understand anything nor did he know until at the end of his meal philomena dressed just as has been said brought him on a plate the head of his son ythis, of which she made a point to him that then thereus knew what his wife had said to him, that is he understood that his son was there. For which treacherous murder thus carried out by his wife on the person of his little son he did not dare to take vengeance because of the shame in the same way which he had for the detestable crime he had committed against philomena. But he spent the rest of his days in tears and tears (*sic*) and weeping and his wife prognes in shame for her so horrible sin from that point on did not come into the royal hall. Thus she remained and spent the rest of her life in the upper rooms and other parts of the house dressed in black without any other color and her sister philomena in equal shame fled to the woods to hide herself where she spent the rest of her life alone.

Miniatures

Each book of the MS. opens with a miniature, which contains two or more scenes surrounded by a conventional 15th century border. The scenes in each miniature are unified in subject and tend to illustrate material that occurs early in their respective book. In general, the scenes seem directly based on the text of the MS. and so a reference to the apppropriate folio and column number is provided in the listing below. In each miniature, except that of Book VIII, chronologically earlier scenes appear on the left side of the miniature, later scenes on the right; scenes in the lower part of miniatures follow scenes in the upper part.

Book VI: f. 2r: Joshua and the crossing into Canaan: four scenes:

1. (upper left): Joshua kneeling, receiving instructions from the Lord (f. 2v, col. 1).
2. (lower left): Joshua instructs his ministers to tell the people to prepare food for the crossing (f. 2v, col. 1).
3. (upper right): Joshua sends out spies to reconnoiter in Canaan (f. 2v, cols. 1-2).
4. (lower right): The Israelites, headed by the Ark of the Covenant and Joshua, cross the Jordan into Canaan (f. 3v).

Book VII: f. 69r: Early events in the life of Oedipus: four scenes:

1. (upper left): Laius receiving the oracle of Apollo (f. 69v, col. 1).
2. (lower left): Birth of Oedipus (f. 69v, col. 1)
3. (upper right): Exposure of Oedipus in the woods with his feet pierced (f. 69v, col. 1).
4. (lower right): Discovery of Oedipus by the shepherd and his presentation to Polybus, King of Corinth. 69v, cols. 1-2).[20]

Book VIII: f. 109v: Two scenes relating to the story of the sack of Troy as presented in Guido delle Colonne's *Historia destructionis Troiae*:

1. (upper third): On left, Jason taming the fire-breathing bulls, with the dragon and golden ram in the background (f. 122r, col. 1), while, on the right, Medea looks on from a tower in the palace (f. 121v, col. 2).

---

[20] With regard to the fourth scene, the text states that the child was given by the shepherd to a merchant who in turn gave it to Merope, wife of Polybus, not directly to Polybus as illustrated in the miniature.

2. (lower two-thirds): The Greeks and Trojans in battle (Book VIII, *passim*).

Books IX-X: f. 1r: Story of Dido and Aeneas: two scenes:
1. (left): Meeting of Dido and Aeneas (f. 3v, col. 2).
2. (right): Departure of Aeneas, while Dido looks on from a high tower (f. 6r, col. 2).

As already stated, with the slight deviation noted above, the miniatures seem to be based closely on the text and created to illustrate it. Since we cannot be sure whether Spencer 41 is the original MS. of the "Fourth Redaction", we cannot know whether the miniatures are original conceptions in their own right or copied from another MS.

Dr. John Plummer of the Pierpont Morgan Library has identified the miniatures as originating in Brittany or Western France. He suggests a date of between 1475 and 1480. As will be seen, knowledge of the original ownership of the MS. narrows the date somewhat further.

The Original Owner

On each of the miniatures appear the arms of Tanguy II Du Châtel (ca. 1425-1477) of Brittany on a banner and those of himself impaled on a woman's shield along with those of his wife, Jeanne de Raguenel, dame de Malestroit.[21] There is no evidence of earlier arms and so it is clear that the first owner of the MS. was Tanguy II Du Châtel.

Tanguy belonged to a distinguished Breton family.[22] His father, Olivier, had been chamberlain of the king and held other important offices. His uncle, Tanguy I Du Châtel, was a major stateman and soldier during the first half of the 15th century, serving Charles VII as Grand Maître de France.

Tanguy II, like his uncle, had a distinguished career in government and in military affairs. Among other positions he held, under Charles VII (king: 1422-1461) he was chamberlain and Grand écuyer de France, and governor of Roussillon under Louis XI (king: 1461-1483) whom he served as an intimate counsellor and leading general. He was mortally wounded by a shot from a falconet at the siege of Bouchain in

---

[21] Léopold Delisle in *Le cabinet des manuscrits de la Bibliothèque Nationale* (Paris 1868-1874) II, 353 lists Tanguy's arms: "fascé d'or et de gueules de 6 pièces, à la bordure fascée de l'un en l'autre" and those of Jeanne de Raguenel: "de gueules à 9 besants d'or, posés 3, 3 et 3".

[22] A short biography of Tanguy can be found in the *Dictionnaire de biographie française* (Paris 1933-) XI, cols. 1180-1181.

May, 1477. He survived up until the end of August, 1477 and perhaps a little after.

The library of Tanguy can in part be reconstructed from information provided by Delisle.[23] The MSS. known to belong to it reflect the interests of a soldier and man of affairs. Twelve MSS., all written or translated into French, are listed by Delisle. Most numerous are works relating to history and biography: St. Augustine's *De civitate Dei* (Bibl. Nat. fr, 25), Boccaccio's *De claris mulieribus* (Vienna, Austrian Nat. Lib. 2555), Leonardo Bruni's *Commentaria tria de primo bello Punico* (Bibl. Nat. fr. 723), *Grandes Croniques de France* (Biblo. Nat. fr. 17270), *Histoire romaine, Sénèque et Cicéron* (Bibl. Nat. fr. 9186), Valerius Maximus' *Dicta et facta memorabilia* (Bibl. Nat. fr. 738), and Vincent of Beauvais' *Speculum historiale* (Bibl. Nat. fr. 6354-6359). Also to be found are three works that include historical content: Honoré Bonet's treatise on the Law of War, *L'Arbre des batailles* (Biblo. Nat. fr. 1276), Brunetto Latini's encyclopedia, *Li Livres dou Trésor* (Bibl. Nat. fr. 569), and Cicero's manual on conduct, *De Officiis* (Vienna, Austrian Nat. Lib. 146). The remaining two MSS. are the *Débat de Fortune et de Vertu devant Raison* (Bibl. Nat. fr. 12781) and a volume of varied content including works by Robert de Sorbon and others (Bibl. Nat. fr. 1608). It is obvious that Spencer 41 fits very well into this library. In fact, the works by Vincent of Beauvais and Valerius Maximus are sources of the "Fourth Redaction."

The Making of Spencer MS. 41

As has already been indicated, the compilation of the "Fourth Redaction" quite certainly dates to after 1449. The date for the miniatures (1475-1480) provided by Dr. John Plummer, assigned incidently before the arms had been attributed to Tanguy II Du Châtel, and the date of Tanguy's death (1477) coincide well and point to a relatively brief period in which our MS. was probably written. In the preceding half-decade (1469-1475), most of the sources of the "Fourth Redaction" additional to the *Histoire ancienne jusqu'à César* first appeared in print in Latin.[24] It is tempting to speculate that the ready

---

[23] *Op. cit.* (above, n.21), 353.

[24] They are: Boccaccio, *De Casibus virorum illustrium* (Strassburg, 1474-75); Boccaccio, *Genealogia deorum gentilium* (Venice, 1472); Guido delle Colonne, *Historia destructionis Troiae* (Netherlands?, ca. 1475); Diodorus Siculus, *Bibliotheca historica* (Bologna, 1472); Esuebius, *Chronicon* (Milan, ca. 1474-75); Josephus, *Antiquitates Judaicae* (-Augsburg, 1470); Justin, *Epitomae in Trogi Pompeii historias Philippicas* (Venice, 1470); Livy, *Ab urbe condita* (Rome, 1469); Orosius, *Historiae adversus paganos* (Augsburg, 1471); Petrus Comestor, *Historia scholastica* (Augsburg, Utrecht, Strassburg, 1473); Valerius Maximus, *Facta et dicta memorabilia* (Strassburg, ca. 1470); Vincent of Beauvais, *Speculum historiale* (Strassburg, 1473).

availability of these books was the impetus to the creation of the "Fourth Redaction" and that Tanguy II Du Châtel was the individual who commissioned it. If this is so, it is one more reflection of the tremendous importance of the printing press as an engine of the Renaissance and the general diffusion of culture. Tanguy's untimely death may explain why the work as a whole was never brought to completion.

Trinity College
Hartford, Connecticut

THE ADULTERY MIME RECONSIDERED

PATRICK H. KEHOE

One of the most popular subjects of the mimic stage of antiquity was adultery, and several versions of adultery mimes are attested.[1] One form, featuring love between a mistress of a household and one of her slaves, occurs in the *Zelotypus* of Herondas, and in a mime actually performed on the stage and called the *Moecheutria* by one of its early editors (Crusius). One of the mimes of Laberius, the *Compitalia*, also seems to have had this theme. Another type contained a love affair between a stepmother and a stepson, a situation which seems to have formed the plot of the *Belonistria* of Laberius. Both of these mimes will be discussed later. A third type, featuring stories of adultery taken from mythology, is especially associated with the names Lentulus and Hostilius, as Tertullian indicates: *despicite apud vos Lentulorum et Hostiliorum sacrilegas venustates, utrum mimos an deos vestros in strophis et iocis rideatis; sed et histrionicas litteras magna cum voluptate suscipitis, quae omnem foeditatem designant deorum.*[2] These mythological mimes were mainly confined to the Empire, but the *Anna Peranna* of Laberius

---

[1] I cite here important works about the mime in general or certain aspects of it. These works will hereafter be cited by the author's name alone. The most important single work on the mime remains the scholarly but wildly speculative book by Hermann Reich, *Der Mimus. Ein litterarentwicklungsgeschichtlicher Versuch* (Berlin 1903). A good survey of the mime which corrects some of Reich's excesses is E. Wüst, art. "Mimos" *RE* XV (1932) cols. 1727-64. The best general exposition in English is *Masks, Mimes and Miracles* by A. Nicholl (London 1931). For the Roman mimes there is the study by C.J. Grysar, "Der römische Mimus" *SBAW* (Phil.-Hist.) 12 (Wien 1854) 237ff. Although severely dated, this work is still worth consulting. For the extant titles, fragments and testimonia about the Roman mimes, an excellent and fairly recent book is *Romani mimi* ed. M. Bonario (Rome 1965). For a recent study and text of the extant Greek mimes see Helmut Wiemken, *Der griechische Mimus. Dokumente zur Geschichte des antiken Volkstheater* (Bremen 1972). For another text see also Otto Crusius, ed., Herondas, *Mimiambi*, 5th ed. (Leipzig 1914). For text, English translation, and commentary for the important mime I have called the *Moicheutria*, see also W. Beare, *The Roman Stage*, 3rd. ed. (London 1964) 314-319. For the adultery mime in particular there is only the influential article by R.W. Reynolds, "The Adultery Mime," *CQ* 40 (1946) 77-84. It will be seen that I strenuously disagree with the general conclusions advanced by Reynolds about the ordinary length and scope of the adultery mimes. For the mimes of Laberius one should also not ignore F. Giancotti, *Mimo e Gnome. Studio su Decimo Laberio e Publilio Siro* (Messina-Florence 1967. *Bibl. cult. contemp.* XCVIII).

[2] Tertull. *ad nat.* 1.10; cf. *id. apol.* 15. See also Nicoll 113, 122-4.

may also have belonged to this category.³ A fourth type depicted a love affair between a Roman or Greek matron and a man from outside the family circle. This is what modern scholars usually mean by the term "adultery mime" and will be the principal focus of this paper.

The most important evidence concerning this last type occurs in the complaint of Ovid (*Tristia* 2.497-500; 505-6):

> quid, si scripsissem mimos obscena iocantes,
>   qui semper vetiti crimen amoris habent;
> in quibus assidue cultus procedit adulter,
>   verbaque dat stulto callida nupta viro
>
> . . . .
>
> cumque fefellit amans aliqua novitate maritum
>   plauditur et magno palma favore datur.

Semper (498) testifies to the popularity of this theme, while *assidue* (499) shows that these mimes possessed a regularity of form. Specifically, they presented a sophisticated young lover (*cultus adulter*) and a clever wife (*callida nupta*) who constantly deceived her stupid husband (*stultus vir*) who was no doubt played by the mimic fool, the *stupidus*. The variations on this basic plot were no doubt due to the ingenious new stratagems contrived by the lovers for this deception. Line 506 shows clearly that the sympathy of the audience was with the adulterous pair.

With time the subject seems to have lost none of its attractions. Juvenal mentions a mime which seems remarkably similar to that which Ovid described (*Met.* 8.196-7):

> quid satius? mortem sic quisquam exhorruit, ut sit
> zelotypus Thymeles, stupidi collega Corinthi?

Clearly the *stupidus,* Corinthus, was the husband and the wife was named Thymele in this mime. Martial mentions Thymele as performing with a mime named Latinus (1.4.5-6):

> qua Thymelen spectas derisoremque Latinum,
>   illa fronte precor carmina nostra legas.

---

³ Giancotti 61-5, thinks it may have resembled the burlesque story of Anna Peranna and Mars in Ovid, *Fasti,* 3.675ff. On this issue see also J. C. McKeown, "Augustan Elegy and Mime," *PCPS* 25 (1979) 76.

The description of Latinus as *derisor* (5) strongly suggests that he was not the *stupidus* in this mime. This suspicion is confirmed by Juvenal's mention of Latinus in discussing a notorious *adulter* of the day (6.42-44):

> si moechorum notissimus olim
> stulta maritali iam porrigit ora capistro,
> quem totiens texit perituri cista Latini?

Here we learn that Latinus played the adulterer in this mime, that regularly he had to hide in a chest (*cista* 44) at the arrival of an unexpected visitor, and that he was discovered when he came out to avoid smothering (*perituri* 44). In Latinus, Thymele, and Corinthus, therefore, we seem to have the same three basic figures mentioned by Ovid nearly a century earlier. In another passage, however, Martial informs us that Latinus appeared with another mime, Panniculus (5.61.11-14):

> O quam dignus eras alapis, Mariani, Latini:
>   te successurum credo ego Panniculo.
> res uxoris agit? res ullas crispulus iste?
>   res non uxoris, res agit iste tuas.

Evidently in this mime Latinus was accustomed to slap the face or box the ears (*alapis* 11) of the hapless Panniculus. Furthermore, since Marianus was a cuckolded husband, it is possible that Panniculus played this role in the mime alluded to. From another, very similar, passage in Martial we learn that this face-slapping was rather vehement (2.72.3-4):

> os tibi percisum quanto non ipse Latinus
>   vilia Panniculi percutit ora sono.

Here again the action of the mime illustrates an occurrence of real life: the face-slapping of Postumus by Caecilius at a banquet. The last line of this poem (8) may be instructive in this connection: *Quid quod habet testes, Postume, Caecilius*? The clever pun on *testes* suggests that Postumus may also be a cuckolded husband.

Since a mimic troupe could have two *stupidi*,[4] it is possible that Panniculus performed with Latinus and Thymele essentially the same

---

[4] As the phrase *stupidi collega Corinthi* (Juv. 8.197) itself indicates. See E. Courtney, *A Commentary on the Satires of Juvenal* (London 1980) on 8.197; *RE* s.v. *stupidus*; Wiemken 179. See also Nicoll p. 47, fig. 31 for a terracotta showing two mimic fools evidently performing together.

adultery mime in which Latinus, Thymele, and Corinthus appeared, and that face-slapping formed a part of this mime. Juvenal's picture of Latinus on the defensive and hiding in the *cista* (6.42-44) constitutes no real obstacle to the supposition that face-slapping formed a part of this mime, since such sudden "turning of the tables" is entirely in the spirit of mime: cf., for instance, Cicero *Phil.* 2.65: *persona de mimo, modo egens, repente dives.* Nevertheless, the total absence of any mention of Thymele in Martial 5.6.11-14 and 2.72.3-4 makes it uncertain whether she appeared in these plays, and the silence about face-slapping in Juvenal 8.196-7 and 6.42-44 compels similar doubt that this detail was a regular feature of the mimes to which he is alluding. Ovid, in his reference to adultery mimes, is also silent about *alapae*, although one suspects that the constant deception of the *stultus vir* by the *amans*[5] was possibly heightened by this detail, which would correspond well enough to the persona of the *derisor Latinus*. It is interesting, however, that the characteristic detail of the adulterer forced to hide in a chest is first mentioned by Horace a generation before Ovid's reference to these mimes (*Sat.* 2.7.58-61):

> quid refert, uri virgis ferroque necari
> auctoratus eas, an turpi clausus in arca,
> quo te demisit peccati conscia erilis
> contractum genibus tangas caput?

It seems very likely that this motif also occurred in the mimes mentioned by Ovid. It is therefore quite possible that the references we have been discussing in Ovid, Juvenal, and Martial point to essentially the same adultery mime.

A mime which has at least two of the three basic figures which we have been discussing is referred to in the *Satyricon* of Petronius. A *rusticus* is speaking of the performers who will soon appear in the gladiatorial shows of his small town (45.7): *Iam Manios aliquot habet et mulierem essedariam et dispensatorem Glyconis, qui deprehensus est, cum dominam suam delectaretur. Videbis populi rixam inter zelotypos et amasiunculos.* The apprehension of a steward and his mistress *in flagranti delicto* reminds the *rusticus* of the mime, but not of the variety involving mistress-slave adultery. He is thinking of the disturbance which will ensue among the members of the audience, and compares this to the *rixa* which evidently was a fairly common scene in the mimes of our fourth type, where the lover is a man from outside the family and the husband is a jealous fool. *Rixa* implies an altercation between

---

[5] *Trist.* 2.505: *cumque fefellit amans aliqua novitate maritum.*

equals or near-equals.⁶ In short, the *rusticus* seems to be referring to mimes like those featuring Latinus, Thymele, and Panniculus/ Corinthus, *zelotypus Thymeles.*⁷

In the second century also, in the time of Marcus Aurelius, we find mimes of adultery which seem very similar to those which we have been considering. About this emperor we read (*SHA, M.Ant.* 29.1-2):

> crimini ei datum est quod adulteros uxoris promoverit, Tertullum et <T>utilium ... ad varios honores, cum Tertullum et prandentem cum uxore deprehenderit. de quo mimus in scaena praesente Antonino dixit, cum stupidus nomen adulteri uxoris a servo quaereret et ille diceret ter "Tullus" et adhuc stupidus quaereret, respondit ille "iam tibi dixi: Ter Tullus dicitur."

Here again we have the husband played by the *stupidus*.

Not only in the first and second centuries, but even as late as the sixth century we hear of mimes featuring the same three basic characters, although we do not hear of their stage names: the stupid husband, the unfaithful wife, and her lover.⁸ There are, however, differences from the earlier plot: upon discovery of the adulterer, the husband becomes angry, calls a slave, and tells him to bring a knife,⁹ but then he changes his mind and summons the guilty pair before a court. Yet these differences may be only apparent. The mimes with Latinus and Thymele may well have included such scenes, as we may infer from the fact that the adulterer found it necessary to hide from the husband.¹⁰ The mockery and physical abuse that Latinus visited upon the *stupidus* may well have followed upon the latter's acceptance of the excuses contrived by the *cultus adulter* and the *callida nupta*, by one of the sudden

---

⁶ Ludwig Friedländer, ed., *Cena Trimalchionis,* 2nd. ed., (Leipzig 1906) 123, translates thus: *Da wird man den Streit des Publikums zwischen den eifersuchtigen Ehemännern und den galanten jungen Herrchen sehn.*

⁷ That such mimes often provoked partisan feeling in the audience is apparent not only from *Trist.* 2.506: *plauditur et magno palma favore datur,* but also from *A.A.* 1.501-2: *et plaudas aliquam mimo saltante puellam / et faveas illi, quisquis agatur amans.* It is easy to see that such feeling could erupt into the *populi rixam* mentioned here in the *Satyricon.*

⁸ Choricius of Gaza, *Ap.m.* 30.

⁹ For the purpose indicated in Plaut. *Mil.* 1394-1425. Wiemken, p. 147, n. 23.

¹⁰ If Heinrich's conjecture of *ut* for the MSS *et* in Juv. 1.36 be accepted, as Courtney proposes (*Comm. Juv.* 93) on the ground that the evidence that Latinus was *delator* is sparse, then we have explicit testimony that Latinus was depicted as fearful (1.35-36): *quem munere palpat / Carus ut a trepido Thymele summissa Latino.*

reversals so beloved by the mime[11] and by popular comedy in general. And it might also be urged that the deceived husband mentioned by Choricius must also have been at least tricked and probably beaten to retain his role as a proper *stupidus*. Likewise, the regular occurrence of a trial scene in the mimes of the days of Choricius did not, as the actor playing the *stupidus* argues, constitute a punishment of adultery: the guilty pair got off free in the end and thus the husband was still mocked (*Ap.m.* 30). We shall see that there is reason to believe that a trial scene may have been associated with mimes of adultery from a date much earlier than Choricius.

Enough has been said of the adultery mimes referred to by the ancient writers, to indicate that cast and plot remained remarkably constant, perhaps for a period of centuries. Indeed, Ovid's complaint was that these plays were already stereotyped in his day. Naturally, therefore, scholars have tried to reconstruct a typical plot of one of these mimes. Such reconstructions are inevitably guesswork, possessing no probative value, but they must be considered, if only because they have served to produce some misleading conceptions about mimic plays in general.

The most detailed of these attempts is that of R.W. Reynolds, who has in mind the plot during the first century A.D. According to Reynolds, mimes probably were short, depending more upon portrayal of character than on development of an intricate story. Consequently, he thinks it unwise to attempt to expand the performance into a play containing several scenes. In his view the mime may have consisted of one scene, set indoors, perhaps in the woman's bedroom. Relying on the information of Capitolinus. (*M.Ant.* 29, 1-3), he thinks that such a mime opened with the husband asking a slave for the name of his wife's lover. Then the husband either left the house himself or he cross-examined the wife. She, however, easily got the better of him, and possibly allayed his suspicions by allowing him to make love to her. Then she could simply concoct some errand that would necessitate his leaving the house. He cites Martial 11, 7 as illustrating a similar situation where the woman wants to absent herself. Reynolds thinks that when the adulterer arrived, there was probably a scene of love, by which he apparently means the representation of sexual intercourse on the stage. After the hypothetical scene of illicit love, however, the adulterer was hidden in a large chest upon the unexpected approach of the husband. A brief conversation referring to the situation probably then ensued. Finally the lover had to come out to avoid asphyxiation, and then the guilty pair had a fictitious story to allay the husband's

---

[11] Cf. Cic. *Phil.* 2.65.

fears. Alternately, the husband might have burst out in clownish rage and bellowed, as in the days of Choricius (*Ap.m.* 55). Here the debonair young man neatly eluded every attack, and the girl used all her feminine ingenuity to speed his escape. Perhaps the clumsy buffoon rushed about wildly, stabbed the empty air, tripped over his own feet, and perhaps even fell into the open chest. Reynolds suggests that farce may have ended on this note.[12]

Reynolds, therefore, thinks that the mime in question usually consisted of a single scene and involved only the three characters mentioned by Ovid, Juvenal, and Martial. In this regard his reconstruction differs from those of Grysar and Reich. To the three basic characters Grysar adds another two: a corrupt slave serving as the intermediary who arranges the adulterous affair, and a person, apparently someone other than the husband, who talks to the wife so long that the adulterer must come out of the chest and be discovered. He also thinks that the mime ended with a reconciliation between lover and husband.[13]

Reich's attempt to reconstruct this plot is characteristically confused. He gives in fact three reconstructions. One apparently is for the plays in which Latinus, Thymele, and Corinthus acted. According to this version, it is the husband who comes (back) and stays so long that the adulterer must come out of the chest. Although Reich does not so indicate, it is likely that he is relying on the scholiast to Juvenal (6.44), who tells us that the unexpected visitor in these mimes was in fact the husband: *qui totiens superveniente marito sub cista celatus est, ut in mimo.* Reich makes no mention of a trial scene, but postulates two intermediaries for arranging the affair: a parasite or trusted slave for the adulterer and a *cata carisa* or crafty woman for the adultress. Reich's second reconstruction is based on the court scene mentioned by Choricius, except that he supposes prior scenes in which the lover approached the woman, seduced her, and was finally caught by the husband.[14] Elsewhere Reich gives a third reconstruction, which combines the evidence of Ovid, Juvenal, and Choricius into one fairly sizeable drama with three scenes, but in a way different from the other two reconstructions: an opening scene in which the wanton wife and the stupid husband are depicted, after which the adulterer is admitted to the house by the *cata carisa* and meets the wife, apparently while the husband is still at home; a second scene, featuring the deception of the

---

[12] Reynolds 82-83.
[13] Grysar 253-4.
[14] Reich 89-91.

husband by several tricks, and the hiding and discovery in the chest; and the finale, consisting of the trial scene and the acquittal.[15]

All of these reconstructions are seriously flawed. Grysar's loses dramatic force by supposing that it is someone other than the husband who stays too long, and that the farce ended with the wife caressing her husband into forgiveness. He obtains the evidence for this ending only by reading *ut* for the *et* of the mss. in Juv. 1.36. Thus lines 35-36 in this poem become:

> quem Massa timet, quem munere palpat
> Carus ut a trepido Thymele summissa Latino.

Even if this uncertain expedient be adopted, it is unlikely that the giving of a gift by Latinus to the *stupidus* by means of Thymele would form the finale. This would be an intolerably flat and unfarcical ending. The various reconstructions of Reich are mutually contradictory and obviously contain a large amount of guesswork. Reynolds' reconstruction is the most significant, but it too is seriously defective. There is no evidence for the supposition that the mime began with the suspicious husband asking a slave for the name of his wife's lover. This circumstance occurred in the adultery mime of Marullus to set up the *Ter Tullus* joke which obviously applied only to the situation of Marcus Aurelius. Likewise, his hypothesis that mimes of adultery regularly simulated a scene of sexual intercourse seems incredible, at least for the early part of our period and in particular for the reign of Augustus.[16]

---

[15] Reich 563ff.

[16] Let us for example consider the audience whom Ovid reports as watching these mimes (*Trist.* 2.501-506; 511-14). It is difficult to imagine Augustus, that stern would-be reformer of Roman morals, banisher not only of Ovid but of his own adulterous daughter, watching nonchalantly (*lentus* 514), surrounded by married women and men, boys, girls, and senators, as scenes of sexual intercourse are simulated by stage adulterers. There is no mention here of the bed described by Chrysostom at a much later date (Chrys. 6.558 τὴν κλίνην). The critical line, 504 (*adsuescunt oculi multa pudenda pati*) must be interpreted in a less drastic sense, coming as it does immediately after mention of the contamination of the ears by lewd words (*incestis ... vocibus* 503). It would be sufficient to imagine a clever farce no more destructive of morality than the *Amphitruo* of Plautus, which also deals with an (unwitting) adultery and has in fact much in common with the mythological mimes of adultery mentioned earlier (our third type). Ovid's concept of immorality here is clarified a few lines later when he expresses indignation that the most popular part of the *Aeneid* in his day was the book (4) featuring an illicit love (*Trist.* 2.535-6): *nec legitur pars ulla magis de corpore toto / quam non legitimo foedere vinctus amor.* Surely this is a surprising *volte-face* for the author of the *Amores, Ars Amatoria*, and *Metamorphoses*!

A better reconstruction of these mimes is offered by Wiemken.[17] As he observes, the sparse testimony of the authors allows us to trace the plot only in the roughest outline. Assuming, like Reynolds, that mimes were probably usually short and simple pieces, he says nothing about a scene in which the two lovers-to-be meet each other for the first time, but thinks that the farce may have started with the wife surprised by her husband while engaged in a "tender tête-à-tête" with her lover.[18] The lover then succeeds in hiding in a nearby trunk, in which he then is forced to listen to the dialogue of the husband and wife. Wiemken observes that Juvenal does not give a resolution of the situation, but adds that there are two possibilities: either the lover succeeds in escaping[19] or the events detailed by Choricius (*Ap.m.* 30, 55) continue the action. As noted earlier, the husband in this case discovers the lover, summons the slaves, commands someone to bring a knife, but then changes his mind and summons the evildoers before a court. He thinks that the court scene would occur according to the example given by Apuleius (*Metam.* 10.2-12). except that in the time of Choricius the trial scene came to a merry end. Wiemken comments that subordinate motifs could be introduced, citing Juv. 6.275-8 and the scholion to show that the husband's discovery of incriminating letters in his wife's desk addressed to the lover could give the possibility of further development. He adds that it is uncertain whether still other roles (besides the basic three) occurred in these mimes, and observes that the letter motif would support such a notion.

The points at issue in these reconstructions revolve around the number of actors and scenes in the typical adultery mime. The answers given vary from only three actors and one scene (Reynolds) to many actors and many scenes (Reich). Since adultery mimes seem to have constituted a large part of the mimes presented on stage,[20] a resolution of this question will be important for generalization about the mimes. The influential article of Reynolds states this rather explicitly: "In many cases it [the adultery mime] is spoken of as a theme typical of the

---

[17] Wiemken 146-8.

[18] Yet in a footnote (p. 146, n. 20) he says "or better *in flagranti*" citing Augustine *Conf.* 3.2 to prove that mimic adulteries were staged very realistically: *in theatris congaudebam amantibus, cum sese fruebantur per flagitia, quamvis haec imaginarie gererent in ludo spectaculi.*

[19] On p. 147 n. 21 he compares Cic. *pro Cael.* 65.

[20] Cf. Val. Max. 2.6.7, who relates that the mimes were banned in Massilia in the time of Tiberius because the inhabitants disapproved of productions *quorum argumenta maiore ex parte stuprorum continent actus. Stuprorum actus* certainly includes adultery. Cf. Accius ap. Cic. *ND* 3.27.68 *qui non sat habuit coniugem inlexe in stuprum;* Livy 10.31.9 *matronas ad populum stupri damnatas pecunia multavit;* Hor. *C.* 4.5.21ff. *nullis polluitur casta domus stupris ... laudantur simili prole puerperae.*

mime as a whole." Furthermore, "It is possible, however, to form a fairly definite conception of a plot of this class [adultery mimes] which was famous during the earlier part of this period, and which may be taken as typical of them all."[21] If the adultery mime was really "typical of the mime as a whole," it will be instructive to consider what evidence there is that large-scale mimic dramas were staged. The existence of such large-scale productions would imply that many mimes of adultery were also productions of some size.

In view of the relative scarcity of information about the mime, the amount of evidence on this question is surprising. Testimony extending over our entire period (third century B.C. - sixth century A.D.) shows that many mimic dramas required more than three actors and one scene and were often quite large scale productions. A mimic play of the second century A.D. which was clearly a large-scale production is preserved on *P. Oxy.* 413. It is an imitation of the *Iphigenia in Tauris*.[22] It will not do to call this production a farce instead of a mime or to term it a crossing of the mime with higher forms such as comedy and even tragedy.[23] In one of the main characters we recognize the mimic fool, and there is no doubt that this production was called a mime in antiquity. Nicoll counts seven principal characters here, with, in addition, a number of attendants, barbarian guards, and Amazons. He estimates that a production of this play would call for not less than twenty people, even if the modern practice of "doubling" were allowed. Likewise, the Christian mimes described in some accounts of the martyrs included, besides the hero, such varied characters as a friend, a judge and his attendants, a bishop and his acolytes, and such subordinate roles as soldiers, guards, neighbors, and Christians. Further evidence of the large scope of at least some mimic productions exists in the form of an inscription erected at Bovillae in A.D. 169 and honoring the mime-director L. Acilius Pomtinus Eutyches. After the praise of Eutyches there follows the list of his company, containing no less than sixty names.[24]

Large-scale mimic productions are attested not only for the second but even for the first century after Christ, the very time when — according to Reynolds — the adultery mime regularly involved no more than three actors and one scene. Plutarch, in mentioning a type of

---

[21] Reynolds 77, 81.

[22] For the text of this, with a German (and English) translation, see Wiemken 48-59, and Nicholl 115-18 for an English translation and commentary. See also A. Lesky, *A History of Greek Literature* 2nd. ed. tr. J. Willis & C. de Heer (New York 1966) 809-10.

[23] Crusius, "Ueber das Phantastisches im Mimus" *NJb* 25 (1910) 100.

[24] *CIL* XIV. 2408; Nicholl 85-6.

mimic production called *hypothesis,* tells us explicitly that it was unsuitable for performance at banquets διὰ τὰ μήκη τῶν δραμάτων καὶ τὸ δυσχορήγητον. (*Quaest. conviv.* 7.8.4). He is evidently thinking of the same kind of mime when he tells us that he witnessed a mime in the theater of Marcellus with a πλοκὴ δραματικὴ καὶ πολυπρόσωπος (*de soll. an.* 19). The presence of the aged Vespasian in the audience allows us to date this performance to about A.D. 79. Another such large production was the *Laureolus* of the mimographer Valerius Catullus,[25] which was performed in the year A.D 41. According to the reconstruction by Reich, the story of the robber Laureolus began with a scene in which he runs away from the house of his master and joins a gang of robbers. Other scenes then showed how he became leader of the robbers, and performed all sorts of feats of banditry. Finally, he was arrested, hauled before a court, and executed on a cross. Martial (*Spect.* 7) tells us of a performance in A.D. 80 in which a condemned criminal played the part of Laureolus and was actually crucified. A crucifixion scene, therefore, is well attested for this mime. There must also have been, at the very least, one scene in which Laureolus was arrested and another in which he was condemned to death. This latter scene probably took the form of a trial since we know from Philo (*Embassy to Gaius* 359) that such scenes were common in the mimes of his day. A trial would naturally involve a rather large cast. In addition, Suetonius (*Calig.* 57.4) in referring to this mime mentions several mimes in secondary roles: *et cum in Laureolo mimo, in quo actor proripiens se ruina sanguinem vomit, plures secundarum certatim experimentum artis darent, cruore scaena abundavit.* Since the activity narrated here does not seem to fit scenes of arrest, trial, or crucifixion, it must come from yet another scene. The *plures secundarum* are no doubt other robbers in the gang of Laureolus. So, even if one cannot agree that this mime had as many scenes and characters as Reich argues, it is clear that many characters and at least four scenes were necessary.

To the *Laureolus* and *hypothesis* mentioned by Plutarch we may add two other references to apparently large-scale mimes in the first century: the first of these is the *mimicum naufragium* mentioned by Seneca (*de ira* 2.2.5) as a typical mimic scene in his day. A shipwreck implies a crew and passengers, and almost certainly involved more than

---

[25] For the name Valerius Catullus, see Bonaria 133; for the *Laureolus*: id. 134-5 and Reich 88-89, 198, 564.

three actors and one scene. The second reference occurs in the *Satyricon* (80.9):

> grex agit in scena mimum: pater ille vocatur,
> filius hic, nomen divitis ille tenet.

As Reich points out (p. 565) we have here only the three main roles; there is no mention of feminine roles or the no doubt numerous secondary roles. Although this citation comes from a work of fiction, it is likely meant to reflect contemporary mimic productions.

Mimes requiring more than three roles and one scene seem to have been performed also in the first century B.C. Consider, for example, the meager fragments of the *Ephebus* of Laberius:[26]

I

> idcirco ope nostra dilatatum est dominium
> togatae gentis.

II

> licentiam ac libidinem ut tollam petis
> togatae stirpis.

Both fragments seem clearly the words of a god. Fragment I is cited by Macrobius (6.5.15) as an earlier occurrence of the expression *gens togata,* put by Vergil into the mouth of Jupiter in the great prophecy of *Aeneid* I (282). Since Vergil's scene is probably indebted to some degree to earlier Roman epic, the god speaking these lines in the *Ephebus* is probably Jupiter, and the scene is set at Olympus. Fragment II is cited in the same place by Macrobius to show that Laberius substituted *togata stirps* for *gens togata.* This fragment bears an obvious similarity to the first one. The *dominium togatae gentis* is described by an interlocutor hostile to the Romans as *licentiam ac libidinem ... togatae stirpis.* The interlocutors, therefore, are probably Jupiter and Juno, and the whole scene may by a parody of a scene from earlier Roman epic, possibly from the *Annales* of Ennius. We know that *Annales* I contained a famous *concilium deorum* on the Homeric pattern. A literary model for such a procedure was to hand: Laberius may have drawn on the *concilium deorum* in Lucilius' first book, which was probably a parody of the Ennian scene. And there were probably other popular versions of this theme as well. The title *Ephebus,* like most of the other

---

[26] Bonaria 49.

Laberian titles, seems to refer to daily life.[27] Thus it is very unlikely that the *Ephebus* was entirely about gods. Probably the *ephebus* of the title was a human being or a hero like Aeneas or Romulus.[28] Thus, on the analogy of the epic convention of the *Iliad, Odyssey, Annales* and *Aeneid,* the *Ephebus* probably contained two sets of characters, one divine and one human or heroic, and at least two scenes, one on Olympus and one on earth.

Another mime of Laberius, the *Tusca,* also seems to have required more than three roles and one scene.[29] Let us consider the slender remains of this mime:

I

bipedem bliteam beluam

II

concitata mobilitatem mente maestas

III

dominus <est> noster tua
luculentitate captus.

IV

inridenter petit.[30]

---

[27] Cf. *Centonarius, Augur, Belonistria, Carcer, Fullo.*

[28] We may note that Lucilius uses the *concilium deorum* to make a personal attack on Cornelius Lentulus Lupus. Therefore, it is tempting to speculate that Laberius was likewise making a personal attack on an eminent Roman, represented in this play possibly by the *ephebus.* If so, then the person attacked was quite likely Julius Caesar, since we know from Gellius (17.14.2) that Caesar found the mimes of Laberius offensive, preferring instead those of his rival Publilius Syrus: *Caesarem ita Laberii maledicentia et adrogantia offendebat, ut acceptiores et probatiores sibi esse Publilii quam Laberii mimos praedicaret.* The claims of Caesar to be a man of destiny descended from Jupiter by way of Venus were well known. Moreover, his conquests had significantly extended the *dominium togatae gentis* (frag. I), and his character seemed to his enemies to be one of surpassing *licentia ac libido* (frag. II).

[29] On the significance of the title cf. Wölfflin, *P. Syri mimi* (Leipzig 1869) p. 7, n. 1, as cited in Bonaria, p. 124: *utrum haec fabula indicet in Tuscia natam an potius intelligenda sit meretrix vici Tusci videant alii.* Bonaria adds that one should recall that in the *corpus glossar.* (t. 5., p. 413, 61) *lena toscia* is found.

[30] Bonaria 656.

Fragment III shows the use of a slave or freedman (cf. *dominus noster*) intermediary to arrange an amorous affair. Thus it seems very likely that this mime had at least four roles. Besides the intermediary, the *Tusca* and the *dominus,* the exigencies of drama require at least one other person to establish a dramatic conflict. Who this was depends on the social position and circumstances of the *Tusca,* which cannot be determined. If she was a *meretrix vici Tusci,* we would expect a rival suitor, a father of the *dominus,* a mercenary *leno/lena,* or an injured wife. If she was a married woman, this may have been an adultery mime with a *zelotypus maritus.* Also, the scene of fragment III is plainly preliminary, and is incomplete without at least one other scene to resolve the situation. Furthermore, fragment I "a two-legged, useless beast" looks like part of a furious denunciation of one character by another, and would fit well as the utterance of an offended wife/ lover or possibly the *Tusca.* It seems likely, therefore, that this mime required at least four roles and two scenes.

Long before Laberius, however, mimic plays seem to have existed containing more than three roles. One piece of evidence is a lamp published by Watzinger and dated to the end of the third century B.C. Although found on the Acropolis of Athens, it has been thought to derive ultimately from the Greek East, probably from Alexandria.[31] Three male figures are depicted on it, and the central one, with his huge ears and bald head, is obviously the mimic *stupidus.* Beneath them is the inscription:

μιμόλογοι
ἡ ὑπόθεσις
Ἑκυρά

This lamp, then, is our earliest example of a mimic *hypothesis.* It has, however, been pointed out that there was presumably one more role, that of the mother-in-law of the title, and that this role no doubt was played by a female colleague of the three male actors.[32]

Thus far we have found abundant evidence that from at least the third century B.C. to the second century A.D. many mimes contained at least four roles and more than one scene, and many of these mimes were clearly large-scale productions. Some of them may have involved the theme of adultery. This is likely true, for instance, of the *hypothesis* seen by Plutarch (*de soll. an.* 19) and described as πολυπρόσωπος,

---

[31] Watzinger, *Ath. Mitt.* 26 (1901) 1ff. for the Alexandrian provenience see Wiemken 39; see also Beare 153.

[32] Beare 153.

w p o ts$, since the dog mentioned seems to have been used as a sort of guinea-pig for a concoction of poison or a sleeping drug.[33] Since it is clear that adultery was a very common mimic theme, perhaps the most common one, it is reasonable to conclude that many adultery mimes also contained more than three roles and one scene. There is, in fact, good evidence, from the first century B.C. to the sixth century A.D. that some mimes clearly about adultery fit this description. For the latter end of this span I have already mentioned the mimes discussed by Choricius, where an adultery theme involved a trial and thus a large cast.

Of the mimes of Laberius, the *Belonistria* and the *Compitalia* were both mentioned earlier as instances of varieties of adultery mime. The *Belonistria*, to judge from its sole surviving fragment,[34] seems to have required more than three roles and one scene:

> domina nostra privignum suum
> amat efflictim.[35]

Here clearly a slave or freedman (cf. *domina nostra*) is talking to somebody else about two other people: the mistress and her stepson. Clearly a minimum of four roles is required. If, as seems likely, the person addressed is not the *dominus,* we must have at least five roles. Furthermore, the use of the third person for the stepmother and stepson implies their temporary absence from the stage, so that there may have been more than one scene. Similar conclusions emerge from an analysis of the fragments of the *Compitalia:*

II

> nunc tu lentu's nunc tu susque deque fers:
> mater familias tua in lecto adverso sedet,
> servos sextantis utitur nefariis verbis.

---

[33] For the connection of drugs with adultery plots cf. the *Moicheutria* and the involved story narrated in Apuleius, *Met.* 10.2-12. For other possible references to drugs in the plays of Laberius cf. also *Sorores*, frag. I (Bonaria 62): *Ecastor, mustum somniculosum* (drugged wine?); cf. also references to (possibly drug-induced) sleep in other mimes of Laberius, e.g. *Aulularia,* frag. I (Bonaria 41): *homo ebriacus somno sanari solet,* and *Aquae Caldae,* frag. I (Bonaria 39): *et iam hic me optimus somnus premit / ut premitur glis.* Very important also is a specific reference, in an erotic context (*amorem*), to *veneficia: ad amorem iniciendum delenimenta esse delerimenta, / beneficia autem veneficia* (Laberius, line 121, *ex incertis fabulis,* Bonaria 67).

[34] Lines 185-87 among the *fragmenta incerta* of Laberius (Bonaria 77) have been not implausibly ascribed (Giancotti 66) to this mime: *uxorem tuam / et meam novercam consectari lapidibus / a populo video.*

[35] Bonaria 41.

III

                        quo quidem
me a matronali pudore prolubium meretricium
progredi coegit.[36]

These two fragments seem to belong to two different scenes. In fragment II someone apparently is informing a husband that his wife is committing adultery with a slave. The wife and the slave are both spoken of in the third person and thus are presumably not present. Fragment III seems to represent the wife's rueful confession of her error. She is probably addressing her husband. Of the other two fragments, not given here, fragment I is unimportant and inconclusive, but fragment IV, a crude criticism of the Cynic philosophy, seems to have no connection with the other fragments, and may belong to yet another scene. Thus the evidence suggests at least four roles (husband, wife, slave, and informant) and at least two, possibly three or more scenes.

Thus far we have been considering evidence more or less explicitly referring to contemporaneous mimic productions. One should not, however, overlook the valuable evidence afforded by various literary passages which, although not directly alluding to the mimic stage, seem strongly influenced by it. These passages, extending at least from Livy to Apuleius, uniformly point to the existence over this period of mimes of adultery containing more than three roles and one scene. Sudhaus long ago suggested that an involved story narrated by Apuleius (*Metam.* 10.2-12) on the Phaedra theme was probably derived from the mimic stage.[37] This tale, concluding in a highly dramatic courtroom scene in which a doctor becomes a sort of ancient Perry Mason to free the innocent and convict the guilty, clearly would require a large cast in order to be presented on stage. Similarly, it has been acutely suggested that the trial scene in the *Satyricon* featuring Eumolpus as a lawyer defending his two reprobate companions (107) is also of mimic derivation.[38] Not only is this whole episode replete with mimic motifs,[39] but Lichas is also explicitly described as a wronged husband (106.2): *sed Lichas memor adhuc uxoris corruptae contumeliarumque quas in Herculis porticu acceperat, turbato vehementius vultu proclamat* etc. The rage of Lichas,

---

[36] Bonaria 46-7.

[37] S. Sudhaus, "Der Mimus von Oxyrhynchus" *Hermes* 91 (1906) 262ff.

[38] G. N. Sandy, "Scaenica Petroniana," *TAPA* 104 (1974) 345.

[39] When Eumolpus and Giton have their heads shaved, the whole procedure is described as a *fallacia* (103.3). When Lichas discovers the trick, he speaks of himself and Tryphaena as attacked and mocked by trickery characteristic of the mimic stage (106.1): *nunc mimicis artibus petiti sumus et adumbrata inscriptione derisi.*

here said to be apparent from his facial expression (*turbato ... vultu*), reminds us of the similar rage of the wronged husband described by Choricius (*Ap.m.* 55). Lichas himself acts like a prosecutor: "*noli,*" inquit, "*causam confundere,*" and refutes Eumolpus (107.7-11). He is only placated with difficulty. This trial scene takes place in the middle of the ship of Lichas. The mimic original of this scene no doubt required the whole crew to be in attendance. In fact the trial scene in the *Satyricon* quickly progresses to a melee involving the entire personnel of the ship (108.3-9). Beatings formed, of course, a stock motif of the mimic stage.

Trial scenes seem also to have occurred earlier in the mimes. Philo compares his unfair treatment at the court of Caligula to scenes from the contemporary mime in which the judge takes on the role of accuser and the accusers the role of a bad judge with eyes only for his enmity (*Leg.* 359). We have seen that the *Laureolus* of the mimographer Valerius Catullus was also performed during the reign of Caligula and very likely included a trial scene. That Livy also, or even Valerias Antias, his annalist source, may have been acquainted with comedies or mimes featuring courtroom scenes is suggested by a detail from the story of Verginia, who is made to appear before the court of the evil Appius Claudius. This scene is called by Livy a *fabula* (3.44.9): *Vocat puellam in ius. Auctoribus qui aderant ut sequerentur, ad tribunal Appi perventum est. Notam iudici fabulam petitor, quippe apud ipsum auctorem argumenti, peragit.* Moreover, the second mime of Herondas, the *Pornoboskos,* is good evidence that mimic courtroom scenes occurred as early as the third century B.C. This mime, with its two speaking roles, purports to be the speech of the plaintiff against a man who broke into his house and tried to steal one of his *pornai.* Although a "literary" mime, it might derive from a popular mime delivered by one performer. Surely, however, it could easily be expanded, and would then be very suitable for peformance by a mimic ensemble, which would have to be fairly numerous.

Two other literary passages, depending more or less indirectly upon the mimic stage, allow a similar conclusion concerning the mimes of the Augustan age. Here there is evidence that adulterous liaisons in these mimes usually required the services of an intermediary to set them up, so that once again we must have more than three roles and more than one scene. We have already inferred from the surviving fragments of his text — miserably sparse as these fragments may be — that Laberius used intermediaries to set up similar liaisons in his plays. Our first passage is Horace, *Sat.* 2.7.60ff., already considered as the earliest surviving evidence for the stock motif of the adulterer forced to hide suddenly in a large jar, chest, or tub at the unexpected arrival of the husband. We learn that the adulterer is directed to this hiding place by the lady's maid, who is said to be involved in the whole affair (60): *quo te demisit peccati conscia erilis*. Similarly, the Ovidian adulterer confronting the same predicament[40] avails himself of the help of a maid who is even more obviously a guilty accomplice of the erring wife (*A.A.* 3.607): *callida prosiliat dicatque ancilla "perimus."* *Callida* reminds us of the *callida nupta* who, Ovid tells us, was a fixture in the adultery mime. The preceding line (*A.A.* 3.606), addressed to the adulterous wife, is an exhortation for her to *play her part* well: *inque tuo vultu signa timentis habe*. The emphasis on facial expressions (*vultu*) no less than the prominence here of such words as *fallere*[41] point also to mimic inspiration.

In conclusion, we may say that there is abundant evidence that the common mimic theme of adultery was treated in productions which were very often quite elaborate, demanding more than the bare minimum of three roles and one scene which Reynolds claims as the norm for this variety of mime. This evidence extends from as early as the third century B.C. (Watzinger's lamp) to the sixth century after Christ (Choricius), and is discoverable both directly from the surviving mimic texts and inscriptions, and indirectly from literary passages which seem heavily indebted to the mime.

Wichita State University
Wichita, Kansas

---

[40] McKeown (above, n. 4) 76, thinks that this passage is ultimately dependent on the adultery mime.

[41] Note 3.616 *fallas*; 618 *verba dabis*; 627 *fallitque*; 629 *fallet*.

THE RHETORICAL VALUE OF THE SIMILES IN LUCRETIUS

ANNE LEEN

De Rerum Natura is a poem of persuasion. It has at its center three reasons for being: to elucidate the physical, moral and ethical principles of the Epicurean system, to impress the reader with the rightness and truth of the argument, and to convince him to accept the philosophy of Epicurus as the *vera ratio* and only means to happiness. Yet, far from being a grim philosophical tract, *DRN* is at times purely poetical, as the fact that it is read primarily for its famous "purple patches" bears ample testimony. It is, indeed, Lucretius' intention, proudly and lyrically proclaimed (1.921-50), to teach and to delight his reader through the charming medium of verse. Lucretius' three-fold task, therefore, is identical to that of the orator: *docere, delectare, movere*. In relationship to these goals, the poem can be considered a rhetorical work.

This paper will focus on the rhetoric inherent in Lucretius' poetic mode of presentation. Specifically, I shall examine the rhetorical value of the extended poetic similes which adorn the poem from its opening to its closing verses, after a preliminary discussion of the various types of illustrations in the poem, their background and the purposes they serve.

The poetry of *DRN* is not separate from the philosophy, nor can the illustrations which embellish the poem be distinguished from its philosophical mode of enquiry and exposition. It is, however, important to separate the poetic from the philosophic strands woven into the texture of each comparative illustration in order to appreciate their function in the poem.

The visual and descriptive elements derive in part from traditional Epicurean methods of clarification and proof. In his arguments Lucretius strives to render the unseen visible and the hypothetical concrete by means of empirical analogies drawn from close personal observation. It was upon this form of evidence, gathered and evaluated sensorily, that the Epicurean theory of knowledge rested.[1]

The comparisons in *DRN* frequently differ, however, from the brief analogies we find in Epicurus, in the amount of descriptive detail which Lucretius includes. The embellished simile could, in fact, find

---

[1] See, e.g., *Vita Epicuri*, D.L. 10.31; *DRN* 4.379-468.

no parallel in the περὶ φύσεως, given Epicurus' views on poetry.[2] In this respect, then, Lucretius is truer to the traditions of epic poetry than to the practice of his master. He opts to amplify illustrations and comparisons beyond the scope of the simple, straightforward analogy and to offer multiple examples of his meaning. His similes are not strictly ornamental, and thus quite unlike Homer's.

The device of comparison in *DRN* therefore clearly has a complex pedigree. In the form of analogy it derives from Epicurean methodology, and as simile from the epic genre. Both analogy and simile in turn have a persuasive purpose and as such are based in rhetoric.[3] It is rhetorical theory which reconciles Lucretius' varied and creative uses of analogy and simile.

The comparisons and illustrations in *DRN* reveal an ability of the author to see sameness in very different things, an ability characteristic of the poet, philosopher and orator, but Lucretius' method in the selection and composition of illustrations is particularly rhetorical. A poet composes similes for their emotional effect, while a philosopher selects analogies of didactic import. Lucretius does both in an effort to combine pleasure and instruction in a convincing appeal.[4]

I. Analogy

The comparative illustration at its most basic level is the brief, unadorned analogy.[5] Many single analogies, such as the likening of the soul to smoke (3.456, 583), are both poetic and functional. Throughout the third book, the soul, which is composed of tiny, round, and mobile atoms (179-88), is consistently compared to similarly insubstantial essences like the bouquet of wine (221), perfume (222), frankincense (327), and clouds (428). This last analogy is strengthened by the company of two others, water, and again, smoke. The cumulative effect of these images is as much persuasive as descriptive of the principal argument that the soul is corporeal and therefore mortal.

---

[2] See e.g., D.L. 10.121b.

[3] M. McCall, *Ancient Rhetorical Theories of Simile and Comparison* (Cambridge, Mass. 1969) 70; B.P. Wallach, *Lucretius and the Diatribe Against the Fear of Death. DRN III. 830-1094* (Leiden 1976) 20; Aristotle, *Ars Rhet.* 1.1355a, 17 and 1359b. 30-3.

[4] Lucretius' originality and the extent to which he borrowed from his sources are not the issues here.

[5] Even in the writings of other Epicureans, analogy serves a rhetorical purpose, a practice which contradicts their anti-rhetorical stance. Wallach (above, note 3) 20 observes that "one might assume that Lucretius uses analogy because he is an Epicurean, but it is interesting to note that, although the school allegedly disparaged rhetoric, its methodology of reasoning has much in common with rhetorical theory."

Often several analogies are collected into one argument, which clearly points their value as brief but apposite *confirmationes.* To explain the concepts of "properties" and "accidents" in Book One, Lucretius offers five quick examples of properties (453-4) and six of accidents (455-6). These introduce the contentious argument that time is also an accident, illustrated in the elaborate (and to Lucretius, unhistorical) *exemplum* of the Trojan War (462-82). The analogies act as preliminary proofs to the sustained descriptive argument. Likewise in Book Four, in a discussion of "idols," five analogies explain the concept (54-62) and function also as anticipatory proofs that idols do in fact exist (63-4). A more detailed proof follows with the example of the colors streaming from the awnings of a theater and flooding the faces of the audience and the stage below (75-86).

An argument may consist entirely of such analogies, as when Lucretius argues that the mind is susceptible to false inferences. Thirteen separate examples of optical illusions (4.387-461) amply reinforce the point. The sixth book is devoted to meteorological and terrestrial phenomena and abounds in earthly analogies whose familiarity is intended to breed contempt for supposed supernatural wonders. The *Averna loca,* fatal to birds passing overhead, have a naturally toxic atmosphere, Lucretius argues, and to prove this he relies heavily on a catalogue of analogies; various effluences which are poisonous to human beings (781-817); and relatively little expository proof (818-29). Visual proof is hard to refute; as Lucretius confidently asserts, *manifesta docet res* (6.139).

II. Lucretius, Vergil, and the Single Simile

It is the extended poetic simile, rather than the brief analogy, which constitutes the element of descriptive proof unique in this Epicurean treatise.[6] Lucretius here most radically departs from Epicurean literary theory and closely emulates his predecessors in epic poetry, among them Empedocles and Ennius. Since neither of these authors survives in more than fragmentary form, a comparison with Vergil is

---

[6] Of necessity the term "simile" will be loosely construed. Lucretius does not always preface his illustrations with the traditional comparative particles, such as *ac veluti.* Conversely, not every simile, formal or otherwise, serves a didactic purpose. Some are purely poetic images, such as Lucretius' comparison of his sweet discourse to the brief song of the swan (4.180-2, 909-11). Lucretius is frequently most metaphoric in prologues to books or new discussions, such as 1.936-50, 1114-17; 2.55-61; 6.1-41. See W.S. Maguinness, "The Language of Lucretius," in *Lucretius,* ed. D.R. Dudley (London 1967) 86; G. Townend, "Imagery in Lucretius," also in *Lucretius* (above) 103.

desirable to determine the differences which set Lucretius apart from other epic poets.

The point of departure for this discussion is the extensive work of David West on the similes in both Vergil and Lucretius. In his book, West argued for a close connection in *DRN* between the similes and the main narrative, in terms both of language and of thought.[7] West followed his study with a series of articles on Vergil in which he successfully proved that, contrary to traditional thinking, the similes in the *Aeneid* are not similes *à queue longue,* a single point of comparion embellished with poetic but extraneous matter, but rather share multiple correspondences of detail with the main narrative.[8] West also investigated the simile in Vergil's predecessors and concluded that, while Homer and Apollonius exhibit the same kind of correspondences on a lesser scale, Lucretius is the only "classical author in whom the correspondences between simile and context are as complex, elaborate, and multifarious" as in Vergil. He found differences as well. Vergil is essentially creating a generalized image whose value lies in its aesthetic and emotional effects. Lucretius, however, is more restricted in his choice of illustration and in the adaptation to the narrative of embellishing details, since the logic of the argument must determine their suitability. In short, Vergil "seems to care more for the words and Lucretius ... for the matter."[9]

There is some truth to this. Like Vergil, Lucretius does not compose a lengthy simile in the Homeric manner. Again, like his successor, he exhibits a careful regard for those details which link comparison to narrative. Yet the fundamental difference in their poetry derives from their respective intentions. Since the *Aeneid* is an epic poem, we do not find detailed didacticism in any form. Even the *Georgics* features similes which, as we shall see later, are in the epic manner. In *DRN,* on the other hand, Lucretius is explaining a philosophical system and his similes are functional. The normal function of these similes is to explain the invisible by an appeal to the visible.

This is not to say that Lucretius seems not to care for the words. Lucretius cares as much for his language as Vergil, but for different reasons. To the Epicureans language is atomic, and words are highly charged units of meaning. The letters of the alphabet are, as

---

[7] D. West, *The Imagery and Poetry of Lucretius* (Edinburgh 1969).

[8] West, "Multiple-correspondence Similes in the *Aeneid,*" *JRS* 59 (1969) 40-9; "The Poetry of Lucretius" *PCA* 66 (1969) 34; "Virgilian Multiple-correspondence Similes and their Antecedents," *Philologus* 114 (1970) 262-75.

[9] West, "Virgilian Multiple-correspondence Similes" (above, note 8) 272, 274-5.

Friedländer says, "an image of the atoms producing the world,"[10] a doctrine cast by Lucretius in a simile which both literally and figuratively illustrates the principle (2.1013-22). Lucretius therefore consistently selects similes with their didactic value in mind and embellishes these with verbal and substantive details chosen to clarify distinct aspects of an argument, or piles simile upon simile to achieve the same result. In other words, the dogma does not dictate the wording of the simile. The words matter. The descriptive details are not superfluous, but instructive and persuasive. Herein lies their rhetorical value.

Lucretius

A simile from the first book of *DRN* exhibits many verbal correspondences of the Vergilian type, devised for a thoroughly Lucretian purpose. In 1.400-9 Lucretius describes the intellectual process of the search for knowledge and selects as his point of comparison a picture of dogs hunting wild animals in the forest. The verbal correspondences between this passage and the surrounding narrative are clear since it moves easily from metaphor into simile and back to metaphor. The words *vestigia* (402) and *sagaci* and *caecasque latebras insinuare* (408-9) enclose the simile in a circular structure and in turn find parallels within the simile itself: *vestigia* (406), *naribus* and *intectas fronde quietes* (405). West notes other correspondences: *per quae cetera* and *alid ex alio, cognoscere* and *videre, tute* and *tute.*[11]

The imagery and language of this passage function on yet another level of meaning. The hunt is not simply a metaphor for the search for knowledge in general but is a poet's description of the Epicurean scientific method. The particular chase envisioned involves a search for what is unseen, which is a metaphoric description of the Epicurean's search to understand a system whose foundations rest on invisible physical components. The language of the simile reinforces this application. The phrases *animo ... sagaci* (402) and *per te tute ipse videre ... poteris* (407-8) remind us that this is a rational philosophy whose tenets can be logically and empirically proven. The catchy *alid ex alio* (407) is repeated from the discussion of the eternal supply of matter (1.263) and will recur in both literal (3.970) and metaphorical (1.1115; 5.1035, 1456) contexts (and sounds much like the axiomatic *nil de nilo* which the reader has already heard more than once [1.155-6], 205) in

---

[10] P. Friedländer, "The Pattern of Sound and Atomistic Theory in Lucretius," *AJP* 62 (1914) 17.

[11] West (above, note 7) 75.

more than one form (1.150) and will hear again (2.287). The phrases *talibus in rebus* and *caecas ... latebras* (408) and to a lesser extent, *haec vestigia parva* (402), recall the technical terms *res* (*in rebus* above, 399) and *corpora caeca*. Lucretius has reinforced some fundamental concepts with a clever and careful choice of words.

A simile with the same multiplicity of purposes is the extended comparison (6.655-69) of a human being to the globe of the earth, the prelude to a discussion of volcanic activity. The illustration elaborates the philosophical commonplace that man is a microcosm of the universe, and as such is subject to the same atomic movements and forces which affect the earth and heavens.[12] Meteorological and terrestrial phenomena are consistently explicated here and elsewhere in terms which every reader can understand. As I noted earlier, Book Six abounds in earthly analogies, which have the added effect of reducing these wonders to the commonplace. As Lucretius is quick to remind the reader, in Giussani's words, "il meraviglioso è sempre relativo."[13]

Numerous verbal correspondences between simile and narrative (through 6.702) reinforce the points of similarity between a volcanic eruption and a disease.[14] Since fire is the most visible accompaniment to a volcanic eruption, Lucretius compares men in the grip of fever (655-6) and suffering an attack of what he calls the *sacer ignis* (660-1) (either erysipelas or shingles) as well as other illnesses whose symptoms imitate the physical aspects of an eruption (657-9). He repeatedly stresses the visual and tactile similarity between the fevered warmth of disease and the flames of Aetna: *ignis abundare Aetnaeus* (669), *flamescere* (669), *ardescunt* (670), *incendi* (673), *flamma* (681, 699), *percaluit calefecitque* (686), *calidum flammis ... ignem* (688), *ardorem* (690), *aestum* (695).

Lucretius attributes volcanic eruptions to a violent turbulence of air beneath the earth's surface which soon bursts through the crust. The gradual increase in movement and pressure, as well as the sudden rush of released air, is emphasized in both the object and the subject of the comparison. First the progress of disease is described: *coörtam* (656), *obturgescit enim subito pes* (658), *arripit* (658, 661) *invadit* (659), *exsistit* (660), *repit* (661), *procrescere* (664). In a similar fashion Lucretius describes the subterranean agitation which results in an eruption: *repente tellus concussa moveri* (667), *rapidus percurrere turbo* (669), *coortu*

---

[12] Lucretius has used this simile shortly before, in his discussion of the connection between wind and earthquakes (6.591-5). C. Giussani, ed. *De Rerum Natura* vol. 4 (Turin 1900) 243 rightly detected the relevance of this simile.

[13] Giussani (above, note 12) 243.

[14] West (above, note 7) 75 has pointed out some of these correspondences.

(671), *turbidus* (673, 693), *efflet* (681) *ventus et aer* (684, cf. 685), *excussit... flammis velocibus* (688), *tollit se ac... eicit* (688), *fert... longe longeque* (690), *fluctus aestumque* (695), *penetrare* (698), *efflare* (699), *extollere* (699), *subiectare* (700), *tollere* (700).

Disease penetrates and corrupts as thoroughly as volcanic disorder. Every part of the body is attacked: *in artus* (655), *per membra* (657), *pes* (658), *dentis* (659), *oculus* (659), *corpore* (660), *quamcumque ... partem* (661), *per artus* (661). Similarly the heat and motion of a volcanic eruption produce a reaction which is felt in every part of the area, from subterranean caverns to mountain peaks: *per ... mare ac terras* (668), *ardescunt caelestia templa* (670), *subcava montis natura* (682-3), *cavernis* (683), *speluncis* (684), *omnia circum saxa* (686-7), *montis ad eius radices* (694-5), *ex hoc usque mari speluncae montis ad altas perveniunt* (696-7), *in summo ... vertice ... crateres* (701).

Lucretius' primary and immediate objective is to describe the visual and sensory effects of a volcanic eruption with clarity and accuracy. His other purpose is to recall the fundamental Epicurean doctrine that both man and his world are animate beings subject to the same governing principles. Therefore, while Lucretius endows the simile with a genuine poetic interest, his larger purpose is to instruct the reader and to persuade him to see and accept a greater truth.

The didactic purpose of the formal simile is evident in Lucretius' explanation of mirror reflections, which are actually reverse images (4.292-301). Lucretius preserves the language of the main argument in the simile so that there are both near and exact correspondences between the two. The process of reversal is described twice in virtually identical form (292-6 and 300-1), while *adlidat* (297) recalls *offendit* (294) and *eliditur* (296) is echoed in *elisam* (299). A *persona* (297) is the concrete and tangible form of an *imago* (294), while the surface of the mirror, *planitiem ... speculi* (294), parallels the *pilaeve trabive* (297) in the simile. A plaster mask is entirely appropriate as an explanation of facial reflection in a mirror but its applicability goes beyond the level of the readily visible, since the mask illustrates not only the reversal of an image but also the three-dimensional nature of this image. Bailey reminds us that "Lucretius does not conceive the image coming off the mirror as flat, but with the same prominences as in life. The parallel of the mask is therefore close: e.g., in both cases the nose comes right through and projects again on the other side."[15] In other words, the *comparandum* and the *comparatum* share similarities, some of which are made explicit while others are left unexpressed, but all of which are

---

[15] C. Bailey, ed., C. Lucreti *De Rerum Natura* vol. 3 (Oxford 1947) 1216.

relevant both to the immediate discussion of the behavior of the images in mirrors and to the general concept of the *simulacra*.

Lucretius' similes not only relate clearly to the immediate contexts in which they appear, but they can also be relevant to other arguments. Comparisons are sometimes repeated from one book to another, and when this happens the intention is usually didactic. Later in the sixth book, for example, Lucretius makes an analogic connection between the formation of diseases and clouds (6.1090-1137). He does so by consistently speaking of the atomic particles of disease in terms associated with air or clouds. The reader can thereby envision diseases as billows of contaminated air which envelope and infect helpless persons. The comparison serves another purpose as well. Earlier in Book Six Lucretius had explained the formation of clouds in some detail (451-94). His subsequent association of disease with clouds recalls that explanation and, with true poetic economy, allows him to dispense with a second technical account of the formation of disease, since the reader has been made to see that the processes are identical.

The same principle operates in other similes. West cites Lucretius' comparison of liquids to poppy seeds (2.451-5) as a proof which does not allow for much adjustment of detail, the sole demonstrable point of comparison being their fluidity of movement. The shape of the constituent liquid atoms, however, must be inferred.[16] Yet certain far reaching considerations govern the selection of this illustration. For the argument at hand, firstly, a scoop of poppy seeds poured from the hand visibly resembles the flow of water. Secondly, since the roundness of the individual seeds is easily discerned by the reader, who has just made the connection between seeds and water, he will accept the argument that the invisible components of liquids are smooth and round as well. The comparison ends with a pertinent point about this handful of seeds (455).

This particular detail is significant in a subsequent discussion of a far subtler nature. Lucretius has fixed the association between poppy seeds and liquid atoms on two points: shape and movement but, more precisely, velocity of movement. In the third book, in describing the atomic composition of the mind, he cites the quickness of thought and argues that such speed belongs only to those substances composed of smooth, round, small particles (3.177-205). To prove the point he offers several examples, among these water and poppy seeds (3.186-90, 193-7). Presented with this argument, the reader recalls Lucretius' discussion from the previous book. He remembers the association made

---

[16] West, "Virgilian Multiple-correspondence Similes and their Antecedents," (above, note 8) 275.

there between the poppy seeds and the atoms of liquids, which are invisible to his eye as units, and he is all the more convinced that these sensory data accurately illustrate the shape and movement of the atoms of the soul, which is completely invisible to him. Lucretius depends on the weight of a previous proof, in the form of a simile, to illustrate and bolster a subsequent argument of some difficulty.

Vergil

Single similes are relatively rare in Vergil. Among the few examples which the *Georgics* affords is a comparison of a horse racing over the plains to the North wind sweeping over crops and seas (3.193-201). The principle comparison is between the speed of the horse and the wind. The horse has challenged the winds to a race (*cursibus auras ... vocet*). Vergil describes each as flying (*volans, volat*) and fleeing (*ceu liber harenis, fuga*) over broad expanses (*aperta aequora, aequora*) which may be loosely construed as either the plains of the earth or the open seas. The horse is said specifically to race over the sand (*harena*), while the wind has swept over crops, trees, waves, and surf (*segetes, campique natantes, silvae, longi fluctus, arva*). Each barely grazes the landscape below in its rush through the air (*vix summa vestigia ponat harena, segetes altae, summae ... silvae, aequora verrens*).

In many particulars of thought and diction the simile corresponds very closely to the narrative. These details are primarily descriptive, evoking in their totality an image which is visual and sensual rather than strictly relevant. The simile is expressive rather than didactic: Vergil is more interested in conveying an impression of strength and speed than in explaining the mechanics of motion.

In *Georgics* 4.170-8 Vergil compares the industry and efficiency of the bees to the work habits of the Cyclopes. The Cyclopes' division of labor parallels that of the bees, which Vergil has just described (158-68). Otherwise, Cyclopes and bees have very little in common, as Vergil acknowledges (176). The point of this simile is therefore not a close parallel which would bind it to the narrative, but an unexpected incongruity, a highly emotional contrast, which elicits a smile from the reader as he compares giant Cyclopes to tiny bees. The relevance of the simile lies less in the explanation it offers of the bees' activity than in the variety of reactions which it evokes.[17]

The Cyclopes appear again in the *Aeneid*, this time as the object rather than the subject of the comparison. Venus asks Vulcan to

---

[17] Cf. *Aen.* 1.430-6.

fashion a suit of armor for Aeneas; in compliance, he and his helpers set to work before dawn, like a housewife and her maids (8.407-15). Gransden has noted the vital connection between narrative and simile. Hornsby has also investigated the manner in which Vergil works out the themes.[18] Yet Vergil has explicitly emphasized just a few points of comparison: Vulcan and the woman are alike only in their early rising, the significance to each of their work, and the helpers who attend them; in all else the poet offers the reader surprising contrast.

Vergil is no less concerned with the truth of the details of his comparisons than Lucretius, but these details have a different significance and are neither as exact nor as explicit as those which embellish the similes of *DRN*. Lucretius is concerned to illustrate a technical argument point by point; detailed instruction which is easy and pleasant for the reader to grasp is the *raison d'être* of his similes. In Vergil's poetry, since the connection between the subject and the object of comparison is more diffuse, the effect of similes is quite different. Furthermore, his similes have a literary value different from those in Lucretius. The simile in *Aeneid* 8.408-15 has as its source four similes, two each in Homer and Apollonius.[19] Here, as in the comparison between Cyclopes and bees in the *Georgics*, Vergil is striving for a humorous effect which springs from the incongruity of comparing brawny workers with demure handmaidens. The juxtaposition is most Alexandrian, and touched by a light frivolity inconceivable in Lucretius.

Pöschl has written of the similes in the *Aeneid* that "the emotional content dominates the perceptible content, and the symbolic content dominates the concrete."[20] The same is true of those in the *Georgics*, where we might reasonably expect a difference, but do not find one. In composing his didactic treatise Vergil sought to take advantage of the ornamental value of the simile rather than to exploit its didactic potential. He has none of the passionate zeal for the *natura rerum* which grips his great predecessor and consequently he can abandon his topic for a few lines of pure poetry in a manner which is quite different from that of Lucretius.

To a certain extent, in fact, Vergil is more like Lucretius in the composition of his epic similes. The *Georgics* offers intervals of poetry which relieve the narrative or intensify the emotional color applied to a specific scene. The similes of the Aeneid do this, and more.

---

[18] K.W. Gransden, *Vergil. Aeneid VIII* (Cambridge 1976) 138; R. Hornsby, *Patterns of Action in the 'Aeneid.' An Interpretation of Vergil's Epic Similes* (Iowa City 1970) 14-15.

[19] *Il.* 12.433-5; *Od.* 5.488-90; Apoll. 3.291-5, 4.1062-7.

[20] V. Pöschl, *The Art of Vergil. Image and Symbol in the Aeneid*, trans. G. Seligson (Ann Arbor 1970) 92.

Lucretius' illustrations frequently have a relevance both for the immediate argument and for general philosophic principles which the poet wishes to keep before the eyes of his reader. Likewise Vergil's similes take part in the rhythm of the entire epic. Hornsby has shown that "the similes individually illuminate the various aspects and parts of the *Aeneid,* and through their repetition they define the patterns of action in the poem."[21] Pöschl has demonstrated the symbolic connections which Vergil has carefully crafted between similes sharing the same subject. For example, the idea of regulation is expressed repeatedly in the first book.[22] In one of these scenes, Neptune calms the seas for the safe passage of Aeneas' fleet. Vergil compares him to a respected magistrate who quells a riot in the forum (1.142-56).

The simile shares many verbal and substantive correspondences with the main narrative. The *vir pietate gravis ac meritis* displays the same authority and capacity to impose order which Neptune possesses. He calms a disturbance which arises as suddenly (*coörta*) and rages as violently (*saevit*) as a sea-storm. His weapon is words (*dictis*), while the sea-god wields the trident, and with words the speaker soothes the crowd (*regit ... animos et pectora mulcet*) just as Neptune settles the seas (*aequora placat, temperat aequor*). By implication, the *faces et saxa* are dispersed from the area as effectively as the *collectas nubes* from the sky, the *furor* of the crowd, just as the noise of the wild sea (*fragor*), dies away, and quiet, like the sun, is restored.

Like its Vergilian counterpart, the Lucretian simile is part of the fabric of the entire work. The difference is that where Vergil is deeply poetic and literary, Lucretius is relentlessly didactic. He draws correspondences of details which are unambiguous, sharp, cogent, and more precise than Vergil's because they are differently conceived.

III. Multiple Similes in Lucretius

The difference between Lucretius and Vergil is nowhere more readily apparent than in the use each makes of multiple similes, that is, series of two or more. Lucretius frequently offers several illustrations or comparisons to explain an argument. On the other hand, Vergil pairs similes, but not lengthy ones and not often. In the *Georgics* there are four pairs of similes; two of these are of medium length and two are short, involving only one or two words.[23]

---

[21] Hornsby (above, note 18) 4.

[22] Pöschl (above, note 20) 22-3.

[23] Of medium length, *G.* 2.105-8, 4.312-14; of one or two words, *G.* 4.41, 80-81. These statistics and those for the *Aeneid* were compiled by E. G. Wilkins, "A

The *Aeneid* offers eighteen pairs of similes of at least medium length and ten pairs of short similes, some of these also phrased in very few words. Most of the pairs run to four or five lines (much shorter than Lucretius' usage). Such is the dual comparison describing the attack on Troy, which Aeneas witnesses from the roof of his father's home (2.304-7).

Vergil very rarely places three similes together, and never more than three. In the *Georgics* there is only one group of three similes, which describe the strange buzzing of bees when they are sick (4.261-3). When similes appear as a triad in the *Aeneid* they are short and designed to quicken the pace of the narrative (5.316-19).[24] At the end of the epic Aeneas is described with three brief but evocative images as he hurls his spear at his enemy for the last time (12.919-26).

De Rerum Natura is very different. Wilkinson writes that Lucretius seems to have "enjoyed detailing things for their own sake"[25] and while Lucretius is certainly a zealot, he is a good teacher and persuader as well. We earlier saw that it is not unusual for him to offer a series of two, three, or even more analogic illustrations if the difficulty of a subject, or his own enthusiasm, so requires. The same interest is apparent in his use of multiple similes.

The discussion of the *clinamen* in Book Two is a highly sophisticated piece of argumentation heavily embellished with rhetorical flourishes which support and further the central thesis, that free will in man proves the existence of the swerve in atoms. Art complements argument very persuasively, particularly in the series of illustrations which form the core of Lucretius' case for the *clinamen*. The similes are drawn from the realm of commonly seen or experienced activities and so have an appeal and a validity for Lucretius' readers, whom the poet is anxious, as always, to accommodate. Two distinct sets of comparisons are also essential: to prove free will, Lucretius must not only show 1) how it assents, but also 2) how it dissents. Both are implicated in the general principle. The first simile (263-71) constitutes the first argument and comes from the race-course at the moment when the barriers are first removed from the horses' necks, and proves that *voluntas* is a crucial agent in producing motion.

The second argument consists of two similes and makes two points by describing the same phenomenon twice. The first illustration proves the power of *voluntas* to resist external force (272-6). The second

---

Classification of the Similes in Vergil's *Aeneid* and *Georgics*," *CW* 14 (1921) 170-4.

[24] L. A. Grothaus, "A Study of the Similes in the *Aeneid*" (M.A. thesis, University of Cincinnati, 1949) 7.

[25] L.P. Wilkinson, *The Georgics of Vergil* (Cambridge 1949) 7.

illustration is the logical extension of the first, but shows that, although the will does not assert itself forcefully at the precise moment when the *vis externa* strikes, still it does gradually exert its strength not only to resist, but to overcome (277-83).

The three illustrations stand in close relation to one another. The last two are formally separate, as indicated by the respective introductions *nec similest et cum* (272) and *iamne vides igitur* (277), yet they are complementary and in fact, nearly repetitious. Two similar illustrations are paired to emphasize the crucial fact that an external blow has a more immediate effect on the body (272-6) than the opposing force of the *voluntas* (277-83). Each simile stresses the role of the *voluntas*, with the second clarifying the technical aspects of its mechanics. These two illustrations also complement the first. In all three Lucretius argues 1) that the mind will play a role in producing motion, although 2) this is not instantly apparent, since the will has a somewhat slower reaction time than other force-producing agents. If the reader, therefore, did not understand the first simile, perhaps never having been to the circus or never having observed this particular behavior in racehorses, he could nonetheless grasp the point of the second pair and the essential thesis that the will has its own power.[26] Finally, Lucretius does not ask his reader to accept an abstract argument as proof of a theory which Cicero (*De Fin* 1.6.19) dismissed as *res tota ficta pueriliter*. Nor does he attempt to obfuscate the difficulty with poetic language and imagery. Instead, he addresses the issue squarely and explains the theory as clearly as possible to his reader with carefully chosen and coherent illustrations.

Lucretius follows the same procedure elsewhere. Later in the second book the question of atomic motion arises. The Epicureans argued that the *corpora caeca* were constantly moving, but they faced a difficulty in proving this since these component parts en masse do not seem to move at all. Lucretius anticipates this objection by explaining that the atomic motion in question takes place on a level which eyesight cannot fathom. In support of his thesis the poet offers two illustrations, first of a flock of sheep, and secondly of a military squadron, which each appear to stand still when viewed from a distance, but are actually never at rest (317-22, 323-32).

Lucretius draws upon two characteristically Roman sources of metaphor, and two of the most familiar, agriculture and war. Each simile describes a different aspect of atomic motion-attraction, then

---

[26] Epicurus and Lucretius both provide several different illustrations in the hope that the reader will be convinced by one, and they do not particularly care which one. The section on the causes of fire, 5.1091-4, is a case in point. See also Lucretius' statement of method at 6.703-11.

repulsion — so that the second is clearly designed to complement the first. Similarities between the two illustrations emphasize their joint didactic function. Both the flocks and the legion are seen from a distance, each seems to be standing still, and of each Lucretius comments on the blur of flashing color, which, rather than any movement, is, to the distant viewer, the most noticeable feature. Even the diction and syntax of the verses in which Lucretius sums up these observations is similar (cf. 321-2 and 331-2).

At close range neither the flock nor the legion is ever, in fact, at rest. The sheep creep slowly, but steadily, to represent the affinity of atoms in motion: *reptunt, quo quamque ... invitant herbae,* while the soldiers dart about in a frenzy of incessant activity, reflecting the speed and movement of rebounding atoms: *complent, cientes, circumvolitant, tramittunt, quatientes.*

The similes stand here as proofs of the argument. As always, Lucretius offers evidence that is easily grasped by his readers, all of whom would have observed one of these activities. The illustrations are used both as dogmatic scientific explanations and as readily visible empirical data. Lucretius consistently corroborates arguments in this fashion (cf. 3.186-195, 196-200).

Often illustration follows closely upon illustration not to clarify different aspects of an argument but simply to add the weight of amply documented evidence. A good example comes in a discussion of the variety of atomic shapes in 2.333-477. Lucretius argues from the manifestly different shapes and appearances of different species of animal. Four generic analogies — men, fish, beasts, birds — testify to the truth of the thesis, while four separate illustrations confirm it in more detail: first, the famous description of a mother cow who searches in vain for her lost calf (349-66); second, a quick mention of other young animals who can recognize their parents (367-70); third, the variety of grains in existence (371-3); and fourth, the diverse multitude of seashells which dapple a coastline (374-6). The examples are simple ones from the natural world, particularly the provinces of the shepherd, the farmer, and the sailor (or anyone who had ever visited the seashore).

Such a rich variety of illustrations shows the acuteness of Lucretius' powers of observation, as well as his sensitivity to the apposite example. The sheer number of the analogies and similes springs from a true passion for the subject. It is this which drives Lucretius to add proof to proof, rather than any conventions of ancient scientific method. One or two illustrations could not provide sufficient clarification or enough persuasive appeal.

The most striking example of the effectiveness of multiple similes is the entire mid-section of Book Three (417-829). The mortality of soul is a crucial doctrine in the Epicurean system. To no other topic does Lucretius devote almost an entire book and more than twenty-five proofs, almost every one of which is bolstered by one or more illustrations or is itself an illustration. These proofs relate closely to the immediate context, but also add weight to the sustained plea of which they are a small part. He argues, for instance, that, since the soul is divided when limbs are torn from the body, it cannot be immortal (634-69). Two illustrations argue the point, first a gory picture of arms and legs severed in battle (642-56) and second, a description of the writhing sections of a snake split by a hatchet (657-63).

In another set of arguments (463-525) Lucretius demonstrates that the soul shares experiences with the body, including death. The first argument (463-86) consists of a description of a sick man and the attendant mental disturbances (463-9) and then the effects of wine on the imbiber (476-83). The second argument (487-509) is based on the manifest effects of an epileptic seizure on the mind's processes (487-505). Each picture is vivid, graphically detailed, and relentlessly to the point. The passionate note of urgency never subsides. Later in this section, to prove that the soul is closely connected with the body, Lucretius offers three homely examples of the feelings inherent even in teeth: toothache, the ache of cold water, the pain produced upon biting unexpectedly onto a sharp object (691-4). In short, in this most important matter Lucretius amasses a quantity of arguments and proofs which are designed individually to erode the doubter's resistance and collectively to win him over as a convert. The accumulation of illustrations serves the rhetorical ends of instruction and persuasion.

IV. Structure of the Lucretian Simile

We cannot leave a discussion of the rhetorical values of the similes in Lucretius without considering a regular structural principle which emphasizes their essentially functional nature. When, as often, the purpose of the illustrations is to clarify or prove a technical argument, Lucretius frequently appends a resumé to an illustration, in lieu of or in addition to a formal application or conclusion, which restates the principal argument and thereby relates the simile more clearly to its context. Almost as frequently he provides a pointed introduction to the simile, so that there can be no mistaking its meaning. There is nothing like this in Vergil and nothing which demonstrates as clearly the symbiotic relationship of illustration and argument in the poem.

For example, consider the famous description of motes of dust dancing in a shaft of sunlight, which illustrates the movement of the invisible atoms (2.112-28). Lucretius frames the picture with an introduction (109-11) follows with two statements of method (112-15), and concludes with a reiteration of the main argument (121-28). Typically the language of the illustration reinforces its connection to the argument. The particles of dust are described in the technical terms which Lucretius uses to explain atomic motion: many and tiny (*multa minuta*), they move incessantly through a void (*inane*), colliding, uniting, and dissolving (*conciliis et discidiis exercita crebris*). In a lengthy application of the simile to the point under discussion which follows (129-41), Lucretius argues that not only do the motes of dust illustrate the behavior of the *primordia caeca,* but they are actually the first visible manifestation of the chain of movement which begins with the smallest of these atoms (138-41).

An equally famous simile in the fourth book, in which the *simulacra* are compared to the multicolored reflections of theater-awnings, is set within a similarly tight frame of reference (4.72-86). Verses 72-4 provide the introduction and 54-9 constitute the conclusion.

Poetic adornment complements didacticism in Lucretius' proof of the infinite number of atomic shapes in 2.522-68. At one point he argues from the improbability of the atomic cohesion of a limited number of the right atoms floating about in a limitless universe. He bolsters the argument with an illustration (552-9), painstakingly relates the simile to the context (560-6), and concludes with a pointed statement which restates the principal doctrine (567-8). The didactic function of this simile, if for some reason not absolutely clear to the reader at the outset, becomes quite obvious in the concluding verses. Lucretius entices his reader with a vivid picture, intensified by alliterative sounds and an almost frenzied rhythm, but he does not intend that his reader enjoy the poetry so much that he misses the point. Lucretius is careful, therefore, to lead the train of thought away from the picturesque and metaphorical and back to the concrete.

Almost any simile, arbitrarily chosen, would exhibit the same careful structure. For examples we need only look back at those previously discussed. The comparison of disease to volcanic activity in Book Six is prefaced by a statement of method which, with some modifications, is a good description of Lucretius' approach in general (647-54). The illustration, which is not a formal simile, follows, and in turn is summarized in a formal conclusion which applies it to the argument at hand (665-9). The illustrations proving the existence of the *clinamen* are framed with verses stating and restating the central point (2.261-2 and 284-6). The discussion of mirror reflections (4.292-301), which includes the mask simile, ends with approximately the same statement as it opens (cf. 292-3 and 301-2). Likewise the examples which prove that atoms vary in shape (2.342-76) are framed by nearly identical statement of the principle (336-41, 377-80). These citations should suffice to show the pervasiveness of this method, which is both a didactic device and an organizational principle, and as such is thoroughly rhetorical. There is nothing like this in Vergil. Not even in a didactic poem does Vergil display anything quite like this professorial concern.[27]

Furman University
Greenville, South Carolina

---

[27] For the text of Lucretius, I have used Bailey's Oxford edition of 1947 (above, note 15). An earlier version of this paper was read at the annual meeting of the Classical Association of the Middle West and South in Atlanta, Georgia on April 15, 1982. I would like to thank my colleague, Dr. Benny R. Reece, for his advice and critical comments.

COUNTERFEIT MAN

DANIEL B. LEVINE

Men and metals have been associated in western literature since Hesiod's description of the races of gold, silver, bronze and iron (*Works and Days* 109-201). Homer often associated persons with metals: his Achaeans are bronze-clad, he wishes for a brazen heart to sing well, and goddesses are silver-footed.[1] The English word *metal* is derived through the Latin *metallum* from the Greek μέταλλον 'mine, or its product'. The variant spelling *mettle* means a man's character, which can be shown or tested, as can metal.

Hebrew literature shows parallel imagery. Nebuchadnezzar's dream (Dan. 2.25 ff.) of the idol of gold, silver, bronze, iron and clay, and its interpretation as degenerating stages of world-kingdoms is similar to the generations of man in the *Works and Days*.[2] Job asserts of God: "But he knows the way that I take; when he has tried me, I shall come forth as gold." (Job 23.10). Keeping in mind Sandmel's caution about the dangers of 'parallelomania',[3] this paper is an attempt to trace the Greek idea of men as base and adulterated metals to a similar Hebrew notion.

J.P. Brown has recently pointed out the striking similarities between the Proverbs of Solomon and the Archaic Greek Theognidea.[4] Both are repositories of wisdom with an aristocratic bias and treat such themes as the power of the wealthy, the 'good' and its superiority, justice and wealth, a man's companions, women and wine, enlightened self-interest, the fragility of power, and the oneness of wealth and wisdom. Both collections present their aphorisms in couplets. Brown notes that ancient Greek and Hebrew literature treat the testing of a

---

[1] Stentor (*Iliad* 5.785) is χαλκεοφώνος ; the poet says that without the Muses' help, even if he had a χάλκεον ἦτορ (2.490), he could not sing the catalogue of the ships; Thetis is silver-footed throughout the epic (1.538, 556, 9.410, 16.222, etc.); Achaians are χαλκοχιτώνων (1.371, 2.47, 2.187, etc.).

[2] Scholarship on Hesiod's debt to eastern sources is extensive. Cf. M. West, *Hesiod Theogony* (Oxford 1966) 106-107: "Hesiod and the East", a bibliography, and 18-31: "The Myths" and their eastern parallels. Also cf. West's *Hesiod, Works and Days* (Oxford 1978) for the eastern sources of the metal ages in Hesiod. Cf. J. Fontenrose, "Work, Justice and Hesiod's Five Ages" *CPh* 69 (1974) 1-16; G. Hasel, "The Four World Empires of Daniel 2 against its Near Eastern Environment" *JSOT* 12 (1979) 17-30. It is surprising that Hesiod, with his extensive debt to Semitic sources, does not use the counterfeit or touchstone images with which we are here concerned.

[3] S. Sandmel , "Parallelomania" *JBL* 81 (1962) 1-13.

[4] J. Brown, "Proverb-Book, Gold-Economy, Alphabet" *JBL* 100 (1981) 169-191.

man's character in terms of the testing of gold, and concludes that a class of 'goldsmith-bankers' brought not only their alphabet, but also eastern gold technology and its terminology from the Semitic to the Hellenic world.

His evidence is convincing: the Greek χρυσός comes from a Hebrew word; βάσανος has probable eastern roots; the Greek system of weighing gold adheres to that practiced by the Babylonians; the Hellenic unit of weight between the talent and the drachma, the μνᾶ, is a Semitic word attested in Akkadian, Hebrew and Biblical Aramaic; the term for financial pledge or downpayment, ἀρραβών, is a Hebrew loan-word probably imported by the goldsmith-bankers. Brown treats the archaeological evidence for the working of gold and its westward movement, and also makes good use of the literary touchstone parallels, comparing the images and language of Plato's *Republic* 413e and Theognis 447-52, 417 f.=1105 f. with Proverbs 17.3, Zechariah 13.9 and Job 23.10.[5]

The idea of testing a man's character in order to find out his true nature is congenial to Greek literature. In early Greek poetry there is a dichotomy between γλῶσσα and νόος, 'tongue' and 'mind', that is, between what a man says and what he really believes.[6] Perhaps the best-known Homeric example is in *Iliad* 9.312-313, where Achilles declares to the embassy:

ἐχθρὸς γάρ μοι κεῖνος ὁμῶς Ἀίδαο πύλῃσιν
ὅς χ' ἕτερον μὲν κεύθῃ ἐνὶ φρεσίν, ἄλλο δὲ εἴπῃ.

In Greek poetry the testing of a man's character to show his true worth is a popular theme. It first appears in Theognis, and continues to be used by Pindar, Bacchylides, Aeschylus, Sophocles, Euripides and Plato.[7] Words which re-occur in Greek contexts with this metaphorical use of βάσανος 'touchstone' are those which one would expect from its use as a metallurgical and human-testing term: εὑρεῖν ('find out'),

---

[5] Brown (above, n.4) 176, 181-182, 186.

[6] The Theognidea is filled with cautions against the men who speak well but are not to be trusted. At the same time, the poet urges Kyrnos to deceive others by speaking well but keep his true thoughts to himself. Cf. Theognidea 73-74, 91-96, 115-116, 117-128, 213-218, 301-302, 309-312, 359-360, 363-366, 571-572, 575-576, 643-644, 963-970, 979-982, 1071-1074. Cf. D. Levine, "Symposium and Polis" in a forthcoming volume on Theognis and archaic Greece: (Johns Hopkins University Press).

[7] Cf., for example, the Theognis passages cited above, Pindar P.10.67, N.8.20, Fr. 122.16; Bacchylides *Hyporchemata* Fr. 22 Bergk; Aeschylus *Agamemnon* 385-398; Sophocles *Antigone* 540-541, *Oedipus Tyrannus* 510; Euripides *Medea* 516-519, *Electra* 550-551, *Hippolytus* 616-617; Plato, *Laws* I-II, especially 649d-650d.

δόλος, πιστός, χρόνος, νόος, χρυσός, (παρα)τρίβομαι, μολύβδῳ, καθαρόν, and πειρ.[8]

But βάσανος is not the only term employed in early Greek poetry which has both metallurgical and ethical connotations. Brown's work makes no mention of the κίβδηλος ἀνήρ, an image which makes its debut in Greek literature in the Theognidea (117, 119, 123, 965). This paper will examine the literary uses of the κίβδηλος theme and its Semitic parallels in order to show that the counterfeit man trope — derived from the need to identify falseness in metals — was another import in the baggage of the goldsmith-bankers.

The concept is introduced in this Theognidea distich (117-118):

κιβδήλου δ' ἀνδρὸς γνῶναι χαλεπώτερον οὐδέν,
Κύρν', οὐδ' εὐλαβίης ἐστὶ περὶ πλέονος.

The verb γνῶναι 'know by observation' (117) is often associated with counterfeit because it is just as important to know false coin as it is to see through human façades.[9] This need to know is stressed in the following passage, as is the connection with metals which the word κίβδηλος itself implies:

Χρυσοῦ κιβδήλοιο καὶ ἀργύρου ἀνσχετὸς ἄτη,
   Κύρνε, καὶ ἐξευρεῖν ῥᾴδιον ἀνδρὶ σοφῷ.
εἰ δὲ φίλου νόος ἀνδρὸς ἐνὶ στήθεσσι λελήθῃ
   ψυδρὸς ἐών, δόλιον δ' ἐνὶ φρεσὶν ἦτορ ἔχῃ,
τοῦτο θεὸς κιβδηλότατον ποίησε βροτοῖσιν,
   καὶ γνῶναι πάντων τοῦτ' ἀνιηρότατον.
οὐδὲ γὰρ εἰδείης ἀνδρὸς νόον οὔτε γυναικός,
   πρὶν πειρηθείης ὥσπερ ὑποζυγίου,
οὐδέ κεν εἰκάσσαις †ὥσπερ ποτ' ἐς ὥριον ἐλθών·†
   πολλάκι γὰρ γνώμην ἐξαπατῶσ' ἰδέαι.
                                    (Theognis 119-128).

Notice here that the images are similar to those in passages where the touchstone occurs. νόος occurs twice (121, 125 cf. Adespota Elegiaca 22 West=Stobaeus 1.8.15); ἐξευρεῖν is used (120 cf. 415=1164e), as are δόλιον (122 cf. 416=1164f), χρυσός (119 cf. 418=1164h, 450, 1106) and πειρηθείης (126 cf. 1104a-b). The fact emerges that although the imagery of βάσανος passages is similar to that which

---
[8] Theognis 415-418, 447-452, 1105-1106; Adespota Elegaica 2 West=Simonides 199 Edmonds; Pindar P.10.67, N.8.20, Fr. 122.16; Bacchylides Fr. 22 Bergk; Antiphon Fr. 88 Diels-Kranz; Chilon apud Diogenes Laertius 1.71.

[9] Theognis 124, 128, 500, 968; Archilochus 328 West 18-19; Herodotus 7.10a; Xenophon Memorabilia 3.1.9; Marcus Aurelius 11.5; Bacchylides Fr. 43.

describes the κίβδηλος personality, the two terms are not ever used together. In other words, in Greek literature a touchstone is never figuratively applied to a potentially counterfeit man. By the same token, a βάσανος is never used literally to test metal which is suspected of being κίβδηλος. An attempt to explain this phenomenon will follow below.

The need to know a man's true character is stressed in the following verses of Theognis, where it is stated that only χρόνος can really reveal someone's personality (Theognis 967: cf. Adespota Elegiaca 22 West=Stobaeus 1.8.15):

> Μήποτ' ἐπαινήσῃς, πρὶν ἂν εἰδῇς ἄνδρα σαφηνῶς,
> ὀργὴν καὶ ῥυθμὸν καὶ τρόπον ὅστις ἂν ᾖ.
> πολλοί τοι κίβδηλον ἐπίκλοπον ἦθος ἔχοντες
> κρύπτουσ', ἐνθέμενοι θυμὸν ἐφημέριον·
> τούτων δ' ἐκφαίνει πάντως χρόνος ἦθος ἑκάστου.
> καὶ γὰρ ἐγὼν γνώμης πολλὸν ἄρ' ἐκτὸς ἔβην·
> ἔφθην αἰνήσας πρὶν σοῦ κατὰ πάντα δαῆναι
> ἤθεα· νῦν δ' ἤδη νηῦς ἅθ' ἑκὰς διέχω.
>
> (963-970)

Danger comes from those whose personalities are counterfeit: they can cause destruction.[10] Such men hide by donning ordinary expressions, glazing over, as it were, their true worthlessness with an attractive but false front (cf. Proverbs 26.23, below).

It is generally believed that κίβδος 'dross of silver' is the root of κίβδηλος.[11] Chantraine and Boisacq compare Hesychius' gloss κίβον ἐνεόν· Πάφιοι to the French *pierre sourde* in the jeweler's vocabulary, meaning 'without reflection.' Groselj mentions the German *taub* and Slovenian *gluh* 'deaf' in the sense of non-metal-producing ruck.[12] The scholiast to Aristophanes' *Birds* 158 calls κιβδηλίαν τὸν ἐκ τοῦ ἀργύρου ῥύπον, which also implies μοχθηρίαν καὶ ζηλοτυπίαν. The commentator goes on to relate a story, probably related to the mid-fifth-century Clearchus decree,[13] which called for an end to coin production by individual allied states. Henceforth, all coins of the Athenian empire would be minted at Athens. Chian coins which were

---

[10] The κίβδηλον ἦθος appears again in Marcus Aurelius 4.28 as a synonym for the black, feminine, stubborn, wild, brutish, despotic, cheating, ribald and foolish heart.

[11] E. Boisacq, *Dictionnaire étymologique de la langue grecque* 2nd ed. (Paris, 1923) *s.v.*; P. Chantraine, *Dictionnaire étymologique de la langue grecque* (Paris, 1968-1980) *s.v.*; LSJ *s.v.*.

[12] "Etyma Graeca" *Ziva Ant.* 3 (1953) 200ff.

[13] R. Meiggs, and D. Lewis, *Greek Historical Inscriptions* (Oxford 1969) No. 45.

re-minted and sent back to Chios were called χίβδηλα, which was later changed to κίβδηλα (ἐναλλάξασα τά στοιχεῖα πρὸς τὸ εὐγλωττότερον). However, the earlier attestations of κίβδηλος make such an assertion unlikely.[14]

In the Hecatompedon inscription (*IG* II² 1388.61: late 5th c.), among the dedications of gold, silver, ivory and precious stones, there is a dedication by one Lakon of στατῆρες κίβδηλοι sealed in a box. Apparently there was no stigma attached to a dedication of this sort, which must have consisted of staters of *mixed metal or alloy*. Such coins were not always acceptable, however. A proclamation from Egypt (*P.Oxy.* 1411.2, 3rd c. A.D.) orders defiant businessmen and bank owners to accept all coin except the absolutely παράτυπος 'counterfeit, improperly struck' and κίβδηλος 'adulterated, counterfeit'.

The Hellenistic Jews who translated the Old Testament into Greek used the word κίβδηλος as equivalent to the Hebrew *shaatnez* 'mingling' where purity is stressed in contrast to impure mixing: "You shall not allow two different kinds of beast to mate together. You shall not plant your field with two kinds of seed. You shall not put on a garment woven (*shaatnez*, LXX κίβδηλον) with two kinds of yarn." (Lev. 19.19). "You shall not plough with an ox and an ass yoked together. You shall not wear clothes woven (*shaatnez*, LXX κίβδηλον) with two kinds of yarn, wool and flax together." (Deut. 22.10-11). The Israelite idea of purity as the absence of adulteration was thus by the second century B.C. understood by Greek-speakers as κιβδηλία.[15]

Linguistically, the word can be related to the Zend root -*saepa*- 'fusion (des métaux)', the Latin *caespes* 'turf', the Gothic *haifts* 'struggle, quarrel', Old Norse *heipt* 'hatred, violence', and Anglo-Saxon *haest* 'violence'.[16] Curtius cites J. Grimm as bringing κίβδηλος under the root κοπ– 'cut, strike' attested in κόπτω, κοπή, κόπος, κοπιάω, and κάπων.[17] Lewy[18] suggests a Semitic borrowing, which would seem likely if we are dealing with a metallurgical term brought to Greece,

---

[14] Note also Aristophanes *Acharnians* 515-519, where Dikaeopolis calls his fellow citizens παρακεκομμένα 'badly minted', 'improperly struck coins' for their wrongful treatment of Megara. Cf. Schol. *ad Acharnians* 516, who explains the descriptions in terms of coinage and mentions the expression 'counterfeit orator': παράσημος ῥήτωρ.

[15] In this respect, see the Wisdom of Solomon 2.16 and 15.9, where κίβδηλος refers to the impurity of peoples and idols.

[16] Cf. Boisacq (above, n.11).

[17] G. Curtius, *Principles of Greek Etymology* (Tr. by A.S. Wilkins and E.B. England) volume 1 (London 1875) 187 = para. 68b, citing J. Grimm, *Ueber Diphthongen nach Weggefallnen Consonanten* (Berlin 1845).

[18] H. Lewy, *Die semitischen Fremdwörter im griechischen* (Berlin 1895) 132 f.

like the touchstone, by eastern traders. Furthermore, note the Hebrew word *kibshân* (from *kâbash* 'to subdue, tread down, conquer, force'), 'kiln, smelting furnace' used for reducing metals, and its similarity (KIB) to κίβδος, including the association with violence and metallurgy. The Hebrew word for 'alloy, tin', *bedīl* (from *bâdal*, to separate), shares the BDEL cluster evident in κίβδηλος, and, as will be shown below, is used in contexts similar to corresponding passages dealing with counterfeit in Theognis.

Koehler's assertion[19] that *bedīl* itself is a loanword from the Sanskrit *pātīra* (cf. Latin *pars, partis*) does not necessarily rule out its being returned to Indo-Europeans through their intercourse with the Semitic peoples who had earlier made it their own. We could suggest as a possibility that κίβδηλος might be related to derivatives of Hebrew *kib(shan)* 'furnace' and *bedīl* 'alloy, tin'. A term such as 'furnace alloy' or 'furnace tin' might have been used for waste products of the smelting process, later applied to humans with negative connotations.[20]

While Brown's work deals with the testing of men's characters like gold, there is little or no discussion of the *necessity* for such a trial. We have seen that the Greek use of the motif is based on the inability to trust appearances. It will now be shown that the notion of men — like metals — hiding their impurities is common both to Greek and Hebrew literary traditions.

The Old Testament compares evil men to counterfeit and impure metals. Proverbs 25.4-5: "Rid silver of its impurities (*sīg*), then it may go to the silversmith; rid the king's presence of wicked men, and his throne will rest firmly on righteousness." Psalms 119.119: "Thou regardest the wicked of the world as dross (*sīg*)." Proverbs 26.23-28 bears a strong similarity to the Theognidean passages quoted above, both in regard to its γλῶσσα-νόος contrast and its comparison of the false man to dross of silver: "Glib speech that covers a spiteful heart (LXX δόλου) is like silver dross (*sīg*) spread on earthenware. With his lips an enemy may speak you fair but inwardly he harbors deceit (LXX δόλους); when his words are gracious do not trust him, for seven abominations fill his heart; he may cloak his enmity in

---

[19] L. Koehler, "Alttestamentliche Wortforschung, Bᵉdīl und bᵉdīlīm" *Theologische Zeitschrift* 3 (1947) 155-156.

[20] Cf. Pollux 7.99 κίβδος = dross or alloy of gold, κίβδωνες = μεταλλεῖς 'miners'; Schol. *ad* Aristoph. *Birds* 158; Hesychius κίβδης· κακοῦργος, κάπηλος, χειροτέχνης. On *bedīl* and the smelting process as evidenced in the Old Testament, cf. W. Zimmerli, *Ezekiel 1*, (translated by R. Clements; Philadelphia 1979) 462-464; J. Soggin, "Jeremias 6:27-30" *Vetus Testamentum* 9 (1959) 95-98; G. Driver, "Two Misunderstood Passages of the OT" *Journal of Theological Studies* NS 6 (1955) 84 ff.; K. Keil, and F. Delitzsch, *Commentary on the Old Testament* (translated by James Martin: reprinted, Philadelphia 1973, 1975) volume vi 193, vol. vii 105.

dissimulation (LXX δόλον), but his wickedness is shown up before the assembly. If he digs a pit, he will fall into it, if he rolls a stone, it will roll back upon him. A lying tongue (LXX γλῶσσα ψευδής) makes innocence feel guilty, and smooth words conceal their sting." Such generalities are along the same lines as the κίβδηλος passages in Theognis in that they do not describe a certain fixed time and place, nor do they describe specific people. Other parallels in Greek literature include the following fragments of Demokritos: χαριζόμενος προσκέπτεο τὸν λαμβάνοντα, μὴ κακὸν ἀντ' ἀγαθοῦ κίβδηλος ἐὼν ἀποδῷ. (fr. 93 Diels-Kranz); κίβδηλοι καὶ ἀγαθοφανέες οἱ λόγῳ μὲν ἅπαντα, ἔργῳ δὲ οὐδὲν ἔρδοντες. (fr. 82); εὐλογέειν ἐπὶ καλοῖς ἔργμασι καλόν· τὸ γὰρ ἐπὶ φλαυροῖσι κίβδηλον καὶ ἀπατεῶνος ἔργον. (fr. 63).[21]

Old Testament prophetic writings use the same image of men as impurities in metals, but they are more specific in designating the people of Israel as needing to be cleansed as though they were the adulterated gold or silver. Isaiah 1.21-22 treats the religious life of Judah — and specifically Jerusalem — in the eighth century B.C.: "How the faithful city has played the whore, once the home of justice where righteousness dwelt — but now murderers! Your silver has turned into base metal (dross, sīg, LXX ἀδόκιμον) and your liquor is diluted with water."[22] The southern Hebrew nation's moral degeneration is compared to the dross of silver also in verses 25-26, this time with the Lord's promise to purify the metal/people: "Once again I will act against you to refine away your base metal (dross, sīg) as with potashand purge all your impurities (bedīl);[23] I will make your judges what they were once and your counsellors like those of old.

---

[21] Cf. also Plato *Laws* 917b; Ps.-Plutarch *Epitome* of Aetius' *de Placitis* I.7.9-10; Marcus Aurelius 4.28, 11.5; Aristotle *Rhetoric* I.15.1375a-b; Ps.-Archilochus 328 West 17-21.

[22] Literally, "Your wine is circumcised (or weakened, *mahul*) with water." Compare Pliny *NH* 19.153: *vinum castrare;* Martial 1.18: *juglare Falernum.*

[23] Cf. Keil and Delitzsch (above, n.20) VII.105: "By *bedilim* (from *bâdal,* to separate) we are to understand the several pieces of *stannum* or lead, in which the silver is contained, and which are separated by smelting, all the baser metals being distinguished from the purer kinds by the fact that they are combustible (*i.e.* can be oxidized). *Plumbum nigrum*, says Pliny, *HN* 24.16, is sometimes found alone, and sometimes mixed with silver: *eius qui primus fluit in fornacibus liquor, stannum appellatur.* The reference here is to the lead separated from the ore in the process of obtaining pure silver. In the form of powder this dross is called *bedil*, and the pieces *bedilim;* whereas *ophereth* is the name of solid lead, obtained by simply melting down from ore which does not contain silver. The fact that *bedil* is also apparently used as a name for tin, may be explained in the same way as the homonymy of iron and basalt, and of the oak and the terebinth. The two metals are called by the same name on account of their having a certain outward resemblance, viz. in softness, pliability, colour, and specific gravity."

Then at length you shall be called the home of righteousness, the faithful city." Compare Isaiah 48.10: "See how I tested (smelted, *tsaraf*) you, not as silver is tested, but in the furnace of affliction, there I purified you." The people of Israel, like silver, must be cleansed of their impurities by being melted down in the furnace and purified. Zimmerli[24] has shown that these Isaiah passages are the background to the oracle at Ezekiel 22.17-22 (ca. 589 B.C.) where Israel is conceived of as being in the smelting oven: an alloy of many metals. God must act to melt and purify them: "Then the word of Yahweh came to me: 'Son of man, the people of the house of Israel have become for me dross (*sig* LXX ἀναμεμειγμένοι). They are all copper and tin (*bedīl*) and iron and lead inside a (smelting) oven. They have become dross silver. Therefore speak: Thus has the lord Yahweh spoken: Because you have become dross (*sīg* LXX σύγκρασιν μίαν), see, therefore, I will gather you together in the midst of Jerusalem. As men gather together silver and copper and iron and lead and tin in a (smelting) oven and kindle fire under it, in order to smelt it, so will I gather you together in my anger and smelt you. And I will kindle against you the fire of my wrath, and you shall be smelted in it. As silver is smelted in a (smelting) oven, so shall you be smelted in it (i.e., in the fire of my anger), and you shall know that I — I Yahweh — have poured out my wrath upon you." Noteworthy in respect to Brown's discussion is the fact that it is the refining of silver, rather than gold, which is the paradigm in the visions of Isaiah, the oracle of Ezekiel and the following prophecy in Jeremiah (6.27-30; late 7th-early 6th century): "I have appointed you an assayer of my people: you will know how to test them and will assay their conduct; arch-rebels all of them, mischief-makers — bronze and iron — corrupt to a man. The bellows puff and blow, the furnace glows; in vain does the refiner smelt the ore; lead, copper and iron are not separated out. Call them spurious silver, for the Lord has spurned them." Again we see the image of people as an alloy, an impure mixture of metals, *spurious silver,* which must be purified. The book of Malachi (5th century B.C.), also an oracle, contains a similar image in reference to the arrival of God (3.2-3): "Who can endure the day of his coming? Who can stand firm when he appears? He is like a refiner's fire, like a fuller's soap; he will take his seat, refining and purifying silver; he will purify the Levites and cleanse them like gold and silver, and so they shall be fit to bring offerings to the Lord." Even the priestly class has been infected and must be purified like metals.

---

[24] W. Zimmerli, (above, n.20) 461-464.

One of the differences between the literary use of silver and gold is beginning to emerge. Gold, as Brown has pointed out, is assayed by the touchstone (βάσανος), while silver, if suspected of being counterfeit, is *refined* to rid it of its impurities. Thus, a κίβδηλος man (or silver) would not be tested by a βάσανος, which is only used to test the genuinesses of gold. A parallel passage in Zechariah 13.8-9; 2nd century B.C.) points up this difference: "It shall happen throughout the land that two thirds of the people shall be struck down and die, while one third of them shall be left there. Then I will pass this third through the fire and I will refine them as silver is refined and assay them as gold is assayed. Then they will invoke me by my name and I myself will answer them ... " The touchstone is for gold; dross (κίβδος, sīg) refers to silver and refining. The βάσανος is an instrument for testing that is rubbed, while counterfeit silver is associated with the furnace and fire. A touchstone will tell if gold is genuine or false, while κίβδηλος refers to adulterated, mixed or alloyed metal, usually silver. Thus, a distinction evident in the Old Testament parallels that made in Greek, where κίβδηλος and βάσανος never appear in the same contexts.[25]

The equation of metallic impurity with the crimes and inferiority of specific individuals or groups is paralleled in Greek texts. Anacreon's scathing poem about Artemon condemns a degenerate for his new-found prosperity:[26]

πρὶν μὲν ἔχων βερβέριον, καλύμματ' ἐσφηκωμένα,
καὶ ξυλίνους ἀστραγάλους ἐν ὠσὶ καὶ ψιλὸν περὶ
πλευρῇσι δέρμ' ἤει βοός,
νήπλυτον εἴλυμα κακῆς ἀσπίδος, ἀρτοπώλοισιν
κἀθελοπόρνοισιν ὁμιλέων ὁ πονηρὸς Ἀρτέμων,
πολλὰ μὲν ἐν δουρὶ τιθεὶς αὐχένα, πολλὰ δ' ἐν τροχῷ,
πολλὰ δὲ νῶτον σκυτίνῃ μάστιγι θωμιχθείς, κόμην
πώγωνά τ' ἐκτετιλμένος·
νῦν δ' ἐπιβαίνει σατινέων χρύσεα φορέων κατέρματα

---

[25] This is not to say that the touchstone was the *only* test for gold, but that it was never used for silver. Fire was also used to test both metals. Cf. Proverbs 17.3: "The crucible is for silver and the furnace is for gold, and the Lord tries hearts." Also, cf. Theognis 499-500: "Skillful men recognize gold and silver in the fire, but wine reveals the mind of a man."

[26] Fr. 388 Campbell=43 Page=97 Edmonds=Athenaeus 12.533f-534b. See the commentaries of D. Campbell *Greek Lyric Poetry* (London 1967) 323-325; H. Smyth *Greek Melic Poets* (New York 1963) 290-291.

παῖς Κύκης καὶ σκιαδίσκην ἐλεφαντίνην φορεῖ
γυναιξὶν αὔτως ἐμφερής.[27]

His earlier life (1, πρίν) had been wretched, marked by his wearing rejected shield-hides on his sides (3, πλευρῆσι) and constantly being punished in the stocks, on the wheel, with the lash and by depilation (for adultery). He associated with low-lifes and was himself πονηρός (5), having happened upon a κίβδηλον βίον (6) 'a base way of making a living'. However, the use of κίβδηλος is ambiguous here, for his lifestyle, while bogus by normal standards, was not 'counterfeit' for Artemon, but rather quite appropriate to his low character. His outward appearance matched his inner decrepitude. The word κίβδηλος is proleptic, for when he becomes rich (9, νῦν), Artemon does not stop being vile, but rather hides behind a façade of wealth, which includes golden earrings instead of wood, an ivory parasol and a fancy litter for transport. The contrast between the physical and ethical facts of his life makes Artemon a counterfeit man *par excellence*.

Parallel to this is Ps.-Archilochus 328 (West), a poem explaining why the mind is like a κίναιδος and a wicked πόρνη. After a list of obscene pleasures (1-16), the poet rejects such a debauched life and opts instead for uncounterfeit joy (19, ἀκίβδηλος χαρά), which consists of the pursuit of the Muses, a life which is σαόφρων and has nothing to do with those who enjoy themselves with shameful pleasures (17-21). The purity of such a life reflects the metalurgical *desideratum* of undebased silver; there is no hiding behind false joys, no riotous living being passed off as pleasure in a truly temperate life.[28]

The picture of Artemon and the intemperance which characterizes the immoderate sexuality in the spurious Archilochus poem are reflected in the description of the commons described in Theognis 53-58. Note the wearing of skin garments on their sides (55 πλευραῖσι)

---

[27] Once he went out huddled about in dirty clothes with his hair skimped up, buttons of wood hung in his ears for rings, and the hide of a threadbare ox scrubbed from a cast-off shield to wrap
his bones to keep him warm. For friends all he could get was pastry cooks or girls who walked the streets for fun. He was the lousy Artemon.
He lived the life of a useless bum
He got his neck framed in the pillory, he got whipped till his back was raw, he had hairs pulled out of his head.
Look at him now, Kyke's boy: he rides in a coach and four, and wears gold on his arms, gold on his neck, shaded by ivory parasols,
like some dame in society.
Translation by R. Lattimore, *Greek Lyrics* (Chicago 1971) 46.

[28] On ἀκίβδηλος as the mark of a genuine human nature, cf. also Herodotus 9.7a and Isocrates 1.7.

to characterize their wretched former life (56) and the πρίν ... νῦν contrast (57-58):

Κύρνε, πόλις μὲν ἔθ' ἥδε πόλις, λαοὶ δὲ δὴ ἄλλοι,
οἳ πρόσθ' οὔτε δίκας ᾔδεσαν οὔτε νόμους,
ἀλλ' ἀμφὶ πλευραῖσι δορὰς αἰγῶν κατέτριβον,
ἔξω δ' ὥστ' ἔλαφοι τῆσδ' ἐνέμοντο πόλεως.
καὶ νῦν εἰσ' ἀγαθοὶ Πολυπαίδη· οἱ δὲ πρὶν ἐσθλοὶ
νῦν δειλοί.

Artemon (in his new life) and the upstart Megarians are described as counterfeit: they seem on the outside to be good, but are really base. Their former livelihood was more appropriate to their true natures. The Theognidean warnings about counterfeit men quoted above are amply supplemented, we have seen, by warnings about the dangers of appearance versus reality.[29] The work is characterized by its preoccupation with politics and trust. The topsy-turvy political world of Megara in the 7th-6th centuries B.C. was fertile soil for the implantation of the literary seeds which produced the κίβδηλος ἀνήρ.[30]

The concept of κιβδηλία appears in a similar context in Athenian comedy. In the parabasis of Aristophanes' *Frogs* (717-732) there is a contrast between counterfeit men and their opposite. The chorus urges the citizens to make use of the counsel of the men of old, who were like the good non-debased silver coinage circulating before the Peloponnesian War. The non-counterfeit men (οὐ κεκιβδηλευμένοις 720) are described as the best of all coins, the only ones struck properly and ringing true (720-723). This points out the purity and superiority of the old Athenian coinage, as well as the excellence of the men of old. These men were well-born, temperate, just, καλοὶ κἀγαθοί, brought up in palaestras and choruses and with a good musical education, i.e., properly educated physically, mentally and spiritually (726-728). They are also useful (735).

Aristophanes describes their opposites with the same contempt evident in Anacreon's description of Artemon and Theognis' chagrin at the new *agathoi*. These counterfeit men are wicked bronze — struck recently and from the worst coin (724-725); they are brazen, foreigners, red-heads (Thracian slaves or counterfeit coins of Athena

---

[29] Cf. above, n.6.

[30] On Megarian politics in the Archaic Age, cf. E. Harrison, *Studies in Theognis* (1902), E. Highbarger, *The History and Civilization of Ancient Megara* (1927), L. Jeffery, *Archaic Greece: The City States* (1976); R. Legon, *Megara: The Political History of a Greek City State to 336 B.C.* (Ithaca 1981); S. Oost, "The Megara of Theagenes and Theognis" *CPh* 68 (1973) 186-196; M. West, *Studies in Greek Elegy and Iambus* (Berlin 1974).

with the silver rubbed off the head showing the red bronze beneath?),[31] evil and low-born, recent arrivals whom the city would not even consider using as scapegoat victims because of their ritual impurity (729-732).

Demosthenes concludes his oration against Leptines thus: "And I am amazed that the punishment for those who debase the coinage of Athens is death, but that you will give reason to those who make the entire city counterfeit (κίβδηλον) and untrustworthy." (*In Lept.* 508.15) The association of the counterfeit idea with political as well as moral issues is clear here, in Aristophanes and in Theognis, as well as in the Old Testament prophetic writings. Whole communities are described in metallurgical terms as being false to their polities and to divine and human standards.

The literary parallels outlined here do not, in themselves, prove that the Greeks took their ideas of counterfeit man directly from their eastern neighbors. However, when joined with the observations provided by Brown concerning the probable importation by goldsmith-bankers of proverbial literature, gold-economy and the alphabet, the case for borrowing is strengthened somewhat. The fact that the touchstone and the notion of a κίβδηλος ἀνήρ occur first in Theognis might imply that these words came into Greek poetry after the epic poems had been crystallized into their final forms, but before the final composition of the Theognidea.[32] Since the poetry of Theognis was written down around the time when coinage was making its early appearance in the Greek world,[33] it could thus avail itself of the new words κίβδηλος and βάσανος, and adapt them to a context which was already traditional: namely, that appearances often deceive the mind, and that a

---

[31] This latter suggestion is made by Brown (above, n.3.1) 176, who cites W.B. Stanford, *Aristophanes: The Frogs* (London, 1958) 134-135.

[32] The date of the Theognidea is generally considered to be mid sixth-century. West (above, n.30) dates it to the late 7th century. For further considerations about the date of the collection, cf. the works cited above (n.30).

[33] The date of the introduction of coinage into Greece has not been exactly determined, but most conjectures coincide with the range of speculations on the date of the Theognidea: from the last quarter of the seventh to the middle of the sixth century B.C. C. Starr dates the coins in the Artemision at Ephesus to ca. 625: *The Economic and Social Growth of Early Greece, 800-500 B.C.* (New York 1977) 109. M. Austin, and P. Vidal-Naquet, support this early date: *Economic and Social History of Ancient Greece, an Introduction* (Berkeley 1977) 56-58, cf. 73 notes 14, 15 for further bibliography. Cf. also C. Kraay, *Archaic and Classical Coinage* (1977); M. Price and N. Waggonner, *Archaic Greek Coinage: the Asyut Hoard* (Manchester 1976). D. Kagan's forthcoming article in *AJA*, following Lisa Weidauer, attempts to put the introduction of coinage back to the beginning of the seventh century. Whenever coinage was actually introduced into Greece, it was probably not silver, but rather electrum, the purity of which, however, would be just as crucial to measure.

method of testing for true character is always needed. As advanced metallurgy spread to the west, bringing with it the touchstone and the importance of identifying impure metals, it also brought along the idea of testing people like gold and silver in order to identify counterfeit men.

University of Arkansas
Fayettville, Arkansas

TIME'S MIRROR: A REFLECTION OF PHAEDRA'S ISOLATION AND SELF-CONSCIOUSNESS

CECELIA A. E. LUSCHNIG

Κακοὺς δὲ θνητῶν ἐξέφην᾽, ὅταν τύχῃ,
προθεὶς κάτοπτρον ὥστε παρθένῳ νέᾳ
Χρόνος· παρ᾽ οἷσι μήποτ᾽ ὀφθείην ἐγώ.
(*Hipp.* 428-30)

"An odd confusion," remarks W.S. Barrett in his splendid edition of the *Hippolytus*,[1] commenting on the double use of the mirror here, as both self-revealing and other-revealing. This paper will examine two aspects of Phaedra's character as drawn in the *Hippolytus* and as reflected in this mysterious image: her isolation[2] and her self-consciousness.[3] The confusion of this image is one which plagues Phaedra's every mood and move in the drama, from her first fevered utterances through which she is able to both reveal and keep concealed the cause of her suffering, up to her lying letter through which she hopes to undo the damage done to her reputation, but which ironically brings her everlasting ill-fame[4] and places her squarely in the company of ruined and vicious women she so longed to avoid. Further, these two aspects of Phaedra's personality can be seen reflected in the other two major characters and in the goddesses who frame the play.

Self-consciousness and isolation: the former is emphasized by the mirror itself, the solitary viewer seeing herself and exposed to the world at last, the latter by the speech (the final lines of which I quoted above) wherein Phaedra has disclosed the conclusions of her long, lonely nights of thought (373-430). Phaedra's speech is as it were a second prologue, beginning again with a statement of the way things are. The address is narrower, women of Trozen as opposed to the world in general of Kupris' monologue. The focus is narrower too, Phaedra's own struggle in contrast to Aphrodite's pronouncement of

---

[1] W.S. Barrett, *Euripides: Hippolytos* (Oxford 1964) 328.

[2] On the theme of isolation in the *Hippolytus,* see H.P. Stahl, 'On "Extra-Dramatic" Communication of Characters in Euripides,' *YCS* 25 (1977) 159-76 and C. Luschnig, "Men and Gods in Euripides' *Hippolytus,*" *Ramus* 9 (1980) 89-100.

[3] On the concern over the self as seen by others and by itself, see Harry C. Avery, "My Tongue Swore, but my Mind is Unsworn," *TAPA* 99 (1968) 19-35.

[4] See especially lines 1429-30, on which cf. D.C. Braund, "Artemis Eukleia and Euripides' *Hippolytus,*" *JHS* 100 (1980) 184-5.

the way things are in the universe. But both speeches give step by step plans; both juxtapose or interpose the general and the particular, moving from the general statement to the case at hand, and back to the general. This is not the place for a thorough analysis of this much scrutinized[5] speech, but perhaps a few general comments will not seriously unbalance my argument.

I cannot agree with those who see Phaedra's speech as an admission of guilt[6] nor with those who interpret it as her account of success.[7] The speech is rather an *apologia pro vita sua* and, like so many other things in the play, is ambiguous. Phaedra outlines her plan: she has just failed, very painfully and dramatically, to carry out the first point of her program: to keep silence.[8] She admits that she has failed to overcome her love with σωφροσύνη.[9] But she can still succeed at the one last point: she will die.

This is a rational speech, perhaps the most intelligently rational in the play, but still the reasoning is agglutinative rather than syllogistic. Phaedra has no equal with whom to share these thoughts: reason does not take place in a vacuum; and so the speech points up her isolation. The speech, furthermore, balances — gives the other side of — the Phaedra of the wild fantasy. We certainly do not expect such an intellectual, thoughtful, almost academic Phaedra after her irrational vision of herself, any more than we expect a Medea who, after barbarous behind-the-scenes crimes, gives a set speech on the sorry lot of women, in particular of foreign women, in society. On the other hand the two glimpses of Phaedra share one aspect of her character. In both, self-consciousness, an almost abnormal interest in herself, is apparent.[10] One of the most cogent aspects of the speech is the number of words

---

[5] See among others, David Claus, "Phaedra and the Socratic Paradox," *YCS* 22 (1972) 223-38; Friedrich Solmsen, "'Bad Shame' and Related Problems in Phaedra's Speech," *Hermes* 101 (1973) 420-425; David Kovacs, "Shame, Pleasure, and Honor in Phaedra's Great Speech," *AJP* 101 (1980) 287-303.

[6] Cf. Barrett (above, n.1) 227ff.

[7] Cf. Claus and Kovacs (above, n.5).

[8] On the theme of silence (and speech) see B.M.W. Knox's brilliant piece, "The *Hippolytus* of Euripides," *YCS* 13 (1952) 3-31.

[9] Notice how Phaedra uses ἄνοιαν φέρειν ... νικῶσα (398-9) and Κύπριν κρατῆσαι (401) as synonyms and that she admits failure at this important step of her plan.

[10] Jean J. Smoot comments in some detail on the narcissism of Hippolytus in "Literary Criticism on a Vase-Painting: A Clearer Picture of Euripides' *Hippolytus*," *CLS* 12 (1976) 292-303. The present paper wishes to show a similar trait in all the named characters.

describing mental activity.[11] And most interesting of all are the lines in which she not only examines the lives of men, implicitly comparing her own plight to others' experience, in which she not only sees herself, but those in which she sees herself being seen (404-5, 415-18 in juxtaposition to 419-20, 430). The image of Time's mirror conflates these two and shows how they are related: Phaedra is concerned not only with how she is seen by others[12] but also with how she sees herself. The image makes this clear beyond a doubt, by surrounding the self-revealing mirror with the other-revealing mirror. The παρθένος of the image is vain about her appearance;[13] Phaedra is vain about her moral integrity as Nurse points out.[14] The παρθένος νέα whom Phaedra envisions as likely to admire herself in a mirror is overwhelmed by the other mirror held up by Time. This imaginary girl must not only see herself superficially but also see herself being seen in the revelation of Time. Although the παρθένος cannot literally be Phaedra, she herself makes the connection, "may I not be seen among them" (430), including herself as she does throughout in the generalization, balancing κακούς (428) with ἐγώ (430). One is seen in Time's glass as wicked, only if one is wicked. The image then reflects three ways of seeing the self: the self seen alone by the self, the self seen by others, the self seen by the self in the light of truth and in relation to others.

Not only in her great speech, but throughout her part Phaedra displays the same multiple view of herself. From her entrance we hear her talking about seeing herself. She imagines an idyllic setting and places herself in it, taking a drink of pure water, resting under a tree, cheering on the hounds, brandishing her hunting gear, taming horses, growing more active and aggressive as her fevered courage climbs. That this is not the Phaedra of reality is made abundantly clear by the chorus' solicitous questions, by the querulous nurse whose nagging insistence the real Phaedra has not the strength to resist, and most apparently by the passive Phaedra we see lying on her bed of sickness. Nor does the fantasy reflect Phaedra, the queen, as she ought to be; these are not things that should be uttered in front of a crowd

---

[11] In this speech alone it must be significant that so many of Phaedra's lines include reference to intellectual activity: 376, 377, 378, 379, 380, 386, 387, 388, 390, 391, 392, 396, 398, 399, 401, 402, 405, 411, 412, 413, 425, 427. This is a conservative reading, a bolder reader might wish to include more.

[12] See, for example, C.P. Segal, "Shame and Purity in Euripides' *Hippolytus*," *Hermes* 98 (1970) 278-299; William Sale, *Existentialism and Euripides* (Melbourne 1977) 58-65.

[13] We might compare Phaedra's imaginary παρθένος with Jason's new bride who smiles at her ἄψυχον εἰκώ in the mirror (*Medea* 1160-1162).

[14] Especially at lines 490-496 and 507.

(213-214), as the nurse reminds her mistress. And Nurse does know how to keep up appearances.

Why is Phaedra so ashamed after her lyrical outcry that she feels she must hide her head again? She has seen herself, not acting disgracefully — for she is not conscious of the erotic symbolism of her utterances[15] — but in a dangerous juxtaposition. The double (or even triple) vision of the mirror metaphor is foreshadowed here: Phaedra sees the picture in her fantasy in revealing detail and she is in that picture. She sees her golden hair flowing (220); she sees her hand[16] with the hunting spear in it (221-2). It is as if she were looking at herself in a mirror dressed for the hunt, seeing herself as she would be seen. But the scene is not her boudoir; it is a leafy meadow (210-211), watered by pure streams (208-209): it is no other than the place Hippolytus has just left (cf. 73-4, 78). To be complete, the picture requires a viewer at least. Phaedra sees herself as she would be seen by another, just as one sees oneself in a mirror, and that other is Hippolytus, who, it may be added, also goes about with and is reflected by another unseen viewer. In how many ways does Phaedra see herself in this one painful scene? She fantasizes a self as she wishes she could be, she describes herself as another would see her, and finally she sees clearly and honestly what her vision means in relation to the knowledge she alone holds, the knowledge which we share because we have heard the prologue.

What helper, what friend, what companion can Phaedra have (675-6)? No one can share in her final lonely decision, in her decision not to be alone in shame.[17] To Phaedra's mind outsiders are witnesses (see, for example, 321, 403-4, 420, 430), whether to her goodness or her disgrace: but given her propensity to project her own private knowledge to others, already seen in her reaction to her fantasy, and in her projected fear of the darkness and of the beams of the house (416-

---

[15] This is not to suggest that Phaedra is in every way unaware of the erotic significance of her outcries, described by Justin Glenn in "The Fantasies of Phaedra: A Psychoanalytic Reading," *CW* 69 (1976) 435-442, but that for the present argument, another aspect — that of seeing and being seen — is under examination.

[16] Cf. 200, 317, 325, 335, 814, 856 for the fatal significance of Phaedra's χείρ.

[17] Our interest in Phaedra from the first concerns the knowledge we share with her. Our fullest sympathy is extended when she explains so clearly and honestly what she knows and intends to do. But when she acts on her knowledge to destroy Hippolytus, she loses some of that fellow-feeling. When she claims ignorance (at line 599) it is an indication of her despair and confusion. She has but one hope left: to die. When she adds to her plan (723) something which she hides from us, our fellow-feeling is thwarted. We have been party to all Phaedra's secrets, her passion and her intimate thoughts. Her denial here undoes it all: we cannot feel for her in her last unshared plan. Our knowledge of her knowledge both creates and erases sympathy.

418), she scarcely needs an outside witness. As long as she was able to keep secret her shameful passion, Phaedra had only the self-revealing mirror to worry about. But Hippolytus' view of her does not conform to her ideal self-image, neither to the natural Phaedra of her fantasy nor to the coherent Phaedra who would rather die than continue living with the disgrace of guilty desire. Rather, Hippolytus' denunciation turns out to be a conflation of her fantasy (in which she gives voice to her longing) and her fear (voiced in her similar denunciation of adulterous women). Phaedra's fear of witnesses has become a reality.[18] For witnesses in this play, even if they witness mistakenly, have a way of turning what they witness into reality. Hippolytus' view of Phaedra forces her to put herself into the group of women with ruined reputations (668-669; cf. Barrett *ad loc.*). Because there are now two witnesses (herself and Hippolytus), the mirror can no longer reflect a good reputation, neither to herself nor to the world outside. Her discovery (in line 715) is of a way to destroy both witnesses, by removing herself and by putting the mirror, as it were, in Hippolytus' hand.[19] The reputation for the deed is taken as the equivalent of the deed itself. And it is precisely that, the false reputation, which Phaedra makes Hippolytus share (830-831): that is the illness of which she speaks (in line 730).

Phaedra then is accustomed to seeing herself from the outside as in a picture or a mirror, and she is not alone in so doing. Theseus too sees himself being seen. Immediately after his entrance (790) he is seen seeing himself as not being received as etiquette demands (792). When he has learned of his loss, he sees himself almost as a stage figure wearing the wrong costume, dressed as a $\theta\epsilon\omega\rho\grave{o}s$ with a crown on his head, when his role now is that of bereaved widower. In a self-conscious act, reminiscent of both his son's and his wife's first acts of

---

[18] I prefer the presence of Phaedra on stage during Hippolytus' denunciation, since it is important that we know exactly what she has heard, how many of her own sentiments she has heard Hippolytus repeat: for the tragedy of their inability to communicate is heightened in the face of their similarity of thought by their presence together. That Phaedra also hears Hippolytus agree reluctantly to keep silence does not affect the present argument, since the compelling fact is that he is a witness, however mistaken, to her wrongdoing and he promises to be a watcher (661-2) to a scene she knows she cannot face (415-16). For the aesthetically persuasive suggestion that Phaedra is cowering behind the statue of Aphrodite (where indeed Hippolytus would not turn his gaze), see David Sider, "Two Stage Directions for Euripides," *AJP* 98 (1977) 16-19; cf. Oliver Taplin, *Greek Tragedy in Action* (California 1978) 155 and 199, n. 7.

[19] Hippolytus is forced to see that others see him as $\kappa\alpha\kappa\acute{o}s$, lines 654, 1031, 1071, 1075, 1191; for though we recognize Hippolytus as the most virtuous of all men, again and again we hear the word $\kappa\alpha\kappa\acute{o}s$ predicated upon him and it is from his own lips that we hear it. His $\kappa\alpha\kappa\acute{\iota}\alpha$ is present in the minds of those who hear these words, first Nurse and then Theseus: their false image of him is forced into his consciousness.

self-assertion, he throws off that inappropriate headband (806-7; cf. 73, 201-2). Again, in the debate with his son, we see a self-conscious Theseus, seeing himself as a figure of legend, in need of upholding his past and being true to it (975-980). He too speaks of witnesses, as if witnesses gave reality to his great deeds; and we recall Phaedra's prayer not to have witnesses to her ugly deeds (404). For witnesses are the viewers of Time's mirror. Unless Theseus remains true to himself, the deeds of his past cannot withstand Time's scrutiny. But ironically, the witnesses he cites, being dead or inanimate, are as mute as the halls Hippolytus calls upon to speak for him (1074-5; cf. 1076).

Each of these characters tries to be self-contained, Phaedra in her decision and death, Theseus in his past, Hippolytus in his purity and perfection. Each fails. But Hippolytus comes closest to succeeding. Hippolytus' isolation is self-imposed and is evident even before he enters through Aphrodite's words which point up the unnaturalness of his isolation (an isolation, we may note, which is very similar to that which he wishes to impose on all women). He sees himself as the one virtuous man in a world of κακοί with whom he shares nothing (e.g. 81, 614). His references to the pure meadow give the clearest evidence of his self-consciousness, along with his prayer for continued virginity and perfection, a prayer that is to be answered only through the changelessness of death. But for Hippolytus there is, in the beginning, no confusion about the inner and outer self. He is what we see; he is what he claims to be. When he is confronted by other people, however, the confusion of the two views of self does surface. That the nurse could think him capable of taking part in her scheme (654-5), that his own father could think him guilty, indicate that his life no longer has the integrity he thought it had. This was perhaps true as soon as Phaedra saw him in Athens; but until he became aware that others could see him as a wrongdoer his self-perception remained unaffected. In his understandable, if unkind, outburst, the singling out of certain parts of his body for special comment indicates an inchoate sense of inner alienation: as if his γλῶσσα and φρήν belonged to separable individuals (612); as if by washing out his ears (653-4) he could clean away the stain caused by the knowledge of evil.

Hippolytus shows a singular inability to address persons except in generalities, even when, as far as he can know, his life and future depend on how he presents himself. Hippolytus cannot see Artemis' face; he turns away from his father's; he is not given to knowing intimately his fellow men. And this failing extends even to himself: for when he describes himself and his life, even that is in the most general terms. In his singleness, his simplicity, of character, Hippolytus is most unlike Phaedra, but at the same time the growing confusion over inward and outward self which appears most clearly in certain lines addressed to his father, shows a close similarity between him and Phaedra. The need for a witness like himself; the pity of appearing κακός; the appeal to the house to bear witness for him; and especially the wish to stand outside himself — to be another person, to see himself and weep for himself — show something of the same odd confusion as Phaedra's image of Time's mirror (1022, 1070-1, 1074-5, 1078-9; cf. Barrett p. 363, "this rather odd wish").

Phaedra could not bear to face her wickedness in her reflection, nor could she bear for others to see it in the reflection held up by time.[20] The mirror the young women (of line 429) looks into reveals herself to herself. But a mirror is, in some sense, inherently other-revealing: for the self one sees reflected in the mirror is seen as other and it is the self one will present to others. Phaedra's mirror metaphor refers to herself in a subtle and complex way: the παρθένος νέα (of 429) is the self of the pictorial level of Phaedra's fantasy, the self (no longer in existence) of her imagination who could ride and hunt with Hippolytus as innocently as the maidens who will cut their hair in mourning for him (1125-7). The mirror held up by time — proverbially the bringer of truth to light — of course reveals more than the surface. Time's mirror reveals the inner being, the goodness or wickedness of the person reflected in it. Phaedra's concern is with wickedness and so her words κακούς ... ἐξέφην' reveal her deepest fear and foreshadow her fate. Human beings were reflected by others, by the witnesses mentioned by all the characters, and they reveal themselves through their interactions with others. But like the goddesses in this drama who exist on another plane, apart from the human sufferers, and whose nature is to know and declare their own power and to be discrete, alien to one another, and therefore capable of only a partial view, so likewise the human actors, isolated and unable to comprehend more than that part of the others which reflects some aspect of themselves, are not ever in control of the knowledge the audience holds. Because of this isolation and selective ignorance they are reflected by one another as in a mirror and they use the false or partial image to destroy one another. Time and Artemis do finally reveal the truth to Theseus. But Artemis' truth is only part of the whole. Time reveals a fuller truth than can be acceptable to any of the characters, human or divine. For the fullness of Time's revelation uncovers their communion and complicity in this tragedy.

---

[20] "Living where innocence is a crime, she witnesses with disgust what she will end up being. Seen from the outside, her destiny horrifies her ... she escapes from her terrible future by running away." Marguerite Yourcenar, *Fires* tr. Dori Katz (New York 1981) 5 (originally published in 1936).

Phaedra's image of Time's mirror points both backward and forward, and catches in its oblique light a concern of all persons who share this tragedy and reflects a central question of the play: how is the truth to be known? what witnesses are to be accepted? For finally no single witnesses is enough to lead players or audience to the truth, so that the confusion of the image hints at the relation of audience to the work being performed. The image of Time's mirror is odd, but it is a microcosm of the drama.[21]

University of Idaho
Moscow, Idaho

---

[21] An earlier version of this paper was read at the annual meeting of the American Philological Association in December 1980.

THE STATILIUS-SUBSCRIPTION AND THE EDITIONS OF LATE ANTIQUITY

DONALD E. MARTIN

The gentlemen and scholars of the fourth and fifth centuries of our era who "subscribed" their manuscripts of the Latin classics little realized how enigmatic a legacy their subscriptions would be. As it is now, the areas in the history of book production which they might have been expected to illuminate remain in shadow except where they are clarified from other sources. Giorgio Pasquali asserts, for example, that the texts of the Latin classics were transcribed from rolls to codices at the time that they were subscribed.[1] But it is not from any specific information provided by the subscriptions that he arrived at this conclusion. Nor do the subscriptions explicitly support Dain's thesis that these affidavits mark the era in which the *archétypes latins* were created.[2] The subscriptions support both assertions only indirectly and circumstantially rather than through any concrete data which they might have imparted.

There has always been a general recognition of the importance of the subscriptions found recorded on the manuscripts of classical and Christian Latin authors. The large number of these subscriptions, and the frequency with which they appear on manuscripts regarded as important to a tradition, have prompted numerous attempts to assess their value, both to the textual tradition with which they are associated and to the history of book production in antiquity. In the 17th century Henri de Valois had observed that the subscriptions testified to a historical phenomenon with considerable consequences for textual transmission: the custom had arisen among men of the highest social and political stature to take upon themselves the task of proofing the texts of the ancient authors.[3] De Valois imagined the noblemen of late antiquity laying down their consulships and prefectures in their old age and busying themselves with interpreting and improving the texts of the illustrious writers of antiquity for their own amusement or as a favor for friends. This notion, which seems acceptable enough, suggests in addition the likelihood that a new technique or process of caring for these books might have been initiated by the new class of

---

[1] G. Pasquali, *Storia della tradizione e critica del testo*² (Firenze 1962) 366.

[2] A. Dain, *Les manuscrits*² (Paris 1964) 119.

[3] H. Valesii *Emendationum libri quinque et de critica libri duo* (Amsterdam 1740) 179.

correctors. It also suggests that this humble task took on greater importance than it once had.

In his oft-cited paper of 1851,[4] Otto Jahn collected all the subscriptions known to him and discussed numerous details in dating and prosopography, their contexts, and the manner in which they were preserved to us. The value of this seminal work has been frequently appreciated,[5] for it is here that we can see the startling number and the broad chronological span of these small documents. And it was undoubtedly Jahn's paper which brought to the subscriptions the attention which they subsequently received. Eduard Lommatzsch noted that many of the subscriptions had been entered during the years of the late 4th century.[6] It was during that period that the pagan nobility had experienced a series of catastrophes crucial to their continued existence, most notably the fall of Julian (363); the failure of Procopius (365/6); the removal of the Altar of Victory (384); and the defeat of Eugenius (394). This was undoubtedly a time of stress for the diminishing pagan community, during which, as Lommatzsch suggested, the ancient classics were embraced as though durch Erhaltung dieser Litteratur einen schweigenden Protest gegen das verhässte, siegreiche Christentum einzulegen.[7]

The circulation of the Scriptures in codices could not have failed to catch the attention of the pagan community. They would certainly have been aware of the profound and unifying effect that the Holy Book had upon the Christian cause. The Christians were at that time struggling to establish a canon of texts which, as the Word of God, were regarded as unmarred by human error, hence unvarying and open to but a single interpretation. The editing of the classics had never been subject to such heavy strictures, but the nobility, by selecting and correcting texts, and compiling anthologies, tended toward a canonical body of pagan literature analogous to the Scriptures and similarly unmarred by error.[8] Whether we regard the effort as an act of protest, with Lommatzsch, or

---

[4] O. Jahn, "Ueber die Subscriptionen in den Handschriften römischer Classiker," *Ber. königl. sächs. Ges. d. Wiss. zu Leipzig,* Phil.-hist. Classe 3 (1851) 327-372.

[5] *E. g.,* J. E. G. Zetzel, "Emendavi ad Tironem: some notes on scholarship in the second century A.D." *HSCP* 77 (1973) 225.

[6] E. Lommatzsch, "Litterarische Bewegungen in Rom im vierten und fünften Jahrhundert n. Chr.," *Zeitsch. f. verg. Literaturgesch.,* N. F. 15 (1904) pp. 177-192.

[7] *Ibid.,* p. 183.

[8] H. Bloch, "The conflict between paganism and Christianity at the end of the fourth century" in *The Conflict between Paganism and Christianity in the Fourth Century,* ed. A. Momigliano (Oxford 1963) 213-214. James Zetzel concludes that their aims were considerably more modest: "The Subscriptions in the Manuscript of Livy and Fronto and the meaning of Emendatio," *CP* 75 (1980), p. 49.

as a phase of resistance, with Bloch,[9] it must in any case have represented a striking new departure from the traditional methods and philosophy of book editing. The success of this new departure assured the continuation of the Latin classics. The vitality of the process — whatever it entailed — can be seen in the number of subscriptions preserved and in the eventual acceptance and preservation of pagan literature by the Christians, who took up the task when the pagan resistance faded.[10]

But the motivation behind the text-editing of the fourth century, no matter how compelling, cannot explain the device of subscribing. And of course it cannot account for the first subscriptions preserved to us, for those which Statilius Maximus entered onto his text of Cicero's *De lege agraria* antedate that era by probably a hundred years and perhaps longer.[11] Statilius was a grammarian known in late antiquity for his book *De singularibus apud Ciceronem* as well as works on Sallust and Cato. As a follower in the archaist tradition of Aulus Gellius and Fronto, Statilius' act of subscribing his Cicero edition should, I believe, set him apart from the general run of grammarians and cause us to wonder why he did it. (For my argument it does not matter whether or not Statilius was actually the first to subscribe a text. I argue not so much that Statilius was himself a great innovator, but that subscribing a literary text was a great innovation. He was surely among the first and presumably employed the subscription for the same reasons as any who might have preceded him.)

The accidental preservation of Statilius' subscriptions provides us the opportunity to consider an isolated case. The unique properties of his subscriptions in date, form, and circumstances allow us to see the rest in their earliest stage of development and to suggest at least tentative ways to define these and the later subscriptions, as well as to make a general assessment of their role in the histories of the texts with which they are preserved.

I must review briefly the views of Theodor Birt and of Karl Buchner, which impinge directly upon this matter. Birt assumed that Statilius was following a long-established tradition when he subscribed his Cicero edition.[12] The manuscript which Statilius corrected, according to Birt, bore a subscription which he simply imitated. In general, Birt's argument rested upon the locations of later subscriptions. They often

---

[9] Bloch, p. 194.

[10] Bloch, pp. 216-217.

[11] Zetzel dates Statilius to the latter half of the 2nd century (*art. cit.* above, n.5, p. 228).

[12] Th. Birt, *Das antike Buchwesen* (Berlin 1882) 124.

appeared at the end of increments of the complete work which Birt believed must have corresponded to the ends of individual *volumina*. Otherwise (he asserted) it made no sense for a subscription to be placed anywhere but at the end of the work and their appearance in the middle of a codex could only be accounted for by the scribe's copying the subscription at the end of the roll he was transcribing. In this view the practice of subscribing must have arisen while the roll-form book was still prevalent. But there is no reason to assume that the end of the roll was the only logical place for the subscription. Other criteria, such as the increment of the work done in a session, might as easily account for the location of the subscription. (The displacement of subscriptions in the course of recopying might also be misleading. The Sabinus subscription in Montpellier 212 (A) of Persius is a case in point.)

More recently Karl Büchner expressed the opinion that there were already literary subscriptions in the time of Fronto.[13] One of Fronto's letters reads:

> Quid tale M. Porcio aut Quinto Ennio, C. Graccho aut Titio poetae, quid Scipioni aut Numidico, quid M. Tullio tale usu venit? Quorum libri pretiosiores habentur et summan gloriam retinent, si sunt Lampadionis aut Staberii, Plautii aut D. Aurelii Autriconis aut Aelii manu scripta exempla aut a Tirone emendata aut a Domitio Balbo descripta aut ab Attico aut Nepote. Mea oratio exstabit M. Caesaris manu scripta.
>
> (*Ad M. Caes.* I. 7. 4.)

In this text Büchner assumed that there were tags of subscriptions to be found in *a Tirone emendata, Aelii manu scripta* and *a Domitio Balbo descripta*. That there were respected editions in existence throughout the empire can hardly be disputed. By then there were countless well-established libraries both public and private. And many books must have been inscribed with the names of illustrious previous owners and of scholars who had attended the preparation of the text. *Emendata* does suggest a term often seen in the subscriptions, but on the whole

---

[13] K. Büchner, "Ueberlieferungsgeschichte der lateinischen Literatur des Altertums" in H. Hunger et al, *Geschichte der Textüberlieferung der antiken und mittelalterlichen Literatur*, Bd. I (Zürich 1961) 355.

his wording seems a spontaneous use of common vocabulary, and merely proleptic of the more specialized terminology later in use.[14]

It is not the terminology of Statilius' subscriptions, nor even their location in context, but rather their form that is the key to their origin. A brief reconsideration of what a *subscriptio* actually was will, I believe, make it clear that Statilius did not employ the device out of mere whim. For *subscriptio* at a different level of meaning had several functions in Roman law.[15] The fact that it was primarily a legal formula places Statilius' Cicero edition and the later "subscribed" editions into some sort of relationship, however loose, with the field of law. It is this primarily which I believe permits us to look upon the literary subscriptions as something more than the sum of the literal information that they convey.

The *subscriptio* in the strict sense was a response to the text of a document which required an official answer.[16] With it the magistrate responded to a petition (*libellus*) submitted to him by a private citizen. This process underwent a special evolution in the imperial rescript. Appended to the text of the rescript was the formula of yet another subscription.[17] It is this formula to which I believe the "literary subscription" is related.

By the 2nd century the subscription had come to be employed as a mark of authentication.[18] On some rescripts preserved to us in inscriptions can be seen the words (RE)SCRIPSI. RECOGN(OVI).[19] The form of the verbs is important, as well as the absence of an expressed subject.

The second member of the formula, RECOGNOVI, must have been entered, as Wilcken observed,[20] by a staff member of the office *a libellis*. This term must have been his affidavit confirming the completion of the next step in handling the text, for the nature of the *libellus* rendered it necessary to reproduce it in true copies. Since the rescript was entered onto the petition as submitted, the original document, or at least a copy of it, was probably retained on file. Other copies must have been prepared for distribution to the petitioner(s) and any other qualified recipients. A complex procedure requiring several copies —

---

[14] Cf. Zetzel (above, n. 5) 241 ff.

[15] U. Wilcken, "Zu den Kaiserreskripten," *Hermes* 55 (1920) 1-42.

[16] P. Willems, *Le droit public romain* (7.ed. Louvain 1910) 436.

[17] P. Krüger, *Geschichte der Quellen und Litteratur des römischen Rechts* (Leipzig 1888) 96.

[18] B. G. A. Kübler, *R-E* IVA, col. 497; Wilcken (above, n. 15) p. 7, n. 3.

[19] Krüger, *ibid.*

[20] Wilcken (above, n. 15) p.7, n.3.

the forerunner of the multiple carbons of modern beaurocracy — implies, in the absence of carbons, a sophisticated and effective method of accurate correcting.

I submit that it is to this method that Statilius referred when he entered his first subscription in his Cicero edition. If we examine his wording,

> EMENDAVI AD TIRONEM ET LAECANIANUM,

we will note first of all that he omitted his own name. If he had not returned later to his task, we should never have known who had done the correcting. But that is the correct formula of an authenticating subscription. It is analogous to RECOGNOVI. He had adjusted his terminology to that commonly employed for correcting a literary text, such as we saw in Fronto's letter. When Statilius completed his second perusal of the Cicero text, he noted his oversight and reformulated his subscription:

> STATILIUS MAXIMUS RURSUS EMENDAVI AD
> TIRONEM ET LAECANIANUM ET DOMITIUM
> ET ALIOS VETERES III.[21]

The phrase *Ad Tironem,* etc., identifies the manuscripts which Statilius regarded as authoritative, or, in a sense, as analogous to the original *libellus* in the legal context. He undertook the task a second time when he turned up more manuscripts which shared the authority of his first two. The later subscriptions testify strongly to the essential role of the authoritative source. It is an occasion for apology when this condition of process cannot be met. The *sine antigrapho* of Sabinus and the *sine exemplario* of Eutropius seem to reveal that both were aware that an important aspect of Statilius' technique was being omitted.

Of course we cannot vouch for Statilius' expertise (nor that of any other subscriber). That he used six manuscripts for his edition does not mean that he used them well nor that he was necessarily able to determine which were actually good authorities. The words *Tiro* and *veteres* reveal his chief criteria: the age of his manuscripts and their association with known scholars of the past. This would be characteristic of an "archaist" grammarian of that period. Short of the knowledge and expertise of modern scholarship, however, these criteria at least had the virtue of drawing together that which was then regarded as the best of the tradition. And this was, after all, quite in the spirit of the

---

[21] Zetzel's reconstruction (*art. cit.* above, n.5 p. 230).

editing of legal texts: culling and preserving the best. The Codes and Digests were formed in this manner. Though Cicero's text was presumably not trimmed in any way, there is at least some indication that Statilius attempted to create a text based upon old manuscripts, ones that would be considered superior to the average.

I take the legal formula RECOGNOVI to have designated a mechanical function. Correcting a legal document against its original could not have allowed for any play of erudition or imagination. It was simply a matter of making sure that one copy was exactly like the other. Statilius' subscription betrays an attitude of slavish adherence to his "authoritative texts," and consequently a radical departure from the use of erudition as a tool for correcting his texts. For the latter method there is abundant evidence in the pages of the *Attic Nights*.[22] From his observation of correcting techniques in the government offices, Statilius might have moved from Proban scholarship to mechanical proofing, a step that would have made him as reverent before the ancient texts as was Probus, but without the scholar's propensity to quarrel with and second-guess his author. Pasquali has remarked that the era of the subscriptions did not represent a high point for philology which, he says, cannot flourish unless the culture of which it is a part flourishes also.[23] The activities of the gentlemen and schoolmasters who made our subscriptions were, he says, more like those of a *correttore di tipografia* or a *casa editrice* than that of a philologist-editor. Statilius' method required no philology, only patience and motivation. The drudgery of book-copying was supported by a precise but mindless system of proofing.

Within this context Pasquali says that the editing to which the subscriptions testify included the accurate transcription of texts "... dal papiro sulla pergamena, in forma non più di rotolo ma di codice."[24] The subscriptions themselves never record or even hint at this aspect of the editing. *Emendare, distinguere, legere,* and the other terms used are neutral with regard to book format. The only surmise we can make rests upon the fact that subscriptions were employed at all. The mere fact that distinguished men were involving themselves with the humble task of book correcting betrays at least a strong possibility that there was something special and unique about these books. A freshly copied, corrected and punctuated roll-form book would not have caught the attention in the way that a conspicuous change of format would have. Only something thus visible and charged with meaning for their

---

[22] *E. g. NA* 10.26.1 and 1.15.18.

[23] Pasquali (above, n.1) 366.

[24] *Ibid.*

culture would have justified the participation of the highly stationed gentlemen of the Roman state.

The association of the subscriptions to transcription from roll to codex must remain conjectural. But the strength of this conjecture is great enough to build upon, if not too heavily. It was during the third century that the literature of law was passing through the bottleneck of editorial selection and transcription.[25] The celebrated collection of constitutions made by Gregorius and Hermogenianus appeared in codices during the last decade of that century. The codices in the imperial library to which Bishop Theona referred in his advice to Lucianus were most likely legal in nature, if, indeed, the document preserved by Luc d'Achery dates from the reign of Diocletian.[26] At any rate, Statilius could easily have been involved in his editing project about the time of the first transcriptions of legal texts. Cicero's forensic works, together with his *De re publica* and *De legibus* seem to belong to law as well as to *belles lettres*. Viewed in this way, Statilius' edition of Cicero can be seen as a legitimate part of the change-over from rolls to codices in law and as the pioneer in preserving the classical authors in codices.[27]

finis

Rockford College
Rockford, Illinois

---

[25] F. Wieacker, *Textstufen klassischer Juristen* (Abh. d. Akad. d. Wiss. in Göttingen. Phil.-hist. Kl., 3. Folge, Nr. 45: 1960) 93-95.

[26] Birt (above, n. 12), p. 113, n. 2; Eric de Grolier, *Histoire du livre* (Paris 1954) 25-6.

[27] C. H. Roberts, "The Codex," *Proceedings of the British Academy* 40 (1954) esp. 196, 203-04.

CICERO'S *PRO SESTIO* IN LONDON, BRITISH LIBRARY, MS HARLEY 4927

TADEUSZ MASLOWSKI

In the course of examining manuscripts for a new Teubner edition of Cicero's *Pro Sestio*,[1] I was struck by the poor state of our knowledge of one of the primary manuscripts for this oration, London, British Library, MS Harley 4927 (H), s. xii[2]. H has already been collated twice and it is a pity that the progression, if this is the word to use, has been from bad to worse. Peterson, the first editor to use H, may to some extent be excused his sparse entries in the critical apparatus, as he was intentionally observing the conventions of the OCT series, but it is considerably more difficult to forgive him his fascination with the *recentiores*, manuscripts which on his own showing[2] derive their text from H, and the attributions he makes to them, the credit for which rightfully belongs to their identified parent instead.[3] Cousin, the Budé editor of the *Pro Sestio*[4] and the second collator of H, presents an altogether different problem. His attempt at a full collation of H, apparently intended to fill the gap left by Peterson, is a giant step backward. Even a perfunctory glance at the apparatus reveals Cousin's utter confusion. The attributions to H are mostly erroneous,[5] the indications

---

[1] M.T. Ciceronis *Scripta quae manserunt omnia* 22, *Pro Sestio*, ed. T. Maslowski (Teubner). Forthcoming.

[2] M.T. Ciceronis *Orationes: Cum sen. gr. egit, ... Pro Sestio*, al., ed. G. Peterson (Oxford 1911) x-xii.

[3] For instance, in all the following entries and many more, the ascriptions to k,s,w or an editor are misleading: 24 *cum hominibus*] ante *cum* add. Halm *sic*, Lamb. in mag. *ita*, although *ita* is in H; 40 *non illius* P rell. praeter k in quo est: *non movit illius* ut man. rec. in P, although k's reading is from H; 43 *quis reliqua praestaret* Gulielmius : *quis reliqua irae staret* P rell. (*quis reliquiarum restaret* in P man. rec.) : *quid reliqui restaret* k, but k's variant is from H; 110 *pro vino etiam saepe* PBG : *etiam pro vino saepe* ks : *etiam saepe pro vino* w, for *etiam pro vino saepe* H; 116 *psaltria* k : *psalteria* rell., for *psaltria* H; 117 *infando*] *nefando* ks, for *nefando* H; 143 *dicatur*] *dicitur* k, for *dicitur* H.

[4] Cicéron, *Discours* 14: *Pour Sestius, Contre Vatinius*, ed. and tr. J. Cousin (Paris 1965).

[5] To illustrate this, I quote his notes at *Sest.* 140 on p.218. Cousin records: *iniqui* PG : *at si quos iniqui* H, where H's version should in fact be described as follows: *ac ne quis ... egregium* PG : om. H | *iniqui* PG : *et si quos eorum aut iniqui* H; *procella* PG : *quadam procella* H, for *quaedam procella* H; *ceteri vero* om. H (correct); *aut repentina vi perculsi* PG : *aut aliqua repentina vis perculit* H | *ac tempestate* PG : *aut aliqua tempestate* H, where the two entries ought to have been telescoped and read: *aut repentina vi perculsi ac tempestate populari* PG : *aut aliqua repentina vis ac tempestas perculit popularis* H; *ii* PG : *hi* H (correct);

of omissions followed by quotations from the omitted text are perplexing,[6] and the unexpected stretches of silence are misleading.[7]

This, however, is not the place to embark on a detailed discussion of the merits and demerits of either Peterson's or Cousin's apparatus. My concern is of a different order. The fact that we do not have an adequate collation of a manuscript which is recognized to be an authoritative witness to the text must have far reaching consequences. My study has indeed convinced me that our current knowledge of H does not allow us to assess the impact this witness had on two crucial areas of the critical evaluation of the *Pro Sestio,* namely its contributions to the text of the oration and its influence on the conjectural speculations by textual scholars.

Before I proceed to state the case of H in detail, two points must be briefly discussed: 1) H as a primary witness in the tradition of the *Pro Sestio* and 2) the influence of H on the later tradition of the oration.

The first point concerns the question of H's independence, and it must be stated at the outset that to claim independence for Harley 4927

---

neglexerunt PG : *neclexerunt* H, for *neglexerunt* GH : *neclexerunt* P; *omnes* P²GH : *omne* P¹ (correct); the final entry, ignored by Cousin, ought to have been *dependerunt* PG : *deprehenderunt* H. Thus in one paragraph alone, Cousin neglects to report H's omission of a major portion of the text and one variant, and out of the eight following attributions, five are misleading and only three correct.

[6] To quote a few examples, *Sest.* 26 the seven lines of text, *cum incredibilis ... universus ordo,* are condensed in H to read *senatus et universus ordo flens consulatus mei causa.* Cousin's entry reads *cum ... tempore* om. H | *repraesentabat* PH: -*bant* G, although *repraesentabat* clearly cannot be in H; 36 Cousin puts on record *nam ...* 38 *susceperant* om. H and then two entries further down *expedita* PH : *expedita esset* G; 55 the apparatus reads *illo anno* add. H ante *fuerunt* | *quae ...* 65 *exturbari* om. H. The truth is H does not add anything before *fuerunt* but omits 55 *legum ...* 65 *exturbari,* and then in the following paragraph, 66, instead of *illo anno fuerint* reads *illo anno fuerunt;* 75 the entries *tandem ... concilio* om. H | *concilio* P¹H : *concilii* P²GH make no sense at all and ought to be changed to *tandem* om. H | *concilio* P¹ : *concilii* P²GH; 99 Cousin is not aware of *etenim ... dignitatis* om. H and quotes *cum tutores* PGH : *cum auctores* ed. Ascensiana 1531; 102 Cousin enters *est labor ...* 105 *commonebatur* (for *commovebatur*) om. H and then, still at 102, writes *sed te* P²GH : *et te* P¹; 110 the apparatus reads *deinde ... anagnostae* om. H as well as *dedidit* PH : *dedit* G;111 Cousin indicates *te sororis ... nescio* om. H, which is correct, but subsequently claims *utri* H : *ut ei* PG; 112 one finds *illuc ...* 114 *iudicet* om. H as well as, still at 112, *valetudinis* edd. : *valitudinis* PGH; 118 *nam ...* 119 (for 118) *actor* om. H and immediately after, *concentione* PH : *contentione* G.

[7] To illustrate this, in the following examples - and numerous others could be quoted - Cousin forgets H entirely and leaves the reader guessing as to whether the text exists in H or not: *Sest.* 4 *aut acrius* P (also H) : *aut carius* G; 5 *pertineat* P (also H) : *pertinet* G; 5 *esse videatur* P (also H) : *videatur esse* G; 6 *factus* P² (also H) : *tactum* P¹ : *statutus* G; 7 *at* P²G (also H) : *ad* P¹; 26 *veste* P² (also H) : *vestem* P¹G; lll *tu meo* P² (also H) : *tuo meo* P¹G ; 116 *ludius* P (also H) : *ludos* G; 116 *actor* P (also H) : *auctor* G; 124 *consensio* P¹G (also H) : *consessio* P².

poses a vexing problem.[8] The *Pro Sestio* is one of the nine post-exile orations of Cicero (*Red. Sen., Red. Quir., Dom., Har. Resp., Sest., Vat., Cael., Prov. Cons., Balb.*, headed by the ps.-Ciceronian *Pridie* oration) which derive from a common archetype written in majuscules in late antiquity. There are two recognized independent lines of transmission from this ancient manuscript: one consisting of Paris, B.N., MS lat. 7794 (P), s. ix$^{med.}$, the most authoritative witness of all extant manuscripts, and the other, known from the lost y manuscript as the y branch, consisting of Brussels, Bibl. Royale, MS lat. 5345 (G), s. xi[1], and its sister copy Berlin, Deutsche Staatsbibl., MS lat. fol. 252 (E), s. xii[1]. Unfortunately E, owing to physical damage, lost the leaves containing the *Pro Sestio,* and consequently the y branch for this oration is represented by G alone. It is in the context of these two branches of the tradition that the authenticity of H's testimony is considered. Under normal circumstances the emergence of the third branch of a tradition has a tremendous impact on textual considerations, as the principle of two against one becomes operative and the elimination of errors and interpolations in the recovery of the paradosis, a mechanical operation. On purely textual and historical grounds, in line with other most recent editors I have recognized H's independence, but the creation of this third branch in the manuscript tradition of Cicero's post-exile orations does not make the reconstruction of the lost archetype an automatic procedure. The problem lies in the character of H. Although this may vary from oration to oration, it is no exaggeration to say that in general Harley 4927 resembles a florilegium. For the *Pro Sestio* in particular, what the scribe offers us is not a record of the text he presumably saw in his exemplar, but a certain version of it. Roughly one third of this oration is completely gone and the lacerated text resulting from the omissions has been more or less intelligently altered to create a readable whole. *Sest.* 140, the paragraph for which the relevant part of the apparatus is quoted above in n.5 and the actual text can be deduced from the PG variants, may serve to illustrate the scribe's editorial method:

> [ac ne quis ... civem egregium] <et si quos eorum
> aut> iniqui iudicii <quaedam> procella pervortit
> [ceteri vero] aut aliqua repentina vis ac tempestas
> perculit popularis, per populum tamen ipsum recreati

---

[8] For conclusions stated in this paragraph and full bibliography see M.T. Ciceronis *Scripta quae manserunt omnia* 21: *Orationes post reditum,* ed. T. Maslowski (Teubner 1982), v-xxix; T. Maslowski, "Some Remarks on London, British Library, MS Harley 4927", *RhM* 125 (1982) 141-161.

sunt atque revocati, aut omnino involnerati inviolatique vixerunt.

This redaction is but a faint reflection of the genuine text, to say nothing of the distortion of the author's arguments:

> ac ne quis ... atque hunc (sc. L.Opimium) tamen flagrantem invidia propter interitum C. Gracchi semper ipse populus Romanus periculo liberavit; alia quaedam civem egregium iniqui iudicii procella pervortit. ceteri vero aut repentina vi perculsi ac tempestate populari per populum tamen ipsum recreati sunt atque revocati, aut omnino involnerati inviolatique vixerunt.

A further complicating factor in the assessment of the independence of this branch of the tradition is the presence of contamination in H. Contamination in a twelfth-century witness is something of a fact of life, and in H in other orations it has been recognized by A. Klotz, Wuilleumier, Tupet and myself.[9] However, looking at Cousin's stemma one gets the impression that the scribe suddenly reformed.[10] Is Cousin justified? To answer this question, I call attention first to the following class of PH errors which, I believe, reveal H's relation to P: *Sest.* 6 *ut utrique eorum* G : *utrique eorum* P^1 : *utrique eorum ut (ut* sscr. P^2) P^2H or 17 *illa rei p.* (·*R·P*· P) P^1G : *in illa re p.* (·*R·P*· P) P^2H. P^2 here stands for the second hand in P, a corrector practically contemporary with the original scribe (P^1). Normally the P^2H errors, when supported by G (and in other orations by E), tell us nothing of H's relation to P because P^2, as Cousin also recognizes[11] had access to the lost y (or a similar manuscript) of the second branch and H could also have taken them from that source (see below). However, in the examples quoted above, the P^2 lections represent conjecture, since y, to judge from the testimony of G, had the correct reading. Such isolated P^2H agreements in error suggest that H was influenced by the corrected

---

[9] M.T. Ciceronis *Scripta quae manserunt omnia* 7: *Orationes Cum sen. gr. egit, Cum pop. gr. egit,* al., ed. A. Klotz (Leipzig 1919), xx-xxi ; Cicéron, *Discours* 13: *Au sénat, Au peuple, Sur sa maison,* ed. and tr. P. Wullleumier (Paris 1952) 30; Cicéron, *Discours* 13.2: *Sur la réponse des haruspices,* ed. and tr. P. Wuilleumier and A.-M. Tupet (Paris 1966) 24; Cicero, *Scripta* 21, ed. Maslowski, xxvi.

[10] Cicéron, *Discours* 14, ed. and tr. Cousin, 98; cf. also Cicéron, *Discours* 15: *Pour Caelius, Sur les provinces consulaires, Pour Balbus,* ed. and tr. J. Cousin (Paris 1962) 64 (the stemma).

[11] Cicéron, *Discours* 14, ed. and tr. Cousin, 98 (the stemma); Cicéron, *Discours* 15, ed. and tr. Cousin, 64.

exemplar of P. Another class of conjunctive errors common in the *Pro Sestio* is of the yGH type: *Sest.*7 *filiam L. Scipionis* P : *filiam C. Scipionis* GH : *L. Scipionis filiam* Schol. Bob; 12 *neque umquam* P : *nequaquam* GH; 71 *iudices* P : *iudex* GH; 80 *temere* P : *tempore* GH; 116 *ipse ille* Schol. Bob. P : *ille ipse* GH. This class of errors bespeaks a horizontal flow from, say, the lost y.

Now a contamination by two other streams of a tradition in a manuscript which itself represents an independent textual source seems an unnecessarily elaborate supposition. Still, even if we organize our evidence on different lines of argument, for instance, as an indication that the archetype had variants to begin with, or, better yet, that it suffered correction at the time the split in the tradition had occurred (a case of the "fluid archetype"),[12] the capricious behavior of H does not make for a straightforward application of the three-branch stemma.

These observations on the character of H - the presence of interpolation, contamination and abridgement - are of the first importance in any treatment of H's contributions to the text. On the whole, whenever the PG text is defensible, the evidence of H, unless it is a question of simple correction, must carry little weight with us, and though it may have commended itself to an editor or a textual critic, it is, I think, of no interest other than antiquarian. A number of such H readings, usually known to a scholar from the late manuscripts, are mentioned in the second part of this study. On the other hand, even where PG are clearly in error and H offers a viable alternative, this alternative, in view of H's character, must always be treated with the utmost suspicion. But this is not to suggest that H is of no textual value at all.

The second point to be made is on the influence Harley 4927 exerted on the later history of the text of the *Pro Sestio* (and other post-exile orations). The following annotations in Cousin's apparatus lead me to comment on this aspect of H: *Sest.*85 *a* M : om. PG, despite 84 *nondum erat* ... 85 *mentio nulla* om. H; 93 *profundat* M : *profundant* PG^2 : *profundunt* G^1, despite 93 *cum sciat* ... 95 *Milonem* om. H (Cousin's *cum sciat* ... 95 *neque hic tamen* om. H is incorrect); 112 *abhorreret* M : *abhorret* G : *aborret* P, desipte 112 *illuc revortor* ... 114 *dignissimos iudicet* om. H; 115 *consessus* M : *consensus* PG and 115 *sibilum* M : *sibtum* P^1 : *sibi tum* P^{2}G, despite 115 *comitiorum* ... *necesse est* om. H.

---

[12] Cf. A. Dain, *Éditions des textes classiques. Théories et méthodes* (Association Guillaume Budé, Congrès de Nîmes 1932) 79-80; J. Irigoin, "Stemmas bifides et états de manuscrits", *RPh* 28 (1954) 211-217; L.D. Reynolds, *The Medieval Tradition of Seneca's Letters* (Oxford 1965) 56.

In all of these entries, it is not significant that M allegedly offers the correct reading against the errors of P and G or PG. The corruption in each case is trifling and a fairly intellegent scribe could easily have removed it. What is significant about those reports is that M supposedly has text in those places at all, although H does not (hence my indication of H's omissions). Since M (Halm's S,[13] Peterson's s), Munich, Bayerische Staatsbibl., MS lat. 15734, s. xv, is a *recentior* of Italian origin,[14] this, if true, would make it a worthwhile manuscript.[15]

As Peterson already partially realized,[16] the history of the later manuscripts and the early editions of Cicero's post-exile orations is closely related to that of Harley 4927. Indeed the H branch of the tradition developed at the expense of the other two, P and yG(E), and accounts for the majority of the *recentiores*.[17] Although Harley 4927 is of French origin, written on the Loire, perhaps even at Tours, its text was removed in the mid-fourteenth century to Italy by Petrarch and here it began its spectacular career. The pure H text of the *Pro Sestio* is, as pointed out above, easy to recognize because of the large number of omissions and the peculiar errors or rather wholesale alterations of the original that followed as a result. However, between 1417 and 1421[18] - the years of the new discoveries of classical texts by Italian scholars - a manuscript of the y branch was brought to Italy and began to exert its influence on the H strain of text, producing such hybrids as the Escorial MSS, R.I.12, R.I.15, T.II.4, T.III.22 (V.III.23 does not carry the *Pro Sestio*) and many others, all of Italian origin and dated fifteenth century. MS lat. 15734 quoted by Cousin is one of those hybrid manuscripts and the specific reason why it cannot diverge from

---

[13] M.T. Ciceronis *Opera quae manserunt omnia* 2.2, ed. I.C. Orelli, I.G. Baiter, C. Halm (Zurich 1856).

[14] See C. Halm, F. Heinz, G. Meyer, G. Thomas, *Catalogus codicum manuscriptorum* 4.3 (Munich 1878).

[15] To be fair, Cousin does not claim to have seen MS lat. 15734. Since he was unable to obtain a microfilm of the manuscript, he professes to have availed himself of Halm's collation (see Cicéron, Discours 14, ed. Cousin, 99). But this makes matters even worse, as the readings of M quoted by Cousin are not to be found in Halm's apparatus.

[16] Cicero, *Orationes,* ed. Peterson, x-xii. Peterson, however, did not know how H related to P and G(E) and in general had a confused notion of the stemmatic interrelationship of the members of the tradition. He followed the older view that all manuscripts have somehow been derived from P.

[17] See Maslowski (above, n. 8) and the bibliography there.

[18] That this happened during this period follows from de la Mare's dating of MS Laur.48.25. See A.C. de la Mare, "Humanistic Script: The First Ten Years" in *Das Verhältniss der Humanisten zum Buch,* ed. R. Krafft and D. Wuttke. Deutsche Forschungsgemeinschaft, Kommission für Humanismusforschung. Mitteilung iv (Boppard 1977) 89-110. I am grateful to R.H. Rouse for calling my attention to this study.

H in any significant way in the places listed above (they all derive from the second half of the oration) is this: in the *Pro Sestio* the contamination by the y branch extends only as far as § *74*, which, among other things, means that the omissions peculiar to H have been filled in only up to this paragraph. Following § *74* in some manuscripts, as for example is the case with Escorial, MS R.I.12, there is a major omission extending from 74 *populi quoque Romani* to 80 *primumque resipisset,* while in others, as for instance in MS lat. 15734, the scribes simply continue the H text. But this peculiarity aside, in all these manuscripts the text, whether immediately after § *74* or beginning with §*80,* is thereafter to the end of the oration strictly that of H.

How the merger of the two branches was originally carried out can be perceived from Florence, Bibl. Med. Laur., MS Laur. 48.25, the key manuscript to this whole group. In Laur.48.25 the original text, U^1, is that of H and on the basis of its contents[19] can be dated to the first quarter of the fifteenth century. Later this manuscript was corrected and annotated from another copy representing the y stream of the tradition. The corrections or supplements of the missing text, U^2, are introduced either directly into the text after erasure of U^1 or as marginalia and interlinear additions.[20] On fol. 99^v in the right hand margin at *Sest.*77, U^2 quotes from his y manuscript for the last time in this oration: (74) *Sed post eum ... censere ut ad senatum (senatus* PG) (80) *non se referri iussit.* The words *non se referri iussit,* which belong to *Sest.*80, are underlined and followed by a note: "quere (sc. the underlined words) in sequenti columnella ubi est hoc signum +". The change of PG's *senatus* to *senatum* is deliberate, facilitating the jump over the intervening U^1 (=H) text. The *nota* offers an explanation for the omission of *Sest.* 74-80 which distinguishes some manuscripts in what we may call the H-y group.[21] De la Mare in her study of the early

---

[19] In 1417 Poggio brought back from his travels in France and Germany eight previously unknown speeches of Cicero: the *Pro Caecina, Pro Roscio Comoedo, De Lege Agraria* i-iii, *Pro Rabirio Perduellionis Reo, In Pisonem, Pro Rabirio Postumo* (see R. Sabbadini, *Le scoperte dei codici Latini e Greci ne secoli XIV e XV* i [Florence 1967] 81-82; A.C. Clark, *Inventa Italorum* in *Anecdota Oxoniensia* [Oxford 1909] Classical Series pt. 11. Poggio's autograph copy of the eight Cicero speeches, Vat. Lat. 11458, has been recently identified by A. Campana. See *Codices Vaticani Latini* 7, ed. J. Ruysschaert, [Vatican 1959]). Four of these, *Caecin., Rab. Post., Rab. Perd.* and *Rosc. Com.* appear in Laur.48.25 thus setting for its completion a terminus post.

[20] That U^2 is derived from a y manuscript can be demonstrated by numerous errors which it shares with G: *Sest.*8 *vere* PHU^1 : *vero* GU^2; 11 *adventu* P : om. GU^2 (11 *atque ut illius temporis ...* 12 *defendissent Sestius* om. HU^1, suppl. U^2 in mg.); 28 *advocat* PHU^1 : *et advocat* GU^2, al.

[21] I should also point out that the presence of the y element in the H-y manuscripts varies from copy to copy. For instance, Escorial, R.I.12 is most heavily indebted to y and in fact appears to be an apograph of U. On the other hand MS lat. 15734 (M) is

humanistic script identifies the annotator of Laur. 48.25 as Bartolomeo di Piero Nerucci of San Gimignano, a Dante scholar, who worked for Mattia Lupi of San Gimignano (1380-1468),[22] and suggests that the annotations reflect the new finds of classical texts made by the Italian scholars in the years 1417-1421 as mentioned above.

Thus Italy now possessed two texts of the *Pro Sestio,* the fuller H-y and the pure H text, and these two strains of text passed into the earliest printed editions, the *ed. Romana* (1471) and *ed. Veneta* (1471) respectively, and then into the subsequent editions until all omissions, that is, those from *Sest.* 74 to the end, had been eliminated and the text further improved with the aid of the P branch of the tradition in *ed. Ascensiana* (1531). *Hervagiana* (1534) and *Naugeriana* (1534).[23] It was roughly in this way that the vulgate text of the oration finally emerged, a text which with minor alterations survived into the times of Orelli.[24]

---

influenced by y only to a slight degree. To illustrate this, M shares with H all the major omissions, filling in only a few minor gaps in the text, as at *Sest.* 8 *nihil dico ... sedare voluisse* M : om. H; 9 *cum exercitu* M : om. H; 9 *hominem perditum ... curavit* M : om. H; 9 *qui propter ... adoptavit* M : om. H; 13 et *aliquando ... veniam* M : om. H. Nor does M as a rule change the text of H.

[22] De la Mare (above, n. 18) 98-100.

[23] See M.T. Ciceronis *Pro Sestio oratio,* ed. I.C. Orelli (Heidelberg 1834³), iv-vii; C.F. Hermann, "Disputatio de loco Ciceronis *pro Sestio* c.xxxiii", *Index Scholarum* (Göttingen 1843) 1-13; Cicero, *Orationes,* ed. Peterson, x-xii.

For a description of these and other early editions of Cicero see I.C. Orelli and I.G. Baiter, *Onomasticon Tullianum* 1 (Zurich 1836) 193 ff.

What P branch manuscripts were used in those editions still remains to be investigated. However, for the ed. Ascensiana of 1531 it was, according to the "Praefatio", a book from the abbey of St. Victor in Paris collated by the two *lecteurs royaux* for Greek in the Collége Royal (opened in 1530), Pierre Danès and Jacques Toussain. The most likely candidate that fits the description is B.N., MS lat. 14749, s.xv, but Orelli dismisses this possibility (cf. Orelli and Baiter, *Onomasticon,* 241-242).

For the ed. Hervagiana of 1534 a manuscript of Gabrielus Florentius Talentus, a senator of Milan, was used (cf. Orelli and Baiter, *Onomasticon,* 198-199).

The ed. Naugeriana of 1534 has a history of its own. Andreas Navagero (1483-1529) prepared, properly speaking, only the Aldine edition of 1519 (the text in this edition is that of the corrected Laur. 48.25 without the omission of *Sest.* 74-80). Later, however, he annotated a copy of this edition from an unknown manuscript, and this copy was subsequently used by Petrus Victorius (Piero Vettori, 1499-1585) for the second volume of the Juntine edition of 1534-1537 (cf. Orelli and Baiter, *Onomasticon,* 199-200).

[24] His first edition of the oration is to be found in M.T. Ciceronis *Opera omnia* 2.2, ed. I.C. Orelli (Zurich 1826). He subsequently edited the *Pro Sestio* separately in 1832 and 1833 (for the last edition see n.21). The most important editions published in the intervening period are: M.T. Ciceronis *Opera omnia quae exstant,* 4 vols., D. Lambinus (Paris 1565-1566); M.T. Ciceronis *Opera omnia quae exstant,* 4 vols. ed. J. Gruter (cum notis J. Gulielmii) (Hamburg 1618); M.T. Ciceronis *Opera omnia cum notis variorum,* 11 vols., ed. J.G. Graevius (Amsterdam 1684-1699); M.T. Ciceronis *Opera omnia ex rec. I. Gronovii,* 6 vols., ed. J.A. Ernesti (Leipzig 1737-1739); M.T. Ciceronis *Opera omnia deperditorumque librorum fragmenta,* 20 vols., ed. C.G. Schütz (Leipzig 1814-1823).

This very brief account of the later history of the text of Cicero's *Pro Sestio* teaches us an important lesson. For centuries the base text of the oration had been that of H. Whatever additions, alterations and improvements had been made, the underlying stratum remained the same, but buried ever deeper beneath the fresh layers that formed in the wake of the successive inflows from the y or P branches of the tradition. Considering this unique role of H in the history of the oration, one would think that at least the most recent editors would finally attempt to separate the H text from that of the other two branches of the tradition. Unfortunately this has not yet happened. We look in vain to Peterson's apparatus for assistance and are generally misled by Cousin's. It is no wonder, then, that the H element, so strongly entrenched in the traditional text, remains unrecognized here and there in our modern texts.

It is in the context of these remarks that I offer for consideration the following list of H readings. The selection highlights H's direct contributions to the text of the *Pro Sestio* which for reasons to be stated merit discussion or at least mention, as well as some of its lections which played a part in conjectural emendation now to be rejected outright in view of the stemma and our current knowledge of H. It will be seen throughout that the presence of Harley 4927 as an equal partner in the manuscript tradition of the oration both solves and creates textual problems. In either case, H as the element of uncertainty warrants a fresh look at the text.

The apparatus varies in its explicitness from entry to entry and is strictly contingent upon the point to be discussed.[25]

3   *atque ego sic statuo, iudices, a me in hac causa atque hoc extremo dicendi loco pietatis potius quam defensionis, querellae < quam > eloquentiae, doloris quam ingeni partis esse susceptas.*

a me post *dicendi* transp. H | *hoc extremo* P : *extremo* G : *exercitio* H | *loco pietatis* PG^2 : *locupletatis* G^1 : *locum pietatis* H | *querele* M : *querell*** P^1 : *querellam* P^2 : *querelam* (*quae-* G) GH | *quam* H : om. PG | *eloquentiae* P^{2}G : *-a* P^1 : *-am* H | *doloris* P^{1}G^{1}H : *dolores* P^{2}G^2 | *partis* edd. : *partes* P^{2}GH : *partim* P^1 | *esse* om. G

quam is one of the traditional readings that has always been in the text, and no editor has as yet pointed out that it derives from H. Considering that the text in H is completely revamped, it is probably an insertion by the scribe. Also, *querellae* (spelled *querele*), a simple improvement on H, appears (for the first time?) in M.

---

[25] Henceforward an edition that has been mentioned at least once will no longer be referred to in the notes.

4   *peto a vobis ut tantum orationi meae concedatis quantum et pio dolori et iustae iracundiae concedendum putetis; nam neque officio coniunctior dolor ullus esse potest quam hic meus ..., neque iracundia magis ulla ludanda est quam ...*

   ullus esse potest H : *ullius esse potest* P : *esse ullius potest**** G

Although Madvig[26] expressed surprise at Cicero's employment of *ullius* for *cuiusquam*, the substantival use of *ullus* in the oblique cases is in fact not against Cicero's usage: *Phil*.13,15 *non potest ullius auctoritate tantus senatus populique R. ardor exstingui* (cf. *Mur*.69 (*ullius* MSS : *nullius* Zumpt); *Planc*.64; *Phil*.11,1).[27] But even Stuerenburg, who dealt with the uses of *ullus* at great length and was the first to note its pronominal function in Cicero, objected to *ullius* in the passage before us on the ground that in what follows there is no genitive noun for counterbalance or correspondence: "propterea quod oppositio hominis hoc loco est nulla. Nihil certius lectione *ullus*: quam nonnulli codices praebent, optima etiam editio anni 1480".[28] Klotz's reply to this argument was to deduce the corresponding noun from *meus*.[29] The defense of PG's *ullius*, however, is difficult and two points in particular must be stressed to clarify the problem. One, already mentioned by Madvig, is that Cicero speaks here of sorrow in general and not of "anyone's sorrow", as is evident from the correspondence of *pio dolori et iustae iracundiae* to *dolor ullus* and *iracundia ulla*. Two, is Mueller's observation,[30] that the manuscripts frequently feature a superfluous *i*, as *Sest*.15 *cautorem* P²(?) : *cautiorem* P¹GH; 51 *fere* P²G : *fiere* P¹ : cum pluribus om. H. H's *ullus,* then, will stand.

9   *idem ... venit cum exercitu Capuam ...* ; *C. Mevulanum ... Capua praecipitem eiecit.*

   C. Mevulanum (-*vol*- G²) PG : *et inde Meaulanum* H

H's *et inde ... Capua*, which became the vulgate reading, is clearly spurious. The sentence as attested by PG is parallel to the following

---

[26] J.N. Madvig, *Opuscula¹* (=*Opuscula academica* [Copenhagen 1834]) 435.

[27] For bilbiography see J.P. Krebs (and J.H. Schmalz), *Antibarbarus der lateinischen Sprache* 2 (Basel 1905⁷), s.v. *ullus*. For general information on the use of *quisquam* and *ullus* see K.-S. (=R. Kühner and C. Stegmann, *Ausführliche Grammatik der lateinischen Sprache,* 2 pts. of the 2nd vol. [Hannover 1966]), 2.1, 637-642, esp. 639.

[28] M.T. Ciceronis *De officiis libri tres,* ed. R. Stuerenberg (Leipzig 1834) 200-201. The "nonnulli codices" mentioned by Stuerenburg are some *recentiores* derived from H. The "optima editio anni 1480" is a Venice edition of 1480, a repetition of the Venice edition of 1471. Hence in both cases *ullus*.

[29] M.T. Cicernois *Scripta quae manserunt omnia* 2.3, ed. R. Klotz (Leipzig 1871²) iv.

[30] M.T. Ciceronis *Scripta quae manserunt omnia* 2.3, ed. C.F.W. Mueller (Leipzig 1893) iv.

idemque C. Marcellum ... exterminandum ex illa urbe curavit. Furthermore, *inde* ("from there") in addition to *Capua* ("from Capua") is redundant, and either one or the other must go. It is interesting, then, to see that Bake[31] (who knew H from later manuscripts) opts for *et inde* and deletes *Capua*.

It should also be noted that Cousin's report "*inde Meaulanum* H" is incorrect. The reading of H is as indicated above, *et inde Meaulanum*.

ib.   *huic apud* (*aput* P) *me P. Sestio* PG : *huic P. Sestio apud me* H

P. Sestio was deleted by Manutius, Bake, Kimmig and others as a gloss on *huic*.[32] It was defended by Klotz[33] and Dietrich,[34] and printed by practically all editors (with the exception of Kayser and Eberhard),[35] and rightly so. This collocation of words is strictly rhetorical and *P. Sestio* is placed at the end for emphasis, just as *P. Sesti* three lines further down in *beneficium P. Sesti*. However, trifling as this controversy may be, what leads me to mention it is Cousin's apparatus where we read: *P. Sestio* om. H. To prevent any future speculation, H does preserve *P. Sestio*, albeit in its peculiar word order; H omits *P. Sesti* in *beneficium P. Sesti*.

13   *attulit* (*adt-* edd.) *ad tribunatum P. Sestius* H : *apstulit ad tribunatum P. Sestius* P : *ad tribunatum attulit P. Sestius* G

The credit for *adtulit* (*attulit* H) *ad tribunatum P. Sestius* goes to H, not to "edd.", as Cousin intimates. The later vulgate *ad tribunatum P. Sestius* (Orelli 1826), criticized by Bake,[36] shows the influence of the y branch on H, as evidenced by G.

14   The apparatus should read *perstringerem* (for Cousin's *praestringerem*) H : *prestringerem* P : *perstringere* G.

17   *sed fuit profecto quaedam illa rei publicae fortuna fatalis.*

   quaedam PG : om. H | *illa rei p.* (·R·P· P) P¹G : *in illa re p.* (·R·P· P) P²H

---

[31] J. Bake, *Scholica hypomnemata* 1 (Leiden 1837) 53.

[32] Bake, *Scholica* 1, 54; O. Kimmig, *De Sestianae Ciceronianae interpolationibus* (Freiburg 1882) 16.

[33] R. Klotz, *Emendationes Tullianae* (Leipzig 1832) 26-27.

[34] A. Dietrich, "Ciceros ausgewählte Reden erklärt von Karl Halm. IV Bändchen: die Rede für P. Sestius. Dritte vielfach verbesserte Auflage. Berlin, Weidmannsche Buchhandlung. 1862", *Neue Jahrb*. 87 (1863) 509.

[35] M.T. Ciceronis *Opera quae supersunt omnia* 5, ed. J.G. Baiter and C.L. Kayser. *Orationes* 3, ed. C.L. Kayser (Leipzig 1862); Ciceros *Rede für P. Sestius*, ed. H.A. Koch and A. Eberhard (Leipzig 1877).

[36] Bake, *Scholica* 1, 57.

Bake[37] took the omission of *quaedam* seriously: "Ut *in* interpolatum est, ita *quaedam* non esse Ciceronis affirmo. Mirifice languidam reddit sententiam: si augendi sensu accipiendum exspectabas post *fatalis*". But one might also argue: since *in* is arbitrary, therefore the omission of *quaedam* is also arbitrary. Of course neither argument will do. We must know the interrelationships of the manuscripts and their character, which Bake did not.

24   *et quod videbam quibuscum hominibus <in> interiore parte aedium viveret.*

   in interiore H : interiore P : interiori G | parte aedium edd. : parte naedium P¹ : parte nediu G : parte in aedium P² : edium parte H

These are the actual readings of the manuscripts. *in* before *interiore* is the contribution of H, not of "edd.", as Cousin reports. The vulgate text followed the word order of H.

There is a curious comment on this passage by van den Bruwaene:[38] "*interiore parte in aedium* P², ce P² devait être un rude connaisseur du latin car il n'a pas hésité à restituer une tournure rare mais spécifique (on en trouve une trace dans Kühner L.G. I p.425 Anm.2, pas assez poussé)". Since Kühner and Stegmann (2.1, 425) discuss in the place referred to the use of prepositional phrases as an alternative to the genitive partitive construction, I do not see what relevance this discussion might possibly have to P²'s correction. On the other hand, *interiore parte in aedium* could, I suppose, be viewed as a case of anastrophe of the "noun - preposition - attributive genitive" variety.[39] But this usage is confined to poetry, as Cic. *Div.* 1,106 *obitu a solis* (in poem), *Arat.*201 *parte ex Aquilonis*; Lucr.1,740 *principiis tamen in rerum.*

ib. *sed ita est, iudices: ut, si gladium parvo puero aut si imbecillo seni ac debili dederis, ipse impetu suo nemini noceat, sin ad nudum vel fortissimi viri corpus accesserit, possit acie ipsa et ferri viribus vulnerare, <ita>, cum hominibus enervatis atque exsanguibus consulatus tamquam gladius esset datus, qui per se pungere neminem umquam potuissent, ii summi imperi nomine armati <nuda> tam rem publicam contrucidarunt.*

   *ita*² H : om. PG | *armati <nuda> tam* Imelmann : *armati tam* P¹G : *armati* H : *arma* P²

---

[37] Bake, *Scholica* 1, 61.

[38] M. van den Bruwaene, (Review of Cousin's edition), *L'Antiquité classique* 34 (1965) 611.

[39] See K.-S. 2.1, 587.

Here the presence of H calls for a brief comment on three distinct issues:

1) Strangely enough, A. Klotz's *nutum* for *nudum* in his text, a typographical error, produced the following entry in Cousin's apparatus: *nudum* H : *nutum* PG. In truth, all three manuscripts read *nudum*.

2) Halm proposed *sic* to fill in PG's omission and dismissed *ita* which he knew as the vulgate reading. In Cicero the *ut* - *sic* comparisons are very frequent,[40] but *ut* - *ita* combinations are common in all periods of Latin.[41] There is really not much to go by in choosing between *sic* and *ita*,[42] and we may give H the benefit of the doubt. PG's hint at an ellipsis is hardly convincing in this long and carefully organized sentence, although the phenomenon is not unheard of (cf. *Off*.1,151; *N.D.*2,15; *Clu*.184).[43]

3) Imelmann's conjecture *armati* < *nuda*> *tam*[44] suits the context and imagery of the passage best. Other attempts at a solution include *armati* < *tan*> *tam* Maehly[45] : *armati* < *to*> *tam* Pluygers[46] *armati tum* Halm, Cousin, etc. The vulgate reading is *armati* alone, which won the commendation of Peterson. Hertz,[47] too, supported *armati* (not *armatam* as Peterson reports) on the assumption that *armati tam* originated from a correction in the archetype, *armatam* Although paleographically this makes perfect sense, the close parallelism of expression that characterizes the two *ut* - *ita* clauses calls for a qualification of *rem publicam* to match the corresponding *nudum ... corpus*. Also, we now know that the source of *armati rem p.* is H (ignored by both Peterson and Cousin) and that the scribe of this manuscript does not hesitate to remove textual difficulties.

34 *dilectus* H : *delectus* PG

dilectus is another traditional reading. Cousin thinks that H has *delectus* and attributes *dilectus* to Lambinus.

---

[40] See H. Merguet, *Lexikon zu den Reden des Ciceros* 4 (Jena 1877-1884) 495.

[41] See K.-S. 2.2, 449.

[42] A. Klotz in his edition opted for *sic*, "propterea quod Cicero longiore membro comparativo antecedente *sic* potius quam *ita* scripsisse videtur".

[43] See K.-S. 2.2, 550. For examples other than those in Cicero see W.A. Baehrens, *Beitraege zur lateinischen Syntax, Philologus,* Suppl. 12 (1912) 309-311.

[44] Imelmann, "Zur Sestiana", *Sokrates* 19 (1865), 791.

[45] J.A. Maehly, "Ciceros ausgewählte Reden. Erklärt von Karl Halm. IV. Bandchen, Die Rede für Publius Sestius (Leipzig 1853)", Neue Jahrb. 69 (1854) 42.

[46] W.G. Pluygers, "Lectiones Tullianae (*Oratio pro P. Sestio*)", *Mnemosyne* 9 (1860) 332.

[47] M. Hertz, "Zur Kritik von Ciceros Rede für den P. Sestius", *Neue Jahrb.*, Suppl. 13 (1884) 67.

35   *sed et voce et sententia comprobarentur.*

   et¹ PG : om. H

H's omission of the first *et*, unrecorded by the editors, made an impression on Bake[48] who thought it produced better sense. Cicero, however, clearly employs *et ... et* for emphasis.

38   *quaeque non modo ad singularem meam gloriam sed ad communem salutem omnium civium et prope gentium pertinerent.*

   singularem meam PG : *meam singularem* H | *gentium* PG : *gentium omnium* H

Bake[49] prefers the word order of H, believing that *singularis* ought to occupy the same place as *unius* at, for instance, *Pis.*3 *mea unius opera res publica salva est*. This appears to be true of Cicero's orations: *Red. Sen.*2 *vestro singulari studio*; *Phil.*11,13 *pro tua singulari sapientia*, al. But one wonders what analogy to such expressions as *Cael.*4,11 *singulari quadam humanitate*, *Sest.*13 *singularis illa integritas provincialis*, al.,[50] could do to the collocation in question. Furthermore H is not to be trusted here, as the addition of *omnium* after *gentium* shows the scribe's manipulation of the text.

Neither of these H readings has been noted by the editors, and Cousin incorrectly reports H's omission of *meam*.

39   *omnibus in contionibus illa furia clamabat se quae faceret contra salutem <meam> facere auctore Cn. Pompeio.*

   meam H : om. PG

All editors misread the manuscripts here, reporting the omission of *meam* by G alone. Of course H's *meam* is necessary here since otherwise the *salus* might be taken as that of Clodius.[51]

45   *unum enim mihi restabat illud quod forsitan non nemo vir fortis et acris animi magnique dixerit: 'restitisses, repugnasses, mortem pugnans oppetisses'.*

   enim (*-nim* in ras. P) PG : om. H : *autem* Peterson : *tamen* Keil[52]

---

[48] Bake, *Scholica* 1, 72.

[49] Bake, *Scholica* 1, 73.

[50] For more examples see Merguet, *Lexikon* 4, s.v. *singularis*.

[51] See K.-S. 2.1, 596.

[52] H. Keil, "Bemerkungen zu Cicero's Rede für Sestius", *Eos* (Würzburg) 1 (1864) 17.

This sentence belongs to a lengthy apologia in which Cicero discloses his motives for leaving Rome and going into voluntary exile. It was not cowardice that prompted his decision but his desire to save the State during a situation created by Clodius' actions and legislation as well as the treacherous conduct of the consuls Piso and Gabinius. In § 42 Cicero considers his options under the circumstances and asks: *haec cum viderem, quid agerem, iudices*? In what follows he rejects one of the options, the use of force, because of the disastrous consequences it would have had for the State and himself. In the passage quoted above, however, he returns to his original question and affirms, for rhetorical effect, that the use of force was indeed his only choice. There follows a description of the consequences of this step and Cicero's decision to leave Rome rather than endanger the State (49).

Enim in our passage must mean "indeed" or "in fact", as already suspected by Ernesti. This usage, I note, is common in Plautus.[53] *Enim* would also be intelligible here if it meant *autem*: what was I to do? (42) - Was I to resist and cause civil war or my destruction? (42-43) - And yet this was the only choice left for me ... etc. (45 ff.). Now the adversative force is not completely alien to *enim*, but the passages illustrative of this use of *enim* are hardly parallel to ours: *Caec.* 8 *ac si quis mihi hoc iudex recuperatorve dicat: 'potuisti enim* (="but") *leviore actione confligere'*; *Verr.* 2,1,15 *nam accusandi mihi tempus mea causa datum est ut possem oratione mea crimina causamque explicare; hoc si non utor, non tibi iniuriam facio sed de meo iure aliquid et commodo detraho. 'causam enim* (="but")*' inquit 'cognosci oportet'*.[54] Hence to secure an adversative transition one would have to resort to a more drastic step as Peterson and Keil have done, changing *enim* to *autem* and *tamen* respectively.

Some editors (Graevius, Schütz) eliminate *enim* entirely, and Paul[55] regards it as a dittography of *unum*. What has gone unnoticed by editors hitherto is that H is the oldest manuscript in which *enim* is omitted (Cousin's report that H has *enim* is incorrect). This, I believe, is of some significance. The scribe of H must have seen *enim* in his exemplar, but unable to perceive its meaning removed it.[56] In any case, *enim*

---

[53] See K.-S. 2.2, 120.

[54] For the whole question see F. Hand, *Tursellinus* 2 (Leipzig 1832) 387-396.

[55] W. Paul, "Zu Ciceros Sestiana", *Sokrates* 28 *(1874) 318.*

[56] Another possibility is that he found an unfamiliar abbreviation there, such as the insular abbreviation for *autem* which the copyists frequenlty confused with *enim*. But there are few, if any, such confusions either in P, despite Klotz's insistence to the contrary (cf. Cicero, *Scripta* 7, ed. A. Klotz, vii-x and xxxvi-xxxviii) or in H (cf. Cicero, *Opera* 21, ed. Maslowski, xv).

seems functional and defendable, and to Gardner, the editor of the oration in the Loeb series,[57] goes the credit for its reinstatement.

ib. *penates patriique* (*patrique* Schol.) *dii* (*dei* PG) Schol. PG : *penates dii patrique* H

Bake[58] stated his preference for the word order of H, but PG receive support from the Scholiasta Bobiensis. Cousin does not report H's lection, and only mentions that H has *dei,* which is not the case. Elsewhere, *Sull.*86 and *Har. Resp.*37, Cicero has *di patrii ac penates* and *patrii penatesque di* respectively. In all three places the reference seems to be to "the national ancestral gods of Rome (*di patrii*) and the private household gods of Roman families collectively (*di penates*)".[59]

ib. *multi ex multis locis.*

ex multis PG : *mutlis ex* H

Bake[60] sides with H overlooked by Cousin. H's word order is possible of course, but not necessary.[61] The manuscript authority in such a case counts for everything.

47 *a me tum* PG : *tum a me* H | *definita mors* PG : *mors definita* H

tum a me and *mors definita* are two readings of H (not reported by Cousin) that again played some part in the textual criticism of the oration.[62]

50 *quod si immortale retinetur.*

quod si H : *quid si* PG

quod si is another example of a traditional reading the credit for which goes to H. Cousin's *quod si* edd. : *quid si* PGH is incorrect.

---

[57] Cicero, *The Speeches Pro Sestio and In Vatinium,* ed. and tr. R. Gardner (London-Cambridge, Mass. 1958).

[58] Bake, *Scholica* 1, 78.

[59] See M.T. Ciceronis *De domo sua oratio,* ed. R.G. Nisbet (Oxford 1939) 193-194 (ad *Dom.*144). Cf. Ciceros *Rede für Publius Sestius,* ed. K. Halm (revised by G. Laubmann) (Berlin 1886⁶ 46 (ad *Sest.*45); D.R. Shackleton Bailey, "On Cicero's Speeches", *HSCP* (1979) 266 (ad *Dom.*144).

[60] Bake, *Scholica* 1, 78.

[61] Cf. K.-S. 2.1, 587; Merguet, *Lexikon* 2, s.v. *ex*.

[62] They are supported by Bake, *Scholica* 1, 80.

53   *cum ... furori hominis, sceleri, perfidiae, telis minisque cessissem.*

   minisque PG : *inuiisque* H : *iniuriisque* s

Bake[63] insists on *iniuriisque* of the *recentiores*, but H's error *inuiisque* (ignored by Cousin) brings to light the origin of this variant.

54   *hac tanta perturbatione civitatis ne noctem quidem consules inter meum <casum> et suam praedam interesse passi sunt.*

   casum H : om. P¹G : *discrimen* P³ | *et suam praedam* H : *et suam a praedam* (i.e., librarius omisit *a* delere) P³ : *et summa praedam* P¹ : *et suum a praeda* P² : *et suiamapraeda* G

The text as printed above rests entirely on H. Cousin is the first editor to reveal H's *casum* previously known as a vulgate reading, yet he missed H's *et suam praedam*, attributing it to "edd." Other editors invariably print von Jan's conjecture *interitum*,[64] a likely omission between *inter* and *interesse*, which, as suggested by Seyffert,[65] receives strong support from a similar omission that occurred at *Sest.* 127, where *inter* caused *intersit* to fall out. But paleographical reasons can also be adduced to explain the loss of *casum*, as witness Orelli's speculation (1826): "Poterat tamen *casum* expelli a similibus ductibus lit. *et suam*". Orelli was on the right track. In P the first hand divides *et summa* as follows: *etsum ma*, and the first word has the appearance of *cosum*. Thus the palaeographical environment would seem able to accomodate both *casum* and *interitum*, and this being the case, we must consider the respective claims of these words to authenticity in the framework of Cicero's usage.

The word we are seeking is one denoting exile. Editors printing *interitum* quote two passages in support, *Sest.*44 *a tribuno plebis post interitum <meum> dissedissent, qui eandem horam meae pestis et suorum praemiorum esse voluissent* and *Sest.*51 *quam* (sc. *medicinam*) *omnem, iudices, perdidissetis, si meo interitu senatui populoque Romano doloris sui de me declarandi potestas esset erepta.* Unfortunately neither quotation is relevant to our problem, since in each *interitus* literally means "death", not "exile". *Sest.*44 is a particularly striking example, where Cicero specifically refers to his exile as *pestis,* a word which reappears elsewhere in this sense: *Red. Sen.*17 *ut ne unam quidem horam interesse patereris inter meam pestem et tuam praedam* (cf. also *Red. Sen*16; *Dom.*26; *Sest.*44). This is not to imply that Cicero never uses *interitus* in a figurative sense for personal disaster or ruin, as for example *Vat.*25

---

[63] Bake, *Scholica* 1, 82.

[64] L. von Jan, *Münchener gelehrte Anzeigen* 187 (1847).

[65] M. Seyffert, *Epistola critica ad C. Halmium de Ciceronis Pro P. Sulla et Pro Sestio orationibus ab ipso editis* (Brandenburg 1848), 60-61.

huius etiam filium eodem indicio et crimine ad patris interitum adgregare voluisti. Nevertheless when Cicero wishes to employ a strong term for his own misfortune, he resorts rather to *pernicies*: *Sest.*53 *mihi reique publicae pernicies, Gabinio et Pisoni provincia rogata est* (cf. also *Sest.*25; *Red. Quir.*10; *Pis.*19).

These reservations do not arise in our consideration of *casum*. Wesenberg[66] and Jeep[67] rightly observed that *casus* is one of Cicero's favorite expressions conveying the notion of his sudden downfall: *Sest.*29 *una cum senatu ... casum amici rei publicae lugentem*; 53 *cum meum illum casum ... lugerent*; 60 *flens meum et rei publicae casum*; 123 *casum meum totiens conlacrumavit*; 140 *ac ne quis ex nostro aut aliquorum praeterea casu hanc vitae viam pertimescat*; 145 *quia meum casum luctumque doluerunt*. Then at *Dom.*84 there is the interesting reference to the exile of P. Clodius' father, *ac vide quid intersit inter iniquissimum patris tui casum et hanc fortunam condicionemque nostram*, where the presence of *intersit inter*, as in our passage, is not necessarily followed by *interitum*.

These considerations lead me to believe that H has the right word, conjecture or not. Other attempts to fill the omission of P^1G appears less successful. Madvig's *inter meum exitum et praedam*,[68] resting on the view that *et suum* (now we know that this is P^2's reading)[69] conceals *exitum*, leaves *meum* on a limb and requires the reader to understand *praedam* as "Ciceronis praeda ... id est, de Cicerone capta". Hertz's defense of P^3's *discrimen*,[70] apart from other reasons, was sufficiently refuted by Halm:[71] "res eius tum non in discrimine versabantur, sed iam prorsus afflictae atque perditae erant". Hertz disagreed.

67   *quam* (sc. *rem p.*) *ipse* (sc. *Cn. Pompeius*) *non solum consiliis sed etiam sanguine suo saepe servasset.*

servasset PG : *defendisset* H

---

[66] A.S. Wesenberg, *Observationes criticae in M.T. Ciceronis Pro Sestio orationem, sive censura tertiae editionis Orellianae* (Viburgi 1837) 34-35.

[67] J. Jeep, "Zu Ciceros Reden", *Neue Jahrb.* 82 (1860) 618.

[68] J.N. Madvig, *Opuscula²* (= *Opuscula academica* [Copenhagen 1887]) 359.

[69] My distinction between P^1, P^2 and P^3 in the apparatus is largely based on the testimony of Bern, Burgerbibl. 136, a twelfth-century apograph of P. Before B was copied, P^1 seems to have been corrected only once, by P^2. B has *et suum a praeda*. Other editors, however, assign a different reading here to P^2.

[70] Hertz (above, n. 47) 41 n.7.

[71] M.T. Ciceronis *Orationes* 1.2: *Oratio pro P. Sestio* (Leipzig 1845).

Bake[72] feels *rem p. servare* is too strong an expression for reference to Pompey, a phrase which Cicero normally reserves for himself or C. Marius, and opts instead for H's *defendisset*. Cousin does not record H's reading.

72 *ineunt magistratum tribuni plebis, qui omnes se de me promulgaturos confirmarant.*

   tr. pl. PG : *alii* H | *qui* H : *quod* PG | *se de* PH : *saepe* G | *confirmarant* PG : *confirmarunt* H

H's *qui* will stand, albeit a conjecture, as the other changes in its text indicate. Cousin's notation "*qui* MH" is inept.

73 *cum absens rem publicam non minus magnis periculis quam quodam tempore praesens liberassem.*

   rem p. non minus PG : *non minus rem p.* H

Bake[73] prefers H's word order.

74 *sed post eum rogatus Cn. Pompeius adprobata laudataque Cottae sententia dixit ... adiungeretur.*

   sed G : *set* P : om. H | *adprobata ... sententia* PG : *sententiam Cottae laudavit et approbavit* H | *dixit ... adiungeretur* PG : om. H

Bake[74] supports the omission of *sed*, but H's testimony carries no weight here. In Cousin's apparatus the readings of H are reported inaccurately.

76 *universique destrictis gladiis et cruentis in omnibus fori partibus fratrem meum, virum optimum, fortissimum meique amantissimum, oculis quaerebant.*

   fortissimum meique amantissimum om. H | *fortissimum meique* P : *fortissimumque mei* G

Bake[75] favors the deletion of *fortissimum meique amantissimum,* maintaining that the mention of Quintus' love for his brother is out of place here and that to call *fortissimus* a man who ultimately decided to save his own life is strange. While the latter objection is altogether frivolous (cf. Cicero's eulogies of his brother at *Red. Sen.*.37; *Red.*

---

[72] Bake, *Scholica* 1, 87.
[73] Bake, *Scholica* 1, 91.
[74] Bake, *Scholica* 1, 91.
[75] Bake, *Scholica* 1, 92.

Quir. 5 and 8), Kimmig⁷⁶ properly points out that it was precisely because of Quintus' *amor* for his brother that he become the target of Clodius' men. Had he been Cicero's enemy, he would have been of no interest to them. A variation on this deletion is Kayser's *virum ... amantissimum.* Strangely enough Peterson mentions both under Bake's and Kayser's names respectively, without a word about H. Cousin's apparatus is inaccurate.

ib. *quorum ille telis libenter in tanto luctu ac desiderio mei non repugnandi, sed moriendi causa corpus obtulisset suum, nisi suam vitam ad spem mei reditus servasset.*

in tanto ... causa PG : om. H

Once more, on finding in his *recentiores* the deletion of *in tanto ... causa,* Bake⁷⁷ expressed surprise that no editor followed Ernesti who had suggested it. What allegedly betrays the hand of the interpolator is "inepte dici, *corpus telis obicere repugnandi causa*". I suspect that this objection to the phrase is somehow rooted in Orelli's report (1826) that Hotman found in a manuscript *depugnandi* for *repugnandi.* In any event, Kimmig⁷⁸ rightly observes that there is no issue here worth Bake's trouble and Schroeder⁷⁹ pointed out even before Kimmig that the words *non repugnandi sed moriendi causa* find full justification in *in tanto luctu ac desiderio mei,* that filled with sorrow and yearning for his brother, Quintus was ready to throw himself against Clodius' men, not to fight but to sacrifice his life etc. In the meantime, Kayser attempted to build on Bake's (Ernesti's) idea and proposed bracketing *non repugnandi ... causa.*

Here again Peterson mentions Ernesti's and Kayser's proposals, but not H's reading, nor for that matter does Cousin.

77 *nihil neque ante hoc tempus neque hoc ipso turbulentissimo die criminamini Sestium.*

nihil PG : *nihilque* H | *criminamini* PG : *criminationis esse in* H

With a small adjustment, *criminationis [esse] in,* H's variant became the vulgate reading. The "*criminationis in* H" in Cousin's apparatus is incorrect. H's lection, however, has no authority as it resulted from the following abridgement of the paragraph: *meministis tum, iudices, corporibus civium Tiberim repleri (compleri* G² : *-ere* PG¹*), cloacas refarciri [e*

---

⁷⁶ Kimmig (above, n.32) 28.
⁷⁷ Bake, *Scholica* 1, 92.
⁷⁸ Kimmig (above, n.32) 28-29.
⁷⁹ A. Schroeder, *De interpolationibus in duabus Ciceronis orationibus pro Sestio, pro Plancio habitis* (Bonn 1865) 12-13.

foro ... arbitrarentur] *nihilque neque ante hoc tempus neque hoc ipso turbulentissimo die criminationis esse in Sestium.*

78 *cum praesidio magno.*

   magno H : *magni* PG

   magno is from H, not from "edd.", as Cousin has it.

ib. *gladiatores tu novicios, pro exspectata aedilitate suppositos.*

   tu novicios P : *uno victos* G : *tu* H | *novicios ... aedilitate* om. H | *suppositos* PG : *supponas* H

Bake[80] would again follow H and read *gladiatores tu supponas.* Cousin's apparatus displaying H's *supponas* alone is inadequate.

83 *animo in rem p.* PG : *in rem p. animo* H

Bake[81] prefers H's word order.

ib. *luce palam <a> nefariis pestibus ... esset occisus.*

The preposition *a* is in H. Cousin's apparatus indicating that H omitted *a* is incorrect.

86 *et quid necesse esset*

   necesse esset H : *necesset* PG

Cousin's attribution of *necesset* to H is fallacious.

96 *de qua* (sc. *re*) *pauca, iudices, dicam, et. ut arbitror, nec ab utilitate eorum qui audient, nec ab officio vestro, nec ab ipsa causa P. Sesti abhorrebit oratio mea.*

   vestro PG : *nostro* H

Here is yet another example of H's dominance of the text. *Nostro* (not recorded by Cousin), which became the vulgate reading, stands for *meo.* That this cannot be right was demonstrated by Wesenberg who adopted *vestro* and paraphrased the sentence as follows:[82] "pauca dicam, quae et auditoribus ... utilia erunt nec non proprium *officii vestri,* iudices, erit audire ... neque ab ipsa Sestii causa, i.e., a *meo* omnia, quae ad eam obtinendam pertineant, dicendi *officio,* aliena erunt". Thus the presence of *nostro* would make Cicero refer to his *officium* twice, which is absurd. Similarly in the digression at *Sest.* 119 Cicero lists the jury

---

[80] Bake, *Scholica* 1, 95.

[81] Bake, *Scholica* 1, 98.

[82] Wesenberg (above, n.66) 66.

(*gravitas vestra*), the audience (*advocatio, conventus*), P. Sestius (*dignitas P. Sesti*) and himself (*aetas, honos meus*).

On the other hand there is nothing inapposite in *nostro* on strictly formal grounds, although Wesenberg thought so, invoking Madvig's hasty generalization[83] that Cicero in his orations does not employ the plural with reference to his person alone. Madvig repented of this statement as soon as he found the opportunity.[84]

97   *horum* (sc. *optimatium*) *qui voluntati, commodis, opinionibus in gubernanda re publica serviunt, defensores optumatium ipsique optumates gravissimi et clarissimi cives numerantur et principes civitatis.*

opinionibus Halm : *opinis* PG^1 : *optimis* G^2 : *opinioni* H

Halm's *opinionibus* is still the best solution for the corrupt text. H's *opinioni* seems to be derived from *opinis*. Jacob[85] proposed in its place *opibus*, arguing that to express the notion of political principle Cicero would rather have used *consiliis*. But *opibus* next to *commodis* is too much of the same. Of late, Sydow[86] conjectured *disciplinis*, believing that *dis-* has been swallowed up by the preceding *commo-dis*. Cousin's "opinioni M" is misleading.

106   *quae contio fuit per hos annos, quae quidem esset non conducta sed vera, in qua populi Romani consensus* <*non*> *perspici posset? habitae sunt multae de me* <*a*> *gladiatore sceleratissimo, ad quas nemo adibat incorruptus, nemo integer.*

sceleratissimo PG : *sceleratissimo contiones* H

Cousin's return to the vulgate (H) *contiones* after *sceleratissimo*, so that his text reads: ... *habitae sunt multae ... contiones, ad quas ...,* seems an unwise decision. The presence of the word constitutes one of the "alte Probleme" of the oration, with Madvig[87] and Bake[88] arguing against its authenticity and Orelli[89] defending it. Madvig and Bake were probably right. It is difficult to see why this particular insertion has better claim to authenticity than, for instance *Sest.* 32 *veste* PG : *veste mutata* H; 78 *inmittas* PG : *in forum inmittas* H; 79 *rem publicam* PG : *ut*

---

[83] Madvig, *Opuscula*^{1}, 497.

[84] Madvig, *Opuscula*^{2}, 386 n.1: "Non debebam de hoc sic universe asseverare; vid. *de imp. Pomp.* 47, *in Vat.* 29, *Philipp.* VII,7,XII,24".

[85] F. Jacob, "Bemerkungen zu Cicero's Rede für Sestius", *Philologus* 3 (1848) 712.

[86] R. Sydow, "Kritische Beiträge zu Ciceros Sestiana", *RhM* 89 (1940), 159.

[87] Madvig, *Opuscula*^{2}, 377.

[88] Bake, *Scholica* 1, 112.

[89] Orelli believes (1826) that if the word were a gloss it would be right after *multae*.

suis munitus rem publicam H;[90] 107 *praebuit* Madvig : om. PG : *exibuit* H;[91] 139 *dignitatis* PG : *ordinis et dignitatis* H.

109 *de me ... dicit se legem tulisse.*

dicit H : *dicet* PG

H does not have *dicet*, as Cousin asserts in his apparatus.

137 *qui (sc. maiores nostri) cum regum potestatem non tulissent, ita magistratus annuos creaverunt ut ...*

regum PG : *regiam* H

Since cut and dried rules do not exist for the use of the attributive genitive in place of the atributive adjective or vice versa,[92] editors till the time of Orelli freely printed the vulgate (H) *regiam*. Wesenberg, however, was able to show the superiority of *regum*:[93] "ita enim *reges* melius opponuntur *magistratibus annuis*". Indeed, had Cicero said *regiam potestatem*, he would most likely have continued with *ita annuam creaverunt*, as at *Rep.* 2,56 *uti consules potestatem haberent tempore dumtaxat annuam, genere ipso ac iure regiam* or 2,43 *aliquis perpetua potestate, praesertim regia.*

138 *nam si qui voluptatibus ducuntur ..., missos faciant honores, ne attingant rem publicam, patiantur virorum fortium labore se otio suo perfrui.*

ne PG : *nec* H | *rem p.* PG : *re p.* H | *patiantur* (-cia- P) PHG² : *patiuntur* G¹ | *virorum fortium labore* (-es G) *se otio suo perfrui* PG : *viros laborum patientes frui* H

Anyone inquiring about the manuscript evidence underlying Bake's conjecture *patiantur viros fortes laboribus perfungi*[94] for *patiantur virorum fortium labore se otio suo perfrui*, would receive no assistance from Cousin's apparatus. And yet this conjecture ultimately goes back to H, as was known to Bake from the *recentiores*. Cousin's entries in the

---

[90] This appears to be H's attempt to soften what some critics also perceived as a rather harsh asyndeton in *ut a suis munitus tuto in foro (foro* M : *foro tuo* PGH) *magistratum gereret, rem publicam administraret*, where Madvig, *Opuscula*², 368-369, conjectured *ut a suis munitus tuto in foro, dum magistratum gereret, rem publicam administraret*, while Bake, *Scholica* 1, 96-97 and Eberhard in *Rede für P. Sestius*, ed. Koch and Eberhard, added, with less violence to the text, *et* before *rem p.*

[91] This occurs in *se ... supplicem populo Romano <praebuit>*. H's *exhibuit* (spelled *exibuit*) cannot be right. Phrases such as *se supplicem alicui exhibere* are late Latin. See Madvig, *Opuscula*², 377; Krebs (and Schmalz), *Antibarbarus* 1, s.v. *exhibere*.

[92] Cf. K.-S. 2.1, 209-213.

[93] Wesenberg (above, n.66) 68.

[94] Bake, *Scholica* 1, 132.

apparatus *virorum fortium labore* (*labores* G) PG : *viros laborum patientes* H and *perfrui*PG : *frui* H, implying that H has *se otio suo,* is misleading.

Since the phrase *patior me aliqua re perfrui* (or *frui*) at first sight appears a rather peculiar way to express a simple thought (see below), Bake was happy to find manuscripts in which *otio* was missing and therefore another verb was needed for *perfrui* or *frui* to suit the notion of *labor* and to accommodate *patior.* In Bake's words: "Neque *patior me otio frui* cuiquam probari poterit: longeque diversum est, *aliis permittere otium suum,* Republ. I, 34. Credo veram Ciceronis manum esse, *patiantur viros fortes laboribus perfungi*". Although Bake was troubled by the phrase, Garatoni[95] had offered a satisfactory interpretation long before: "contenti sint otio suo se perfrui per laborem virorum fortium."

University of California
Los Angeles

---

[95] In M.T. Ciceronis *Opera ex rec. I.G. Graevii cum Variorum,* 17 vols., with G. Garatoni's annotations in vols. 3-11 (Naples 1777-1788).

HISTORICAL DEVELOPMENT IN LIVY

RICHARD E. MITCHELL

The major dilemma for Roman historians who work on the early period has always been, to paraphrase Plinio Fraccaro's words, how little of the Roman tradition to accept and how much of it to reject.[1] In order to justify acceptance, historians have constantly searched for an original, archival source of information. Because of the supposed elliptical nature of the annalistic record, the shorter the notice in the history and the less embellished with interpretation and details, the more it was thought to represent an early fragment of the *annales maximi,* which many assumed to be the compilation of the *tabulae dealbatae* of individual *pontifices maximi.* Our sources also contain reports of laws, treaties, religious formulae, and ritual practices which modern historians have pointed to as evidence of authentic records. The physical evidence of monuments, buildings, inscriptional dedications, statues, and countless other private and public objects both reported by our sources and uncovered by modern research are also presumed to be authentic material from early Rome. At times our sources incorrectly explain, garble, or rationalize the true identification of the aforementioned, and modern scholars, while differing widely in their own assessment, have presumed that laws, treaties, rituals, and all such documentation were subject to interpretation and embellishment by the Roman annalists and by the later historians who used their work and who, like Livy, often only worked directly from such developed interpretations and rationalizations of the "evidence."

We can characterize the impression many have about Livy's history by another paraphrase, this time from Thomas B. Macaulay: it is a bad history well done.[2] The benefit of being trained at the University of Cincinnati by men like Donald Bradeen and Carl Trahman was that one was never either subjected to an exclusively "classical" approach to the great artistic beauty and value of Livy or permitted fully to engage in vitriolic assaults on his credulity without close examination. We were

---

[1] Plinio Fraccaro, "The History of Rome in the Regal Period," *JRS* 47 (1957) 59. This essay is part of a larger study dealing with patres and plebs and the struggle of the orders. Citations are kept to the absolute minimum, but additional material is presented in my forthcoming essay, "The Definition of Patres and Plebs: An End to the Struggle of the Orders," *The Conflict of the Orders in Archaic Rome,* ed. Kurt Raaflaub.

[2] As quoted in *Livy, Rome and Italy* (Books VI-X), tr. by B. Radice with intro. by R. M. Ogilvie (New York: Penguin 1982) 7f.

made aware that Livy and others could be both appreciated as "classics" and used as historical sources at the same time. Proving that Livy's work is historically reliable and useful has been far more difficult than showing that it has artistic merit. However, in recent years the pendulum has begun to swing back in favor of Livy.

As commonplace as assaults on his veracity were a few decades ago, it is surprising to see Livy's defenders now taking the field and arguing that he is "generally" more reliable than previously thought. "The wonder is," says P.G. Walsh, "that being neither Senator nor soldier nor avid traveller he got so much right."[3] In the absence of personal experience, Livy "had to rely in part on authorities who were as dishonest as they were inventive."[4] As Robert M. Ogilvie says, "Livy was content to take over a narrative at second hand from an earlier chronicler and reshape it according to his own artistic aim. It rarely crossed his mind that that narrative might be tendentious and largely fictitious."[5] Also, as many have stressed, Livy developed the personalities and characters of the important figures in Rome's past to serve as moral *exempla,* and the clash of these personalities gave structure to his history and permitted the story to move pleasantly and entertainingly along, *ab urbe condita.* "For Livy, the main value of history lay in providing examples of conduct to imitate or avoid, whether for the individual or the state."[6] Livy was preoccupied with the moral decay of Rome, a decay he illustrated by countless examples of individual success or failure. Livy was also excessively concerned with and concentrated upon religious phenomena: "He regards the performance of traditional religious rites as essential for the well-being of the State."[7]

When modern scholars deny the historicity of Livy's focus upon Rome's moral decline and question the material evoked in support of traditional Roman religious beliefs and practices, they often do so by insisting that either Livy or, more likely, his late annalistic sources fabricated much of the evidential material using the forms and styles of limited archival records as their models. Walsh is not alone in his

---

[3] P.G. Walsh, "Livy," *Latin Historians,* ed. T. A. Dorey (New York 1966) 115. (Perhaps such a claim that historians must be men of experience could only come from someone in the British Empire, where men of "classical" education were so frequently men of both action and letters. Livy was part of their curriculum, but he was not part of their model. Here, Thucydides and Polybius held pride of place.)

[4] Walsh, *ibid.*

[5] Robert M. Ogilvie, *Roman Literature and Society* (Penguin 1980) 156.

[6] T.P. Wiseman, *Clio's Cosmetics: Three Studies in Greco-Roman Literature* (Leicester University Press 1979) 38.

[7] Ogilvie (above, n.2) 14.

characterization that, despite these weaknesses, Livy's "outline of the decisive stages can be accepted; but the detail was largely written into the framework by historians and legal authorities in the late second and first century. Later constitutional and legal practices are given ancient precedents."[8] Walsh is referring largely to Livy's account contained in his first decade, his outline of Rome's external historical development which concentrated upon her Italian expansion and on the internal struggle between patricians and plebeians which took place during the same period. The crucial questions about Livy's historical value and importance concern the specific issue of the reliability or authenticity of any of the detailed pieces of information he presented about early Rome's growth and development, together with the reliability of his overall outline or structure of Roman historical developments.

My present purpose is to show that appreciation of Livy's artistry has resulted in a misplaced enthusiasm for the reliability of his outline of general developments and, in particular, of his account of the so-called "struggle of the orders." Furthermore, acceptance of his outline has led to the failure to see the true importance of certain pieces of information which Livy presented in the context of the struggle. I hope to demonstrate the importance of accepting certain specific material as authentic while stripping it of either its annalistic or Livian interpretation as part of the struggle between patricians and plebeians. What this means is rejecting the struggle of the orders while accepting some of the specific evidence and placing it in an entirely different context. This is a reversal of the normal practice of historians.

Part of the problem is the question of what specific information was available to Livy even if it came through an intermediary source. Certainly there were some authentic documents about Rome's early history, and there were some records couched in the style and language of the *pontifex maximus,* and annalistic historians did use the authentic material in their own interpretations of Rome's historical development. The question of Livy's scissors-and-paste method of composition, the issue of whether he used a single source at a time or wove conflicting accounts into a successful, but not necessarily historically reliable, narrative are all ultimately dependent upon the nature of his sources or, more specifically, the nature of the original records available to his sources. In this respect, we must make certain corrections in the common opinion voiced about which sources he employed and what those sources contained.

It is argued that Livy was at the mercy of his sources, in particular annalistic historians who were his near contemporaries: "they

---

[8] Walsh (above, n.3) 126.

conveniently embodied previous research, thereby saving him the trouble of going back to early authorities himself."[9] T.J. Luce criticizes this assumption, maintaining that "on the contrary, it seems prima facie likely and reasonable that Livy had indeed read, for example, Rome's first historian [Fabius Pictor] and that he consulted him in writing his own history."[10] Luce is certainly right, but all such debate is beside the point, since Livy's reputation cannot be enhanced by proving that he did or did not use Pictor directly. There is little proof that Fabius Pictor or his near contemporaries, despite their apparent brevity, were more historically reliable or preserved more authentic records because they engaged in less embellishment. It is not even certain how extensively any annalist, early or late, used the available documentary material. In fact, the fragmentary remains of the early annalists do not inspire much confidence in the authenticity of their accounts. On the other hand, if it is true that these early histories were brief and if the original annalistic records were short, then they could not have contained the elaborate explanations and interpretations found in the pages of Livy and Dionysius of Halicarnassus. It certainly does not follow, however, that the earliest histories contained proportionately more archival material because both they and the documents were limited in scope. Conversely, it cannot be assumed that the eventual publication of the *annales maximi* enriched the narratives of the later annalistic historians precisely because the publication added to the store of information now readily available. Nor can it be established that "the enrichment of material did not depend on the publication of the *annales maximi* but on the new tendency in historical writing to give a literary form and a richness of detail to the events narrated."[11]

Recently, the entire tradition and the actual publication of the annual *tabulae* of the *pontifices* by P. Mucius Scaevola (pontifex maximus in 130 B.C.) has been called into question. Bruce Frier has argued that the yearly *tabulae* were collected into yearly *libri* and were available from 300 B.C. and that the annual *tabula* stopped with Scaevola. There was, in other words, no great influx of annalistic information in the late second century, and correspondingly there is no essential quantitative difference between works written before or after that time.[12]

---

[9] T.J. Luce, *Livy, The Composition of His History* (Princeton University Press 1977) 159.

[10] Luce (above, n.9) 161.

[11] Fraccaro (above, n.1) 2.

[12] Bruce W. Frier, *Libri Annales Pontificium Maximorum: The Origins of the Annalistic Tradition. Papers and Monographs of the American Academy in Rome* 27 (Rome 1979).

The publication of a yearly *tabula* was intended to inform the public of religious and civic events and to record precedents that must be kept in mind for the future. The point must also be made again and again, because it is so often forgotten, that the pontifex and his *tabula* must have been primarily concerned with the primitive law and procedure and with the calendar which permitted public and private activities to take place. Pontiffs controlled the law, directed its use, and for much of the Republic were the only experts in the field. The mistake is to assume that either the law or the *tabula* was essentially religious. "The frequent modern view," says Frier, "that the pontifical notices had at first a predominantly religious tone not only lacks support in the texts, but is without substantiation in theory."[13] Originally, there was little or no differentiation between religion and law, and in fact the *ius sacrum* "touched the ordinary civil law."[14]

Although the *tabulae* of the pontifices were not intended to serve as "historical" records, they "may have constituted a repository of fact from which, at a later date, proper consultation might extract guides and precedents for action."[15] Unfortunately, Frier mars an otherwise acceptable discussion of the *libri annales* by concluding that the keeping of the *tabulae* by the pontiffs did not proceed from "any legal authorization or compulsion stemming from the civil government."[16] As he notes, "in an early period there was no absolute distinction between religion and government ..., then there was likewise no reason why the pontifex maximus should have limited himself to reporting only parochial affairs."[17] Or, as I would add, no reason to prohibit his exercising an official judicial and legal control over "parochial affairs."

Frier has separated the pontifex' original sacred and legal importance from his archival functions. He has criticised those who (like Theodor Mommsen) opt for the view that the *rex sacrorum* and *pontifex maximus* divided the king's authority, with the pontiff receiving a "quasi-magisterial authority" and the rex becoming essentially a priest.[18] True, the schematic depiction of the king's position and authority flowing unchanged to different officials in an attempt to diffuse monarchical power and prevent its renewal is unacceptable, but this criticism should not have obscured the actual "quasi-magisterial

---

[13] Frier (above, n. 12) 96.

[14] H. F. Jolowicz, *Historical Introduction to the Study of Roman Law* 3rd ed. (Cambridge University Press 1972) 89.

[15] Frier 98.

[16] Frier 101.

[17] Frier 97.

[18] Frier 101.

authority" which the pontiff did possess. We should not summarily dismiss his *potestas* any more than we should restrict the functioning of his legal and procedural activities.[19] The pontiff did not set up the *tabula* on his own authority; the keeping of records of all sorts was intimately connected with both his religious authority and the intrinsic importance of religion to all facets of Roman private and public life.[20] Some information preserved was later turned into politically significant evidence by annalists and historians who made the material part of the struggle of the orders. Because much of it appeared legal and "constitutional" to our ancient sources, the original importance of the material as evidence for the as yet undifferentiated institutions of Rome was not apparent, and the details became evidence for the struggle of the orders interpretation. In fact, the *tabulae* were, among other things, the quasi-legal records of a college of quasi-magistrates, who were instrumental in the mediation of disputes between men and between men and gods. By 300 B.C. the cares of men were becoming more important, and the religious influences in, and control over, what were rapidly becoming secular affairs were gradually shifted to more worldly officials.

Elsewhere I have tried to show that the *auctoritas* accorded priests was in no small measure due to their exlusive nature, their expertise, and their originally secret knowledge of law, procedure, ritual, and the proper times to undertake private and public measures as determined by the calendar. The XII Tables show an unmistakable religious and sacred character, and priests and especially the pontiffs, who are customarily throughout the Republic associated with private and sacred law, are in fact also to be associated with the great body of archival information and tradition which served as the precedents for action and embodiment of *mos maiorum*.[21] It is also clear from even a cursory examination of the extant XII Table Laws that the priests did not simply record the original form of the law, or the procedure, but they actively engaged in the application of the law and they changed it by

---

[19] Macrobius, *Saturnalia* 3.2.17.

[20] Frier, 92f. and note 24, is too quick to dismiss the connection between the pontifical archival duties and the annales. See L. H. Jeffery and Anna Morpurgo-Davies, "ποινικαστάς and ποινικάζεν: B. M. 1969. 4-2.1, a new archaic inscription from Crete," *Kadmos* 9 (1979) 118-54 with plates, presenting an inscription concerning the hereditary position of a scribe who was the "recorder in public affairs both sacred and secular" (p. 125). Priesthoods in Rome were most certainly hereditary positions for much of the Republic, and record keeping was more a concern of such families than many realize. See my forthcoming essay (above, n.1) for additional information.

[21] Mitchell (above, n.1), forthcoming.

interpretation.[22] Works devoted to pontifical and augural rules, rituals, and regulations, as well as *commentarii,* were in a very technical sense originally priestly records which contributed to the late Republic's growing collection of legal materials.[23]

Modern scholars have certainly overestimated the effects of the supposed publication of the *annales maximi* upon the later annalistic historians, just as they have underestimated precisely what the pontifical records contained. Livy may not have consulted the *annales maximi* directly, but we must not forget that these earliest records were transmitted by priests, especially but not exclusively pontiffs, and that these records were overwhelmingly legal. in this connection, we can point to Livy's report concerning the *iuris interpretes* surrounding the question of the origins of *sacrosanctitas.*[24] Still other *interpretes* were mentioned concerning legal questions surrounding the authority of consuls and other magistrates.[25] There can be no doubt that whatever Livy's source, his information was primarily legal, which means that if the *interpretes* were in disagreement over the meaning of an original authentic piece of evidence, that evidence could well have existed as part of an archival record which was unembellished by conflicting political assessments of its importance offered by later interpretations. In fact, originally the *interpretes* themselves must have been, or must have preserved, the records of priests. In other words, Livy's history contained interpretations of early Roman quasi-religious-legal documents.

When his sources did not agree or were not convincing, Livy often presented the contrasting interpretations. "It is a recurrent cause for complaint," says Walsh, "that he does not always evaluate the merits of opposing statements, being content to present differing interpretations and to leave the onus of choice to the reader."[26] For example, as Walsh continues, "in the first decade, as Livy knew well, the theme of the struggle of the orders had offered boundless temptations to historians of the second and first centuries who wished to further the Optimate cause or to reinforce the claims of the Populares. He sought to steer a fair course by choosing authorities of opposing views,

---

[22] Jolowicz (above, n.14) 108ff., has an acceptable discussion, but I find Alan Watson, *The Law of the Ancient Romans* (Southern Methodist University Press 1970), lacking in historical sophistication.

[23] A valuable introduction is Fritz Schulz, *History of Roman Legal Science* (Oxford: Clarendon Press 1946; reprint 1967), who gives the proper stress to the religious nature of early Roman law and records but gives too narrow a historical value to such material.

[24] Livy, 3.55.8. Cf. Robert Ogilvie, *Commentary On Livy, Books 1-5* (Oxford: Clarendon Press 1965) 502 f.

[25] Livy, 3.55.11.

[26] Walsh (above, n. 3) 121f.

Valerius Antias and Licinius Macer. The reconstruction of Roman history was an especially lively weapon of propaganda in the hands of Licinius, a vehement supporter of the Populares. Valerius on the other hand favoured the Sullan interests, as well as seeking the maximum glory for the Valerii and their allies."[27] The assumption is that Livy, as a moralist in search of moral examples, found in these annalistic accounts the biased presentations of competing political factions who were not above (or below) fabricating material to make their points. Livy had merely to pick and choose, since the tradition had already "been elaborated with appropriate *color* by both conservative and 'popular' historians."[28] Livy's account was "not so much a reconciliation of opposing views as a combination of distortions from the two polar positions."[29] Timothy P. Wiseman observes that "what never occurred to him was to reject the elaboration to begin with."[30]

Modern historians would not be better served had Livy been successful in "reconciling" the opposing views, and neither Livy nor modern historians have considered rejecting the polar opposites reflected in the struggle of the orders. To be absolutely clear about my own position, that is precisely what must be done. However, we must distinguish between the "struggle" as it appears in the pages of Livy, in particular, and the conflict found in the pages of modern historians. The characteristic features of the former are not those of the latter. The identification and characterization of Livy's major sources for the struggle are far from acceptable. Just as it was incorrectly assumed that Livy did not use Fabius Pictor directly, there is considerable doubt about his presumed indebtedness to a few late sources which greatly influenced the tone and content of his treatment of the struggle between patricians and plebeians. Scholars have concentrated a great deal of attention on the question of annalistic fabrications that found their way into the narrative concerning early Roman developments preserved basically by Livy and Dionysius of Halicarnassus. "This combination of unscrupulous invention on the part of the late-republican annalists and innocent acceptance of their inventions on the part of Livy and Dionysius has not been easy for modern readers to understand. We do not find it too hard to recognize the inventive technique in comparatively unimportant details, but it does not come

---

[27] Walsh 122.
[28] Wiseman (above, n.6) 51.
[29] Walsh 122.
[30] Wiseman 51.

naturally to us to expect the *big* lie as well; ..."[31] It is not altogether clear what Wiseman means by the "big lie," but I think the "big lie" is the struggle of the orders. However, it is not always evident who is the father of the falsehood, ancient or modern author.

It is assumed that "the Annalists certainly had to elaborate the material of the *Annales Maximi* to make it historically intelligible."[32] If the annalists had used such unpromising material as was contained in the priestly records, they must have "interpreted it." Ernst Badian maintains that "the tradition of Roman historiography made plausible lying easy: its true content was to some extent based on archival material, written in simple and archaic style and clamouring for imitation."[33] The annalists did not commonly fabricate documents, according to Badian, but some were invented, and he believes that "with Valerius the invention of 'archival material' seems to have reached new heights."[34]

A.H. McDonald points out that much of Livy's technical vocabulary resulted from "the influence of the traditional style which came to him from the *Annales Maximi* through the Annalists, above all where the vocabulary of the State religion, in its 'augural' and 'sacral' forms, appeared to him to evoke the spirit of early Roman history."[35] Livy took care to present "the full constitutional subject-matter in its appropriate style ..."[36] McDonald assumes that the style and form of the documentary material came from the pontifical records, and they "owed something to conventional elaboration along technical, antiquarian, and sacral lines."[37] He points to "phraseology in Livy that is technical to the point of legalism; it may also bear the marks of antiquarian research; and where the augural aspects of a ceremony become significant, the religious associations are heightened by the sacral vocabulary."[38] It is also argued that Livy frequently worked through his sources rapidly and mechanically, often not making the material part of the structure at all. Some material — brief notices — "did not easily lend themselves to structural or thematic manipulations ... Often Livy appears to have used them as dividers and contrasts to more extensive

---

[31] Wiseman 52.

[32] A.H. McDonald, "The Style of Livy," *JRS* 47 (1957) 156.

[33] E. Badian, "The Early Historians," *Latin Historians*, ed. T.A. Dorey (New York: Basic Books 1966) 21.

[34] Badian 21.

[35] McDonald (above, n.32) 157f.

[36] McDonald *ibid.*

[37] McDonald 156.

[38] McDonald *ibid.*

and important blocks of material ..." and he tended to "string events out in no particular order."[39] The prototypes of these notices, says Luce, were the *tabulae dealbatae* of the *pontifex maximus,* or the published *annales maximi:* "hence the brevity, the technical vocabulary, the antique-looking word here and there, and — above all — the bulletin-like sequence that we suppose characterized the whitened tablets."[40] Livy did not necessarily preserve authentic documents, but "merely couched [them] in a manner evocative of what the *tabulae* were like or thought to have been like."[41] Quite simply, the emphasis of all the above is on the use of annalistic form and not on the use of substance. Supposedly Livy found both legal and religious styles that appealed to him, and his employment of the styles is not necessarily indicative of a reliable content. Several modern scholars have warned that the existence of annalist fabrications makes identification of authentic evidence about Rome's past most difficult because the later annalists fabricated evidence in the archaic forms and styles of the original material. The important historical question to pursue is whether we have any examples of the archival, documentary style which retains its original content.

As a possible candidate for authenticity I want to nominate the *lex Valeria de provocatione* of 300 B.C., which was the third and last such measure passed by a member of the same *gens*.[42] Livy said that beating and beheading someone who employed *provocatio* was forbidden but that the punishment for those who disregarded the prohibition was to declare their deed *improbum*, a "wicked deed," as some translate it.[43] This is a good example of both the moral decline and the religious themes found in Livy, since he maintains that such a sanction was sufficient to deter men of an earlier period but it would not even faze anyone in his day. Ogilvie couples this notice with a speech supposedly given by Cato the Elder on the occasion of the repeal of the lex Oppia, which forbade excessive displays of luxury: "diseases must be known before their cures are found; by the same token, appetites come into being before the laws to limit their exercise."[44] Ogilvie's aforementioned conflation is a good example of how modern criticism has

---

[39] Luce (above, n.9) 191f.

[40] Luce 192.

[41] Luce 192f.

[42] Consult T. Robert S. Broughton, *The Magistrates of the Roman Republic,* I (New York, American Philological Association 1951) 2f, 47f (509 and 449 B.C.) for ancient references to *provocatio* laws. There were also three *leges Porciae* on the same subject!

[43] 10.9.3-6: *si quis adversus ea fecisset, nihil ultra quam "improbe factum" adiecit.* See *Livy, Rome and Italy* for Ogilvie's introduction (p. 14) and Radice's translation (p. 299).

[44] *Livy, Rome and Italy* 14 (cf. Livy, 34.4.8, on the *lex Oppia*).

complicated our understanding of the historical development of Rome in precisely the same fashion as Livy.

It is customary to view the three *leges Valeriae* as, in part at least, the fabrication of Valerius Antias, with only the final law normally accepted as historical.[45] Despite the important role *provocatio* legislation supposedly played in the struggle of the orders and its equally indispensable protection afforded citizens, *provocatio* is so little understood, so much debated, and so infrequently used that modern scholars generally criticize our sources for their failure to fabricate accurately an acceptable historical context and explanation for the various *leges* or to cover accurately the tracks of their fabrication. In fact, in the XII Table Laws, being declared *improbus* is also a punishment for someone who fails to perform as a witness or who fails to give testimony.[46] With good reason we can assume that declaring someone *improbus* was very similar to declaring that he was *sacer*, which involved his "excommunication from the civil community." *Improbus* was then a "primitive legal principle, a condemnation by the community, which, rising to malediction and abandonment to the revenge of Gods and men, excommunicated from the civil fellowship the person who violated the legal principles (*mores*) which were the very foundation of the social order ..."[47] Who declared or judged the person or his deed *improbus*? Certainly not the magistrate, and we have no reason to believe that the tribunes acted in this matter. Most likely the pronouncement came from the *pontifex maximus* or the college of pontiffs, or at least they maintained such a jurisdiction until other kinds of (secular) legal and jurisdictional machinery developed. All admit that this did not happen until sometime after 300 B.C., but both Livy and modern scholars have turned the actual legal pronouncements into evidence either for the moral decay from previous high standards of religious conduct or for one more concession won by the plebeians from the patricians. In fact, the original idea of *provocatio* may not have been the much overused and clearly misinterpreted "appeal" but instead, a challenge, and we know of challenges to both *sacramentum* and *sponsio*.[48] We are told that the

---

[45] R.A. Bauman, "The *lex Valeria de provocatione* of 300 B.C.," *Historia* 22 (1973) 33ff., has collected the evidence and modern argument but has assumed too much about the dictatorship and the question of *provocatio*-free magistracies.

[46] *Fontes Iuris Romani Anteiustiniani*, I (Florence 1941), ed. S. Riccobono *et al.*, p. 62 (= 8.22, which is from Gaius, 15.13.11).

[47] C.W. Westrup, *Introduction to Early Roman Law*, (Copenhagen 1939), Vol. 3, pt. 1, p. 172. Cf. Bauman, (above, n.45) 35f.

[48] On *sacramentum*, see Francis de Zuleuta, *The Institutes of Gaius* (Oxford: Clarendon Press 1946), vol. 1, pp. 234ff., for the text of Gaius (4.13-4) and vol. 2, pp. 232ff., for the discussion. On *sponsio*, see John Crook, "*Sponsione Provocare:* Its Place in

sacramentum was laid *ad pontem* (not *ad pontificem* as emended),[49] and the bridge may well have been the frontier at which a form of trial by challenge and ordeal took place, presided over by the pontifex. Some have considered the procedure of *sponsione provocare* "extra-legal:" it may well have been a challenge that did not have to lead to adjudication.[50] Whatever the case, there is little or no evidence that *provocatio* was the method whereby citizens protected themselves from magisterial *coercitio,* and we know of no secular cases where it was used against a sentence handed down. As A.H.M. Jones pointed out, the only known cases of *provocatio* were those involving disputes between a *pontifex maximus* and those under his authority.[51] These cases are clearly only a vestige of what had been the practice generally for a considerable period of time — namely, that pontiffs were once judicial authorities in every sense of the word, perhaps the only ones.

It should also be pointed out that the *Lex Valeria* of 300 (as well as its predecessors in 509 and 449 B.C.) was probably preserved as part of the pontifical record. M. Valerius, the author of the law in 300 B.C., was a pontiff,[52] and Cicero referred to the fact that his information about *provocatio* came from the *pontificii libri,* and what he found there was confirmed by information obtained from the XII Table Laws and the augural record.[53] The Valerian *gens* may well have preserved the *provocatio* tradition as part of the private records of the family as illustrations of its members' public activities. There is some indication that such records were transmitted within families from father to son and yet also formed part of the official record of public development. This would be especially cogent if some positions were inherited by sons automatically, a fact which seems virtually certain for the major priesthoods.[54]

Roman Litigation," *JRS* 66 (1976) 132ff., for a discussion of its later employment.

[49] Varro, *LL* 5.180.

[50] See Crook, (above, n.48) 132ff., for discussion and bibliography.

[51] A. H. M. Jones, *The Criminal Courts of the Roman Republic and Principate* (Oxford: Blackwell 1972) 10ff., but I cannot accept all of Jones's historical conclusions. What is generally overlooked in the trial of Rabirius (63 B.C.) is the fact that the *duoviri* in the case were C. Julius and L. Julius Caesar. The former was pontiff (perhaps already maximus by the trial) and the latter was augur. Whatever the archaic form of the trial, Rabirius's crime was certainly a form of sacrilege. See R.A. Bauman, *The Duumviri in the Roman Criminal Law and in the Horatius Legend, Historia Einzelschriften* (12 (1969), for a discussion of this mysterious criminal procedure.

[52] M. Valerius, six times consul, was pontiff about 340 B.C., and even if he was the son of the pontiff of 340, he certainly could have succeeded his father in the college.

[53] Cicero, *De republica* 2.31 (54).

[54] I mention only the notice of Dionysius of Halicarnassus, 1.74.4-5, and the discussion of P.A. Brunt, *Italian Manpower (225 B.C.-A.D. 14)* (Oxford: Clarendon Press 1971)

In other words, one reason the Valerii figure so prominently may well be due to the original form of the material preserved. It was part of a Valerian family archive transmitted from father to son as part of the priestly inheritance. Pliny tells us about archive rooms of the important *gentes*.[55] This is not to credit everything that Valerius Antias stated as derived from a private archive with a pseudo-public nature, but merely to suggest that once later political and personal interpretations have been removed from some such material, their fabrication is neither evident nor necessary.

In this respect, we should look at the religious and archival nature of early Roman law and legislation with a view toward removing the most pervasive late interpretation of their importance. That is, we must remove the "big lie," the struggle of the orders. As Badian points out concerning the embellishments of Valerius Antias, "scholars [have tried] to separate the substratum from his additions; and for the early part of Roman history the task is almost hopeless."[56] However true this assessment, I propose to separate the substratum from the historical structures imposed upon the material by both ancient and modern scholars in an attempt to make more headway.

Frier, for example, is only one of the most recent historians to place a modern gloss on the traditional account. He has argued that Licinius Macer confined his *annales* to "the great plebeian revolution, from the origins of Rome down to the Lex Hortensia of 287 and its immediate aftermath in the conquest of Italy."[57] Macer's motives were in part his desire to glorify his plebeian ancestors, in part his general love of plebeian institutions and history, and he called upon "archaic documents such as the *foedus Ardeatinum* and the *libri lintei*" in support of his cause.[58] However, it is not possible to prove that Licinius Macer wrote strongly pro-plebeian *annales* or that he concentrated upon the period of the plebeian revolution down to 287 B.C. So much of the depiction of Licinius Macer's work depends upon accepting still additional modern assumptions about his politics, his family, and his plebeian pride as well as the questionable deduction based upon the

---

26 and 32, as indications of the troublesome background of the census and censors. I cannot follow Brunt in all respects. For additional information see my forthcoming essay, "The Definition of Patres and Plebs," (above, n.1).

[55] Pliny, *Nat. Hist.* 35.2.2.7: *tabulina codicibus implebantur et monimentis rerum in magistratu gestarum.*

[56] Badian (above, n.33) 21.

[57] Bruce W. Frier, "Licinius Macer and the *Consules suffecti* of 444 B.C." *TAPA* 105 (1975) 95. Frier notes that this "is an ex silentio deduction, but an attractive one ...."

[58] Frier 95.

fragmentary remains of his history. The latter, naturally enough, may well have ended with Pyrrhus.[59] Frier, in any event, has committed the cardinal sin of the modern historian: he has taken a modern assumption and presumed that it has ancient standing. In fact, there is not a shred of evidence that Licinius Macer's work concentrated on the plebeian revolution or that he held exclusive populares or plebeian sympathies. Nor do his fragments tell us much about his struggle of the orders. In particular, we do not know when or how he ended his work.

Luce has correctly and conclusively demonstrated how flimsy both the identification and depiction of certain passages of Livy are when assessed according to an argument that he copied a major source that had a major bias.[60] In other words, it is no longer possible to support Ogilvie's view that the unknown, pro-senatorial, and Sullan aristocrat Valerius Antias and the equally monolithic pro-plebeian Licinius Macer were Livy's major sources for his conflicting points of view offered during this description of the struggle of the orders.[61] Tracing the various oligarchic and popular features of the struggle found in Livy back to either Valerius Antias or Licinius Macer has been a favorite pastime of modern scholars, but the practice is very nearly as much a fabrication as anything those two were guilty of creating. "The result," says Luce, "forms a vicious circle in which the theory and the proof for it must come into being simultaneously."[62] In fact, the description of the struggle of the orders given by these annalists is far from clear. Luce warns that "if everything in the first pentad that is pro-senatorial comes from Antias and everything pro-plebeian comes from Macer, their respective versions of the Struggle of the Orders must have been singular indeed: the triumph of the villains in the one case and of the heroes in the other."[63]

As a possible solution, Luce observes, in particular from the Livian passages that derived from Polybius, precisely how much Livy added and changed the emphasis of the original. As a result, he asks if "it might be worth considering whether the dominance of this [struggle] theme in early Roman history, and the interpretation of it, might not

---

[59] This might well be the case since the latest datable fragment deals with Pyrrhus (cf. Hermann Peter, *Historicorum Romanorum Reliquiae*, 2nd ed., (Leipzig 1914) vol. 1, p. 308 (frg. 20). Frier (above, n.57) 95, along with others, rightfully questions the location of the Pyrrhic fragment in Book II of Macer's work.

[60] Luce (above, n.9) 165ff.

[61] In particular, see Ogilvie, *Commentary* 7-16, and the many passages in Livy attributed to the two authors by Ogilvie.

[62] *Livy* 166.

[63] *Livy* 169.

be due to a significant degree to Livy's own historical perspective."[64] I could not agree more but hasten to emphasize that if the struggle is a theme found more in Livy than in any other source, it is also a theme found more in modern historians than in ancient. This fact is made clear by Luce himself, but he is also swept along by the wave of common opinion he advances in support of his view that Livy took a "developmental" approach to Rome's history: "In 509 many fundamental institutions are still waiting in the wings: all the magistracies other than the consulship, together with the tribunate; moreover, the long course that the struggle of the orders took would not be concluded until the Lex Hortensia of 287. The enactment and codification of laws are in the future, together with a host of other social, religious, and political changes."[65] The idea that the "struggle" ended with the Lex Hortensia, though often repeated is not an ancient idea, and it is not part of Livy's developmental process, as the following will make clear.

If the struggle of the orders played an important role in Livy's depiction of Rome's historical development, we might expect to find the chronological features of the struggle emphasized in the tradition. Hortensius' dictatorship is mentioned in *Periocha* XI, but not his legislation,[66] and those who have attempted to analyze the structure of Livy's history do not see a break at this point in the narrative.[67] The law would have been discussed, presumably, toward the end of book XI, and we might expect some break between books XI and XII if the struggle of the orders had been given much significance. In other words, Livy's historical development, as reflected in book divisions, was not structured around the struggle of the orders. A defense has been offered for a division which stressed the cohesiveness of books I, II-V, and I-XV,[68] but it would appear that no major break exists between books X and XI, let alone between XI and XII. Although this is not my primary concern, as an illustration of how much modern opinion has colored our impression of Livy's history, I want to point out that in book VI we have Livy's own claim that now *clariora deinceps certioraque ab secunda origine velut ab stirpibus laetius feraciusque renatae*

---

[64] *Livy* 169.

[65] *Livy* 241. Luce also correctly stresses (contra Collingwood) "that the Roman desire to put things in a historical context proved so strong that even the stuff of myth, fable, and invention is delineated in well-articulated stages of accretion and development" (p. 241).

[66] *Plebs propter aes alienum post graves et longas seditiones ad ultimum secessit in Ianiculum, unde a Q. Hortensio dictatore deducta est; isque in ipso magistratu decessit.*

[67] Philip A. Stadter, "The Structure of Livy's History" *Historia* 21 (1972) 287ff., and Luce, *Livy* 3f.

[68] Stadter, (above, n. 67) 287ff., and Luce, *Livy* 3f.

urbis gesta domi militiaeque exponentur (6.1.3). The argument that book XVI marked another beginning because the *Periocha* mentioned *Origo Carthaginiensium et primordia urbis eorum referuntur* is without merit for the simple reason that the break and new beginning that do occur between books V and VI are not clear from the summary, although they are obvious from Livy's own words. The summaries cannot be used to show a break since they frequently have a structure and emphasis of their own.[69]

Nevertheless, to return to our problem, there is no reason to believe that Livy thought the struggle of the orders had come to an end by the end of either book X or book XI. In fact, there is no doubt that Livy saw the conflict as essentially between two constant, inevitable groups of opposing political forces. It was a continuous feature of Roman life.

Once we remind ourselves that the modern analysis of Valerius Antias and Licinius Macer as polar opposites and as Livy's main sources for the struggle are not established facts but merely modern hypotheses at best, we can readily see that a great deal of the struggle was Livy's own creation. The conclusion is confirmed by the fact that he is our only source for so much of its detail.[70] However, the common modern opinion that the struggle began in 494 B.C. with the creation of the plebeian tribunes and ended in 287 B.C. with the Lex Hortensia is not part of Livy's structure. In Livy the struggle began with Romulus' creation of patricians and plebeians.[71] The struggle surfaced several times during the monarchy and the tribunes were created, said Livy, because the patricians now acted like the tyrannical Tarquins.[72] We cannot be certain when, if ever, the struggle ended. The patrician-plebeian struggle that began with Romulus is not unlike the conflict between *equites* and senators (or *populares* and *novi homines* with *optimates* and *nobiles*) that characterizes the late Republican tradition.[73] The struggle certainly continued, but its contestants were redefined. In a very

---

[69] See Luce 10f., and notes for bibliography and discussion.

[70] Luce, 165f. and 230f.: "The prominence given to the struggle of the orders and the strong thread that runs from the initial clashes early in Book 2 through Book 4 and *beyond* [my emphasis] doubtless owe much to Livy's selectivity and personal outlook" (p. 245).

[71] In Book 1 we find the multitude (1.15.8), plebs, and exercitus already favored by Romulus (1.16.8) and suspicious of the *patres*, who were the interreges and one hundred times worse than a single master (1.17.7). The *patres* were already engaged in factional politics as well (1.17.1).

[72] Livy, 2.21.5-6, but 2.21-33 for the entire story.

[73] Cf. P. A. Brunt, *Social Conflicts in the Roman Republic* (New York 1971) 72f., and R.E. Mitchell, "The Aristocracy of the Roman Republic," in *The Rich, The Well Born, and the Powerful*, ed. Frederic C. Jaher (Urbana: University of Illinois Press 1973) 45.

similar fashion Livy saw Regal authority and institutions change by flowing directly into Republican.[74] Mommsen was certainly right to recognize this as the tradition but certainly wrong to attempt to build "historical" legal structures on the basis of that tradition.[75] Modern scholars have rightly criticized Mommsen's system, but in the process they have denied the possible existence of authentic materials which the ancients might have used to "fabricate" their own interpretations and structures. To illustrate the point, one can do no better than use Mommsen's own view of the Lex Hortensia as the standard characterization of the law's position in modern scholarship: "The two hundred years' struggle [i.e. 494-287 B.C.] was brought at length to a close by the law of the dictator Q. Hortensius which was occasioned by a dangerous popular insurrection, and which declared that the decrees of the plebes should stand on the absolute footing of equality – instead of their earlier conditional equivalence – with those of the whole community .... The struggle between the Roman clans and commons was thus substantially at an end."[76]

The assumption is that the plebeians could not legislate without patrician approval (*patrum auctoritas*) until the Lex Hortensia.[77] There were two other occasions on which *plebiscita* were also made binding

---

[74] Livy, 2.1.2-3, which illustrates Luce's "developmental" interpretation (*Livy*, 238ff.). Luce also points out that the kings were all seen as "versatile and many-sided (p. 239 n. 20)." In this respect also take note of J.P.V.D. Balsdon, "Dionysius on Romulus: A Political Pamphlet?," *JRS* 61 (1971) 18-27, where Romulus is seen in the guise of the typical founding father. It was commonplace for all things to begin at the beginning (cf. Ogilvie, *Commentary* 87: "It was a *fable convenue* of Roman constitutional history that the power of the kings had been transferred in some form to the consuls.") In fact, that modern scholars are equally guilty is clear from the familiar but badly understood origins of the *lex curiata de imperio* which is often left in the shadows of Rome's regal past despite obvious "constitutional" problems.

[75] The process is particularly clear in Mommsen's *Römisches Staatsrecht*, 3rd ed. (Leipzig 1887) vol. 2. For the example of the presumed transition from royal religious powers to pontiff and *rex sacrorum*, see Frier, *Libri Annales* 101f., and notes. The most difficult questions concern *imperium* and *coercitio* and the problem of "political" and "constitutional" authority. I will deal with some of these questions in my forthcoming essay (see n.1), but an abbreviated bibliography and debate can be found in Jolowicz, *Historical Introduction* 305ff., where he discusses the distinction between the approaches of Mommsen and Kunkle concerning criminal law and jurisdiction. For the decline of another of Mommsen's "Platonic distinctions" between a *lex rogata* and a *lex data,* see M. Frederiksen, "The Republican Municipal Laws: Errors and Drafts," *JRS* 55 (1965).

[76] Theodor Mommsen, *The History of Rome* I, 4th ed. tr. Rev. Wm. Dickson (New York 1875), vol. 1, p. 386.

[77] As an example, I offer Arnaldo Momigliano, "An Interim Report on the Origins of Rome," *JRS* 53 (1963) 117: "It is easy enough to believe that after the fall of the monarchy the patricians could, and did, usurp the right to veto on laws and elections made by the Comitia (which is what the *patrum auctoritas* amounted to)."

(449 and 339 B.C.), these have been characterized as either annalistic fabrications or legislation which gave qualified approval to *comitia* acts in some fashion.[78] Livy mentioned the *secessio* of the plebeians about 287 B.C., and the dictator Hortensius, but he did not mention the Lex Hortensia.[79] Gaius (*ut plebiscita universum populum tenerent*), Pliny (*ut quod plebs iussisset omnes quirites teneret*) and Gellius (*ut eo iure quod plebs statuisset omnes quirites tenerentur*) are our major sources for the Hortensian law.[80] Livy did, however, preserve the other two measures of 449 B.C. (*ut quod tributim plebs iussisset, populum teneret*) and of 339 B.C. (*ut plebiscita omnes quirites tenerent*).[81] In all the aforementioned the formulae are similar. Did some inventive annalist make up the various measures to demonstrate an ancestor at work, to prove that the plebeians always had the right to do what they struggled two hundred years to achieve, and is there any truth to any of it?

In another passage from Livy, M. Fabius Ambustus, as interrex in 356 B.C., was called upon to settle a dispute. Livy reported that Fabius said the following was the law of the XII Tables: *ut quodcumque postremum populus iussisset, id ius ratumque esset; iussum populi et suffragia esse*.[82] In other words, Fabius quoted the XII Tables to the effect that "whatever the populus decided last was binding law, and votes of the assembly (*suffragia*) were commands of the populus too and therefore binding." This fragment of the XII Tables is often placed in the final table, perhaps as the last measure, for the simple reason that it permitted changes to be made in the law — specifically changes that included popular decisions.[83] What we are dealing with, essentially, is a formulaic statement that proclaims the most recent measure passed to be the operative law on a subject. If we remove the elements of the struggle and do not load the translations of the aforementioned passages with political overtones, we are left with a body of laws which, in each

---

[78] Bibliography and discussion can be found in E. S. Staveley, "Tribal Assemblies before the *Lex Hortensia*," *Athenaeum* 33 (1955) 3-31, and in Robert Develin, "*Comitia tributa plebis*," *Athenaeum* 53 (1975) 302-37. Develin rightly concludes from the evidence that only one tribal assembly existed (contra Staveley) but then completely abandons this promising start by placing his conclusion within the context of the struggle. I reached a different conclusion in my own forthcoming essay (see n.1), which I can only briefly summarize. Only one *comitia tributa* legislated because only one form of legislation was known — the plebiscite. Develin and others often try to analyze the *comitia* evidence without satisfactorily answering the question of what distinguished patres from plebs.

[79] Livy, *Periocha*, 11.

[80] Gaius, *Inst.* 1.3; Pliny, *Nat. Hist.* 16.10 1537; Gellius, 15.27.4. See the references and discussion in Giovanni Rotondi, *Leges Publicae Populi Romani* (Milano 1912) 238ff.

[81] Livy, 3.55.3; 8.12.15.

[82] Livy, 7.17.12. Also Livy 9.33.9, 9.34.6 and 7 contain the same language.

[83] Riccobono, *FIRA, I*, p. 73 (= n. 5).

instance, are stated to be the final measures on their respective subjects. The formulaic passages (*ut quod plebiscita* ... etc.) have nothing to do with the struggle. This fact should have been clear from the "alternate tradition" concerning the Lex Hortensia.

We are told that the Lex Hortensia permitted judicial proceedings and legal transactions to take place on *nundini;* in other words, market days were now days on which secular business could be undertaken. The change was away from considering market days *nefasti,* or, in another sense, they were no longer to be religious holidays, days of rest (*feriae*), days on which sacred, but not secular, activities were permitted. Macrobius reported a tradition that *nundini* were sacred to Jupiter — days on which sacrifices were offered: *sed lege Hortensia effectum ut fastae essent, uti rustici, qui nundinandi causa in urbem veniebant, lites componerent.*[84] Only a short time before, in 304 B.C., Cn. Flavius (it is reported) *civile ius, repositum in penetralibus pontificum, evulgavit fastosque circa forum in albo proposuit, ut quando lege agi posset, sciretur.*[85] That is, Flavius published the civil law, which had been deposited in the secret store rooms of the pontiffs, and he published the *fasti* put up on whitened boards around the *forum* so that all would know when legal proceedings could be undertaken. Flavius had evidently published the *dies fasti,* the calendar which informed those who wished to know when they could undertake certain kinds of secular business. Their undertaking was greatly changed by reducing the exclusive control over the law and legal procedure exercised by the pontiffs. In 287 B.C., Hortensius' measure merely extended the right to engage in secular business to those who wished to take advantage of the market day. Such days were now taken out of the hands of priests who had stressed the ritual and ceremonial aspects of such days. What was meant by stating that the Lex Hortensia now declared *ut plebiscita universum populum tenerent,* or some such variation, was that this was now the law of the land; it was the *postremum* word on the subject.

In sum, the importance of the Lex Hortensia for the secularization of Roman law and society should not be obscured by the desire to have the measure made the final act in the struggle of the orders. Opening market days for legal and public activity meant that those who came into the city could now have recourse to legal advice and procedure which had previously been unavailable. The change may well reflect the fact that the law was no longer a priestly monopoly and, therefore, that the Roman law and procedure began to take on a more secular and public aspect. However, pontiffs continued to be important figures in

---

[84] Macrobius *Saturnalia,* 1.16.30.
[85] Livy, 9.46.5-6, cf. Macrobius, *Saturnalia,* 1.15.9-10.

the growth, development, and interpretation of the law, and publication and secularization probably meant no more than a certain amount of differentiation was taking place in Roman life.[86] The change did not occur because the plebeians were hostile to the continued control by the patrician priests over the law; it occurred because Roman society was growing and developing in such a rapid fashion that it outpaced the priests, who were unwilling or unable to continue their exclusive control. The change was not the result of political conflict, but the natural and inevitable result of Rome's increased urban, economic, and secular sophistication.

In conclusion, there is absolutely no evidence that Licinius Macer or any other ancient author, including Livy, focused upon the Lex Hortensia as the final act of the struggle of the orders. The Lex Hortensia is itself a poorly reported document in the pages of our authors, and it has presented a considerable puzzle to modern historians, who have never fully understood or satisfactorily explained it. Neither Hortensius nor his dictatorial office can easily be explained or placed into any acceptable political historical context. Perhaps the shortcoming is the lack of Livy's complete text, but the problem is more complicated than merely the absence of historical information. In fact, the emphasis placed upon the alternate or supplemental tradition about the Lex Hortensia threatens to turn the measure into a much more workable piece of legislation, but at the same it promises to remove it from the pages of the struggle. The law has been the final act of the struggle for so long that it might be considered sacrilegious to question it.

Interpreting much of Rome's early historical development in terms of the struggle of the orders certainly has been one way of seeing the importance of those features of the tradition which were considered authentic, but it also has resulted in not seeing the potential, perhaps essential, importance of such features. If legal and religious information are really among our most reliable sources of evidence, we have been remiss in applying that principle to early Roman history. Both the three *leges provocationis* and the three laws making *plebiscita* binding can be interpreted as features of early Roman development without making them part of an artificial, admittedly highly embellished, struggle between patricians and plebeians. The emphasis on the struggle of the orders has obscured our vision. There has been a general tendency to deny the historicity of *plebiscita* passed before 287 B.C. on the grounds that plebeians could not legislate without approval of the *patres*. The

---

[86] The single example of Q. Mucius Scaevola will serve to illustrate the point (cf. Cicero, *de legibus*, 2. 19(47)-21(53). Cf. Schulz, *History of Roman Legal Science*, esp. p. 8f.

effect of this conclusion has been to deny, qualify, or misinterpret much of Rome's early legal and constitutional history. We would have little early Roman history without such *plebiscita* and still less without politically active tribunes of the plebs. By placing measures within their proper religious and legal context, we can begin to see their true importance and begin to understand how totally fabricated, misleading, and unsuccessful the attempts have been to place such material with the context of the struggle.[87]

Arnaldo Momigliano once commented that "if religion, economics, politics and law are considered together the probability of multiplying errors is increased. A wrong interpretation of economic or religious fact can easily lie at the root of a wrong interpretation of legal facts, and vice versa."[88] It is my contention that just such an error lies at the root of the common historical depiction of early Roman internal political development as essentially the product of a political struggle between poorly defined patricians and plebeians.

University of Illinois
Urbana, Illinois

---

[87] I deal more extensively with this point and all others made in this essay in my forthcoming essay (above n.1).

[88] "The Consequences of New Trends in the History of Ancient Law," *Studies in Historiography* (London 1966), 243 (= *Rivista Storica Italiana*, 76 [1964] 133-49).

CLODIA IN CICERO'S *PRO CAELIO*

EDWIN S. RAMAGE

Although much has been written about the *Pro Caelio* and Clodia's connection with the case, no one seems to have looked closely at the way in which Cicero manipulates her in the speech.[1] This lack has led in at least one instance to the discovery of difficulties that probably do not exist.[2] The purpose in what follows, then, is to show how Cicero handles Clodia in the *Pro Caelio* and how his treatment of her contributes to his defense of Caelius.

Concealment and Visibility

By the time Cicero rose to defend his client, five speakers had preceded him. Atratinus, Balbus, and Publius Clodius had presented the case for the prosecution, and Caelius and Crassus had spoken for the defense. This surely meant that most of the formal legal aspects of the

---

[1] C.J. Classen cites most of the bibliography on the *Pro Caelio* in the notes of his long article "Ciceros Rede für Caelius," *Aufstieg und Niedergang der römischen Welt*, ed. H. Temporini (Berlin: Walter De Gruyter, 1973), I. 3, pp. 60-94. Cf. R. G. Austin, *M. Tulli Ciceronis pro M. Caelio oratio³* (Oxford: Oxford University Press, 1960), pp. xxviii-xxxii, 162 (hereafter referred to as Austin). The following should be added: C. Deroux, "L'identité de Lesbie," *ANRW* I. 3, pp. 390-416; K. Geffcken, *Comedy in the Pro Caelio* (Leiden: Brill, 1973: *Mnemosyne* Suppl. 30); M. Volpe, "The Persuasive Force of Humor: Cicero's Defense of Caelius," *Quarterly Journal of Speech* 63 (1977), 311-23.

Austin's text of the *Pro Caelio* is used here. It is the text of A. C. Clark, *M. T. Ciceronis orationes pro Sex. Roscio*, etc. (Oxford, 1905: OCT) with one change (see Austin, p. xxi).

The orator has no problem getting Clodia into the speech. Perhaps she was the prime mover in prosecuting Caelius, as he would have us believe, but it is difficult to know how involved she was. T. A. Dorey, "Cicero, Clodia, and the *Pro Caelio*," *G & R* 2 ser., 5 (1958), 175, suggests that her part was "important," but "only a subsidiary one." R. Y. Tyrrell and L. C. Purser, *The Correspondence of Cicero²* (Dublin: Dublin University Press, 1914), vol. 3, p. xlv, assert that "the prosecution was certainly instigated by Clodia and her brother ..." R. Heinze, "Ciceros Rede pro Caelio," *Hermes* 60 (1925) 197, says that Cicero succeeds in leaving the impression that Clodia is heart and soul of the whole process, as if the complaint came from her alone.

There are four points in the *Pro Caelio* where Cicero suggests that the prosecution mentioned Clodia: 30 (*Aurum sumptum ... ut dicitur.*); 35 (*idemque significant ... invita dicere.*); 50 (*Sed ex te ... se habere.*); 53 (*Vidit hoc ... aurum quaerere*). The fact that the prosecution had mentioned her at all would be excuse enough for Cicero's introducing her in his speech. They may also have suggested an involvement for Clodia and a dependence on her that Cicero chose to magnify for his own purposes.

[2] See below, note 4.

trial had been covered and that Cicero could expect to enjoy a certain leeway in preparing his part of the case. He chose boldly to attack Clodia and her hidden support of the prosecution with the idea of turning what should have been an advantage enjoyed by his opponents into a liability for them and a benefit for himself and the defendant. But the orator seems to have had a problem, for as the speech develops it is clear that he has nothing fresh and to the point to use against her. And so he resorts to character assassination. The particular tack he takes is the natural one of revealing what lies hidden, and in doing this he plays with the motif of concealment and visibility on a number of levels. How he uses this idea in dealing with Clodia is what will interest us here.

Although the exordium (1-2) is brief, it not only suggests Clodia's importance for the speech, but it also shows how the orator is going to treat her. Cicero focuses the jury's attention on this woman by referring to her three times, though he is careful not to mention her by name. In fact, he does not even use a noun to refer to Clodia at this point; her identity is indicated by adjectives (1: *meretriciis, muliebrem*) and by a pronoun in which person and sex are undefined (2: *alicuius*). After these three references, the orator hints at her presence once again when he opens up the possibility that Atratinus is prosecuting out of necessity, since he has been ordered to do so (2). All of this vagueness and anonymity is reinforced by the fact that Caelius is also referred to but not named, and that this whole scene is being viewed through the eyes of a stranger who is unfamiliar not only with Caelius and Clodia, but with the whole Roman legal system as well.

Cicero is surely creating suspense and anticipation for the jury here, since they know full well that he is talking about Clodia and that she will be an important part of his defense. Their expectations are heightened by the fact that right at the start the orator also shows how he will present her. On the one hand she appears as a wrathful attacker or besieger (*oppugnari*), while on the other she is a prostitute with lustful ways that are out of control (*meretriciis, libidinem muliebrem, libidine*). Needless to say, the two are closely connected.

After this first step in the process of exposure, it is perfectly natural that Clodia should now disappear completely from the speech (though not from the minds of the jurors), as Cicero attacks the specific charges that the prosecution has made against Caelius (3-18). Every now and then, however, there appear to be vague hints that she lies behind the scene. The most pointed of these is Cicero's allusion to the people who wanted Atratinus to prosecute the case (8). This recalls what Cicero has already said in the exordium about the young man's serving as prosecutor out of necessity.

At the end of this section there is a clear reference to Clodia again (18), when the orator takes advantage of the prosecution's having mentioned Caelius' rented house on the Palatine Hill to bring her in as his client's neighbor. Cicero still does not name her, but comes closer to doing so than before by cleverly adapting (or perhaps we should say readapting) a quotation from Ennius that his colleague Crassus had used earlier. He follows this with the well-known description of Clodia as the Medea of the Palatine who had caused so many problems for Caelius. This must have raised much laughter among the listeners who had surely been expectantly waiting for the next allusion to this woman. But the comment is meant also to increase the jury's anticipation, since once again she is not named and the verbs *reperietis* and *ostendam* show that discovery and revelation really lie in the future.

The process of exposing the hiding Clodia, then, has proceeded another step, but it still has some distance to go. We should also notice that what Cicero will expose about Clodia is the fact that she is the cause of all the ills that have befallen Caelius and all the gossip about him that is circulating in Rome. He will presumably reveal her, then, not only as the hidden hand behind the prosecution but also as the chief cause of Caelius' notorious way of life. Concealment and visibility move on two levels here.

Although he now ostensibly returns to the separate allegations involving the life and ways of Caelius, he is soon drawn back in the direction of Clodia as he insists that he will ask the prosecution's senator-witness from what source (*ex quo fonte*) he has sprung (19). The words *opes* and *nitor,* which in the next sentence characterize the hidden force behind the prosecution, recall these same words used in the exordium to describe Clodia's relationship to the accusers. They leave us in no doubt, then, as to who is supplying the resources. We should notice, however, that Cicero has pushed Clodia back into the shadows. She had a somewhat clearer identity when presented as the Medea of the Palatine, but now has become an impersonal source of influence and wealth.

But Cicero is not yet finished with Clodia, and the process of depersonalization that he has begun continues in the next paragraph (20). If we miss the clear allusion to Clodia in the substance of what Cicero is saying here, the words *oppugnationis* and *oppugnatur* as well as the military metaphor of the last two clauses provide a direct connection with *oppugnari* as it was used in the exordium to describe Clodia's attack on Caelius.

With this statement Clodia has become totally depersonalized and is completely hidden (*clam*) again. It is the last step in a sequence, then, by which Cicero first dangles his Medea of the Palatine in front of the jury and then with certain interruptions draws her back into the shadows and finally hides her completely. There is a certain cleverness and perhaps a touch of irony in the third and last stage (20). For, while Clodia has become invisible, this is at the same time the most explicit statement thus far of her connection with the prosecution. It is worth emphasizing the fact that Cicero uses a balance between visibility (*palam*) and concealment (*clam*) to characterize this alliance.

When Clodia next appears, the orator thrusts her forward into broad daylight, stressing her direct connection with the charges involving the money and poison (30). He draws attention to his discovery of her and her visibility when he insists: "I see the author of these two charges; I see the source (*fontem*); I see a definite name and origin (*caput*)" (31). *Fons* and *caput* here remind us of the unnamed source of the senatorial witness mentioned earlier (19). Moreover, the verb *video*, repeated three times in quick succession, underlines Clodia's visible presence, and its use here is reinforced a little later by two further occurrences of the word as the orator indicated his awareness of an intimacy and ensuing rift between Clodia and Caelius. Clodia's visibility is further intensified by the fact that she is also singled out four times as the one person connected with these charges (30, 31, 32 [twice]).

We should also notice that Cicero is playing with the hidden-visible motif when he suggests that if she is removed there will be no charges and no resources for attacking Caelius (32). As he produces her, then, he metaphorically hides her again for a moment. Here also *opes* and *oppugnare* remind us of the role she was given in the exordium.

Clodia, then, has been revealed as lying behind the prosecution. But this is only part of the revelation that Cicero wants to make. He indicates as much almost immediately by ignoring the two charges of which he has made such an issue to concentrate on Clodia herself. It soon becomes clear that the charges have been used simply to focus attention on this woman in as vivid a manner possible so that the orator can now begin revealing her true nature.

To do so, Cicero places Clodia at center stage and brings on various people to remonstrate with her (33-38). Here the orator borrows from drama and visualizes himself as a playwright who makes his characters appear and disappear as he wishes.[3] This is another variation on the theme of concealment and visibility, of course. Now, however, it is

---

[3] Words which suggest this dramatic movement are *excitandus, exsistat, exstiterit* (33); *personam induxi, persona introducta* (35); *removebo* (36); *sumam* (36,37); *suscipio* (37). The orator also quotes from the comedians after mentioning the playwright Caecilius (37-38). On the relationship between the *Pro Caelio* and Roman comic drama, see Geffcken (above, note 1), esp. pp. 1, 11-18, 43-56.

not Clodia who is revealed and removed, but people who are related to her.

Not only does the motif run on this general level, but the orator also makes use of it in a more specific way in the scene with Appius Claudius (33-34). The type of beard worn by Appius is to be seen (33: *videmus*) on the statues in the city; Appius "appears" (33: *exsistat, exstiterit*); he is blind (33: *Caecus ille*; we should remember that *caecus* can also mean "hidden"). There is a clear reference to Clodia's concealment when Cicero suggests a reason for choosing Appius the Blind (33): "for he who doesn't see her (*non videbit*) will feel the least distress." Again Appius gives visibility to Clodia's illustrious forbears by asking her if she had not seen them (33: *non videras*), and he ends with her in plain sight frequenting (34: *celebrares*) the Appian Way with other women's husbands.

Just as Cicero seems to be warming to the challenge of characterizing Clodia she disappears again. At first it appears that Cicero is just shifting to another topic, for he says in a simple and straightforward way that he is returning to Caelius (37). But after three brief quotations from comedy we are reminded of Clodia's presence when the orator chooses a combination of lines in which one father asks his son why he moved next door to a prostitute and another father wants to know why his son came to know "any strange women" (37). At this point Cicero surprises us a little. For after pointing to the fact that anyone living near "that woman" might expect to be the victim of gossip (38), he substitutes an anonymous woman for Clodia to make his point that Caelius can be easily defended against these stories. He goes on to characterize Clodia's replacement as a thoroughgoing prostitute and suggests that a man who is intimate with her can hardly be called an adulterer (38).

Cicero accomplishes two things here. First of all, for the first time since the exordium he has suggested that Clodia is a *meretrix* or prostitute, although he has been leading up to this throughout this part of his speech. But even at this point Cicero does not choose to accost Clodia directly. He substitutes a straw woman, continues to avoid using the noun *meretrix*, limits himself to one long sentence of description, and makes the whole thing a logical argument in his defense of Caelius. Cicero is playing cat-and-mouse with Clodia and to some extent with the jury as well.

The second thing that Cicero accomplishes here is to draw Clodia gradually off the stage. As we have seen, he focuses his attention on Caelius, brings in two prostitutes from comedy, has Clodia appear briefly as Caelius' neighbor, and finally substitutes the anonymous woman for her. And the withdrawal is complete; there is no reference to her for three and a half pages of the Latin text (39-47). After vividly producing her at the beginning of the scene, then, Cicero has allowed her to drop from sight again, and the way in which he does it shows that it is a calculated disappearance.

When she next appears (47) her immorality is quite literally displayed in full light. She has not sought isolation and darkness as screens for her depravity, but courts open publicity in the brightest daylight. Here again Cicero exploits the hidden-visible motif on two levels. First, he has once more produced Clodia. Secondly, when he describes Clodia's true character, words of concealment (*solitudinem, tenebras, integumenta*) balance those of clarity and visibility (*frequentissima celebritate, clarissima luce*). In other words, the orator has brought to light a Clodia who in turn brazenly brings out into broad daylight actions which would normally remain hidden from view.

Cicero now wants to elaborate this relationship between Caelius and Clodia and surprises us once again by not carrying on with Clodia, but by insisting that he is not going to name any woman; he will leave it all anonymous (48). The disguise is quite thin, however, for after a vivid account of this unnamed woman's meretricious ways (49), Cicero turns to Clodia (50) and names her for the first time in a long while, thus effectively identifying her with the "bold, lewd prostitute" of the sentence before (49). And as he talks to her about the anonymous woman (50), he gradually makes the equation in a series of parenthetical comments. First he describes the woman as "quite unlike you;" in the next sentence he ironically draws them closer together with a proviso: "if you are not she, as I prefer;" almost immediately he all but makes the identification using another conditional clause: "If they mean that she is you ..."[4]

Here again by presenting Clodia, then replacing her, and finally bringing her back Cicero is using another variation on the hidden-visible motif to amuse and to tease his audience. By the time he is

---

[4] Once again we should notice the conscious visibility that the orator gives to the unnamed prostitute (49: *palam, celebritate, oculorum, videatur, explere, videatur*). The anonymity which Cicero repeats here has bothered some commentators. Austin, p. 109, *n. ad* 48-50, calls it "certainly curious," but will not go as far as Heinze (above, note 1), pp. 241-44, who supposes that the repetition is one of a number of indications that sections 39-50 were added when the speech was being edited for publication. The duplication can be satisfactorily explained as part of Cicero's exploitation of the fact that Clodia lies behind the prosecution. He produces and removes her as it suits his purpose, making her a little more visible each time, not only because it raises suspense for his listener, but also because it distracts them from the fact that he really has nothing to say against her.

finished he has established her as an out-and-out *meretrix*. We have seen him leading up to this, and here at last she is fully characterized. This is probably the reason he names her at this point; she has been revealed completely. From here on there is no further description of Clodia's character as a whole, but Cicero makes full use of what everyone now knows about her. He has laid the groundwork, then, for his treatment of the two charges involving the money and the poison, but we should also notice that he has kept his promise to the jurors that he would show them how this Medea of the Palatine was the cause of all Caelius' problems (18).

In spite of the fact that he has revealed Clodia for what she is both as far as the prosecution and her morals are concerned, Cicero is not finished applying the motif of concealment and visibility to her and her actions. He had made a false start at treating the specific charges earlier (30-32), and it is only at this point (51), more than halfway through the speech, that he approaches them seriously. And his approach is strikingly similar to the one he used earlier as he focuses on the two charges and draws attention to Clodia by using her name a number of times. It appears five times in the first three paragraphs (51-53), so that Clodia gains the same high visibility in connection with the charges that she had earlier.[5]

But it is in his rebuttal of the poison charge (56-69), which is certainly the climax of the speech, that Cicero gives most play to concealment and visibility. Here the motif appears once again on a number of levels. At the first stage there is Clodia lying behind the prosecution, as everyone knows. But on a second level she is also behind the ambush in the baths. Not only does she have the idea and do the planning, but she may even have bribed the bathkeeper, also behind the scenes (62). Because she is not a direct participant, her role in the stratagem is precisely parallel to the part she plays in the prosecution of Caelius: she is the hidden mover.

---

[5] There is a clever use of the hidden-visible motif at the beginning of 53. Cicero has stated that Clodia was an accessory if she gave money to Caelius after being told what it was for. "Balbus," Cicero says, "saw this (*vidit hoc*) and said Clodia had been kept in the dark (*celatam esse Clodiam*)." Clodia, then, is once again metaphorically hidden right in the middle of a passage in which she is at her most visible. It reminds us of Cicero's use of *ista muliere remota* in 32.

On a third level there is the plan itself which is to *hide* people in the baths with a view to *revealing* the *hidden* plot.[6] This was the kind of scheme that could be expected from Clodia who understood hiding so well. But ironically the witnesses, who should have been so good at concealment, *revealed* themselves too soon (63-64), thus spoiling the plan.

Cicero's running commentary on this episode represents a fourth and final level on which the motif operates. It is dangerous to read too much into words that do not directly reflect concealment and visibility, but the orator's frequent use of various forms of *invenio* with a negative (56, 62, 64 [twice], 65; cf. *reperietur* [66] shows that for him the whole matter remains confusing, unclear, and in essence hidden.

There are other scattered elements of concealment and visibility in this scene that are not part of these four levels. Perhaps the most striking of these is to be found in the piece of obscenity with which Cicero caps this part of his speech (69). He plays with concealment when he shows a false reluctance to tell the story in detail: "You have long since come to realize (*percipitis*), gentlemen of the jury, what I would like or rather what I would not like to say." In other words, Cicero is going to conceal a story that is perfectly clear to everyone. It may not be a true story, he goes on to say, "But even if it is made up and not in dreadfully good taste, it is a fairly witty lie. And certainly people wouldn't have given their mental and verbal approval unless every tale involving any ugliness at all seemed (*viderentur*) to suit her perfectly." As the last word before the peroration, *viderentur* leaves Clodia and her immorality in full view.

Cicero uses *videatur* in much the same way in his final sally at Clodia in the peroration (78). Here the verb is once again the last word in the period and leaves Clodia clearly revealed as desiring to rescue the lowest of criminals and suppress the finest of young men.

Cicero's Purposes

To complete our study of Cicero's manipulation of Clodia in the *Pro Caelio* we should consider what his use of the hidden-visible motif

---

[6] In the first announcement of the plan (62), Cicero plays upon the hidden-visible motif: the poison is to be caught red-handed (*manifesto*) by people hiding (*delitescerent*) who are to leap out (*prosilirent*) and seize Licinius. These words and words with similar connotations occur frequently in this scene: 62: *latebra, laterent*; 63: *manifesto; contruderentur, delituerunt, prosiluerunt, evolasse*; 64: *oculis esset testatior, manifesto, prosiluisse, manifesto*; 65: *prosilire, evasissent, vidisse, vidisse, videre, se ostenderunt*; 66: *multorum oculis, crimen expresserint, inlustrari*; 67: *videre, in insidiis ... conlocatos, latuerint, texerit, videtis, processerint, explicabunt, conspectus, lux ... solis ... lychnorum, prodierint, ostentent.*

contributes to his defense of Caelius. The orator has two good reasons for focusing on Clodia as he does. First, and perhaps most obviously, it enables him to undercut the prosecution. Clodia represents the resources (1, 19, 32: *opes*) or foundation on which their case rests, and if she falls, it falls. And we see it tottering throughout the speech. Atratinus is pleading out of necessity; he has been ordered to do so (2, 8). Thus he is ill-suited to the task that has been given him (7) and he pleads hesitantly and without conviction (8). The witnesses who will come forward at Clodia's instigation are the kind who want to "please" her because of her influence and resources (19) or else they are "fine" young men who are her intimates in this immoral existence (67). Even the slaves who have their part to play as informers and go-betweens are tainted by living with her (57). And, finally, the charges against Caelius which involve the money and the poison and which stem from her alone (30, 51) are to be laughed out of court because they are ultimately the product of Clodia's unreasoning anger and her grotesque machinations, both of which may be traced to her less than savory ways (56-69). How can this woman, for example, who is rumored to be the poisoner of her husband, dare to bring a charge of attempted poisoning against Caelius (60)?

Cicero's second reason for focusing on Clodia's immorality is to effect a comparison with Caelius. The most important issue of the *Pro Caelio* is not the actual charges, but the characters of the leading personalities. The defense has a serious problem with Caelius' less than sterling reputation, and the prosecutors have evidently seen this and have taken full advantage of it for their own purposes.[7] Cicero has to offer rebuttal by presenting his client in as favorable a light possible. He approaches the problem from two directions: the orator describes Caelius as positively as he can (e.g., 28-30, 39-97, 72-78) and at the same time attacks Clodia for her moral degeneracy. By introducing Clodia he shows the reason for any immorality that may be found in Caelius (18, 47, 75) and at the same time provides a comparison by which Caelius appears to be the better of the two.

---

[7] This is implied by the length of time Cicero devotes to rebutting the arguments from character (3-18). He also tells us that Balbus had dwelt on Caelius' habits; the orator spends some time dealing with his opponent's arguments (25-30).

R. Reitzenstein, "Zu Ciceros Rede für Caelius," *Nachrichten von der Gesellschaft der Wissenschaften zu Göttingen, Philologisch-historische Klasse* (Göttingen, 1925), 26, says that the greatest danger for Cicero lay not in the legal part of the case, but in the life of Caelius and what he calls *die moralische Verkommenheit*. On Caelius, see Austin, pp. v-xvi; G. Boissier, *Cicéron et ses amis*[13] (Paris: Librarie Hachette, 1905), pp. 167-219 (trans. A. D. Jones, *Cicero and His Friends* [New York: Cooper Square, repr. 1970], pp. 159-208); Tyrrell and Purser (above, note 1), vol. 3, pp. xxxvii-lx.

This is not the place for a detailed analysis of Cicero's treatment of character in the *Pro Caelio,* but what has been said will perhaps enable us to come to some kind of conclusion as to why Cicero chose concealment and visibility in dealing with Clodia. In the first place, as has been pointed out often enough above, use of the motif enables Cicero to treat Clodia and her charges in a light and humorous way. This, of course, is entertaining for the jury, and along with the suspense created early in the speech, helps to keep their interest and win their support.[8] The listeners enjoy seeing Cicero playing cat-and-mouse with Clodia and also enjoy having him play cat-and-mouse with them. They are at the same time distracted from the fact that the orator really has nothing to say against Clodia.

This is part of a more general humorous treatment of Clodia by which Cicero ultimately reduces his protagonist and her charges *ad absurdum.* The way in which he deals with her is to be contrasted with what he does with Caelius. For when he talks about his client, the orator is deadly serious - so much so, in fact, that his descriptions at time border on the tedious. This contrast serves a number of purposes. First of all, a variety of mood is created whereby the serious - which usually involves Caelius--becomes more tolerable. Secondly, the contrast in character is underlined with an essentially good Caelius being treated seriously and a thoroughly bad Clodia being laughed at. The hidden-visible motif by itself suggests a third purpose in all of this, for as he uses it Cicero is in essence drawing attention to Clodia's underhand ways of working, whereas Caelius remains thoroughly visible and above board throughout.[9]

Before leaving the subject we should notice that elements like humor, suspense, and character are components of formal rhetoric and are discussed as such in the rhetorical treatises.[10] On the other hand, attacking the opposition at its point of strength and using a device like the hidden-visible motif to do this do not seem to have a place in that tradition. They are what might be called strategies developed by the individual orator for the particular situation. The choice of such

---

[8] On humor in the *Pro Caelio* see Geffcken (above, note 1). Regarding suspense in the exordium, she comments (p. 12): "Such phrases as *oppugnari autem opibus meretriciis* and *libidinem muliebrem,* so shrewd in their vagueness, introduce suspense, hint at scandal to be revealed, entertainment to be provided, and titillate the listeners."

[9] Words of visibility cluster about Caelius as the speech proceeds. A few examples will suffice for present purposes: *inlustri ingenio* (1); *nemo ... vidit nisi* (9); *candor* (36); *ingenium elucere eius videbatis* (45); *inspectante populo Romano* (47); *inlustri accusatione* (73); *ardor* (76); *splendor, nitor* (77).

[10] Cf. *Rhet. ad Her.* 2.5; Cicero, *De Inv.* 2.32-37. Cicero and Quintilian both discuss wit at some length (*De or.* 2.217-290; *Inst. or.* 6.3).

strategies and the development of them within a speech were surely among the factors contributing to the special flavor of each speaker's work as well as to the reputation he enjoyed.[11]

Indiana University
Bloomington, Indiana

---

[11] This is not to say that such strategies could not be repeated elsewhere, however. In the *Pro Roscio Amerino,* for example, Cicero takes his own inexperience, his client's naïete, and the power of the prosecution, and parlays them into a successful defense.

THE CUP AND THE LIP

JAMES S. RUEBEL

Epicureanism endured serious, critical, sustained attacks in antiquity, at the time of its greatest philosophical influence waging (historically speaking) losing battles against Stoicism and other spiritualistic doctrines,[1] finally vanquished (until the seventeenth century) by Christianity.[2] Such conflict in fact, would have been the chosen fate of its most impressive spokesman, the Roman poet Lucretius.[3] It is therefore incongruous that none of these (as it were) professional assaults has wrought more lasting damage to his reputation as poet and thinker than the vexatious report by Jerome, which resides in his *Chronicle* somewhat uncertainly under the year corresponding to 94/3 B.C.:[4]

> T. Lucretius poeta nascitur, qui postea amatorio poculo in furorem versus, cum aliquot libros per intervalla insaniae conscripsisset, quae postea Cicero emendavit, propria se manu interfecit anno aetatis XLIIII.

The spectacular details of this story were long thought to derive ultimately from a credible, or at least knowledgeable, source such as Suetonius, on whom Jerome drew heavily. This supposition has been seriously questioned, especially after K. Ziegler's exhaustive analysis of the *testimonia* uncovered no trace of a madness-suicide tradition for Lucretius earlier than Jerome himself: those authors dwell instead on either the majesty of his verse or the perniciousness of his doctrine.[5]

---

[1] T. Maslowski, *Lucretius and Cicero* (Diss. Cincinnati 1969) 22f., 46-115, 184-87.

[2] G.D. Hadzits, *Lucretius and His Influence* (New York 1934 [1963]) 198-283.

[3] *DRN* 2.1040-43: desine quapropter novitate exterritus ipsa
 exspuere ex animo rationem, sed magis acri
 iudicio perpende et, si tibi vera videntur,
 dede manus, aut, si falsum est, accingere contra.

[4] The mss. vary among 96, 94, and 93 B.C. But Jerome's dates are approximations at best; they are wrong for Lucilius, Catullus, and Messala Corvinus, and probably also for Livy: pertinent references in T.P. Wiseman, "The Two Worlds of Titus Lucretius," *Cinna the Poet and Other Roman Essays* (Leicester 1974) 11-43 at 40 n. 98.

[5] K. Ziegler, "Der Tod des Lucretius," *Hermes* 71 (1936) 421-440; the line of argument was already suggested by S. Brandt, "Lactantius und Lucretius," *Jahrbücher für Philologie und Paedagogik* 143 (1891) 225-51. See also F.H. Sandbach, "Lucreti Poemata and the Poet's Death," *CR* 54 (1940) 72-77.

Lactantius was singled out as an enemy of Lucretius who would surely have exploited a rumor that would call into question Lucretius' mental stability, if such had been known to him, for he frequently invokes the terminology of madness against Lucretius on spiritual, rather than clinical, grounds.[6] These onslaughts against Lucretius' spiritual delusion are, in fact, the first explicit allegations in the tradition of derangement of any kind. Lactantius was in this respect fully within the Christian tradition wherein "madness" metaphors are regularly invoked against theological opponents.[7] The metaphorical value of this terminology was not always distinguished from its literal force; in this atmosphere, the story of a pagan materialist "driven" to literal insanity might be well received. On the other hand, Christian writers are not alone in this method, which had a long classical pedigree and in which Lucretius himself freely indulged.[8]

Ziegler has demonstrated beyond doubt that the *silentium*, out of which Jerome must be assailed, is complete. Indeed, I do not see how Vergil could have written (*Georg.* 2.490-92) the triumphant lines,

>felix qui potuit rerum cognoscere causas
>atque metus omnes et inexorabile fatum
>subiecit pedibus, strepitum Acherontis avari,

in the face of Jerome's tale: his tribute would become grotesque.[9] Be that as it may, not even a total *silentium* has persuaded all scholars, and the spectral authority, such as it is,[10] of Suetonius has been resurrected

---

[6] Cf. Maslowski (above, n.1) 23-36 (correcting the notion that Lactantius' understanding of Lucretius was superficial); F. Jackson Bryce, *The Library of Lactantius* (Diss. Harvard 1973) 225-26, however, points out that Lactantius (and Arnobius) had probably not read Suetonius, to whom Lactantius makes not a single reference; his silence is consequently irrelevant to the question of a Suetonian authority for Jerome, but not to the existence of a tradition of madness-suicide.

[7] I offer an incomplete but suggestive collection: Boethius, *Eut.praef.* 32,33; 4.46 *duos vero esse dicere Christos nihil est aliud nisi praecipitatae mentis insania;* and Augustine's *Confessions: delirans* (3.6); *dementia* (1.13; 4.7; 5.5; 5.9); *insania* or *insanire* (3.2; 6.7,8; 7.14; 8.8; 9.2,4; 10.37); *vesania* (2.2; 5.5). On Lactantius' predilection for the metaphor, cf. Ziegler 428-30.

[8] *DRN* 1.692 (*perdelirum*), 698 (*delirum*), 704 (*dementia*) against Heraclitus; 2.985-90 (*delira, furiosa*); cf. 3.800-802 (*desipere*).

[9] This point is also made by M.F. Smith in his revised Loeb edition of Lucretius (1975), p. xxi.

[10] Ziegler (above, n.5) 431-32: "Gross wäre diese Autorität nicht, denn wir kennen den Mangel an Kritik und die Vorliebe des Sueton für jede Art von Klatsch ja gut genug aus seinen Kaiserbiographien."

to salvage the "substance" of Jerome's biography;[11] pressed to its logical conclusion, this stance must leave us approximately in the position of C. Bailey: rejecting the insanity but finding evidence for it in passages not understood, unhappy about the love-potion but conceding that such devices were not rare, perhaps accepting the suicide.[12]

It would seem fruitless to attempt again to crack this aged chestnut, but scholars persist in trying to raise trees from it. T.P. Wiseman tries to exercise, so to speak, historical criticism on Jerome's story by combining it with his own reconstruction of a statement in Donatus:[13] Lucretius' suicide occurred on the same day that Vergil assumed the *toga virilis* in his seventeenth year (which ran from October 15, 54 B.C. through October 14, 53 B.C.), the precise period during which G. Memmius (the addressee of Lucretius' poem) was suffering political disgrace by indictment for bribery and corruption: "[Lucretius'] hopes for the salvation of Memmius and of mankind lay in ruins. At some time during that year Lucretius, a highly unstable man whose hold on sanity was at best precarious, took his own life, leaving unperfected the great work into which he had put so much of his experience."[14] The fragility of spirit taken for granted here may be the most startling outcome of this fantastic concoction; it is hard to see how an objective reading of *De Rerum Natura* could label its author as "an unstable man whose hold on sanity was at best precarious." Perhaps it is pusillanimous to take Wiseman to task for his apparent *jeu d'esprit*,[15] but it typifies an attitude toward Lucretius, resting ultimately in Jerome, that the poet need not always be taken seriously. Examples could be

---

[11] Wiseman, "Two Worlds," 40-41, citing D.B. Gain, *Latomus* 28 (1969) 545-53.

[12] C. Bailey, *C. Lucreti Cari De rerum natura* (Oxford 1947) vol. I, pp. 8-12.

[13] Donatus, *Vita Verg.* 6: *initia aetatis Cremonae egit usque ad virilem togam, quam septimo decimo anno natali suo accepit, isdem consulibus duobus quibus erat natus, evenitque ut eo ipso die Lucretius poeta decederet.* As transmitted, this text says simultaneously that Vergil assumed the *toga virilis* on his seventeenth birthday (October 15, 53 B.C.) and that it was in the second consulship of Pompey and Crassus (55 B.C.). Wiseman accepts the alternative reading *septimo decimo anno aetatis suae* and rejects the synchronization with the consular list. Donatus, of course, does not say that Lucretius committed suicide.

[14] Wiseman (above, n.4) 43. The association of the Memmius scandal with the suicide of Lucretius is attributed (40 n. 96) to P. Brind'amour. Wiseman will not speculate on a specific day for the suicide; but having ventured thus far, why not suggest the Liberalia, the day on which the ceremony of the *toga virilis* was, at least later on, customarily carried out: hence, March 17, 53 B.C.?

[15] But P. Green, "The Penumbra of Power" (review of Wiseman's *Cinna the Poet*), *Times Literary Supplement* May 2, 1975, p. 478, believes that Wiseman has set up "an ineluctable chain of circumstances in which Lucretius's traditional suicide becomes the natural end to the story: not, as St. Jerome thought, because of a mind-fuddling love-potion, but as the response of a highly-strung creative artist to the total destruction of his world," the whole essay is "a bravura performance."

multiplied, but not all would be so obvious as the willingness of Giussani to transpose whole sections of text on the ground that, Lucretius being mad and the work unfinished, one must make the most coherent poem possible from what has come down to us; rather, the attitude lurks in every failure to come to grips with the poem, every abandonment of the principle that Lucretius wrote precisely what he meant, that he was at all times in full control of his argument, his thought, his imagery, his language. As E.J. Kenney remarks, "The monumental certainty of the Lucretian message is severely weakened, if not irredeemably compromised, by the presence of a psychological Fifth Column sapping and mining within the poet's mental citadel."[16] Moreover, it is depressing to observe a scholar, who has labored so tirelessly to raze the petrified forest of Catullan scholarship,[17] become so thoroughly entangled in the similarly fossilized flora of Lucretian.

It is possible, however, to follow an entirely different tack, to treat Jerome's *testimonium* from a strictly literary point of view. Ziegler hinted at this in 1936, but his concern was with independent substantiation rather than with internal structure.[18] I suggest that the entire *testimonium,* insofar as it pertains to the personality and death of Lucretius, was a deliberate fabrication, fashioned in the mold of the scholiastic biographical tradition which scrutinized the works of ancient authors for supposed autobiographical references, and created "lives" by sheer invention.[19] Far from misunderstanding, say, the meaning of *furor* applied to Lucretius by Statius or *delirat* by Lactantius,[20] the author[21] has willfully misread certain passages in *De Rerum Natura* to construct, one might say, a satire on Lucretius, to use his own metaphors against him, to defuse the atomic warhead into a *pétard* with which to hoist a pagan enemy. If such a method for the composition of

---

[16] E.J. Kenney, *Lucretius. Greece & Rome* New Surveys in the Classics No. 11 (Oxford 1977) 7-8.

[17] T.P. Wiseman, "Catullus, his Life and Times (review of F. Stoessl, *C. Valerius Catullus. Mensch, Leben, Dichtung* [Meissenheim am Glan 1977])," *JRS* 69 (1979) 161-62: "Catullan scholars have been wandering in a kind of petrified forest, an enchanted land where creatures of imagination take bodily form and may not be exorcized by reason."

[18] Ziegler 422: "Die Frage, ob der Bericht des Hieronymus der Wahrheit entspricht oder nicht, ist eine reine philologische, d.h. es kommt nur darauf an, ob er so gut bezeugt ist, dass er Glauben verdient, oder so schlecht, dass er verworfen werden muss."

[19] Cf. J.A. Fairweather, "Biographies of Ancient Writers." *Ancient Society* 5 (1974) 231-76; Lucretius makes a brief appearance at p. 244.

[20] Statius, *Silvae* 2.7.76 (*et docti furor arduus Lucreti*). On Lactantius, above, nn.6-7.

[21] Maslowski 44 proposes, correctly in my view, that the author was Jerome himself; but he regards Jerome's "authorship" for the most part as passive misunderstanding, and therefore guileless: my own opinion is less reverent.

Jerome's *testimonium* can be rendered plausible, we can then decisively dismiss it from serious historical and biographical investigation.

A source for Lucretius' supposed madness has often been sought in *DRN* 3.828-29:

> adde *furorem animi proprium* atque oblivia rerum,
> adde quod in nigras lethargi mergitur undas.

Proprium, on this thesis, has been misunderstood to mean "my own" rather than "the special." But more is involved than misunderstanding. Lucretius, as noted above (n. 8), uses madness as a metaphor for misguided philosophical opinion; he also associates it with foolish babbling as a result of disease in his "proofs" of the mortality of the soul in 3.463-64 (*avius errat / saepe animus; dementit enim deliraque fatur*), and with epilepsy, from which the victim periodically recovers.[22] But the key word in Jerome is *furor,* which Lucretius does not normally associate with insanity. He uses the noun and its verb *furere* a combined total of ten times, the meaning in general restricted to violent physical movement, mostly of wind,[23] but also of fire and of human beings out of control.[24] The purely psychological sense of the word is in the background, unless specifically evoked, as in 3.828 (*furorem animi*).[25] The adjective *furiosus,* on the other hand, has psychological implications in both of its appearances.[26] The two spheres of the word *furor* overlap in a most significant way in Book IV, where it applies to

---

[22] *DRN* 3.499-505: desipientia fit, quia vis animi atque animai
conturbatur et, ut docui, *divisa seorsum*
disiectatur eodem illo *distracta veneno.*
inde ubi iam morbi reflexit causa reditque
in latebras acer corrupti corporis umor,
tum quasi vacillans primum consurgit et omnis
paulatim *redit in sensus animamque receptat.*

It is possible that the use of the word *venenum* and the description of periodic loss of rationality were suggestive, but I believe that each of these elements in the Jerome-*testimonium* has a more specific source.

[23] *furere:* 6.49, 111, 687, 1045. *furor:* 6.49. So also *furibundus* in 6.367.

[24] Fire: 2.593 (*furere*). Bacchants: 2.621 (*furor*); lovers: 4.1069, 1117 (*furor*).

[25] Where the physical sense is also appropriate in view of the recent demonstration that the nature of the *animus* is atomic, and is similar to wind (e.g., 3.128: *calor ac ventus vitalis*).

[26] 2.985; 6.1185: in the latter, a *furiosus vultus* is a *mortis signum* for those suffering from the plague.

the violent dislocation of rationality under the influence of *amor;* in 4.1068-69, love is a wound:

> ulcus enim vivescit et inveterascit alendo
> *inque dies gliscit furor* atque aerumna gravescit.

In 4.117, lovers have spent their passion, trying vainly to merge their bodies into one, and are momentarily at peace:

> inde redit rabies eadem et furor ille revisit.

In view of the way Lucretius uses *furor* elsewhere in the poem, the dominant image must be frenzied movement, but the psychological dimension is by no means absent. As evidence of the *insania* of a pagan enemy, however, these two passages are highly suggestive: not only a *furor proprius* (3.828), but one which recurs (4.1117) and grows stronger with time (4.1069); and the cause of this *furor,* significantly, is *amor.*

The idea of the love-philtre may also have been suggested by those two contexts, for at 4.1058-60 Lucretius compares love to a chilling liquid:

> haec Venus est *nobis,* hinc autemst nomen amoris,
> hinc illaec primum Veneris dulcedinis in cor
> stillavit gutta et successit frigida cura.

Of interest is *nobis,* by which Lucretius refers to people in general but which could be read tendentiously as autobiographical.[27] But there is a better source for the love-philtre. At the beginning of Book IV, Lucretius explains why he has sweetened his doctrine with verse (4.11-18):

> nam veluti pueris absinthia taetra medentes
> cum dare conantur, prius oras *pocula* circum
> contingunt mellis dulci flavoque liquore,
> ut puerorum aetas improvida ludificetur
> labrorum tenus, interea perpotet amarum
> absinthi laticem deceptaque non capiatur,
> sed potius tali pacto recreata valescat,
> *sic ego nunc ...*

---

[27] So also with the onset of love's physical symptoms described at 4.1030-36, after which Lucretius remarks (4.1037) *sollicitatur id in nobis.*

The image was famous in antiquity,[28] and the first-personal reference was too tempting; the main satiric thrust of the Jerome-*testimonium* is at Book IV, which is, one might say, structurally summarized: *amatorio poculo in furorem versus* picks up key elements from the beginning and end of the Book and turns them against their creator; the author then expands upon *furorem (per intervalla insaniae)* on the basis of his deliberate misinterpretation of the two passages in Book IV where *furor* occurs, associated there specifically with the harmful effects of love.

A similar pattern, I believe, informs the detail of the suicide, although there is no intrinsic reason to reject that information and nothing shameful from an Epicurean perspective about that mode of death.[29] In this instance, the target is Book III. Near the beginning of the book, Lucretius expounds the striking paradox (3.79-82):

> et saepe usque adeo mortis formidine vitae
> percipit humanos *odium lucisque videndae*
> ut *sibi consciscant* maerenti pectore letum,
> obliti fontem curarum hunc esse timorem.

A few lines later he compares this fear, which is the result of ignorance, with fear of the dark by children: *sic nos in luce timemus* (3.88). Again, the generalizing *nos* could be read against the author, particularly in combination with the famous diatribe against the fear of death which closes the Book; there Lucretius mentions with approval the suicide of Democritus and points to the inevitable death of even the godlike Epicurus (3.1039-44); why, therefore, cling to life when life is beset on every side with cares (3.1045-52)? An autobiographical connection to Lucretius' own demise was discovered in 3.1076-77:

> denique tanto opere in dubiis trepidare periclis
> quae mala *nos* subigit vitai tanta cupido?

All the sensational details of Jerome's account, therefore, can plausibly be traced to a satiric, invective reversal of putative autobiographical remarks in the poem itself: the love-potion, love-engendered insanity, suicidal tendencies.[30] Probably no reliable information can be

---

[28] Quint. *Inst.Or.* 3.1.4; 8.6.45. On the repetition from Book I, cf. C. Bailey *Comm.* II, 757-58.

[29] C. Bailey, *Comm.* I, 8.

[30] I do not see how the detail *quae postea Cicero emendavit* could derive from the poem, nor can I see any polemic point to be gained either from it or from the statement that Lucretius' death occurred in his 44th year. Lachmann's idea that Quintus Cicero was meant has invariably been dismissed; but if the tradition were genuine, the loss or

extracted from Jerome about Lucretius, unless it be a rough indication of the dates of his birth and death (96-53 B.C.). If that information is right, Lucretius was still alive in 54 B.C., when our only clear contemporary reference to him was written, an afterthought in Cicero's letter *Ad Q.Fr.* 2.10(9). But not very much can be made of Cicero's conventional judgment,[31] though it apparently contains sophisticated, multi-level word plays and a joke at the expense of Sallustius.[32]

Oddly enough, one other contemporary allusion to Lucretius may actually be ensconced in the unlikely heat of factional politics. In the course of a note on senatorial procedure, Asconius finds occasion to quote, verbatim (in indirect discourse), the summary in the *Acta* of a remark delivered on March 1, 52 B.C. by the Tribune T. Munatius Plancus (Asc. 44.16-19C):

> Q. Hortensium dixisse ut extra ordinem quaereretur apud quaesitorem; existimare futurum ut, cum pusillum dedisset dulcedinis, largiter acerbitatis devorarent.[33]

It is true that the wording of Munatius Plancus is not remarkably similar to that of Lucretius' image, quoted above, on the honey-rimmed cup, and that the sentiment is probably proverbial. On the other hand, direct quotation *in contione* of a newly published philosophical poem might have been politically unwise, and certain features of the image as written by Lucretius distinguish his version from earlier ones known to

---

alteration of the praenomen could be easily accounted for. On the other hand, this detail is probably no more than an ancient guess, based on Marcus's well known remark about Lucretius to his brother (*Q.Fr.* 2.10[9].3).

[31] L. A. Holland, *Lucretius and the Transpadanes* (Princeton 1979) 90-97 shows in convincing fashion that the two principal motives behind Cicero's comment were to close the letter with a tension-relieving witticism and to fill up empty space; the contrast of *ingenium* with *ars* was already trite.

[32] Cf. Holland 92-93. Cicero's comparison with the *Empedoclea* of Sallustius suggests that he is thinking of Book I (especially 1.716-33); there may thus be a pun on *lumina* (images of which are prominent in Book I and especially dense in the Empedocles section). The joke *homo/vir*, while not quite logical, would have worked in context (D. R. Shackleton Bailey, *Cicero: Epistulae ad Quintum Fratrem et M. Brutum* [Cambridge, Mass. 1980] 191) whether or not it is also a play on a standard Stoic paradox (J.L. Moles, "A Note on Cicero, *ad Quintum fratrem* 2.10(9).3," *Liverpool Classical Monthly* 7 [1982] 63-65).

[33] This version of the passage follows the mss. of Asconius against Clark and Giarratano, as argued convincingly by G.V. Sumner, "Asconius and the Acta," *Hermes* 93 (1965) 134-35.

us:[34] Lucretius sets the potion in a cup only the rim of which is coated with honey; the two elements are not mixed, and his purpose is not to dilute the bitter element but to disguise it long enough to be ingested: the rim is sweet, but the potion remains bitter.[35] Plancus also insists on this division of elements: a *pusillum dulcedinis* was to precede a large dose of *acerbitas,* but only long enough so that the *acerbitas* would have to be swallowed, like it or no; in this instance, he argues, the deception failed (cf. n. 36). In content, then, Plancus' contrast is closer to Lucretius than any earlier use of the image.

Plancus himself was a politician who embodied the very worst that one could expect from that way of life, as Lucretius saw it. The poet could hardly have found a more apt example of the evils of politics:

> certare ingenio,[36] contendere nobilitate,
> noctes atque dies niti praestante labore[37]
> ad summas emergere opes rerumque potiri ...
> (*DRN* 2.11-13)

> consimili ratione ab eodem saepe timore
> macerat invidia ante oculos illum esse potentem
> illum aspectari, claro qui incedit honore,[38]
> ipsi se in tenebris volvi caenoque queruntur.
> (*DRN* 3.74-77)

If Plancus did allude to *De Rerum Natura,* a distinct possibility in view of the similarity of content and of the very recent publication of the

---

[34] D. Parker, *Epicurean Imagery in Lucretius' De Rerum Natura* (Diss. Princeton 1952) 90-92, studied the history of the image. In the event, he uncovered only two persuasive parallels earlier than Lucretius: Menander, frg. 708K (ἀψινθίῳ κατέπασας Ἀττικὸν μέλι) and Plato, *Leg.* 659e (καθάπερ τοῖς κάμνουσίν τε καὶ ἀσθενῶς ἰσχουσιν τὰ σώματα ἐν ἡδέσι τισὶ σιτίοις καὶ πώμασι τὴν χρηστὴν πειρῶνται τροφὴν προσφέρειν); the fragment of Euripides cited (581K: ὁ δ' αὖ Σοφοκλέους μέλιτι κεχριμένου / ὥσπερ καδίσκου περιέλειχε τὸ στόμα) is dubious, since it is unclear that any contrast is implied with bitter contents.

[35] Parker 92 points out that the parallel passages from Plato and Menander (see n. 34) assume (even require) mixing the sweet and bitter elements; the process envisioned there is dilution of the bitterness.

[36] Asc. 44-45C: *adversus hominem ingeniosum nostro ingenio usi sumus; invenimus Fufium qui diceret 'divide'; reliquae parti sententiae ego et Sallustius intercessimus.*

[37] Asc. 51.9-11: *Q. Pompeius Rufus, C. Sallustius Crispus, T. Munatius Plancus, cum cotidianis contionibus suis magnam invidiam Miloni propter occisum Clodium excitarent ...*

[38] Asc. 37.18-38:1C: *inter primos et Q. Pompeius et C. Sallustius et T. Munatius Plancus tribuni plebis inimicissimas contiones de Milone habebant, invidiosas etiam de Cicerone, quod Milonem tanto studio defenderet ... Plancus autem infestissime perstitit, atque in Ciceronem quoque multitudinem instigavit.*

poem, it would be an extraordinary irony that such a man should provide us with our first contemporary witness.[39] For Lucretius, this would have been a bitter draught indeed.

Iowa State University
Ames, Iowa

---

[39] T. Munatius Plancus Bursa made little impact on history apart from his disruptive term in office as Tribune; upon leaving office he was prosecuted and convicted *de vi,* an event which Cicero says gave him more pleasure than the death of Clodius (*Fam.* 7.2); he later returned from exile and fought for Caesar, and was with Antony as late as Mutina; Cicero casts an obscure aspersion on his literacy in *Fam.* 9.10.2 (*ne* [*non*] *habeat Bursa Plancus apud quem litteras discat.*)

THE WRATH OF AENEAS: TWO MYTHS IN *AENEID* X

ROBIN R. SCHLUNK

Given the violent abruptness of the conclusion to the *Aeneid* and the controversy that has swirled about it, it seems only logical to speculate on the possible significance of the *inimicum insigne* of Pallas' sword belt which Turnus had snatched from the young man's corpse and was wearing on his shoulder when he was suddenly dispatched by Aeneas (XII, 938ff.).[1] As Vergil emphasized, it is the appearance of this sword belt that causes Aeneas to abandon thought of sparing his fallen and defenseless antagonist:

> ...stetit acer in armis
> Aeneas volvens oculos dextramque repressit;
> et iam iamque magis cunctantem flectere sermo
> coeperat, infelix umero cum apparuit alto
> balteus et notis fulserunt cingula bullis
> Pallantis pueri, victum quem vulnere Turnus
> straverat atque umeris inimicum insigne gerebat.
> ille, oculis postquam saevi monimenta doloris
> exuviasque hausit, furiis accensus et ira
> terribilis: 'tune hinc spoliis indute meorum
> eripiare mihi? Pallas te hoc vulnere, Pallas
> immolat et poenam scelerato ex sanguine sumit.'
> (XII. 938-949)

The description of the fateful sword belt, when Turnus stripped it from Pallas, is as follows:

> ... et laevo pressit pede talia fatus
> exanimem rapiens immania pondera baltei
> impressumque nefas: una sub nocte iugali
> caesa manus iuvenum foede thalamique cruenti,
> quae Clonus Eurytides multo caelaverat auro;
> quo nunc Turnus ovat spolio gaudetque potitus.
> (X. 495-500)

---

[1] On the controversy, see for example G. K. Galinsky, "Vergil's *Romanitas* and his Adaptation of Greek Heroes," *ANRW* II.31.2 (1981) 987-998, and H.-P. Stahl, "Aeneas - an 'Unheroic' Hero?" *Arethusa* 14 (1981) 157-177.

Vergil continues with an ominous apostrophe:

> nescia mens hominum fati sortisque futurae
> et servare modum rebus sublata secundis

and adds that there will come a day when Turnus will rue his despoliation of the corpse.[2]

Because of the obvious importance of the *impressum nefas*, the Danaids' slaughter of their husbands on their wedding night, one wonders if there is any significance to the heraldic device other than the mood of bloody violence on this extraordinary occasion. With few exceptions, commentators have been reticent on this question; for example, Otis tersely comments,"Fitting booty for the breaker of a marriage treaty," while Knauer observes that Turnus pillages not only the belt, but the "crime" as well ... "Hier bleibt noch manches zu klaren."[3]

One immediately thinks of Lucretius' allegorical use of the Danaid myth and the *vas pertusum* (III, 1003ff.), but Conte has pointed out that the punishment of the Danaids, far from being emphasized in this brief, one-and-one-half line description, is not even mentioned.[4] Conte notes (as did Donatus) that the emphasis is solely on the dramatic moment of the slaughter of the young husbands on their wedding night, "murdered corpses and everywhere their blood." He adds that the tone which underlies the whole is given by *foede,* and that Vergil has seized upon the "sorrow-laden correspondence" between the husbands slain on their wedding night, full of ingenuous expectation of joy, and the death of a young man on his first day of battle, full of hope and confidence in his valor. The relationship between the tragic scene represented on Pallas' belt and his death is simply the "lyric contact" between them underscored by Vergil's effective expression of pity: lyric rapport between the myth and the fate of Pallas.

Although the Lucretian allegory of the Danaids as symbols of those never satisfied with the pleasures of life seems at best only obliquely germane to the action of the *Aeneid*, it should be remembered that the myth enjoyed great popularity in the Augustan age in art and literature,

---

[2] For Turnus' pitiless boast over Pallas, see R. Hornsby, "The Armor of the Slain," *PhQ* 45 (1966) 347-359.

[3] B. Otis, *Vergil: A Study in Civilized Poetry* (Oxford, 1963) 356; G. Knauer, *Die Aeneis und Homer* (Göttingen, 1964) 303 n. 1. See, too, V. Pöschl, *Die Dichtkunst Virgils* (Innsbruck, 1950) 244.

[4] G. B. Conte, "Il Balteo di Pallante," *RFIC* 98 (1970) 292-300. He rightly points out the close association of those who die an untimely death and the unmarried in funerary inscriptions. See following note.

and it is possible that the myth had something more to do with the death of Pallas than the tragic consonance of mood. Unfortunately we do not know the iconographic significance, if any, of the statues of the Danaids in the portico of the Apollo temple dedicated in 28 B.C., and the numerous literary references seem equally to shed no light on the matter.[5]

The myth of the Danaids, or rather, water carriers in Hades, had had a long association with those who had died before their time (ἄωροι), or died unmarried (ἄγαμοι), or had died before initiation into the mysteries. Some have thought that the Lucretian Danaids derive in some way from the water carriers mentioned in Plato's *Gorgias,* 493a-d, though here the damned are not Danaids, and perhaps do not even include women. At any rate, the association of the Danaids with the water carriers was common by the end of the first century, and the term *nox Danai* had become at some point proverbial for a "bloodbath."[6]

Let us look briefly at the allegory of the water carriers as it appears in the *Gorgias.* In their debate over whether a ruler should be able to rule himself and not merely others, Socrates and Callicles turn their thoughts to the repression of desires, and whether this is only an instance of the weaker attempting to curb the stronger by "popular morality." In his rebuttal of Callicles' assertion that it is best for the ruler to gratify rather than repress his desires and that otherwise it would be better to be dead, Socrates resorts to a view he had once heard to the effect that we are in reality the dead, that the body is our tomb, and that those who suffer most are those who have been condemned to an eternal quest to gratify their desires. This, Socrates continues, is the meaning of the myth of the water carriers in Hades: the soul, because it is easily persuadable (πιθανόν τε καὶ πειστικόν) was called a jug (*pithos*), and the unknowing, the uninitiated (τοὺς δ' ἀνοήτους ἀμυήτους). Hence, in the unknowing, or uninitiated, the part of the soul in which the desires dwell was compared to a leaky jug because it can never be filled, and these souls are accordingly represented in Hades as carrying water in a leaky sieve and pouring it into a similarly leaky jug.[7]

Socrates concludes that he has recounted his myth in an attempt to persuade Callicles to choose a well-ordered and contented life over an

---

[5] E. Keuls, *Water Carriers in Hades* (Amsterdam, 1974), presents a thorough study of the whole topic. See especially 46-7 and 116.

[6] See also G.S. West, "Are Lucretius' Danaids Beautiful?" *CP* 77 (1982) 144-7, and Statius, *Theb.* IV, 132.

[7] See E.R. Dodds, *Plato: Gorgias* (Oxford, 1959) 296-304.

insatiate and unbridled one (ἀντὶ τοῦ ἀπλήστους καὶ ἀκολάστως ἔχοντος βίου). Perhaps, too, this is a reason why Vergil chose the myth as a symbol for Turnus' violent act of despoiling Pallas' corpse, for it is indeed the act of an ἀνόητος who knows no restraint, as Vergil's apostrophe, immediately following the description of the sword belt, expressly states (500-502):

> quo nunc Turnus ovat spolio gaudetque potitus.
> *nescia mens hominum* fati sortisque futurae
> et *servare modum* rebus sublata secundis.

After the death of Pallas, Aeneas rages over the field, brutally killing and mercilessly taunting all who come in his path. In this he is reminiscent of Achilles after the death of Patroclus, and his actions, in general, have not been condoned.[8] The passage most seized upon in support of the view that Vergil condemned Aeneas' momentary savagery is the simile which likens him to Aegaeon (X, 565-570):

> Aegaeon qualis, centum cui bracchia dicunt
> centenasque manus, quinquaginta oribus ignem
> pectoribusque arsisse, Iovis cum fulmina contra
> tot paribus streperet clipeis, tot stringeret ensis:
> sic toto Aeneas desaevit in aequore victor
> ut semel intepuit mucro.

In some versions of the myth, Aegaeon (or Briareus, as he was also known) had fought with the Titans in their battle against Jupiter, which for Horace (*Odes* III. 4. 41ff.) represented the conflict between *vis consili expers* and the gods' *vis temperata*. "It is very significant," R.D. Williams observed, "that Aeneas, given over as he now is to rage and frenzy, should be compared with a barbaric figure symbolising violence and brutality."[9]

A. Thornton, however, sees Aeneas' actions as "justified by the situation, being firmly grounded on moral obligations of a complex nature." She also points out that "Aeneas' fighting is approved by Jupiter (X, 610) ... It would be strange if we were to judge an action contemptible which Jupiter judges worthy of praise."[10] She also noted that Vergil calls Aeneas *pius* (X, 591) in the midst of the slaughter, but

---

[8] E.g., R. Hornsby, *Patterns of Action in the Aeneid* (Iowa City, 1970) 109, who, despite his generally favorable view of Aeneas' actions, sees the simile as hinting at "dire consequences for such frenzy."

[9] *Virgil: Aeneid* VII-XII (London, 1973), ad loc., p. 359.

[10] *The Living Universe: Gods and Men in Virgil's Aeneid* (Leiden, 1976) 133.

feels constrained to admit that the comparison of Aeneas with Aegaeon is "a real difficulty" in her efforts to exonerate him. Her view is that the simile "expresses Aeneas' gigantic might as a fighter ... and does not represent (him) as hateful to Jupiter."[11] Apart from the problematic simile, it should also be remembered that Aeneas' fury leads to the breaking of the siege around the Trojan camp and the rescue of his son (602-5). It is easy to forget that Aeneas is fighting not so much "against" an enemy as he is for the very lives of his own beleaguered people.

The Aegaeon simile was also somewhat problematic in antiquity. Servius, for example, noted that Aegaeon was also said to have helped Jupiter against the Titans, and that at another time he had come to the aid of Jupiter when Juno, Neptune, and Minerva had wished to chain him.[12] The latter is, of course, a reference to the myth in *Iliad* I, 399ff., in which Thetis summons to Zeus' aid the "hundred-handed one, whom the gods call Briareus, but men, Aegaeon." Vergil's simile, however, says nothing about this or the occasion of Aegaeon's action. Still, it is clear that Servius felt uneasy about Aegaeon represented as Jupiter's enemy, and accordingly sought, unconvincingly, to explain away the hostile force of *contra*:

> ... et forte aut suum ignem, aut Iovis acceptum spirasse pro eo, ut sit 'contra' non adversus Iovem, sed similiter, a pari, ut Terentius in *Adelphis* in capite comoediae (I, 1, 25), 'ille ut item contra me habeat facio sedulo.' (*ad* x.567)[13]

For the allegorists the Aegaeon (or Briareus) myth had a far-reaching, cosmic significance. In all versions when he comes to the aid of Zeus, the myth represents in some way, as Buffière points out, "a drama of hot and cold."[14] The bT scholia, for example, on *Iliad* I, 399ff., tell us

---

[11] *Ibid.*, 205, n. 88. Perhaps, too, the simile implies little more than that Aeneas fights "with a blazing fury like one possessed," which seems to be the sole force of an analogous simile used of Tydeus when he battles out of the ambush in Statius, *Theb.* II, 595ff.

[12] Serv. *ad Aen.* VI, 287 and X, 565. For Aegaeon as ally of Zeus, see Hesiod, *Th.*, 713ff. See, too, Macrobius, *Sat.* V.16. 9, who notes Vergil's inversion of Homeric materials in the *Aeneid*. For Aegaeon as enemy of Zeus, see schol. to Ap. Rhod. I.1165 (Eumelus, *Titanomachy*), the Verona Schol. *ad Aen* X, 565 (Antimachus, *Theb.* III), and Lydus, *Mens.* IV, 3 (Pherecydes of Syros).

[13] The Verona Schol., *ad* 566, attempted to see a pause (*mora*) after *Iovis* rather than before, though it is difficult to see what change this would make in the sense.

[14] *Les Mythes d'Homère* (Paris, 1956) 173-9. For Cornutus (*Theol. Gr.* 17, p. 27, 11-17), Briareus represented the power that regulates the exhalations of the earth.

that the enchainment of Zeus represents the winter solstice when the sun has departed to the south and the cold threatens our very existence. Without going into the details, the appearance of Briareus as an ally of Zeus (= pure heat) marks the return of the sun (= Briareus), presumably in spring. Indeed, the scholia of the *Theogony,* 148, saw in the name of Briareus the root *bruein,* hence the season, Spring. In every version, naturally, Briareus is far from an impious, irrational monster; if anything, he is an impassive and objective force of nature whose function is order, not chaos, and is a symbol of balance in the universe, as indeed Nonnus called him in Psamathe's prayer to Zeus, "Aegaeon, protector of your laws" (τεῶν χραισμήτορα θεσμῶν).[15] Even in the one version that regarded Briareus as, this time, winter, and as the enemy of the sun (Zeus), according to Pherecydes of Syros - even so, the more Briareus combats Zeus, the more he becomes his ally.[16]

Apart from Servius' efforts to see Aegaeon as an ally of Jupiter in *Aen.* X, 565, and his interpretation of *contra,* there is one reason to believe that Vergil may have had some version of the allegorists in mind when he composed the simile. Here, as in his apostrophe to the Danaid myth, Vergil seems to have provided a hint in the apodosis of the simile so that we need not be constrained to see the comparison as a symbol of Aeneas' "violence and brutality":

> sic toto Aeneas desaevit in aequore victor
> ut semel intepuit mucro. quin ecce *Niphaei*
> quadriiugis in equos adversaque pectora tendit.
> atque illi longe gradientem et dira frementem
> ut videre, metu versi retroque ruentes
> effunduntque ducem rapiuntque ad litora currus.
> (X.569-574)

Although it can be rash to make too much of etymologies of names in ancient authors, still, given the uniqueness of Niphaeus' name and its use at this particular moment, it is perhaps not too far-fetched to see the name and its root meaning, snow, as a continuance of the blazing power of the figure of Aegaeon: the snows of winter scattered to the shores before the onslaught of the sun in spring. Far, then, from

---

[15] *Dion.* XLIII. 361ff., where Thetis also is invoked. See XXXIX. 285ff., where Aegaeon protects Zeus from the Titans.

[16] Lydus, *de Mens.* IV, p. 66, 3. See Buffière, (above, n.16) 178f. Again, it is the moist substance that becomes an ally of the warmth.

representing Aeneas as a hellish force, the simile may serve rather to equate him at this crisis with an instrument of the powers of natural equilibrium.

University of Vermont
Burlington, Vermont

ENCOLPIUS AND ASIANISM (*SATYRICON* 2.7)

BRENT W. SINCLAIR

The rhetorician Agamemnon has wandered into a garden adjacent to the school where he has just finished declaiming a *suasoria,* and Encolpius, posing as a connoisseur of scholastic rhetoric, has followed him outside in hopes of impressing him and securing an invitation to dinner with Trimalchio.[1] As our text of the *Satyricon* opens *in mediis rebus,* Agamemnon listens while his associate criticizes teachers of declamation for nurturing their students on subjects unconnected with reality (1.1-3) and encouraging a sententious, inflated style (1.3; 2.2,6) which originated in the east and had the most pernicious of effects: *nuper ventosa istaec et enormis loquacitas Athenas ex Asia commigravit animosque iuvenum ad magna surgentes veluti pestilenti quodam sidere afflavit, semelque corrupta regula eloquentia stetit et obmutuit* (2.7).[2] His point is clear enough — the subversion of the Atticist *genus dicendi* by its blustering Asiatic rival has stifled eloquence[3] — yet the sentence ranks among the most controversial in all the *Satyricon.*

A question of fundamental importance is whether or not Encolpius' comment reflects Petronius' position on the issue of Atticism and Asianism. More than a few critics have suggested that it does. P.B. Corbett, for example, remarked that Petronius had grown tired of the excesses of Asianism, that here he "takes a brief opportunity to expound his own conviction."[4] Others would disagree, primarily

---

[1] G. Kennedy, "Encolpius and Agamemnon in Petronius", *AJP* 99 (1978) 171-178; P. G. Walsh, *The Roman Novel* (Cambridge 1970) 83. On Encolpius' penchant for role-playing see F. Zeitlin, "Petronius as Paradox: Anarchy and Artistic Integrity", *TAPA* 102 (1971) 667ff.

[2] The text is that of K. Müller, *Petronii Arbitri Satyricon* (München 1961) who opted for Haase's emendation in preference to the *corrupta eloquentiae regula* of the MSS. E. Burriss, "Two Notes on Petronius" *AJP* 62 (1941) 357-358 had attempted in vain to reinstate it; the context forbids that *loquacitas* be the subject of *stetit et obmutuit.*

[3] W. Kissel, "Petrons Kritik der Rhetorik (*sat.* 1-5)" *RhM* 121 (1978) 314-315 was mistaken in following L. Alfonsi, "Petronio e i Teodorei" *RFIC* 26 (1948) 50 n. 2, who sought to deny Encolpius specific reference to Atticism and Asianism. Surely *Athenas ex Asia* is explicit in view of 2.5,8 where mention is made of the Atticist models Plato and Demosthenes, Thucydides and Hyperides. Kissel's claim 314 that the latter pair "lassen sich ebenfalls nicht einfach unter der Bezeichnung Attizisten zusammentun" is obviated by Cicero, *Brut.* 285-287.

[4] P.B. Corbett, *Petronius* (New York 1970) 47. Note also E.T. Sage, "Atticism in Petronius", *TAPA* 46 (1915) 57; J.P. Sullivan, *The Satyricon of Petronius* (Bloomington 1968) 164. For the notion that the author endorses Encolpius' point of view throughout

on grounds of method: it is incorrect to suppose that Petronius' views can be disentangled from any of the statements made by Encolpius or any other of his characters;[5] besides, in chapters 1-2 the author seems to undercut his protagonist by assigning him a style which contradicts the ideals of the rigorous Atticism that he appears to be advocating.[6] Although this last observation merits more attention than it has received, the key to our question lies far outside the narrow confines of the text.

There is much that remains unknown about the celebrated debate over Atticism and Asianism[7] but all available evidence indicates that it was of short duration. It was probably in full swing by the fifties B.C.[8] Cicero's *Brutus* and *Orator* attest to its continued liveliness through 46, yet after his sarcastic dismissal of the Atticists one year later (*Tusc. Disp.* 2.3) we hear little more about it. The comment of Dionysius of Halicarnassus (*Orat. Vett.* 2.4-5, ed. G. Aujac) that by his own time Asianism had been vanquished everywhere but in a few cities of Asia was in all likelihood premature: that vestiges remained in Rome itself is apparent from Seneca the Elder, who calls the declaimer Craton

---

his opening speech see E. Paratore, *Il Satyricon di Petronio* 2 (Firenze 1933) 6; J.W.H. Atkins, *Literary Criticism in Antiquity* (Cambridge 1934) I.161; E. Cizek, "A propos des premiers chapîtres du *Satyricon*", *Latomus* 34 (1975) 201 and "Face à face éloquent: Encolpe et Agamemnon", *PP* 30 (1975) 101. Kissel (above, n.3) 327 did not go quite so far but saw in the speech "eine ernste Natürlichkeit".

[5] E.g., M. Coffey, *Roman Satire* (London 1976) 187; G. Williams, *Change and Decline* (Berkeley 1978) 288; G. Anderson, *Eros Sophistes* (Chico 1982) 99-100; R. Beck, "The *Satyricon*: Satire, Narrator, and Antecedents", *MH* 39 (1982) 207-209. The passage most commonly adduced in arguments to the contrary is 132.15 but see Zeitlin (above, n. 1) 676; C. Gill, "The Sexual Episodes in the *Satyricon*", *CP* 68 (1973) 183-185.

[6] P.A. George, "Style and Character in the *Satyricon*" *Arion* 5 (1966) 351, 359 n.10; Walsh (above, n.1) 84-85. A.D. Nock, *CR* 46 (1932) 173 and G. Bagnani, *Arbiter of Elegance* (Toronto 1954) 8, while holding that Petronius is not completely serious here, declined to elaborate their position in any detail; see also E.J. Barnes, "Petronius, Philo and Stoic Rhetoric" *Latomus* 32 (1973) 797-798.

[7] W.R. Johnson's assessment, *Luxuriance and Economy: Cicero and the Alien Style* (Berkeley 1971) 1 n. 1 ("a literary controversy ... about which we are not likely to learn anything new") was altogether too pessimistic: on the Greek background see now A. Dihle, "Der Beginn des Attizismus", *A&A* 23 (1977) 162-177; T. Gelzer, "Klassizismus, Attizismus, und Asianismus", *Entretiens Hardt 25: Le classicisme à Rome aux Iers siècles avant et après J.-C.* (Genève 1979) 18-31. For a brief summary of major difficulties, A. Desmouliez, " Sur la polemique entre Cicéron et les Atticistes", *REL* 30 (1952) 68-69; G. Kennedy, *The Art of Rhetoric in the Roman World* (Princeton 1972) 97-98, 241-242.

[8] Dihle (above, n.7) 164. Many including Gelzer (above, n.7) 14-15 and A.E. Douglas (ed.), *M. Tulli Ciceronis Brutus* (Oxford 1966) xiii made much of the fact that there is no certain reference to Atticism or Asianism in Cicero's *De Orat.*, written in 55-54; but see G. Bowersock, "Historical Problems in Late Republican and Augustan Classicism", *Entretiens Hardt* 25 (above, n.7) 62.

professus Asianus qui bellum cum omnibus Atticis gerebat (*Contr.* 10.5.1).[9] Craton's dates are uncertain but even if we admit the possibility that he was a younger contemporary of Seneca and still active in the thirties A.D. he was evidently one of only a stubborn few who persisted in taking the matter seriously.[10] Neither the author of the treatise *On the Sublime* nor the younger Seneca so much as mentions it. Tacitus (*Dial.* 18) speaks of it only in its Republican context — that is, Atticist criticism of Cicero — and Quintilian clearly regarded it as long obsolete.[11] On the basis of these facts Wilamowitz arrived at the only reasonable inference: the debate pitting *Attici* against *Asiani* lasted for no more than two generations and ceased to be of active interest in the reign of Tiberius.[12]

To return to the *Satyricon*. Given the transience of the controversy to which our sentence refers, the belabored question of Petronius' involvement is reduced to *cui bono*. In the middle sixties when he wrote the work[13] there was no longer any practical reason for anyone to issue a serious condemnation of Asianism: that movement, if movement it was,[14] lay quietly in its grave. The effect of assuming that Petronius was prepared to take such a position is to saddle him with a critical principle which was risibly out of date and would have pointed ultimately to his own ignorance. It makes far better sense to acknowledge that 2.7 belongs solely to Encolpius, that for his local purposes the author is impersonating his narrator without identifying with what he says.[15] This approach does not diminish the discrepancy —

---

[9] The MSS have *asinius;* Bursian's emendation to *Asianus* is unquestionable. Other references to Asianism include *Contr.* 1.2.23, 7.6.16, 9.1.12.

[10] J. Fairweather, *Seneca the Elder* (Cambridge 1981) 296. E. Norden, *Die antike Kunstprosa* 1 (Leipzig 1898) 263ff. had attempted to demonstrate, in part on the strength of *Satyricon* 2.7, that the declamatory style was a manifestation of Asianism; for a detailed reappraisal of all the evidence see Fairweather 243ff.

[11] *Inst.* 12.10.16: *et antiqua quidem illa divisio inter Atticos et Asianos fuit*. Although he acknowledges the existence of some 'Atticists' in his own day (12.10.14) he leaves no doubt that they were living anachronisms (12.10.15).

[12] U. von Wilamowitz-Moellendorf, "Asianismus und Atticismus" *Hermes* 35 (1900) 7-9; see also R. G. Austin (ed.), *Quintiliani Inst. Or. Liber XII* (Oxford 1948) *ad* 12.10. A.E. Douglas, "M. Calidius and the Atticists" *CQ* N.S. 5 (1955) 241ff., argued that it had an even shorter duration but took too little account of the evidence in the elder Seneca.

[13] For the traditional Neronian date see, e.g., K.F.C. Rose, *The Date and Author of the Satyricon* (Leiden 1971); Sullivan (above, n.4) 21-33.

[14] Wilamowitz (above, n.12) 7 suggested that it was no more than "ein Schlagwort"; for amplification of his view see Gelzer (above, n.7).

[15] Eumolpus' patently erroneous sketch of Greek philosophers and artists in ch. 88 demands a similar interpretation: see Beck (above, n.5) 208; more importantly, Walsh (above, n.1) 96-97.

the datable allusions in the *Satyricon* leave little doubt that "the date of action is Neronian, and roughly contemporary with the date of composition"[16] — yet allows the responsibility for it to be shifted. Petronius may well be parading inadequacy here but it is surely not his own.[17]

The wording of Encolpius' statement has proved troublesome on two accounts. First, that he speaks of the arrival of Asianism at Athens (*Athenas*) rather than Rome is inappropriate to his circumstances and the immediate message he is attempting to convey: the setting for his encounter with Agamemnon is Roman Campania[18] and his criticism must be understood as directed at Roman rhetoricians.[19] Second, the infamous *nuper* at the beginning of the sentence can carry two distinct meanings. While A. Collignon was able to find support for his suggestion that it denotes 'some time ago'[20] Sage took it in the more usual sense and made the apposite comment that in the sixties "Asiatic oratory was not recently introduced into Athens or very recently into Rome."[21] On a related point, however, there has been a modicum of agreement: 2.7 bears indication, in *nuper* or *Athenas* or both, of being owed to a Greek source.[22] This seems a likely proposal since the flavor of Encolpius' tirade is decidedly Greek[23] and it is quite possible that he is regurgitating something he has read or heard. The identity of his source is a more difficult matter.

The only candidate to have been nominated is Dionysius of Halicarnassus who in the preface to *De oratoribus veteribus* compares Atticism to a temperate Greek wife whose prerogatives have been

---

[16] K.F.C. Rose, "Time and Place in the *Satyricon*", *TAPA* 93 (1962) 408.

[17] The possibility that 2.7 was intended to contribute to the characterization of Encolpius did not escape Coffey (above, n.5) 192.

[18] Probably Puteoli: see Rose (above, n.16) 402ff.; Sullivan (above, n.4) 46-47.

[19] This is apparent not so much from his own speech as from Agamemnon's reply (ch. 3-5), in particular his suggestion (5.20) that all students read Cicero; see Fairweather (above, n.10) 299.

[20] A. Collignon, *Etude sur Pétrone* (Paris 1892) 83. More recently, see Rose (above, n.13) 15 and n. 3.

[21] E.T. Sage (ed.), *The Satyricon* (rev. by B. B. Gilleland, New York 1969) 146. For much the same interpretation see Bagnani (above, n.6) and Kennedy (above, n.7) 462. The style which came to be labeled Asianist had probably begun to make its presence felt in Greece by the late fourth century: for the evidence see Gelzer (above, n.7) 29-30.

[22] E.g., see Collignon (above, n.20) 84; Sage (above, n.4); Bagnani (above, n.6). Rose (above, n.13) 16 and Kissel (above, n.3) 314 n. 17 dissented, the latter on the grounds that Petronius was not so careless as to leave a source unadapted. But Encolpius is speaking here and if anyone is guilty of negligence it is he.

[23] The point was made succinctly by Kennedy (above, n.1) 177: "He mentions no Latin writer. As far as he is concerned, it would seem that literature ended with Hyperides."

temporarily usurped by a shameless harlot from Asia (1.6-7): ἡ μὲν Ἀττικὴ μοῦσα καὶ ἀρχαία καὶ αὐτόχθων ἄτιμον εἰλήφει σχῆμα, τῶν ἑαυτῆς ἐκπεσοῦσα ἀγαθῶν, ἡ δὲ ἔκ τινων βαράθρων τῆς Ἀσίας ἐχθὲς καὶ πρώην ἀφικομένη, Μυσὴ ἢ Φρυγία τις ἢ Καρικόν τι κακόν, [ἢ βάρβαρον] Ἑλληνίδας ἠξίου διοικεῖν πόλεις ἀπελάσασα τῶν κοινῶν τὴν ἑτέραν, ἡ ἀμαθὴς τὴν φιλόσοφον καὶ ἡ μαινομένη τὴν σώφρονα. The Greek context is the same and *nuper* invites comparison with ἐχθὲς καὶ πρώην which C. Iannelli, who first noticed the resemblance, translated with *heri et nuperrime*.[24] It is tempting to accept the kinship of the two sentences on these grounds, for then the case could be argued that Petronius is both parodying Dionysius and further undercutting Encolpius: from the arrival of the Asianist style at Athens the one was almost as remote as the other. If ἐχθὲς καὶ πρώην denotes *heri et nuperrime*, however, it is a mistake quite uncharacteristic of Dionysius; what is more, it contradicts his strong suggestion earlier in the same treatise (1.2-3) that the Asianist invasion took place not long after the death of Alexander.[25] Clearly a different meaning is required. While it is true that in the μέν-δέ construction ἐχθὲς καὶ πρώην stands in contrast to ἀρχαία as ἔκ τινων βαράθρων τῆς Ἀσίας does to αὐτόχθων, the point of Dionysius' elaborate allegory is simply that Asianism was an interloper, an alien upstart infringing on territory of which Atticism had long been the occupant. The phrase has a relative rather than an absolute significance — Dionysius means that Asianism was a newcomer to the cities of Greece not in his own day but relative to the antiquity of Atticism itself[26] — and thus fails to support the view that in *Satyricon* 2.7 Encolpius is referring unequivocally to a very recent event. There may be doubt that the two accounts are related at all,[27] but if they are and

---

[24] C. Iannelli, *Codex Perottinus MS. Regiae Bibliothecae Neapolitanae* (Neapoli 1809) 142. See also Fairweather (above n. 10) 299, though she is misleading in calling attention solely to πρώην.

[25] S. Usher (ed.), *Dionysius of Halicarnassus: The Critical Essays* 1 (Cambridge Mass. 1974) 7 n. 1 recognized the problem but provided no satisfactory solution: "in referring to the hostile Asianic Rhetoric as 'arrived only yesterday' he has left the way open for an interpretation which accords with the historical facts: that the controversy itself was of recent origin at the time of writing."

[26] For ἐχθὲς καὶ πρώην used in a similar way see Herodotus 2.53; Plato, *Leg.* 677 D; Josephus, *C. Ap.* 7; also, Plato, *Gorg.* 470 D1 with the comment of T. Gray as cited by W. H. Thompson (ed.), *The Gorgias of Plato* (London 1894) *ad loc.*: "these words must be taken in a larger sense, as we say of a thing long past, 'It happened but the other day', when we compare it with more ancient times".

[27] Unquestionable reminiscences are lacking. *Pudica* in the description of ideal style in 2.6 (*grandis et ut ita dicam pudica oratio* ...) is possibly an echo of σώφρων. The word is absent from the critical vocabulary of Republican theorists and appears again in the same application only in Fronto (*Fum. et Pulv.* 5, ed. van den Hout). On the other hand,

Encolpius has not misunderstood Dionysius, his *nuper* must be interpreted along the same lines. He has been talking about Plato and Demosthenes (2.5) and is just about to mention Thucydides and Hyperides (2.8); since the immigration of Asianism to Athens occurred after their time its arrival was, in a comparative sense at least, recent.[28]

However that may be, Dionysius was certainly not Encolpius' only source or even his major one. J.K. Schönberger recognized long ago that his speech to Agamemnon is riddled with words and sentiments taken from none other than Cicero himself:[29] to cite but a single example, his *omnia quasi eodem cibo pasta non potuerunt usque ad senectutem canescere* (2.8) echoes Cicero's *cumque ipsa oratio iam nostra canesceret haberetque suam quandam maturitatem et quasi senectutem* (*Brut.* 8). In this light it is not unreasonable to seek precedent for Encolpius' remark on Asianism in Cicero's *rhetorica,* specifically in passages devoted to the history of Greek oratory. There is no need to look far. Near the beginning of the *Brutus* he pauses briefly to discuss the pursuit of eloquence outside of Greece and comments, *nam ut semel e Piraeo eloquentia evecta est, omnis peragravit insulas atque ita peregrinata tota Asia est, ut se externis oblineret moribus omnemque illam salubritatem Atticae dictionis et quasi sanitatem perderet ac loqui paene dedisceret* (51). Encolpius' imitation is far from slavish but his *semel ... eloquentia stetit et obmutuit* is a sure reminiscence of *semel ... eloquentia ... loqui paene dedisceret*. Moreover, with *commigravit, corrupta regula* and *veluti pestilenti quodam sidere afflavit* he recalls the ideas conveyed in *peragravit, se externis oblineret moribus* and *omnemque illam salubritatem Atticae dictionis et quasi sanitatem perderet*.[30]

Encolpius' display of erudition is not lost on Agamemnon: the old rhetorician responds with not only an enthusiastic appraisal of his taste (3.1) but in addition a pair of direct references to Cicero (3.2; 5.20) and, eventually we must suppose, an invitation to dinner with

---

the qualifying force of *ut ita dicam* cannot be underestimated.

[28] Compare the use of *nuper* in Cicero, *De Nat. Deor.* 2.126 and see the remarks of A. S. Pease (ed.), *M. Tulli Ciceronis De Natura Deorum* 2 (Cambridge, Mass. 1958) *ad loc.*.

[29] J.K. Schönberger, "Nochmals Petron c. 1-5" *PhW* 59 (1939) 478-480, 508-512, in particular 511: " ... kein Gedanke und fast kein Wort in diesen Kapiteln steht, die sich nicht aus vielen Cicerostellen belegen liessen." See also "Petron c. 1-5", *PhW* 58 (1938) 174-176, 219-222.

[30] If K.F.C. Rose, "The Petronian Inquisition: An Auto-da-fé", *Arion* 5 (1966) 294, was correct in supposing that the original audience of the *Satyricon* was a coterie of literary sophisticates attuned to recognize and savor allusions of all sorts no imitation more belabored than this was necessary; see also Gill (above, n.5) 177 and, for the richness of such fare, E. Courtney, "Parody and Literary Allusion in Menippean Satire" *Philologus* 106 (1962) 92-100.

Trimalchio.[31] Petronius' own intentions are somewhat less clear. Characteristically he places Encolpius' speech against a recognizable literary backdrop, so to provide a level of entertainment which goes well beneath its surface.[32] Although parody is not out of the question, the echoes of Cicero in 2.7 and adjacent sentences look more like straightforward pastiche. Their purpose is probably humor, in particular that which stems from the incongruity between the character of Encolpius and the manner in which on this occasion he has chosen to present himself: he parrots Cicero but is in effect a sort of absurd anti-Cicero, a *vir perditus dicendi peritus* whose eloquence serves no higher goal than the sating of his appetite. He drastically overplays his part.[33] Thus, like the declaimers whom he criticizes (1.2) he too is temporarily *in alium orbem terrarum delatus* — a distant and unreal world occupied not by pirates, tyrants and pestilence (1.3) but by Demosthenes, Hyperides and pestilential Asianism.[34]

Smith College
Northampton, Massachussetts

---

[31] As Kennedy (above, n.1) 176 noted, "Encolpius has marked out his man and what he says should be regarded as *ad hominem* argumentation". Encolpius could have become aware of Agamemnon's fondness for Cicero in the course of hearing his *suasoria*.

[32] On this aspect of Petronian technique see, e.g., Gill (above, n.5) 176-179; P.G. Walsh, "Was Petronius a Moralist?", *G&R* 21 (1974) 186.

[33] For the view that the *Satyricon* is "the narrative equivalent of a stage farce" featuring "ham-actors playing risible stage parts and exchanging absurdly inflated repartee" see Walsh (above, n.32); more specifically on the influence of the mime, M. Rosenblüth, *Beiträge zur Quellenkunde von Petronius' Satiren* (Berlin 1909).

[34] To Professor Gareth Schmeling I owe thanks for advice and encouragement.

PSEUDOLUS AS SOCRATES, POET AND TRICKSTER

EVA STEHLE

Plautus was interested in slaves, to judge by their prominence in his plays, and he delighted in the comic figure of the intriguing slave. Of the twenty plays preserved, the plot turns on a deception in thirteen, and of those ten are carried out by slaves. The deception may or may not work, but the slave is in either case a paragon of self-confidence, not to say cheekiness, in pursuing his scheme. This confidence is only the more striking in the five plays in which the slave's schemes are directed toward his master.[1]

The clever slave has been claimed as Plautus's most original character, the figure on which he lavished the most elaborate reworking of the Greek original.[2] Terence's plays have no slaves to match Plautus' best — Pseudolus, Chrysalus (in the *Bacchides*), Epidicus. It is not yet clear how central or how vivid the slaves were in the Greek comedies from which Plautus translated, but at the very least Plautus has chosen to translate plays that have a slave in the central role and has embellished his speeches.[3]

Scholars have suggested different reasons for Plautus' predilection. Fraenkel perhaps speaks for the general view when he remarks that Plautus needed 'robust comic effects' to engage his restless audience and that the *dominus gregis* would have wished a good leading part for himself.[4] Erich Segal argues that Roman comedy is patterned on the Saturnalia, during which slaves reclined at dinner, served by their

---

[1] The ten plays with slave deceptions are *Asinaria, Bacchides, Captivi, Casina, Epidicus, Miles Gloriosus, Mostellaria, Persa, Poenulus*, and *Pseudolus*. The five in which the deception is directed at least in part against the master are *Bacchides, Epidicus, Miles Gloriosus, Mostellaria, Pseudolus*. The number is six if the *Casina* is counted, in which the husband is beaten up by his wife's slave. In the remaining plays the deception is directed toward a merchant or a pimp.

[2] The major study of Plautus' alterations is E. Fraenkel, *Elementi Plautini in Plauto* (Florence 1960). On Plautine slaves see chapter VIII, 223-41.

[3] Plautus' originality in creating the slave who dominates his comedy has been disputed by e.g. P. W. Harsh, "The Intriguing Slave of Greek Comedy," *TAPA* 86 (1955) 135-42. W. T. MacCary, "Menander's Slaves: Their Names, Roles, and Masks," *TAPA* 100 (1969) 277-94, goes over the fragments of Menander and does not find evidence of successful intriguing slaves or of slaves' parts of the scope of Plautus'; see especially 293. But Manilius 5.473 speaks of "Elusosque senes agilesque per omnia servos" as found in the plays of Menander. The evidence is hard to assess.

[4] Fraenkel (above, note 2) 239-41.

masters. The essence of comedy, he holds, is to break all of society's most tenaciously held rules and turn the social system on its head. Thus *pietas* is mocked by the lovelorn youths, and money is of no interest to any but the anti-comic figures. Likewise the hierarchy which placed the head of the household at the top and the slaves at the bottom must be turned upside down. On the following day all will return to normal, but for the holiday wit is supreme, and the slave excels in wit.[5]

These explanations stand on the assumption that jokes, boasting, and impudence are what Plautus added to his slave figures. And they may be right. But we may perhaps get a better sense of what Plautus' slaves meant to the Romans if we start with a subtler view of "translation" and "originality." A comedy of manners or situation comedy, as the Greek new comedy was, refers constantly to the social milieu in which it is produced. Part of the humor is in the familiar problems and characters, daily life (conventionalized and abstracted, made sharper or more dreamy) reflected back from the stage. Translating comedy into a different social setting means that it will interact differently with the audience and become a different comedy. If successful, it will be funny for different reasons. Plautus surely knew this and exploited it. The lines he translated, then, and the lines he added or changed are both part of one act of creation by which he elicited different absurdities and incongruities from the original ones.[6]

One aspect of Roman society which Plautus exploited in his recasting of the Greek plays was ambivalence toward Greek culture and people. In the late third and early second century BC the Romans were becoming intimately acquainted with both. Greeks were being brought to Rome as slaves in increasing numbers. And, not coincidentally, Romans were starting to read Greek literature, in translation and in the original, to see Greek plays, and to enjoy Greek luxuries. The reaction to this foreign invasion must have been complex, a distinction between Greek culture and Greek individuals on the one hand and ambivalent feelings toward each on the other. Plautus' slaves were well placed to play on the half-articulated web of suspicion and fascination that the current state of affairs probably provoked in many Romans' minds. But before considering Plautus' slaves, specifically Pseudolus, from this

---

[5] E. Segal, *Roman Laughter* (Cambridge, Mass. 1968).

[6] Both P. Spranger, *Historische Untersuchungen zu den Sklavenfiguren des Plautus und Terenz* (Mainz 1961) 99, and K. Gaiser, "Zur Eigenart der römischen Komödie: Plautus und Terenz gegenüber ihren griechischen Vorbildern," in *Aufstieg und Niedergang* I 2, 1030-32, see Plautus' plays as wholes in which the Greek and Roman elements are not separable. Gaiser emphasizes that translation and rewriting work together to create a new original.

point of view, I would like to mention what evidence we have for Roman reactions to things Greek in the early second century and explore the connections between Greek slaves and Greek literature.

Some Roman aristocrats were unabashedly philhellene, at least by mid-century. During the famous visit of the three philosphers to Rome in 155 BC, not only did the young men flock to hear them, but a notable senator, Gaius Acilius, insisted on doing the translating when they spoke to the senate (Plutarch, *Cato mai.*22. 4-5).[7] Aulus Postumius is reported by Polybius to have been so enthusiastic about Greek culture that he made interest in it irritating to the older and more eminent Romans (39. 1. 3-4). Greek culture was an affectation that could easily be overdone.

Apart from such incidental anecdotes we know mainly about the attitude of Cato the Elder, and his views were probably closer to the general feeling than those of Acilius and Postumius.[8] As Astin makes clear in his biography, Cato did not react with unrelieved hostility to everything of Greek origin. But a persistent tradition portrays him as opposing Greek philosophers, critical of Socrates, dismissive of Isocrates.[9] These people have in common the use of language to persuade. The Greek discovery that language is an independent entity, manipulable in its own right and having no simple relationship to reality is, I think, what Cato instinctively found dangerous. According to Plutarch (*Cato mai.* 12. 5) Cato thought that by and large the words of the Greeks came from their lips, those of the Romans from their hearts.

The excerpt from Cato's *Letter to his Son* preserved by Pliny (*Nat. hist.* 29. 13f.) is very interesting in this regard and has a bearing on the effect of Plautus's plays. I quote most of the excerpt:

> Dicam de istis Graecis suo loco, M. fili, quid
> Athenis exquisitum habeam et quod bonum sit
> illorum litteras inspicere, non perdiscere, vincam.
> nequissimum et indocile genus illorum ... : quan-
> doque ista genus suas litteras dabit, omnia conrum-
> pet, tum etiam magis, si medicos suos hoc mittet.
> iurarunt inter se barbaros necare omnes medicina, et

---

[7] The evidence for the Roman attitudes toward the Greeks is collected by J.P.V.D. Balsdon, *Romans and Aliens* (Chapel Hill 1979) ch. 3. He opens the chapter with the sentence, "With the Greeks the Romans had a love-hate relationship" (30). His catalogue of Roman remarks amply bears out the statement, though most of the evidence is much later than the second century BC.

[8] See A. E. Astin, *Cato the Censor* (Oxford 1978) ch. 8, who thinks that Cato's attitude, like that of most Romans probably, was an inconsistent mixture of acceptance and hostility (180-81).

[9] Citations in Astin (above, note 8) 169-70.

> hoc ipsum mercede faciunt ut fides is sit et facile disperdant. (I shall speak about those Greeks in their proper place, Marcus my son, as to what I know as the result of my inquiries at Athens, and I shall demonstrate what benefit there is in looking into their literature, but not in studying it thoroughly. Theirs is an utterly vile and unruly race ... : when that race gives us its literature it will corrupt everything, and all the more so if it sends here its doctors. They have taken an oath among themselves to kill all barbarians by their medicine, and this very thing they do for a fee, so that they should be trusted and may destroy with ease.)[10]

The qualified interest in Greek literature combined with utter condemnation of the people does not need to be specially pointed out. But, more illuminating, the link between literature and doctors implies that Cato saw them as related dangers. The doctors are not called inept or extortionist, but they are said to be *putting on an act*. They carefully go through the fiction of healing, but in fact it is only a well-orchestrated deception. Fiction likewise makes a persuasive "reality" out of word and gesture, but nothing lies behind it except the plot of the manipulative author. If we may trust the run of Cato's thought, he considered Greek literature likely to wreck everything for the same reason that the doctors will: it will inveigle its victim into trusting it.[11]

If the Romans had inconsistent and ambivalent reactions to Greek literature, philosophy, and rhetoric, they must have found confrontation with individual Greeks more immediately anxiety-producing. The dazzling Greek philosophers and the Greek doctors have been mentioned. They were welcomed with honors, if not without suspicion. But a great many of the Greeks who came to Rome in the late third

---

[10] Text and translation from Astin (above, note 8) 170-71.

[11] Cf. Plutarch, *Cato mai.* 22. 4, on Cato's fear that the philosophers would teach the Roman youth to prefer a reputation for speaking to renown for martial deeds. According to Pliny (*Nat. Hist.* 7. 112), Cato said that when Carneades was discoursing it was not easy to discern what the truth was. Here again Cato seems to be objecting to the independence of language. Fiction does the opposite of Cato's *rem tene, verba sequentur*; it finds the words and out of them makes the thing (fact, reality, case).

There are other scattered facts expressive of Roman ambivalence toward Greek culture in the second century. Two Epicurean philosophers were expelled from Rome in 173 and a number of philosophers and rhetoricians in 161 (Baldson, above, note 7, 36), but the Macedonian royal library was brought to Rome (in private hands, it must be admitted) shortly after 168 (Astin [above, note 8] 167). In 151 a permanent theater was begun, but pulled down before it was finished for fear it would undercut military hardihood (Livy, *Epit.* 48). The feared effect must have been more psychological than physical.

and early second centuries came as slaves.[12] Among the slaves were skilled and educated men, a fact which added a further element of confusion to the status to be accorded a particular Greek. Livius Andronicus is the founder of Latin literature. The first public primary school in Rome, says Plutarch, was set up in the mid third century by a former Greek slave.[13] A Greek education became popular; Cato owned a Greek *grammatistes* named Chilon who taught many boys, though not Cato's own son (Plutarch, *Cato mai.* 20. 5). In his sketch of the growth of education at Rome, Suetonius mentions that more than twenty grammar schools existed at one time or another.[14] In the late second century Q. Lutatius Catulus paid 700,000 sesterces for Lutatius Daphnis, apparently because his teaching was so remunerative, and soon set him free (Suet., *De gramm.* 3; the price may be wrong but Daphnis was definitely expensive; presumably he reimbursed Catulus out of his earnings).[15]

These examples serve to show not only the conflicts in status to be assigned to Greek slaves, but also illustrate the connection for the Romans between Greek slaves and Greek literature: each entailed the other, for the slaves provided access to the literature and were desirable for that reason (among others).[16] Another manifestation of the same paradox is found in the location of Greek intrusions into the Latin language. Greek enters Latin from the bottom as part of street slang (presumably an effect of the Greek slaves, traders, and floaters) and from the top as an expression of aristocratic polish.[17]

A Roman, therefore, sizing up a Greek slave will have been subject to a variety of conflicts. The status of a slave, a "speaking instrument," "property with a soul," is ambivalent to begin with.[18] He or she is property, but human, part of the community and yet not. In addition the Greek is an alien at the heart of Roman life, defeated but

---

[12] See M.I. Finley, *Ancient Slavery and Modern Ideology* (New York 1980) 83-84; T. Frank, *An Economic Survey of Ancient Rome,* vol I: *Rome and Italy of the Republic* (Patterson, NY 1959) 100-02 and 187-88.

[13] *Roman Questions* 278E, cited by K. Hopkins, *Conquerers and Slaves* (Cambridge 1978) 76, who imagines that public instruction must have been available before that.

[14] On Suetonius' *De grammaticis* and the growth of education at Rome see Hopkins (above, note 13) 76-80; also C. A. Forbes, "The Education and Training of Slaves in Antiquity," *TAPA* 86 (1955) 338-39.

[15] On the duties of ex-slaves to their former masters, see Hopkins (above, note 13) 129-31.

[16] B. Gentili, *Theatrical Performances in the Ancient World* (Amsterdam 1979) 94-95, connects the Roman interest in literature with the presence of Greek slaves who brought not only cultural sophistication but books with them.

[17] B. Devoto, *The Langauges of Italy,* tr. V. L. Katainen (Chicago 1978) 89-93.

[18] See the interesting discussion in Finley (above, note 12) 95ff.

coming from a more sophisticated culture, perhaps despising his new master. These ambivalences are intersected by another set concerned with the Greek command of language. The Greek slave who learns Latin commands the general discourse but also another, inaccessible one — unless the master submits to being taught by his slave. The Greek is a deceitful, untrustworthy creature, but the bearer of the great fictions of literature and theatre. To put it starkly, a new kind of power was being revealed to the Romans by slaves whose intentions were veiled by their language, their character, and their command of fiction.

Had Plautus then faithfully translated a Greek play with a clever slave as the central character he would have created a new play, for the slave would have appeared very different to Roman eyes than to his original audience. And Plautus (at the very least) heightens his new effect by giving his slaves speeches claiming Roman military and political efficacy (that is, they comprehend Roman culture and values), while at the same time he marks them as Greek in comparison to the other characters in the plays.[19] To the same end he emphasizes their ability to redefine reality through language: to deceive, to create fiction. The Plautine clever slave is the loquacious, prevaricating attitudinizer of disdainful Roman stereotype, but is also the poet. He thinks up the plot and directs the action. As the audience watches him working his deceptions on the other characters they themselves are drawn into the "deception" that is the play acted on the stage. So all the Romans' ambivalences, about slaves, Greeks, language, fiction, are stimulated and add their force to the provoking of laughter.[20]

The *Pseudolus* is the play in which the slave most clearly appears as Greek, trickster, and artist. But before turning to it I want to point out a technique of Plautus, the creation of illusion in the course of

---

[19] On the Romanization see Fraenkel (above, note 2) 232 and note 2. On Plautus' strengthening of Greek elements in the plays, specifically those characteristics that the Romans thought of as especially Greek, as well as Plautus's mixing of Greek and Roman elements, see Gaiser (above, note 6) 1079-80.

[20] The question how the Roman audience would see the characters in relation to themselves is a difficult one. Donatus (*ad* Terence, *Eun.* 39) made the remark that *comoedia palliata* is permitted to show a slave cleverer than his master while *comoedia togata* is not. Presumably the former was considered safely foreign. Spranger (above, note 6) 112 warns that to suppose the Roman *paterfamilias* saw himself in the old man of comedy is to misunderstand the plays. Likewise G. E. Duckworth, *The Nature of Roman Comedy* (Princeton 1952) 318, says, "To the Roman audience, the concept of an intriguing, impertinent, domineering slave would clash violently with the realities of everyday life, and to have him boast of heroic achievements would strike them as highly incongruous ..." On the surface I think these remarks are true, but as Segal points out, the foreign setting conceals some very Roman attitudes and relationships (above, note 5, 31ff). I think that there is probably much more interplay in the audience's mind between the Greeks on the stage and the Greeks who have been absorbed into Roman society.

admitting to it, in two or three simple manifestations. Plautus tells his audience that the play is an ephemeral thing, made of words. *Apporto vobis Plautum, lingua non manu* says the Prologue-speaker of the *Menaechmi*. Later he says, gesturing to the stage,

> haec urbs Epidamnus est, dum haec agitur fabula;
> quando alia agetur, aliud fiet oppidum (72-73).

The location is only a fiction; and yet, no town at all exists there on the stage, only some doors. The town is created in the spectators' minds as they consider how easily it changes its identity.

Another example appears to break the dramatic illusion even more sharply, but in fact furthers it in a more important way. The Prologue-speaker of the *Casina*, describing the girl Casina, says,

> ea invenietur et pudica et libera,
> ... neque quicquam stupri
> faciet profecto in hac quidem comoedia.
> mox hercle vero, post transactam fabulam,
> argentum si quis dederit, ut ego suspicor,
> ultro ibit nuptum, non manebit auspices. (80-86)

It is a rude joke, admitting that the sweet girl is played by a loose actress. But, of course, the character Casina never appears in the play. The apparent moment of shared salaciousness is a joke on the audience; they've been tricked into imagining, however briefly, a possible tumble. On the other hand, the joke perversely induces belief in the character Casina, who takes on a flesh and allure in imagination that she would not otherwise have had.

One more example. In the *Casina* prologue just before the lines I quoted, the speaker assures the audience that slave-weddings do take place in Greece, Carthage, and Apulia (71-72); in fact, more attention is given to them there than to marriage among the free. The speaker seems to feel that the audience doubts his assertion; nevertheless he will bet on it, so long as a Greek, Carthaginian, or Apulian can be the judge: these were people known for their unreliability.[21] In the course of insisting on a fact, the speaker gives the audience ample reason to believe that it is not true. The question turns out to be irrelevant because the girl will be found to be freeborn. But by this ploy Plautus allows his audience to accept a given of the play without the irritation

---

[21] See W.T. MacCary and M.M. Wilcock, *Plautus, Casina* (Cambridge 1976) 108-09 *ad* 76. It is not clear what reaction the Romans would have to the mention of Apulians, but their untrustworthiness may be the point here.

they might feel at serious thought of such privileges for slaves (Slaves married, indeed! What is the world coming to?).

These examples show Plautus at work constructing his fiction.[22] But within the play the clever slave uses similar tricks against his victim. Pseudolus builds his fictions the same way, and to that play we now turn. Early in the play Pseudolus warns everyone not to trust him: *in hunc diem a me ut caveant, ne credant mihi* (127). They all do, of course, from the audience to Calidorus to Simo to Ballio. Rather, they all trust that they understand what he is doing. Simo and Ballio go wrong because they trust his advice not to trust him, and so he weaves his web of fiction.

Pseudolus is characterized in three ways in the play. He is a Greek, a poet, and a trickster. The combination creates his success. He is distinguished as Greek early in the play.[23] When Simo and his friend Callipho approach Pseudolus to ask whether Simo's son is indeed trying to buy his girlfriend and Pseudolus helping find the money, Simo warns Callipho:

> conficient iam te hic verbis ut tu censeas
> non Pseudolum, sed Socratem tecum loqui.
>
> (464-65)

Pseudolus means "liar" in Greek. This liar's lies will be so effective that he will seem to be the most famous seeker after truth, one of the most famous of Greeks. Only a Greek liar could lie that well, in Roman eyes.[24] Furthermore, the usual effect of Socrates' truth-seeking was to leave his interlocutors dazed; perhaps Pseudolus will have this effect also. After a bit of sparring Pseudolus agrees to give *Delphis ... responsum* (480). It was the Delphic oracle that called Socrates the wisest man of all. And Delphi is the Greek institution which shares

---

[22] The section of the *Casina* prologue from which I have drawn the examples is considered to be Plautus' own work. See MacCary (above, note 21) 97.

[23] All the characters in the play are Greek, of course, but attention is drawn to the fact only in Pseudolus' case. The audience's reactions to Greek people would have been focussed on Pseudolus because he is marked as Greek, and because he was the slave, the position in which Romans were perhaps most familiar with actual Greek people.

[24] This is a good example of the case I discussed earlier in which direct translation could produce a new effect on the new audience. The remark about Socrates may well have been in the original, but would have had a different effect from the Romans' reaction, given their preconceptions about overtalkative, philosophizing Greeks who play word games. For the Romans there was probably a kind of plausibility in the notion that Pseudolus and Socrates might come to the same thing that would make it a different joke. For a contemporary image of these philosophizing Greeks see Plautus' *Curculio* 288ff., which Fraenkel (above, note 2) 123-34, following Leo, considers Plautine in composition.

Socrates' reputation for misunderstood truth-telling. To the following questions Pseudolus does answer like the Delphic oracle — in Greek. When Simo later calls Pseudolus *meus Ulixes* (1063) it is but icing on the cake. Pseudolus is long established as a Greek whose truth or falsehood is a matter of profound concern.

Pseudolus is also a poet at work constructing the plot of this play. In his first monologue, after he has undertaken to get the young man either the girl or money to buy her, Pseudolus admits that he has no idea what he is going to do. But he will think of something:

> sed quasi poeta, tabulas quom cepit sibi,
> quaerit quod nusquam gentiumst, reperit tamen,
> facit illud veri simile quod mendacium est,
> nunc ego poeta fiam: viginti minas,
> quae nunc nusquam sunt gentium, inveniam tamen.
> (401-05)

Later, when his plot is all worked out, Pseudolus exclaims, *em tibi omnem fabulam!* (754) This is the point at which Pseudolus creates a tricky slave to carry out the final deception; at the end of the scene he goes off to coach his man.[25] And just as Pseudolus seems to take over his play from within, so his creation, Simia, dressed and rehearsed for his part, acquires independence. *Quippe ego te ni contemnam, / stratioticus homo qui cluear?* (917-18) No clever slave is entirely under control, even by another clever slave. Pseudolus can only watch the last trick from the wings, as it were, while his actor performs.

Pseudolus realizes his need for a complete (Greek) plot after his first encounter with Ballio, the pimp in possession of the girl. Pseudolus and the young man reason and plead with the pimp to hold off selling the girl to a soldier and give the young man more time to find money to pay for her himself. Naturally they fail, so as a last resort they take to shaming, the old Italian custom of *flagitatio*.[26] Their insults recall the Fescennines also, the pre-dramatic Italian ritual. It does not work; Ballio is not abashed. The Italian method of direct attack, the Catonian *rem tene,* is inadequate as a way of manipulating the world. Only a use of words which redefines reality can cause Ballio

---

[25] This is pointed out by J. Wright, "The Transformations of Pseudolus," *TAPA* 105 (1975) 413-14, who traces the theatrical metaphors through the play and suggests that through his versatility Pseudolus becomes an actor playing a clever slave and finally becomes Plautus himself.

[26] That this scene is a *flagitatio* was pointed out by Usener, quoted by G. Williams, "Some Problems in the Construction of Plautus' *Pseudolus,*" *Hermes* 84 (1956) 432.

to modify his behavior. So it is that Pseudolus constructs a play around Ballio and Simo.

Pseudolus decides to become a poet right after his encounter with Ballio and right after that meets Simo and Callipho and hears himself compared to Socrates. That is the hint he needs to begin his fabrication: he will be a distracting truth-teller. He takes up the hint with his reference to Delphi and answers *nai* (the Greek affirmative, with quite possibly an intended play on its similarity to *non,* or *ne*) to the questions whether he is trying to get money for the young man. Simo points out that Pseudolus will not be able to weasel the money out of him because he (Simo) is now on guard and will also warn everybody else not to loan money. "You will give it to me" is Pseudolus' reply, to Simo's astonishment. Pseudolus insists, warns Simo to watch out, offers to take a beating if he does not get it from Simo. And *then* Pseudolus says, "Do you want me to tell you something you will wonder at even more?" (522). By this time the old men are completely engrossed. "I am anxious to hear, by god, for I enjoy listening to you" (523), says Callipho. The new wonder is that Pseudolus will steal the girl from the pimp. Here comes the trick. Simo says that if Pseudolus accomplishes *istaec opera* (note the plural) he will outshine Agathocles, but if he doesn't he should be sent to the mill (531-34). Replies Pseudolus,

> sed si ecfecero,
> dabin mi argentum quod dem lenoni ilico
> tua voluntate?
>
> (535-37)

Simo agrees at Callipho's urging. Pseudolus' verb *ecfecero* has no object; he does not specify what he has to do in order for Simo to give him the money. Simo's *istaec opera* referred vaguely to two things: if you get the money out of me *and* get the girl, then you will outshine Agathocles and I will give you the money to pay the pimp. But Pseudolus has just accomplished the first of the two things. What Simo's promise amounts to is this: if you get the girl and talk me into paying the amount needed for the pimp, then I will pay the amount needed for the pimp. Pseudolus has just talked him into paying the amount needed for the pimp.[27]

---

[27] This scene has elicited much discussion. Scholars tend to feel that Plautus has somehow distorted a logical Greek plot in which Pseudolus did trick Simo out of money *and* collect on the bet or that he conflated two plays or that he added either the bet or Pseudolus' claim that he would trick Simo (i.e., that the Greek play contained either a bet or a tricking of Simo following Pseudolus' boast, but not both). See Duckworth

Pseudolus' trick consisted in telling (what he hoped would be) the truth in such a way that Simo did not believe him. The insistence, exaggeration, boasting destroyed all credence for Pseudolus' claims and created an atmosphere in which Simo felt perfectly safe in making such a promise. Like Socrates and the Delphic oracle Pseudolus said things that his hearers assumed to be jokes because obviously they were not true. Obviously Pseudolus wouldn't be able to get the money out of Simo, so Simo felt no danger in promising to give it to him.

The performance of this "Socratic" trick was a performance, and another way of describing Pseudolus' success is to say that he began to create a fiction and drew the old men into it. Simo and Callipho, on the one hand feeling no threat because Pseudolus' fantastic claims were not real, on the other hand wanted to see the play. By the end of the scene desire to watch the performance has won out over considerations of money. *Lubidost ludos tuos spectare, Pseudole* (552) says Callipho - 'so if he doesn't give you the money, I will, rather than that it should not take place.'

Had Pseudolus been able to get the money in hand, he could simply have paid for the girl. As things have worked out, he can only get the money if he already has the girl, so the plot must develop further. Pseudolus' second trick is more straightforward than his first but also an actor's trick, an improvisation. When Pseudolus sees the emissary from the soldier coming to collect the girl, he poses as one of Ballio's slaves and gets, not the five minas still owing on the girl, but what is more valuable to one who deals in fiction, the *sumbolus*. The *sumbolus* is the token by which Ballio is to recognize the emissary, the symbol of reality. The pedestrian emissary, oblivious to the use of symbols in fiction, hands it over without second thought while clinging obstinately to the cash (which Pseudolus makes a great show of wanting).

Possibly the actor who played Pseudolus in the original production emphasized the relationship between the trick and the actor's art by

---

(above, note 20) 162-63, who thinks there is inconsistency but that it would not be noticed by the audience; Fraenkel (above, note 2) 236; Williams (above, note 26) 424-39, who thinks that Plautus introduced inconsistencies when he enlarged the slave role and Romanized the plot in various ways (particularly by introducing a Roman form of contract); E. Lefèvre, "Plautus-Studien I, der doppelte Geldkreislauf im Pseudolus," *Hermes* 105 (1977) 441-54, who analyses the monetary transactions to deduce the logical scheme of the Greek original in which everyone was paid off at the end. Plautus does seem to have disrupted the financial logic of the original but in the interest of the kind of trick he liked, manipulating the audience into believing a fiction while ostensibly admitting what he was doing. Pseudolus' trick could have been made more obvious by the acting than it is in the text. But since Plautus is usually more careful to clue the audience into what he is doing he may have been working more from instinct in this play than in others.

changing his acting style for as long as he was "Syrus," the putative slave of Ballio's. Be that as it may, Pseudolus collects "spectators" after his second trick, just as he had after his first. The young man returns with a friend, and full of enthusiasm they help with the props for the third act. Pseudolus has graduated to stage manager and sends out a slave trickier than himself to pose as the emissary and carry off the girl, as I mentioned before.

Simia's imposture as the military emissary requires a more skillful bit of acting than Pseudolus' imposture as a slave of Ballio's. Pseudolus had only to act the part of an impudent slave, after all. Simia carries off his role as a military type beautifully: he is rude, short, and suspicious. His ommission of greetings turns out to be echoed by the letter (the *sumbolus*).

The real emissary, Harpax, is a faithful slave and an even-tempered man. When he returns, wondering why he has not been summoned to hand over the money and take the girl, Ballio decides that he must be a fake. He and Simo decide to make a show of him (*ludos facere,* 1167). But theirs is a poor show. They cannot create fiction, and it gradually dawns on them that they have themselves been unwilling participants in someone else's fiction.

Pseudolus' tricks are rather like Plautus' in the *Casina* prologue. He creates suspicion and resistance in his opponents, fosters their conviction that they can match wits with him by his infuriating arrogance, and under cover of their misdirected wariness works his tricks. Simo and Callipho, like the audience, are drawn by desire to enter the fiction so long as their conscious, calculating minds feel sure that no real challenge lies therein. For Ballio the *sumbolus* guarantees the fiction woven around it; given the *sumbolus* he sees a military emissary.[28]

As he takes over the plot construction Pseudolus works the same trick on the audience. As he turns to the problem of stealing the girl he turns to the audience and says:

> suspicio est mi nunc vos suspicarier,
> me idcirco haec tanta facinora promittere,
> qui vos oblectem, hanc fabulam dum transigam,
> neque sim facturus quod facturum dixeram. (562-65)

---

[28] H. E. Wieand, *Deception in Plautus* (Boston 1920) 52-62, lists lies and impersonation as the two principal means by which tricks are carried out. Terentian slaves are neither so given to erecting screens of verbiage behind which to operate nor so successful in their tricks as Plautine slaves.

Pseudolus admits that he does not know how he will pull the trick off, but that he will.[29] For Pseudolus reality can always be made to yield to fiction. The audience, its suspicions acknowledged, is only the more open to Pseudolus' claims. When he returns to the stage after a suspenseful interval (with only the flute-player on stage) and announces that he's got a magnificent plan, relief and eagerness must greet him. But what the plan is we never learn, for the emissary appears and the plan is scrapped in favor of deceiving him. Was there a marvellous plan, now lost forever, or was Pseudolus putting the audience on? We'll never know, but either way we are persuaded that Pseudolus is in control rather than a beneficiary of a lucky accident, the arrival of the emissary.

If Pseudolus is a slave but also the poet, if he is Socrates, Agathocles, Ulysses, if he is a Roman general and politician whose orders others obey, then who is he? When the emissary asks him his status, slave or free, Pseudolus replies, *nunc quidem etiam servio* (610). At some other moment he might rearrange things and be someone else. And rearrange them he does at the end of the play when he persuades Simo to go off drinking with him. Surely it is not that Simo degrades himself by socializing with his slave but that Pseudolus is what he chooses to be, and no external definition of him will ever be adequate.

Wheaton College
Norton, Massachussetts

---

[29] E. W. Handley, "Plautus and his Public: Some Thoughts on New Comedy in Latin," *Dioniso* 46 (1975) 127-28, speaks of breaking the dramatic illusion as a device more beloved by and more effectively used by Plautus than by Menander or Terence.